The Inaugural Addresses of the U.S. Presidents

美国历届总统就职演说

岳西宽 张卫星 刘 禹

图书在版编目（CIP）数据

美国历届总统就职演说：精选本：英汉对照/(美)华盛顿等著；岳西宽，张卫星，刘禹译. —北京：中央编译出版社，2023.9（2023.11重印）

ISBN 978-7-5117-3551-5

Ⅰ.①美… Ⅱ.①华…②岳…③张…④刘… Ⅲ.①英语—汉语—对照读物②总统—就职演说—汇编—美国 Ⅳ.①H319.4：D

中国版本图书馆CIP数据核字(2019)第084642号

美国历届总统就职演说（精选本·英汉对照）

责任编辑	李小燕
责任印制	李 颖
出版发行	中央编译出版社
网　　址	www.cctpcm.com
地　　址	北京市海淀区北四环西路69号（100080）
电　　话	（010）55627391（总编室）　（010）55627301（编辑室） （010）55627320（发行部）　（010）55627377（新技术部）
经　　销	全国新华书店
印　　刷	北京时捷印刷有限公司
开　　本	880毫米×1230毫米　1/16
字　　数	519千字
印　　张	31.75
版　　次	2023年9月第1版
印　　次	2023年11月第2次印刷
定　　价	88.00元

新浪微博：@中央编译出版社　微　信：中央编译出版社（ID:cctphome）
淘宝店铺：中央编译出版社直销店（http://shop108367160.taobao.com）
（010）55627331

本社常年法律顾问：北京市吴栾赵阎律师事务所律师　闫军　梁勤
凡有印装质量问题，本社负责调换，电话：（010）55627320

目 录

乔治·华盛顿（George Washington）..................1
George Washington / First Inaugural Address 2
华盛顿总统首次就职演说 3

约翰·亚当斯（John Adams）..................11
John Adams /Inaugural Address 12
亚当斯总统就职演说 13

托马斯·杰斐逊（Thomas Jefferson）..................25
Thomas Jefferson / First Inaugural Address 26
杰斐逊总统首次就职演说 27

詹姆斯·麦迪逊（James Madison）..................37
James Madison /First Inaugural Address 38
麦迪逊总统首次就职演说 39

詹姆斯·门罗（James Monroe）..................47
James Monroe / First Inaugural Address 48
门罗总统首次就职演说 49

约翰·昆西·亚当斯（John Quincy Adams）..................67
John Quincy Adams / Inaugural Address 68
亚当斯总统就职演说 69

安德鲁·杰克逊（Andrew Jackson）..................85
Andrew Jackson /First Inaugural Address 86
杰克逊总统首次就职演说 87

扎卡里·泰勒（Zachary Taylor）..................95
Zachary Taylor /Inaugural Address 96
泰勒总统就职演说 97

詹姆斯·布坎南（James Buchanan）..................103
James Buchanan / Inaugural Address 104
布坎南总统就职演说 105

美国历届总统就职演说
THE INAUGURAL ADDRESSES OF THE U.S. PRESIDENTS

亚伯拉罕·林肯（Abraham Lincoln） 121
    Abraham Lincoln / First Inaugural Address 122
    林肯总统首次就职演说 123
    Abraham Lincoln / Second Inaugural Address 140
    林肯总统第二次就职演说 141

尤利西斯·辛普森·格兰特（Ulysses Simpson Grant） 147
    Ulysses Simpson Grant /First Inaugural Address 148
    格兰特总统首次就职演说 149

格罗弗·克利夫兰（Grover Cleveland） 155
    Grover Cleveland / First Inaugural Address 156
    克利夫兰总统首次就职演说 157

威廉·麦金莱（William Mckinley） 167
    William McKinley / First Inaugural Address 168
    麦金莱总统首次就职演说 169

西奥多·罗斯福（Theodore Roosevelt） 189
    Theodore Roosevelt / Inaugural Address 190
    罗斯福总统就职演说 191

伍德罗·威尔逊（Woodrow Wilson） 197
    Woodrow Wilson / First Inaugural Address 198
    威尔逊总统首次就职演说 199

赫伯特·胡佛（Herbert Hoover） 209
    Herbert Hoover /Inaugural Address 210
    胡佛总统就职演说 211

富兰克林·罗斯福（Franklin Roosevelt） 233
    Franklin Roosevelt / First Inaugural Address 234
    罗斯福总统首次就职演说 235
    Franklin Roosevelt / Second Inaugural Address 244
    罗斯福总统第二次就职演说 245
    Franklin Roosevelt / Third Inaugural Address 254
    罗斯福总统第三次就职演说 255

目录 Contents

哈里·杜鲁门（Harry Truman）...... 263
Harry Truman / Inaugural Address 264
杜鲁门总统就职演说 265

德怀特·艾森豪威尔（Dwight Eisenhower）...... 277
Dwight Eisenhower / First Inaugural Address 278
艾森豪威尔总统首次就职演说 279
Dwight Eisenhower / Second Inaugural Address 290
艾森豪威尔总统第二次就职演说 291

约翰·肯尼迪（John Kennedy）...... 301
John Kennedy / Inaugural Address 302
肯尼迪总统就职演说 303

林登·约翰逊（Lyndon Johnson）...... 311
Lyndon Johnson /Inaugural Address 312
约翰逊总统就职演说 313

理查德·尼克松（Richard Nixon）...... 323
Richard Nixon / First Inaugural Address 324
尼克松总统首次就职演说 325
Richard Nixon /Second Inaugural Address 336
尼克松总统第二次就职演说 337

吉米·卡特（Jimmy Carter）...... 349
Jimmy Carter /Inaugural Address 350
卡特总统就职演说 351

罗纳德·里根（Ronald Reagan）...... 359
Ronald Reagan / First Inaugural Address 360
里根总统首次就职演说 361
Ronald Reagan / Second Inaugural Address 372
里根总统第二次就职演说 373

乔治·布什（George Bush）...... 389
George Bush / Inaugural Address 390
布什总统就职演说 391

美国历届总统就职演说
THE INAUGURAL ADDRESSES OF THE U.S. PRESIDENTS

比尔·克林顿（Bill Clinton） 403
- Bill Clinton /First Inaugural Address 404
- 克林顿总统首次就职演说 405
- Bill Clinton /Second Inaugural Address 412
- 克林顿总统第二次就职演说 413

乔治·沃克·布什（George Walker Bush） 427
- George Walker Bush /First Inaugural Address 428
- 布什总统首次就职演说 429
- George Walker Bush / Second Inaugural Address 436
- 布什总统第二次就职演说 437

巴拉克·奥巴马（Barack Obama） 451
- Barack Obama /First Inaugural Address 452
- 奥巴马总统首次就职演说 453
- Barack Obama / Second Inaugural Address 464
- 奥巴马总统第二次就职演说 465

唐纳德·特朗普（Donald Trump） 477
- Donald Trump /Inaugural Address 478
- 特朗普总统就职演说 479

约瑟夫·拜登（Joseph Biden） 489
- Joseph Biden / Inaugural Address 490
- 拜登总统就职演说 491

乔治·华盛顿
George Washington

乔治·华盛顿（George Washington）

生平简介 >>

乔治·华盛顿是美国第一任总统，是美国的国父。他于1732年2月22日出生在弗吉尼亚州，11岁时丧父，所受教育很少。1753年，弗吉尼亚州遭到法国士兵的入侵，他被召去担任民兵中校，22岁晋升为陆军上校，并在战争中统领弗吉尼亚的全部军队。

1758年退役后，经过三次竞选他当选为弗吉尼亚州议员。1774年，华盛顿被选为弗吉尼亚州的7名代表之一，参加费城的大陆会议。1775年6月15日，大陆会议任命他担任联军最高司令。

独立战争结束后，他当选为制宪大会主席，倾向于联邦政府，尽力让宪法获得批准。宪法刚一被批准，选举团就一致投票选举华盛顿为总统。他于1789年2月4日当选，4月30日站在纽约华尔街联邦大厦的阳台上宣誓就职。1792年，他获选连任。这时政府所在地已于1790年从纽约迁至费城。这次就职演说是美国历史上最短的就职演说。

第二任期满后，华盛顿坚决拒绝再次连任。他隐退到芒特弗农的农场老家。1799年12月14日，华盛顿病故，终年67岁。

美国历届总统就职演说
THE INAUGURAL ADDRESSES OF THE U.S. PRESIDENTS

George Washington
First Inaugural Address

April 30, 1789

Fellow-Citizens of the Senate and of the House of Representatives:

 Among the vicissitudes incident to life no event could have filled me with greater anxieties than that of which the notification was transmitted by your order, and received on the 14th day of the present month. On the one hand, I was summoned by my country, whose voice I can never hear but with veneration and love, from a retreat which I had chosen with the fondest predilection, and, in my flattering hopes, with an immutable decision, as the asylum of my declining years — a retreat which was rendered every day more necessary as well as more dear to me by the addition of habit to inclination, and of frequent interruptions in my health to the gradual waste committed on it by time. On the other hand, the magnitude and difficulty of the trust to which the voice of my country called me, being sufficient to awaken in the wisest and most experienced of her citizens a distrustful scrutiny into his qualifications, could not but overwhelm with despondence one who (inheriting inferior endowments from nature and unpracticed in the duties of civil administration) ought to be peculiarly conscious of his own deficiencies. In this conflict of emotions all I dare aver is that it has been my faithful study to collect my duty from a just appreciation of every circumstance by which it might be affected. All I dare hope is that if, in executing this task, I have been too much swayed by a grateful remembrance of former instances, or by an affectionate sensibility to this transcendent proof of the confidence of my fellow-citizens, and have thence too little consulted my incapacity as well as disinclination for the weighty and untried cares before me, my error will be palliated by the motives which mislead me, and its consequences be judged by my country with some share of the partiality in which they originated.

乔治·华盛顿
George Washington

华盛顿总统首次就职演说

1789年4月30日

参议院和众议院的先生们：

在人生的沧桑沉浮中，没有任何事情能比在本月14日这天接到你们向我发出的命令这件事更令我焦虑不安了。一方面，国家在召唤我，对于她的召唤，我永远只能肃然从命，诚挚热爱，然而我曾选择隐退，还下定决心满怀希望地想以此作为我晚年的归宿。由于生活习惯难以改变，健康也随着岁月逐渐消损，隐退对我来说，已是刻不容缓的事。另一方面，祖国召唤我担负的责任如此巨大而艰巨，即便是国内最明智、最富经验的贤明之士，也势必对这样的重任怀有谨慎与恐惧之感，从而时时考虑自己是否有资格担此重任，更何况像我这样一个天资愚钝和在行政管理方面没有经验的人，就更应意识到自己的缺陷与不足，以免有负重托。在这种矛盾的心情下，我所能保证的是尽量正确地评估可能影响我职责的每一种情况，来完成我应尽的职务。同时，我唯一能希望的是，如果在履行职务的过程中，因陶醉于往事，或因由衷感激公民给予我的信任，因而受到过多影响，以致我在处理未经历过的大事时，忽视了自己的无能，我的错误将会因使我误入歧途的各种动机而减轻，而大家在评判这些错误的后果时，也会适当宽容这些动机所带来的偏颇。

Such being the impressions under which I have, in obedience to the public summons, repaired to the present station, it would be peculiarly improper to omit in this first official act my fervent supplications to that Almighty Being who rules over the universe, who presides in the councils of nations, and whose providential aids can supply every human defect, that His benediction may consecrate to the liberties and happiness of the people of the United States a Government instituted by themselves for these essential purposes, and may enable every instrument employed in its administration to execute with success the functions allotted to his charge. In tendering this homage to the Great Author of every public and private good, I assure myself that it expresses your sentiments not less than my own, nor those of my fellow-citizens at large less than either. No people can be bound to acknowledge and adore the Invisible Hand which conducts the affairs of men more than those of the United States. Every step by which they have advanced to the character of an independent nation seems to have been distinguished by some token of providential agency; and in the important revolution just accomplished in the system of their united government the tranquil deliberations and voluntary consent of so many distinct communities from which the event has resulted can not be compared with the means by which most governments have been established without some return of pious gratitude, along with an humble anticipation of the future blessings which the past seem to presage. These reflections, arising out of the present crisis, have forced themselves too strongly on my mind to be suppressed. You will join with me, I trust, in thinking that there are none under the influence of which the proceedings of a new and free government can more auspiciously commence.

By the article establishing the executive department it is made the duty of the President "to recommend to your consideration such measures as he shall judge necessary and expedient." The circumstances under which I now meet you will acquit me from entering into that subject further than to refer to the great constitutional charter under which you are assembled, and which, in defining your powers, designates the objects to which your attention is to be given. It will be more consistent with those circumstances and far more congenial with

乔治·华盛顿
George Washington

  遵从民众的呼唤，带着上述信念，我来到此地接受任命，而在我今天的宣誓就职仪式中，如果没有对万能的上帝热切祈求，那将是非常不当的。上帝统治着宇宙，统辖着列国，他的帮助能弥补人类的不足。愿上帝赐福，保佑美国人民自由、幸福，并神圣不可侵犯，美国人民就是以此崇高目标而组建自己的政府的；保佑美国政府的各项行政措施在我负责之下成功地发挥其作用。在向创造公共利益和私人利益的造物主表示敬意方面，我相信诸位及广大公民都不亚于我。没有人能像美国人那样决意去承认和景仰那掌管人间事务的上帝。美国人民在迈向国家独立的进程中，似乎每一步都受到了上帝的影响。在通过建立联合政府制度而完成的重要革命中，诸多不同地区所具有的冷静思考与自愿赞同，是其他许多政府的组建方式所不能比的，在作这种比较时，我们也应心怀虔诚的感恩，并以谦卑的心情去期待过往预示的未来的幸福。这些来自现存危机的思考，强烈地占据我的心，使我难以抑制。我相信，你们和我都一致认为，除了仰仗上帝的力量外，没有别的办法更能使一个新的自由政府顺利地展开工作。

  根据行政部门赖以建立的宪法条款规定，总统有责任将其认为必要且妥善的措施提请国会审议。在这个我们欢聚一堂的隆重仪式中，我要提到你们所赖以集会、规定你们的权利、指明我们共同目标的宪法条文，来开始有关这个主题更深入的讨论。我想若是能免去一些仪式上的歌功颂德的辞藻，代之以切实可行的建议措施，将更能体现这盛典的真正意义，也更能反映我此刻内心的激情。而那些赞扬与颂辞应该给予那些才华横溢、正直及富有爱国心的人。也只有从这些高尚的品格中，我见到了最可靠的保

the feelings which actuate me, to substitute, in place of a recommendation of particular measures, the tribute that is due to the talents, the rectitude, and the patriotism which adorns the characters selected to devise and adopt them. In these honorable qualifications I behold the surest pledges that as on one side no local prejudices or attachments, no separate views nor party animosities, will misdirect the comprehensive and equal eye which ought to watch over this great assemblage of communities and interests, so, on another, that the foundation of our national policy will be laid in the pure and immutable principles of private morality, and the preeminence of free government be exemplified by all the attributes which can win the affections of its citizens and command the respect of the world. I dwell on this prospect with every satisfaction which an ardent love for my country can inspire, since there is no truth more thoroughly established than that there exists in the economy and course of nature an indissoluble union between virtue and happiness; between duty and advantage; between the genuine maxims of an honest and magnanimous policy and the solid rewards of public prosperity and felicity; since we ought to be no less persuaded that the propitious smiles of Heaven can never be expected on a nation that disregards the eternal rules of order and right which Heaven itself has ordained; and since the preservation of the sacred fire of liberty and the destiny of the republican model of government are justly considered, perhaps, as deeply, as finally, staked on the experiment entrusted to the hands of the American people.

　　Besides the ordinary objects submitted to your care, it will remain with your judgment to decide how far an exercise of the occasional power delegated by the fifth article of the Constitution is rendered expedient at the present juncture by the nature of objections which have been urged against the system, or by the degree of inquietude which has given birth to them. Instead of undertaking particular recommendations on this subject, in which I could be guided by no lights derived from official opportunities, I shall again give way to my entire confidence in your discernment and pursuit of the public good; for I assure myself that whilst you carefully avoid every alteration which might endanger the benefits of an united and effective government, or which ought to await

证：第一，将不再有地域的偏见、分歧或党派倾轧[1]，来干扰我们对这个由不同地区、不同利益所形成的伟大社会所应该具有的全局观、公平观。第二，国家的政策将奠定于纯洁而坚定的个人道德之上，而且自由政府的卓越体现在它的所有优点之中，而这些优点不仅得到了本国人民的拥戴，同时也赢得了世界的尊敬。我对国家的一片热爱之心激励我满怀喜悦地展望这幅远景。因为真理告诉我们：在经济与自然发展过程中存在着不朽的结合——美德与幸福不可分；责任与利益不可分；诚实高尚政策的真正准则与民众繁荣幸福的真实回报不可分。我们应该相信，一个国家如果漠视上帝所确立的关于秩序和公理的永恒法则，那么上帝慈祥的笑容就不会光顾这个国家。同时大家也有充分的理由相信：维护自由的圣火与维护共和政府的命运这两件事，全掌握在美国人民自己的手中。

除了托付你们关照的一般事务外，宪法第五条所赋予的临时权力的执行范围，将由你们去判断它在现行法令下究竟有多大益处[2]，可根据反对这个制度的理由或根据产生反对意见的不满程度。这个问题，我无法从过去担任过的职务中得到借鉴，所以我不想就这个问题提任何建议，但我愿再度表示完全信赖你们的洞察力以及对公众利益的追求。因为我明白，在

---

[1]当时美国已有两党制的雏形，即联邦党和共和党。前者代表大资产阶级和大种植园主利益，主张集中权力于联邦政府；后者代表中小资本家、南部某些种植园主及广大小农，主张分权于各州或地方政府。华盛顿对政党现象是持否定态度的，信赖公民投票选出的政府。
[2]华盛顿就职时，联邦党人嫌联邦宪法不够完善而拟修改宪法，以扩大民众所获得的自由保证。宪法修改条款于1791年12月经足够的州联合签署后正式生效，即所谓"权利法案"。

the future lessons of experience, a reverence for the characteristic rights of freemen and a regard for the public harmony will sufficiently influence your deliberations on the question how far the former can be impregnably fortified or the latter be safely and advantageously promoted.

To the foregoing observations I have one to add, which will be most properly addressed to the House of Representatives. It concerns myself, and will therefore be as brief as possible. When I was first honored with a call into the service of my country, then on the eve of an arduous struggle for its liberties, the light in which I contemplated my duty required that I should renounce every pecuniary compensation. From this resolution I have in no instance departed; and being still under the impressions which produced it, I must decline as inapplicable to myself any share in the personal emoluments which may be indispensably included in a permanent provision for the executive department, and must accordingly pray that the pecuniary estimates for the station in which I am placed may during my continuance in it be limited to such actual expenditures as the public good may be thought to require.

Having thus imparted to you my sentiments as they have been awakened by the occasion which brings us together, I shall take my present leave; but not without resorting once more to the benign Parent of the Human Race in humble supplication that, since He has been pleased to favor the American people with opportunities for deliberating in perfect tranquility, and dispositions for deciding with unparalleled unanimity on a form of government for the security of their union and the advancement of their happiness, so His divine blessing may be equally conspicuous in the enlarged views, the temperate consultations, and the wise measures on which the success of this Government must depend.

乔治·华盛顿
George Washington

谨慎避开每种或许能危及联合和有效力的政府所有利益的改变，或有待未来验证的改变之时，大家对自由人特有权利的敬重及对国家和谐的关注都会影响诸位思考这个问题：自由人的特有权利能够确实加强到何种地步？国家的和谐又能够安全而有益地促进到何种程度？

除此之外，我还有一项要补充。这项意见最适于向众议院提出，它与我有关，因此我尽量讲得简短一些。在我第一次奉召为国效力之时，也正是国家为争取自由而艰苦奋斗之际，正是在这种情况下，在考虑到我的职责时，我决定放弃任何俸禄。自从下此决心后，我从未违背过，当时使我下此决心的想法现在仍敦促着我，要我必须放弃我那份个人津贴，而这种个人酬金或许会不可避免地被列入行政部门的正常经费。因此，我必须恳求各位，在我执政期间，预估我就任的这个职位所需要的费用时，应该以公共利益所需的实际支出为限。[1]

现在，我已将有感于我们这次相聚的想法奉告各位，我就要离开这里了。但是在我离开前，我还要再次以谦卑的心情向上帝祈求。因为他向来乐于赐给美国人民机会，使他们能够深思熟虑；也乐于赐给他们支配权，去决定一个巩固他们的联盟并促进幸福的政府体制。所以，在开阔视野、平和协商及采取明智措施这些使这个国家赖以成功的重要因素方面，我们都可以看到同样显著的上帝之神的赐福。

[1]华盛顿这里是指防止有人仅仅为了获得高额报酬而进入政府任职。

约翰·亚当斯
John Adams

约翰·亚当斯（John Adams）

生平简介 >>

约翰·亚当斯是美国第二任总统。他于1735年10月30日出生在马萨诸塞州。他年轻时就投身于爱国事业，并就读于哈佛大学法律专业。

亚当斯是第一届和第二届大陆会议的最强有力的代表之一。在独立战争后期，他大部分时间从事外交工作。他在法国、荷兰任职，并协助和平条约的谈判。从1785年到1788年，他是驻英国公使。回国后，他即被选为华盛顿手下的副总统。1796年当选为总统。

1826年7月4日，亚当斯死于布伦特里自己的家中。这一天恰是由他主要负责起草的《独立宣言》发表50周年。更为凑巧的是，他的老朋友和同僚托马斯·杰斐逊也于同一天去世。

亚当斯还是第一位住进白宫的总统，时间是1800年11月。

John Adams
Inaugural Address

March 4, 1797

When it was first perceived, in early times, that no middle course for America remained between unlimited submission to a foreign legislature and a total independence of its claims, men of reflection were less apprehensive of danger from the formidable power of fleets and armies they must determine to resist than from those contests and dissensions which would certainly arise concerning the forms of government to be instituted over the whole and over the parts of this extensive country. Relying, however, on the purity of their intentions, the justice of their cause, and the integrity and intelligence of the people, under an overruling Providence which had so signally protected this country from the first, the representatives of this nation, then consisting of little more than half its present number, not only broke to pieces the chains which were forging and the rod of iron that was lifted up, but frankly cut asunder the ties which had bound them, and launched into an ocean of uncertainty.

The zeal and ardor of the people during the Revolutionary war, supplying the place of government, commanded a degree of order sufficient at least for the temporary preservation of society. The Confederation which was early felt to be necessary was prepared from the models of the Batavian and Helvetic confederacies, the only examples which remain with any detail and precision in history, and certainly the only ones which the people at large had ever considered. But reflecting on the striking difference in so many particulars between this country and those where a courier may go from the seat of government to the frontier in a single day, it was then certainly foreseen by some who assisted in Congress at the formation of it that it could not be durable.

Negligence of its regulations, inattention to its recommendations, if not

约翰·亚当斯
John Adams

亚当斯总统就职演说

1797年3月4日

早先,当有识之士初次意识到,在将自己的全部主权交付外国立法机关和主权彻底独立之前,美利坚没有中间道路可走,他们并不害怕抵抗外国强大的海军和陆军,他们更为担心的是,在这个疆域辽阔的国家应当建立何种形式的全国和州政府,这必然会引起种种斗争和分歧。然而,这个国家当时人数仅为现在一半的代表们凭着他们纯洁的动机、正义的事业以及人民的正直和智慧,在建国伊始就格外保护这个国家的伟大神明的指引下,不仅粉碎了正在锻制的锁链和铁棍,并且毅然冲破一切束缚,将它们投诸无边的大海之中。

在独立战争期间,全民的高涨热情,不但奠定了政府的地位,而且也暂时维持了社会的稳定秩序。人民早就觉得有必要成立合众国,并根据荷属印尼(Batavian)和瑞士(Helvetic)这两个邦联的模式着手准备。这两个邦联是历史上具体而明确地保存至今的联邦制的唯一样板,它们当然也是一般民众加以考虑的对象。不过,荷属印尼与瑞士这两个邦联的领土较小,邮差在一天之内便可将消息自首府传送至边境,而我们领土广阔,两者差别很大。出席国会筹建合众国的某些人士,也预见到这些明显的差异,从而断言合众国无法维持长久。

果然,很快就出现了个人与各州均无视联邦规定和不听联邦劝告的现

disobedience to its authority, not only in individuals but in States, soon appeared with their melancholy consequences — universal languor, jealousies and rivalries of States, decline of navigation and commerce, discouragement of necessary manufactures, universal fall in the value of lands and their produce, contempt of public and private faith, loss of consideration and credit with foreign nations, and at length in discontents, animosities, combinations, partial conventions, and insurrection, threatening some great national calamity.

In this dangerous crisis the people of America were not abandoned by their usual good sense, presence of mind, resolution, or integrity. Measures were pursued to concert a plan to form a more perfect union, establish justice, insure domestic tranquility, provide for the common defense, promote the general welfare, and secure the blessings of liberty. The public disquisitions, discussions, and deliberations issued in the present happy Constitution of Government.

Employed in the service of my country abroad during the whole course of these transactions, I first saw the Constitution of the United States in a foreign country. Irritated by no literary altercation, animated by no public debate, heated by no party animosity, I read it with great satisfaction, as the result of good heads prompted by good hearts, as an experiment better adapted to the genius, character, situation, and relations of this nation and country than any which had ever been proposed or suggested. In its general principles and great outlines it was conformable to such a system of government as I had ever most esteemed, and in some States, my own native State in particular, had contributed to establish. Claiming a right of suffrage, in common with my fellow-citizens, in the adoption or rejection of a constitution which was to rule me and my posterity, as well as them and theirs, I did not hesitate to express my approbation of it on all occasions, in public and in private. It was not then, nor has been since, any objection to it in my mind that the Executive and Senate were not more permanent. Nor have I ever entertained a thought of promoting any alteration in it but such as the people themselves, in the course of their experience, should see and feel to be necessary or expedient, and by their representatives in Congress and the State legislatures, according to the

约翰·亚当斯
John Adams

象,这即便不算违背联邦权威,但也带来了令人忧郁的后果——各州普遍存在着怠惰、嫉妒和敌对情绪;海运及商业衰落;必需品的制造受到影响,土地及农产品的价格普遍下降;公私双方都对合众国失去信心,并丧失了对外国的尊敬与信任,最后在不满、仇恨、派系勾结、存有偏见的政党大会以及暴乱中,发展成为全国性的大灾难。[1]

在这种危急的情况下,美国人民仍保持着他们特有的良知、冷静、决心和正直。他们想尽办法拟订计划,以组成一个更完美的联盟,确立公理与正义,保障国内安定,提供联合防卫力量,促进大众福利,并确保自由幸福。人民经过探索、讨论和深思熟虑,最终制定了目前这部令人满意的政府宪章。

在这个发展进程中,我因公被派驻国外,在异邦首次看到了美国宪法。既不见文辞争执,又不见公开辩论,也未闻党派争斗,在这种种激励之下,我满意地阅读了这部宪法。我认为它是一批热心的有识之士的杰作,较之人们提出或建议实行的其他任何实验,均更切合美国,以及美国人民的智慧、特性、环境和各种关系。该宪法所规定的一般原则与主要纲领,与我过去最推崇的政府组织是一致的,而且某些州对建立这样的政府制度做出了贡献,尤以我的故乡所在的州[2]为最。和我的同胞一样,我也要求采用投票来决定接受或拒绝一部管理我与他们的子孙万代的宪法。但不论在公开的还是私下的场合,我都会毫不迟疑地表达出我对这部宪法的认可。无论是在当时还是以后,我从未有过行政部门和参议院不能维持长久的想法;我更未有过任何改变宪法的念头,除非美国人民经过多年实践验证,觉得修改宪法是必要的,并由国会或州议会的议员根据宪法做出相应的修正。

[1]亚当斯属联邦党人,一向主张强化联邦政府的权力。
[2]指马萨诸塞州。

Constitution itself, adopt and ordain.

Returning to the bosom of my country after a painful separation from it for ten years, I had the honor to be elected to a station under the new order of things, and I have repeatedly laid myself under the most serious obligations to support the Constitution. The operation of it has equaled the most sanguine expectations of its friends, and from an habitual attention to it, satisfaction in its administration, and delight in its effects upon the peace, order, prosperity, and happiness of the nation I have acquired an habitual attachment to it and veneration for it.

What other form of government, indeed, can so well deserve our esteem and love?

There may be little solidity in an ancient idea that congregations of men into cities and nations are the most pleasing objects in the sight of superior intelligences, but this is very certain, that to a benevolent human mind there can be no spectacle presented by any nation more pleasing, more noble, majestic, or august, than an assembly like that which has so often been seen in this and the other Chamber of Congress, of a Government in which the Executive authority, as well as that of all the branches of the Legislature, are exercised by citizens selected at regular periods by their neighbors to make and execute laws for the general good. Can anything essential, anything more than mere ornament and decoration, be added to this by robes and diamonds? Can authority be more amiable and respectable when it descends from accidents or institutions established in remote antiquity than when it springs fresh from the hearts and judgments of an honest and enlightened people? For it is the people only that are represented. It is their power and majesty that is reflected, and only for their good, in every legitimate government, under whatever form it may appear. The existence of such a government as ours for any length of time is a full proof of a general dissemination of knowledge and virtue throughout the whole body of the people. And what object or consideration more pleasing than this can be presented to the human mind? If national pride is ever justifiable or excusable it is when it springs, not from power or riches, grandeur or glory, but from conviction of national innocence, information, and benevolence.

约翰·亚当斯
John Adams

经过十年与祖国痛苦的分离之后,我又重新回到她的怀抱。[1]在新的情况下,我有幸荣登总统职位,所以我不断提醒自己身负维护宪法的重任。在支持者的殷切盼望下,宪法开始实施了。我时常关注宪法,对它的执行情况感到满意,并对它在国家和平、秩序、繁荣、幸福等方面产生的功效感到喜悦,所以,我对宪法拥有一种自然的依赖和崇敬之情。

的确,还有哪一种政体能如此值得我们这样尊敬与热爱呢?

在古老的观念中,人们聚集在一起形成城市与国家,在有知识的人眼中是最令人愉快的事。当然,这种想法或许不完全对。不过,可以肯定的是,对善良的人类心灵来说,任何其他国家所呈现的景象,都比不上在我们的国会及州议会经常出现的情景那样庄严、高尚和令人敬畏:政府的行政权力和各州议会的职责,由各地在一定时期内选出的公民来行使,以大众利益为目标,制定或执行法律。官服和钻石除了装点门面之外,难道还能为此增加任何实质性的东西吗?那种由偶然继承所得,或出自远古时代确立的权威比一个诚实文明的民族根据自己的意志及判断力而不断更新的权威更可亲、更可敬吗?主权属于全体人民,不论在何种合法的政体下,它都反映出全民的权力与最高权威,并且对人民有利而无害。像我们这样的政府,不论存在多久,都是全人类知识与道德普遍传播的证明。在人类心灵中还会出现什么比这更令人愉快的事情呢?只要民族自豪感不是来自权势与富贵,而是来自国家的纯净、知识与仁爱的信念,那么这份荣誉便是正当的,可以理解的。

---

[1]自独立战争时起,亚当斯即受命去欧洲,担任驻法国、荷兰的使节,驻英国公使,并参与制定对英和约,直到1788年奉召回国。

In the midst of these pleasing ideas we should be unfaithful to ourselves if we should ever lose sight of the danger to our liberties if anything partial or extraneous should infect the purity of our free, fair, virtuous, and independent elections. If an election is to be determined by a majority of a single vote, and that can be procured by a party through artifice or corruption, the Government may be the choice of a party for its own ends, not of the nation for the national good. If that solitary suffrage can be obtained by foreign nations by flattery or menaces, by fraud or violence, by terror, intrigue, or venality, the Government may not be the choice of the American people, but of foreign nations. It may be foreign nations who govern us, and not we, the people, who govern ourselves; and candid men will acknowledge that in such cases choice would have little advantage to boast of over lot or chance.

Such is the amiable and interesting system of government (and such are some of the abuses to which it may be exposed) which the people of America have exhibited to the admiration and anxiety of the wise and virtuous of all nations for eight years under the administration of a citizen who, by a long course of great actions, regulated by prudence, justice, temperance, and fortitude, conducting a people inspired with the same virtues and animated with the same ardent patriotism and love of liberty to independence and peace, to increasing wealth and unexampled prosperity, has merited the gratitude of his fellow-citizens, commanded the highest praises of foreign nations, and secured immortal glory with posterity.

In that retirement which is his voluntary choice may he long live to enjoy the delicious recollection of his services, the gratitude of mankind, the happy fruits of them to himself and the world, which are daily increasing, and that splendid prospect of the future fortunes of this country which is opening from year to year. His name may be still a rampart, and the knowledge that he lives a bulwark, against all open or secret enemies of his country's peace. This example has been recommended to the imitation of his successors by both Houses of Congress and by the voice of the legislatures and the people throughout the nation.

On this subject it might become me better to be silent or to speak with

约翰·亚当斯
John Adams

如果任何偏见或外来事物影响到我们纯洁、自由、公正和独立的选举，我们的自由就会陷入危险之中；如果我们对此视而不见，一味沉溺于这些美妙的想法，那我们就未免自欺欺人。如果选举是以一人一票的多数票来决定胜负，那么一个政党便可能通过计谋或贿赂等不当手段获取胜利，那么这样选举出来的政府则可能成为政党为达到一党私利，而不是国家为了全国利益所做出的选择。假使其他国家的势力利用谄媚胁迫、欺诈暴力、阴谋贿赂等伎俩在这个一人一票的选举中获胜，那么这个政府就不是由美国人民选出的，而是外国的选择。那时我们将会沦为异邦统治，而不是由我们全体人民统治。正直的人们将会感觉到，在这种情况下选举与赌博就相差无几了。

这就是八年来美国人民在一位伟大公民领导下向世界展示的一种亲切而有趣的政府制度，它引起各国有识之士的赞赏，当然也有不安。这位公民通过自己的模范行动运用谨慎公正、自制刚毅的法则，领导着一个同样为美德所鼓舞，为爱国精神所激励，并且热爱自由、独立与和平的民族去增加财富和走向空前的繁荣。这八年来他对国家的贡献，实应受到全国同胞的感激，博得各国的最高赞誉，并定能流芳百世。

在他自愿退职之际，我希望他能长寿，永远沉浸在为国辛勤奉献的美好回忆中，接受人类的感激，以及他们呈献给他和全世界的幸福果实。这果实将与日俱增，而这个国家未来前途的光明远景也将随着时间的推移而展现出来。他的英名将是一道坚强防线，他的长存将筑成一座堡垒，抵御一切危害国家和平的公开或隐蔽的敌人。他为我们树立的榜样已经由国会两院、各州议会和全国人民的同声推荐而成为继任者效仿的典范。

关于能否效仿前任典范的问题，我最好保持沉默，或者不要过于自信

diffidence; but as something may be expected, the occasion, I hope, will be admitted as an apology if I venture to say that if a preference, upon principle, of a free republican government, formed upon long and serious reflection, after a diligent and impartial inquiry after truth; if an attachment to the Constitution of the United States, and a conscientious determination to support it until it shall be altered by the judgments and wishes of the people, expressed in the mode prescribed in it; if a respectful attention to the constitutions of the individual States and a constant caution and delicacy toward the State governments; if an equal and impartial regard to the rights, interest, honor, and happiness of all the States in the Union, without preference or regard to a northern or southern, an eastern or western, position, their various political opinions on unessential points or their personal attachments; if a love of virtuous men of all parties and denominations; if a love of science and letters and a wish to patronize every rational effort to encourage schools, colleges, universities, academies, and every institution for propagating knowledge, virtue, and religion among all classes of the people, not only for their benign influence on the happiness of life in all its stages and classes, and of society in all its forms, but as the only means of preserving our Constitution from its natural enemies, the spirit of sophistry, the spirit of party, the spirit of intrigue, the profligacy of corruption, and the pestilence of foreign influence, which is the angel of destruction to elective governments; if a love of equal laws, of justice, and humanity in the interior administration; if an inclination to improve agriculture, commerce, and manufacturers for necessity, convenience, and defense; if a spirit of equity and humanity toward the aboriginal nations of America, and a disposition to meliorate their condition by inclining them to be more friendly to us, and our citizens to be more friendly to them; if an inflexible determination to maintain peace and inviolable faith with all nations, and that system of neutrality and impartiality among the belligerent powers of Europe which has been adopted by this Government and so solemnly sanctioned by both Houses of Congress and applauded by the legislatures of the States and the public opinion, until it shall be otherwise ordained by Congress; if a personal esteem for the French nation, formed in a residence of seven years chiefly among them, and a sincere

约翰·亚当斯
John Adams

地说些什么。不过大家都期待我有所表示,因而我希望在这个场合大胆发表见解,而不致冒天下之大不韪。只要按原则所选出的政府,是在依事实展开公平认真的调查后,经过长时期的审慎考虑所组成;只要对美国宪法的忠心与支持(支持它直到人民希望要求修改它的时候)的那份诚实的决心在宪法规定的形式中表达出来;只要能尊重各州的法律,并时时关心各州政府;只要大家对联邦内各州的权利、利益、荣誉、幸福等持同等和公正的态度,不管它是东、西、南、北任何一方,也不管各州的地位和在一些次要问题上所持的各种不同的政治意见以及他们个人的好恶;只要所有的党派都荐贤举德;只要大家都热爱文学与科学,并尽力振兴各级学校、学院、大学专门研究机构,使它们在各阶层民众中传播知识、道德与宗教思想,因为这不只是为了使学校能对各阶层及一切社会形式的幸福生活产生良好影响,也因为这是保护我们的宪法的唯一方式,使其免受各种天敌的危害,例如诡辩、党派、阴谋等风气,贪污受贿,以至行为不检,外来影响的渗透,从而导致民选政府的瓦解;只要国内行政是出自对平等法律、公理及人性的爱;只要有为了需要、方便与防卫而改进农、工、商的要求;只要对待美洲的原始居民和印第安人能持以平等人道的精神,并使他们相信,如果他们对我们友好,我们也会平等相待,从而来改善印第安人的状况;只要我们以坚定不移的信念,与世界上所有国家恪守和平与互不侵犯的誓约;只要政府在欧洲交战国之间采取中立,这种中立政策是由国会两院郑重批准,并受到各州议会与民意一致赞成,直到国会另做决定时为止;只要我个人对法国怀有敬意——这种敬意是因在那里居住了七年而养成的,并且热诚渴望要维系双方互敬互利的友谊;只要在保护美国人民的荣誉与其所有权利的前提下,能尽力查清每个问题的正当原因,并消除一切冠冕堂皇的抱怨;只要我们在同胞的商业活动受到任何一国侵害时,愿意以和平谈判寻求补救,如果失败了,我们愿意将事实真相呈交立法机关,由它来考虑保护政府荣誉、利益和选民要求的进一步措施;只要我们决心随时以公正的态度对待所有国家(关于这一点,我的责任甚重),并与全球维持和平、友谊和仁慈待人;只要我们对美国人民的荣誉、精神、资源等方面具有坚定的信心,在这方面我常常冒险,但从未失望过;只要我国命运的崇高意念和我对国家应尽职责的崇高意念,根植于对人民的道德准则与智力利用的认识之上——这一观念在我早年时就已铭刻在心,不但未晦暗失色,反而随时间、经验的积累而增强;此外,在谦卑恭敬的心情下,我觉得补充

desire to preserve the friendship which has been so much for the honor and interest of both nations; if, while the conscious honor and integrity of the people of America and the internal sentiment of their own power and energies must be preserved, an earnest endeavor to investigate every just cause and remove every colorable pretense of complaint; if an intention to pursue by amicable negotiation a reparation for the injuries that have been committed on the commerce of our fellow-citizens by whatever nation, and if success can not be obtained, to lay the facts before the Legislature, that they may consider what further measures the honor and interest of the Government and its constituents demand; if a resolution to do justice as far as may depend upon me, at all times and to all nations, and maintain peace, friendship, and benevolence with all the world; if an unshaken confidence in the honor, spirit, and resources of the American people, on which I have so often hazarded my all and never been deceived; if elevated ideas of the high destinies of this country and of my own duties toward it, founded on a knowledge of the moral principles and intellectual improvements of the people deeply engraven on my mind in early life, and not obscured but exalted by experience and age; and, with humble reverence, I feel it to be my duty to add, if a veneration for the religion of a people who profess and call themselves Christians, and a fixed resolution to consider a decent respect for Christianity among the best recommendations for the public service, can enable me in any degree to comply with your wishes, it shall be my strenuous endeavor that this sagacious injunction of the two Houses shall not be without effect.

With this great example before me, with the sense and spirit, the faith and honor, the duty and interest, of the same American people pledged to support the Constitution of the United States, I entertain no doubt of its continuance in all its energy, and my mind is prepared without hesitation to lay myself under the most solemn obligations to support it to the utmost of my power.

And may that Being who is supreme over all, the Patron of Order, the Fountain of Justice, and the Protector in all ages of the world of virtuous liberty, continue His blessing upon this nation and its Government and give it all possible success and duration consistent with the ends of His providence.

以下这点是我的责任,那就是,只要我们对宗教——一个自认、自称为基督徒的民族所信仰的宗教——抱有敬意;并且只要我们在推荐公职最佳人选时,能坚定不移地适当考虑其是否敬重基督教,那么我在任何事情上,都能满足你们的愿望,并将全力完成两院制定的法律和法令!

在我面前已有一位伟大的表率,而当初立誓要拥护美国宪法的美国人民,仍然抱有同样的思想和精神,同样的信念和荣誉,同样的责任和兴趣,因而我保证:我将对美国宪法的永久性毫不怀疑,而且我也毫不犹豫地决定献身于这项最神圣的职责,尽我最大的力量去保护和捍卫宪法。

愿至高无上之神,秩序的守护神,正义之源,善良自由世界的保护神,继续降福于我们的国家和我们的政府,并赐予它一切可能的成功,使其与上帝同样永世长存。

托马斯·杰斐逊
Thomas Jefferson

托马斯·杰斐逊（Thomas Jefferson）

生平简介 >>

托马斯·杰斐逊是美国第三任总统。他于1743年4月13日出生在弗吉尼亚州。

1769年他当选为弗吉尼亚州下议院议员。1774年，他写的《英属美洲的权利概述》为殖民地的自治提出了坚定明确的要求。1776年，他出席费城大陆会议，并被推为《独立宣言》第一稿的执笔者，并因此而出名。1789年，他担任华盛顿总统内阁的国务卿，这时他发现总统在大部分重要问题上采取汉密尔顿的方针，而他与汉密尔顿的矛盾分歧却越来越深，于是在1793年12月底辞职。1796年，他成为共和党总统候选人，但败在约翰·亚当斯手下，只得屈就副总统之职。

1800年，他和艾伦·伯尔在总统大选中获得了相同的选票，经众议院投票，杰斐逊以一票的优势当选总统。当选后他毅然从法国手中买下路易斯安那州，从而使美国的面积扩大了一倍。1804年11月，他再次当选总统。

1826年7月4日——美国独立50周年纪念日，他病逝于弗吉尼亚州蒙蒂塞洛山顶上自己的家中。

美国历届总统就职演说

THE INAUGURAL ADDRESSES OF THE U.S. PRESIDENTS

Thomas Jefferson
First Inaugural Address

March 4, 1801

Friends and Fellow-Citizens:

Called upon to undertake the duties of the first executive office of our country, I avail myself of the presence of that portion of my fellow-citizens which is here assembled to express my grateful thanks for the favor with which they have been pleased to look toward me, to declare a sincere consciousness that the task is above my talents, and that I approach it with those anxious and awful presentiments which the greatness of the charge and the weakness of my powers so justly inspire. A rising nation, spread over a wide and fruitful land, traversing all the seas with the rich productions of their industry, engaged in commerce with nations who feel power and forget right, advancing rapidly to destinies beyond the reach of mortal eye — when I contemplate these transcendent objects, and see the honor, the happiness, and the hopes of this beloved country committed to the issue, and the auspices of this day, I shrink from the contemplation, and humble myself before the magnitude of the undertaking. Utterly, indeed, should I despair did not the presence of many whom I here see remind me that in the other high authorities provided by our Constitution I shall find resources of wisdom, of virtue, and of zeal on which to rely under all difficulties. To you, then, gentlemen, who are charged with the sovereign functions of legislation, and to those associated with you, I look with encouragement for that guidance and support which may enable us to steer with safety the vessel in which we are all embarked amidst the conflicting elements of a troubled world.

杰斐逊总统首次就职演说

1801年3月4日

各位朋友和同胞：

我受托担任我国最高行政首长的职务，借诸位同胞在此集会之机，对大家寄予我的期望，表示深深的谢意。同时，诚挚地说，我意识到这项任务非我能力所及，其责任重大，而本人能力浅薄，自然使我就任时感到忧惧交加。一个新兴的国家，在一片广阔而物产富饶的土地上成长，带着其丰富的工业产品横渡大洋，与那些只知强权、忘记正义的国家进行商业贸易[1]，向着世人无法预见的天命疾奔。当我注视这些远大的目标，并看到我们所热爱的国家，它的荣誉、幸福与希望，都系于今天所发生的盛典，我便不敢再想下去，在这宏图大业面前，我自感十分渺小。的确，如果不是今天我在这里见到的许多人士提醒我，无论遇到什么困难，都可以向宪法规定的国会两院寻求智慧、美德和热诚，我一定会心灰气馁。因此对于从事神圣的立法工作的各位先生们和有关人士，我鼓起勇气期待着你们给予我指点与支持，这将使我们能够同舟共济，在充满矛盾和冲突的世界中平安地航行。

---

[1]这里指英国仗着其海上霸权，阻拦美国与欧洲的贸易。

美国历届总统就职演说
THE INAUGURAL ADDRESSES OF THE U.S. PRESIDENTS

During the contest of opinion through which we have passed the animation of discussions and of exertions has sometimes worn an aspect which might impose on strangers unused to think freely and to speak and to write what they think; but this being now decided by the voice of the nation, announced according to the rules of the Constitution, all will, of course, arrange themselves under the will of the law, and unite in common efforts for the common good. All, too, will bear in mind this sacred principle, that though the will of the majority is in all cases to prevail, that will to be rightful must be reasonable; that the minority possess their equal rights, which equal law must protect, and to violate would be oppression. Let us, then, fellow-citizens, unite with one heart and one mind. Let us restore to social intercourse that harmony and affection without which liberty and even life itself are but dreary things. And let us reflect that, having banished from our land that religious intolerance under which mankind so long bled and suffered, we have yet gained little if we countenance a political intolerance as despotic, as wicked, and capable of as bitter and bloody persecutions. During the throes and convulsions of the ancient world, during the agonizing spasms of infuriated man, seeking through blood and slaughter his long-lost liberty, it was not wonderful that the agitation of the billows should reach even this distant and peaceful shore; that this should be more felt and feared by some and less by others, and should divide opinions as to measures of safety. But every difference of opinion is not a difference of principle. We have called by different names brethren of the same principle. We are all Republicans, we are all Federalists. If there be any among us who would wish to dissolve this Union or to change its republican form, let them stand undisturbed as monuments of the safety with which error of opinion may be tolerated where reason is left free to combat it. I know, indeed, that some honest men fear that a republican government can not be strong, that this Government is not strong enough; but would the honest patriot, in the full tide of successful experiment, abandon a government which has so far kept us free and firm on the theoretic and visionary fear that this Government, the world's best hope, may by possibility want energy to preserve itself? I trust not. I believe this, on the contrary, the strongest Government on earth. I believe it

托马斯·杰斐逊
Thomas Jefferson

在过去的意见争执中[1]，大家激烈地讨论，极力发挥所长，以致有时情况相当紧张，强迫那些不习惯于思想自由的人，把他们所想的说出来或写出来。但如今这种争论已由全国的民意做出决定，而且根据宪法的规定予以公布。大家当然会在法律的意志下消除分歧，并且团结一致为共同的利益而努力。大家当然也不会忘记那个神圣的法则，这就是在任何情况下，事情是由多数人的意志决定的，但是那些意见必须合理而公正。而且其他少数人的意见也拥有同样的权利，平等地受到法律的保护；如果不是这样，那无异就是高压手段。因此，同胞们，让我们一心一意地团结起来。让我们恢复社会的和谐与友爱，因为没有它们，自由甚至生活本身，就将成为枯燥而无味的事情。让我们仔细想想，那些使人类长期流血、受苦的宗教偏见，已被我们驱逐于国土之外。如果我们让政治上的偏见存在，使之成为与宗教上的不宽容一样的专制与邪恶，就会造成同样的痛苦与血腥的迫害，那么我们努力所得到的成果就差不多付诸东流了。当旧的世界处在痛苦和动乱之时，当愤怒的人在挣扎着想通过流血和战争寻找他们失去已久的自由时，毫不奇怪，这种波涛般的骚动，甚至会冲击到遥远而和平的此岸。人们对此的感触和忧虑不会一样，因此，对安全的衡量，就会有不同的意见。但是，每一个意见上的差异都不是原则上的差异，只是在同一原则上，我们有不同的说法罢了。我们都是赞成共和制的人，我们也都是联邦主义者。如果我们当中有人想解散这个联邦，或改变它的共和形式，我们也不会干扰他们，以便为安全树起一种标志，以此表明只要理智能够自由地进行对抗，即使错误的意见也应容许存在并同它斗争。我知道，事实上，有些正直的人士担心一个共和政府不可能强大，生怕我们的政府不够强大。[2]但是，难道这些诚实的爱国者，在大量的成功的试验面前会因一种理论和空想的疑惧，就以为这个被全世界寄予希望的政府，可能缺乏力量维护自己，放弃这个到目前为止带给我们自由和幸福的政府吗？我相信不会。相反，这是世界上最坚强的政府。我相信，在这个政府之下，任何一个人，一经法律的召唤，就会按照法律的要求，像对待切身利益那样，迎击侵犯公共秩序的举动。人们总是说，自己管理自己是不可靠的，那么，难道受别人

---

[1]联邦成立之初，以杰斐逊为首的共和党人和以汉密尔顿为首的联邦党人对国家政策常有争议。如在内政上，杰斐逊重视发展农业，汉密尔顿侧重发展工业。在外交上，杰斐逊比较亲法，汉密尔顿比较亲英。值得一提的是，联邦党人的亲英政策导致美国人民对其极度反感，在19世纪20年代，该党消失。此为后话。

[2]联邦党人一向主张建立联邦政府的优越地位，而共和党人则重于强化州政府的功能。

the only one where every man, at the call of the law, would fly to the standard of the law, and would meet invasions of the public order as his own personal concern. Sometimes it is said that man can not be trusted with the government of himself. Can he, then, be trusted with the government of others? Or have we found angels in the forms of kings to govern him? Let history answer this question.

Let us, then, with courage and confidence pursue our own Federal and Republican principles, our attachment to union and representative government. Kindly separated by nature and a wide ocean from the exterminating havoc of one quarter of the globe; too high-minded to endure the degradations of the others; possessing a chosen country, with room enough for our descendants to the thousandth and thousandth generation; entertaining a due sense of our equal right to the use of our own faculties, to the acquisitions of our own industry, to honor and confidence from our fellow-citizens, resulting not from birth, but from our actions and their sense of them; enlightened by a benign religion, professed, indeed, and practiced in various forms, yet all of them inculcating honesty, truth, temperance, gratitude, and the love of man; acknowledging and adoring an overruling Providence, which by all its dispensations proves that it delights in the happiness of man here and his greater happiness hereafter — with all these blessings, what more is necessary to make us a happy and a prosperous people? Still one thing more, fellow-citizens — a wise and frugal Government, which shall restrain men from injuring one another, shall leave them otherwise free to regulate their own pursuits of industry and improvement, and shall not take from the mouth of labor the bread it has earned. This is the sum of good government, and this is necessary to close the circle of our felicities.

About to enter, fellow-citizens, on the exercise of duties which comprehend everything dear and valuable to you, it is proper you should understand what I deem the essential principles of our Government, and consequently those which ought to shape its Administration. I will compress them within the narrowest compass they will bear, stating the general principle, but not all its limitations. Equal and exact justice to all men, of whatever state or persuasion, religious or political; peace, commerce, and honest friendship with all nations,

托马斯·杰斐逊
Thomas Jefferson

的管理就会可靠吗?难道我们曾见过以国王的身份而出现的天使来管理人们吗?让历史来回答这个问题吧!

因此,让我们以勇气和信心,践行我们自己的联邦与共和的原则,热爱我们的联邦和代议制政府。我们由于大自然及大洋的阻隔,幸免于地球另一区域毁灭性的灾难。[1]我们品格高尚,不能容忍他人堕落。我们拥有一个伟大的国家,足以容纳我们千万代的子孙。我们充分意识到,在运用自己的才智,拥有我们自己的工业产品,博取同胞对我们的行为而不是对我们的出身背景的尊敬与信心等方面,都享有同等的权利。我们有良好的宗教,虽然教派不同,形式各异,但它们都教导人们诚实、坦白、自制、感恩和博爱。我们承认并崇拜无所不能的上帝,由于他的支配管理,这里的人们享受着幸福而且直到永远。有了这所有的祝福,还会有什么比这更能使我们成为一个快乐与繁荣的民族呢?同胞们!还有一点,那就是我们仍需要一个廉明的政府,来制止人们互相伤害,使人们自由地从事其实业及改良活动,而且不剥夺任何人以劳动赚取的报酬。这是一个良好政府的要义,也是我们取得圆满幸福所必需的。

各位同胞,我即将开始履行职责,它包括一切对你们而言宝贵而有价值的事情。此时你们应当了解,什么是我们政府所坚持的主要原则,以及组成行政班子的主要原则。我将把这些原则简要地加以讲述,只讲一般原则,而不讲其种种限制:不论其地位或观点,宗教的或政治的派别,大家一律平等和公正;与各国和平相处,加强商业往来,并保持真诚的友谊,

---

[1]指欧洲的战争。法国革命后,在欧洲大陆上爆发了多次法国与欧洲的封建势力的战争。

entangling alliances with none; the support of the State governments in all their rights, as the most competent administrations for our domestic concerns and the surest bulwarks against anti-republican tendencies; the preservation of the General Government in its whole constitutional vigor, as the sheet anchor of our peace at home and safety abroad; a jealous care of the right of election by the people — a mild and safe corrective of abuses which are lopped by the sword of revolution where peaceable remedies are unprovoked; absolute acquiescence in the decisions of the majority, the vital principle of republics, from which is no appeal but to force, the vital principle and immediate parent of despotism; a well disciplined militia, our best reliance in peace and for the first moments of war, till regulars may relieve them; the supremacy of the civil over the military authority; economy in the public expense, that labor may be lightly burdened; the honest payment of our debts and sacred preservation of the public faith; encouragement of agriculture, and of commerce as its handmaid; the diffusion of information and arraignment of all abuses at the bar of the public reason; freedom of religion; freedom of the press, and freedom of person under the protection of the habeas corpus, and trial by juries impartially selected. These principles form the bright constellation which has gone before us and guided our steps through an age of revolution and reformation. The wisdom of our sages and blood of our heroes have been devoted to their attainment. They should be the creed of our political faith, the text of civic instruction, the touchstone by which to try the services of those we trust; and should we wander from them in moments of error or of alarm, let us hasten to retrace our steps and to regain the road which alone leads to peace, liberty, and safety.

I repair, then, fellow-citizens, to the post you have assigned me. With experience enough in subordinate offices to have seen the difficulties of this the greatest of all, I have learnt to expect that it will rarely fall to the lot of imperfect man to retire from this station with the reputation and the favor which bring him into it. Without pretensions to that high confidence you reposed in our first and greatest revolutionary character, whose preeminent services had entitled him to the first place in his country's love and destined for him the fairest page in the volume of faithful history, I ask so much confidence

托马斯·杰斐逊
Thomas Jefferson

但不与任何国家结盟；维护各州政府的一切权利，使其成为我们内政上最胜任的机构，并成为同一切反共和倾向斗争的坚强堡垒；维护联邦政府在宪法上的地位，作为对内安定与对外安全保障的最后依靠；努力维护人民的选举权——对于在缺乏和平手段的革命中所产生的权利滥用，要以一种温和而安全的方式予以矫正；不赞成多数统治这个共和制的最重要原则，并由此而实行的强暴统治，这就是独裁政治的主要和直接的根源；维持一支训练有素的民兵，作为和平时期和战争初期的最好依靠，直到正规军来接替；文官权力高于军队权力；节省公共开支，以减轻公民负担；诚实偿付我们的债务，以维持人民对政府的信心；鼓励农业，并促进商业发展以协助农业；传播知识，并在公共理性的审判席上控诉一切弊端；保障宗教自由及出版自由，并根据人身保障法保障民众自由；公正地选出陪审员以从事审判和判决。这些原则，在革命和改革时期，已成为我们的座右铭。先哲们的智慧和英雄们的鲜血，都贡献给了他们的崇高事业。它们应当是我们政治信仰的信条、公民教育的范本、检验我们工作的试金石。如果因为一时的错误想法或在危急时刻背弃了这些原则，就应该赶快停止我们的脚步，重返这唯一通向和平、自由与安全的大道。

　　同胞们！我现在开始担负起你们所委派给我的职务。根据以往在其他较低职位中所获得的经验，我已觉察到这是所有任务中最艰巨最困难的一项。我知道，一个不尽完美的人，当其卸任时，很少能够得到他上任时所享有的声望与荣誉。我并不奢望大家对我也能像过去对我们的第一位也是最伟大的革命元勋一样给予高度的信任，因为他卓越的功绩，最受全国人民的爱戴，他的英名在历史上享有最崇高的地位。我仅要求大家给我相当的信任，使我在依法管理你们的事务时，能够满怀信心、坚定不移并卓有成效。由于判断失误，我可能会时常出现差错。即使我的想法是对的，那

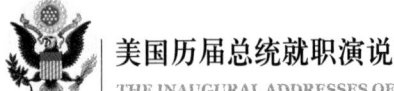

only as may give firmness and effect to the legal administration of your affairs. I shall often go wrong through defect of judgment. When right, I shall often be thought wrong by those whose positions will not command a view of the whole ground. I ask your indulgence for my own errors, which will never be intentional, and your support against the errors of others, who may condemn what they would not if seen in all its parts. The approbation implied by your suffrage is a great consolation to me for the past, and my future solicitude will be to retain the good opinion of those who have bestowed it in advance, to conciliate that of others by doing them all the good in my power, and to be instrumental to the happiness and freedom of all.

Relying, then, on the patronage of your good will, I advance with obedience to the work, ready to retire from it whenever you become sensible how much better choice it is in your power to make. And may that Infinite Power which rules the destinies of the universe lead our councils to what is best, and give them a favorable issue for your peace and prosperity.

托马斯·杰斐逊
Thomas Jefferson

些不是站在统筹全局的立场上看问题的人，也会认为我是错的。我希望大家能宽容我——绝不是有意地——犯的错误；也希望大家能支持我反对他人也许因未能从大局着眼而产生的错误。从大家的投票结果来看，我知道我过去的表现已获得大家的赞许，这使我感到莫大的安慰。未来我所渴望的是，如何使那些已经给我嘉许的人，继续保持对我的良好印象；对其他人，如何在我的权力范围内尽最大的努力，以博得他们对我的好感与尊敬。同时，我要为所有同胞的幸福与自由而努力。

最后，仰承你们的好意，我将尽忠职守，一旦大家感觉你们有能力做更好的选择，我便准备辞去此职。同时，祈求主宰宇宙命运的神灵，使我们的行政机构日臻完善，使人民实现和平与昌盛。

詹姆斯·麦迪逊
James Madison

詹姆斯·麦迪逊（James Madison）

生平简介 >>

詹姆斯·麦迪逊是美国第四任总统。他于1751年3月16日出生在弗吉尼亚州。他毕业于新泽西学院(后改名为普林斯顿大学)，是革命的活跃分子，但是身体太弱，没有资格参军。1776年，他曾出席"弗吉尼亚制宪会议"。他还是出席大陆会议的代表、北部联邦党人文件的起草人之一、众议院议员、民主共和党的组织者、杰斐逊总统的国务卿。

麦迪逊和汉密尔顿、约翰·杰伊在宪法诞生后，一起写了一系列的文章，为宪法的批准做出了重大的贡献。

麦迪逊连任两届总统，时间为1809年3月4日至1817年3月4日。这八年是令人灰心和充满困难的八年，美国在许多事情上都很不顺利。这时，英美关系恶化，1812年美国对英宣战，但由于美国没有做好准备，战况不佳，最后安德鲁·杰克逊将军在新奥尔良取得了巨大胜利，才确保了美国人在这次战争中获得胜利。

1836年6月28日，麦迪逊在弗吉尼亚州的庄园中去世。

James Madison
First Inaugural Address

March 4, 1809

Unwilling to depart from examples of the most revered authority, I avail myself of the occasion now presented to express the profound impression made on me by the call of my country to the station to the duties of which I am about to pledge myself by the most solemn of sanctions. So distinguished a mark of confidence, proceeding from the deliberate and tranquil suffrage of a free and virtuous nation, would under any circumstances have commanded my gratitude and devotion, as well as filled me with an awful sense of the trust to be assumed. Under the various circumstances which give peculiar solemnity to the existing period, I feel that both the honor and the responsibility allotted to me are inexpressibly enhanced.

The present situation of the world is indeed without a parallel, and that of our own country full of difficulties. The pressure of these, too, is the more severely felt because they have fallen upon us at a moment when the national prosperity being at a height not before attained, the contrast resulting from the change has been rendered the more striking. Under the benign influence of our republican institutions, and the maintenance of peace with all nations whilst so many of them were engaged in bloody and wasteful wars, the fruits of a just policy were enjoyed in an unrivaled growth of our faculties and resources. Proofs of this were seen in the improvements of agriculture, in the successful enterprises of commerce, in the progress of manufacturers and useful arts, in the increase of the public revenue and the use made of it in reducing the public debt, and in the valuable works and establishments everywhere multiplying over the face of our land.

詹姆斯·麦迪逊
James Madison

麦迪逊总统首次就职演说

1809年3月4日

我不愿背离最受人尊敬的前任总统所树立的典范，我要利用这个机会表达我接受国家召唤，即将在庄严神圣的仪式下宣誓就职、担负重任之时我内心的深刻感受。我国自由和公正的人民在这次审慎的选举中，对我表达了鲜明而强烈的信赖，这不仅使我对将要承担的重任满怀敬畏，也能在任何情况下激起我的感激之情和奉献之心。在此时此刻特别隆重庄严的情景下，我深深感到加诸我身上的荣誉与责任，正在无形地增长。

目前的世界形势的确比较特殊，我们国家的情况更是困难重重。这些压力非常大，因为它是在国家的繁荣达到前所未有的高峰时来临的；这种变化与从前的对比更显强烈。在我们的共和体制影响下，当世界各国致力于血腥毁灭的战争时，我国却能与各国维持和平状态，我们因而得享正当政策的成果，我国的财富与实力一度获得了无可比拟的增长。这可以从农业改良、企业成功、产品及实用技术的进步、财政收入的增加并用增加的财政收入减少公共债务，以及各种有价值的工程设施在祖国大地处处兴建的情况中得到证实。

美国历届总统就职演说
THE INAUGURAL ADDRESSES OF THE U.S. PRESIDENTS

It is a precious reflection that the transition from this prosperous condition of our country to the scene which has for some time been distressing us is not chargeable on any unwarrantable views, nor, as I trust, on any involuntary errors in the public councils. Indulging no passions which trespass on the rights or the repose of other nations, it has been the true glory of the United States to cultivate peace by observing justice, and to entitle themselves to the respect of the nations at war by fulfilling their neutral obligations with the most scrupulous impartiality. If there be candor in the world, the truth of these assertions will not be questioned; posterity at least will do justice to them.

This unexceptionable course could not avail against the injustice and violence of the belligerent powers. In their rage against each other, or impelled by more direct motives, principles of retaliation have been introduced equally contrary to universal reason and acknowledged law. How long their arbitrary edicts will be continued in spite of the demonstrations that not even a pretext for them has been given by the United States, and of the fair and liberal attempt to induce a revocation of them, can not be anticipated. Assuring myself that under every vicissitude the determined spirit and united councils of the nation will be safeguards to its honor and its essential interests, I repair to the post assigned me with no other discouragement than what springs from my own inadequacy to its high duties. If I do not sink under the weight of this deep conviction it is because I find some support in a consciousness of the purposes and a confidence in the principles which I bring with me into this arduous service.

To cherish peace and friendly intercourse with all nations having correspondent dispositions; to maintain sincere neutrality toward belligerent nations; to prefer in all cases amicable discussion and reasonable accommodation of differences to a decision of them by an appeal to arms; to exclude foreign intrigues and foreign partialities, so degrading to all countries and so baneful to free ones; to foster a spirit of independence too just to invade the rights of others, too proud to surrender our own, too liberal to indulge unworthy prejudices ourselves and too elevated not to look down upon them in others; to hold the union of the States as the basis of their peace and happiness; to support the Constitution, which is the cement of the Union, as well in its

詹姆斯·麦迪逊
James Madison

  如果认为我们国家从繁荣状态走到目前令人沮丧的情景[1]，只是政府政策上的失误，那是不正确的。而且我相信，这也绝非政府的本意。坚决反对任何侵犯他国权利或扰乱其安宁的行为，坚持正义、维持和平，在战争时期以最谨慎、最公正无私的态度贯彻中立政策，而得到各国的尊重，这才是美国的真正荣耀。如果世界还有公正可言，这些论断的真实可信将不会受到怀疑，至少子孙后世对此会给予公正的评价。

  但这种无可挑剔的行为，并不能有效地制止交战国的残暴行为。它们相互疯狂敌视，或受直接动机的驱使，它们所持的报复的原则，已完全违背了一般理性与公认的法律。尽管美国并没有给这些报复原则以任何口实，尽管美国以公正自由去废止这些逻辑，但我们仍然无法预料它们这些专横的法令还将持续多久。[2]我相信，在任何变化下，国家的坚定精神和团结一致的国会将会保护国家荣誉及其根本利益。因此，在我赴任之际，除了担心自己能力不足以胜任这一职位所负有的崇高责任之外，便不再有其他忧虑。如果说我还没有完全丧失信心的话，是因为我从伴随我履行这项艰巨任务的目标中得到了鼓舞，从我所坚守的原则中得到了信心。

  维护与那些有共同立场国家的友好关系，对交战国保持中立态度，以友好协商与理性调停的方式解决分歧，而不诉诸武力，消除对所有国家不利并对自由国家有害的阴谋与偏见，培养独立精神，使其公正而不致侵犯他人权利，使其自重而不放弃自身权利，使其自由而不致沉溺于自己的毫无价值的偏见，使其高尚而不轻视他人，把维护各州的团结作为和平幸福的基

[1]当时英法正在交战中，美国宣布中立，英法却想方设法进行干扰，特别是阻碍美国与欧洲的通商贸易。美国因而于1807年底对欧洲实行禁运，以示报复，但此举反而遭到英法更强烈的反报复，使得美国国内依赖出口的工商界大为不满。杰斐逊总统终于请求国会于1809年初取消禁运法令，但禁运已使美国工商业走向萧条。

[2]1808年4月拿破仑颁布《贝尤诏令》(Bayoune Decree)，扣押没收泊于法国港口的美国船只，以报复美国实施禁运。

limitations as in its authorities; to respect the rights and authorities reserved to the States and to the people as equally incorporated with and essential to the success of the general system; to avoid the slightest interference with the right of conscience or the functions of religion, so wisely exempted from civil jurisdiction; to preserve in their full energy the other salutary provisions in behalf of private and personal rights, and of the freedom of the press; to observe economy in public expenditures; to liberate the public resources by an honorable discharge of the public debts; to keep within the requisite limits a standing military force, always remembering that an armed and trained militia is the firmest bulwark of republics — that without standing armies their liberty can never be in danger, nor with large ones safe; to promote by authorized means improvements friendly to agriculture, to manufactures, and to external as well as internal commerce; to favor in like manner the advancement of science and the diffusion of information as the best aliment to true liberty; to carry on the benevolent plans which have been so meritoriously applied to the conversion of our aboriginal neighbors from the degradation and wretchedness of savage life to a participation of the improvements of which the human mind and manners are susceptible in a civilized state — as far as sentiments and intentions such as these can aid the fulfillment of my duty, they will be a resource which can not fail me.

It is my good fortune, moreover, to have the path in which I am to tread lighted by examples of illustrious services successfully rendered in the most trying difficulties by those who have marched before me. Of those of my immediate predecessor it might least become me here to speak. I may, however, be pardoned for not suppressing the sympathy with which my heart is full in the rich reward he enjoys in the benedictions of a beloved country, gratefully bestowed or exalted talents zealously devoted through a long career to the advancement of its highest interest and happiness.

But the source to which I look or the aids which alone can supply my deficiencies is in the well-tried intelligence and virtue of my fellow-citizens, and in the counsels of those representing them in the other departments associated in the care of the national interests. In these my confidence will under every

詹姆斯·麦迪逊
James Madison

础，支持用来巩固联邦的宪法，拥护其规定与权威；尊重国家和人民所拥有的权利，这是构成整个社会的一部分，也是整个社会得以成功的基本要素。避免哪怕是最小程度上对良心的权利或宗教的功能的干预，如此便能明智地免除民事裁决，全力保障那些对民事与人身权利有益的条款；公共开支要厉行节约，偿还公共债务，开发公共资源；在必要范围内保持常备军事力量，时刻不忘受过良好训练的国民军是维护共和体制的坚强堡垒，如果没有常备军队，自由将遭受危害，大多数人的安全也会受到威胁。提出合理的方案改进农业、工业，以及国内外商业；用类似的方式促进科学发展和知识普及，将其作为真正的自由的最佳滋养品。实行多种有价值的慈善计划，以使我国的原始居民摆脱落后野蛮的生活，从而转向接触进步的文明；使人们的意识与行为在文明开化的地域内受到熏陶。上述这些想法与意向都可帮助我履行职责，是使我不致失败的源泉。

此外，我非常幸运，因为在我即将踏上的路途上，已有许多位前辈成功地克服了极大的困难，树立了光辉的榜样，为我们指引即将奔赴的道路。对于刚刚卸任的前任总统的成就，我不在此一一叙述。但请原谅，我无法抑制我内心的一种强烈的情感，他在这个国家的祝福中得享丰厚的回报，人们感谢他在漫长生涯中，为了推进这个国家的至高利益和幸福，满腔热忱地奉献了自己的卓越才干。

但是，我所寻求的力量，或者说用来弥补我的不足的，则是同胞们几经磨炼的才华与美德，以及那些其他负责国家利益的部门的意见与忠告。因此，不论在多么困难的情况下，我都怀有最大的信心。况且，在全能的上帝的保护和引导下，我们的信心更受到激励和鼓舞。他的力量决定着国

difficulty be best placed, next to that which we have all been encouraged to feel in the guardianship and guidance of that Almighty Being whose power regulates the destiny of nations, whose blessings have been so conspicuously dispensed to this rising Republic, and to whom we are bound to address our devout gratitude for the past, as well as our fervent supplications and best hopes for the future.

家的命运，他的祝福也明显地降赐予这个新兴的共和国，而且我们必须为过去所取得的一切向他表示虔诚的感谢，也为未来向他表明我们的热切祈祷与美好期望。

詹姆斯·门罗
James Monroe

詹姆斯·门罗（James Monroe）

生平简介 >>

詹姆斯·门罗是美国第五任总统。他于1758年4月28日出生在弗吉尼亚州。

1790年他当选为美国参议院议员。1794年到1796年，他任驻法国公使。1803年，再度被杰斐逊总统派往法国，参加购买路易斯安那州的谈判。1811年，门罗受到麦迪逊总统的赏识，担任国务卿。

1816年，他成为共和党的总统候选人，并顺利当选。四年后，在仅有一张反对票的情况下，再度当选。

身为总统，门罗不认为自己应主动立法，因此他将立法权完全委托给国会。他担任总统期间所做的重大贡献是在外交领域，针对当时欧洲的一些封建专制帝国援助西班牙以重新获得其原有殖民地的企图，他给美国和南北美洲各国留下了一项基本政策，即南北美洲不允许由外来者开发，这项政策就是著名的"门罗主义"。

1831年7月4日，门罗逝世于纽约，享年73岁。

James Monroe
First Inaugural Address

March 4, 1817

I should be destitute of feeling if I was not deeply affected by the strong proof which my fellow-citizens have given me of their confidence in calling me to the high office whose functions I am about to assume. As the expression of their good opinion of my conduct in the public service, I derive from it a gratification which those who are conscious of having done all that they could to merit it can alone feel. My sensibility is increased by a just estimate of the importance of the trust and of the nature and extent of its duties, with the proper discharge of which the highest interests of a great and free people are intimately connected. Conscious of my own deficiency, I cannot enter on these duties without great anxiety for the result. From a just responsibility I will never shrink, calculating with confidence that in my best efforts to promote the public welfare my motives will always be duly appreciated and my conduct be viewed with that candor and indulgence which I have experienced in other stations.

In commencing the duties of the chief executive office it has been the practice of the distinguished men who have gone before me to explain the principles which would govern them in their respective Administrations. In following their venerated example my attention is naturally drawn to the great causes which have contributed in a principal degree to produce the present happy condition of the United States. They will best explain the nature of our duties and shed much light on the policy which ought to be pursued in future.

From the commencement of our Revolution to the present day almost forty years have elapsed, and from the establishment of this Constitution twenty-eight. Through this whole term the Government has been what may emphatically be called self-government. And what has been the effect? To whatever object we turn our attention, whether it relates to our foreign or

詹姆斯·门罗
James Monroe

门罗总统首次就职演说

1817年3月4日

　　如果我对同胞们以极大的信任召唤我来担任这一崇高职务而无动于衷的话，那么我就是个没有感情的人了。我感谢你们对我的公职行为的好评，也只有那些尽其所能了解我的功绩而褒奖我的人，才能体会到我的感激之情。由于正确估计到这种信任的重要性和该职务的性质及责任范围，特别是履行这一职务与我们伟大自由的人民的最高利益紧密相连，我更感到惶惑。因我自身的弱点所限，所以在着手履行职责时，我不能不对将来的结果抱有极大的不安。面对公正的责任感，我将永不退缩。我过去担任其他职务所得的经验证明，只要有信心又有计划地尽自己最大努力去实现公众利益，我的动机将得到恰当的评价，而我也从来没有在恰当的责任面前退缩过。

　　历任总统在其开始负起行政首长的责任之前，都有一个惯例——把各自的施政纲领解说清楚。在遵循他们令人尊敬的先例时，我的注意力自然集中于那些已经促成美国目前良好情况的重大原因上。这些原因将最能解释我们的职责的性质，并且有助于指明未来我们所要实行的政策。

　　从独立战争爆发迄今已近40年了，宪法的制定也已有28年。在这期间，美国政府被认为是个自治政府。那么，效果如何呢？不管我们将注意力集中在什么目标上，国内的也好，国外的也好，我们都有足够的理由为我们卓越的制度感到庆幸。在充满艰辛和重大事件的岁月里，我们的国家仍能空前繁荣。人人安居乐业，国泰民安。

domestic concerns, we find abundant cause to felicitate ourselves in the excellence of our institutions. During a period fraught with difficulties and marked by very extraordinary events the United States have flourished beyond example. Their citizens individually have been happy and the nation prosperous.

Under this Constitution our commerce has been wisely regulated with foreign nations and between the States; new States have been admitted into our Union; our territory has been enlarged by fair and honorable treaty, and with great advantage to the original States; the States, respectively protected by the National Government under a mild, parental system against foreign dangers, and enjoying within their separate spheres, by a wise partition of power, a just proportion of the sovereignty, have improved their police, extended their settlements, and attained a strength and maturity which are the best proofs of wholesome laws well administered. And if we look to the condition of individuals what a proud spectacle does it exhibit! On whom has oppression fallen in any quarter of our Union? Who has been deprived of any right of person or property? Who restrained from offering his vows in the mode which he prefers to the Divine Author of his being? It is well known that all these blessings have been enjoyed in their fullest extent; and I add with peculiar satisfaction that there has been no example of a capital punishment being inflicted on anyone for the crime of high treason.

Some who might admit the competency of our Government to these beneficent duties might doubt it in trials which put to the test its strength and efficiency as a member of the great community of nations. Here too experience has afforded us the most satisfactory proof in its favor. Just as this Constitution was put into action several of the principal States of Europe had become much agitated and some of them seriously convulsed. Destructive wars ensued, which have of late only been terminated. In the course of these conflicts the United States received great injury from several of the parties. It was their interest to stand aloof from the contest, to demand justice from the party committing the injury, and to cultivate by a fair and honorable conduct the friendship of all. War became at length inevitable, and the result has shown that our Government is equal to that, the greatest of trials, under the most unfavorable circumstances.

詹姆斯·门罗
James Monroe

在宪法指导下，国际间和州际间的商务管理得很好；新州经过批准加入联邦；领土也通过公平和可信的条约而扩大[1]，给原有的州带来许多利益；各州都感受到了联邦政府的温暖和保护，从而免于外国的威胁；另外，由于合理的分权，各州在它们的管辖范围内享有相应的主权，各州加强了警察力量，扩大了它们的居住领域，也促进了州本身的力量和成熟。这足以证明健全的法制得到了很好的贯彻。如果我们观察每个公民的情况，那将是多么值得骄傲的情景啊！有谁曾受到联邦的任何压迫？有谁曾被剥夺人身及财产的自由？又有谁被禁止以其喜欢的方式去向神立誓？大家深知每个人都享受着上帝的无限祝福，我个人对我们已不再用死刑去惩处犯有叛国罪的人，感到特别的满意。

有些人可能承认，我们的政府具备履行这些善行责任的能力，但他们也许会怀疑，政府的力量及效能在国际社会能否经得起竞争和考验。经验为我们提供了最有力的证明。当这部宪法要付诸实施时，欧洲几个强国正动乱不安，有的甚至面临着严重的灾难。毁灭性的战争随之而来，直到最近才停止。在这些冲突过程中，美国蒙受了来自几个不同方面的伤害。美国主要关心的是远离战争，向伤害它的集团讨回正义，并且通过合理公正的途径培育相互间的友谊。然而战争终不可免，而战争的结果却显示出我们的政府即使在最不利的情况下，也能经得起艰巨的考验。这些都应归功于人民及陆军和海军以及民兵所表现出来的英勇战斗精神。

[1]1810年，美国种植园主侵入西班牙属地西佛罗里达，并派兵占领该地；1818年，又出兵侵占东佛罗里达。1819年，美国政府以500万美元的"代价"强购佛罗里达半岛，完成了一桩"左轮枪口下的买卖"。

Of the virtue of the people and of the heroic exploits of the Army, the Navy, and the militia I need not speak.

Such, then, is the happy Government under which we live — a Government adequate to every purpose for which the social compact is formed; a Government elective in all its branches, under which every citizen may by his merit obtain the highest trust recognized by the Constitution; which contains within it no cause of discord, none to put at variance one portion of the community with another; a Government which protects every citizen in the full enjoyment of his rights, and is able to protect the nation against injustice from foreign powers.

Other considerations of the highest importance admonish us to cherish our Union and to cling to the Government which supports it. Fortunate as we are in our political institutions, we have not been less so in other circumstances on which our prosperity and happiness essentially depend. Situated within the temperate zone, and extending through many degrees of latitude along the Atlantic, the United States enjoy all the varieties of climate, and every production incident to that portion of the globe. Penetrating internally to the Great Lakes and beyond the sources of the great rivers which communicate through our whole interior, no country was ever happier with respect to its domain. Blessed, too, with a fertile soil, our produce has always been very abundant, leaving, even in years the least favorable, a surplus for the wants of our fellow-men in other countries. Such is our peculiar felicity that there is not a part of our Union that is not particularly interested in preserving it. The great agricultural interest of the nation prospers under its protection. Local interests are not less fostered by it. Our fellow-citizens of the North engaged in navigation find great encouragement in being made the favored carriers of the vast productions of the other portions of the United States, while the inhabitants of these are amply recompensed, in their turn, by the nursery for seamen and naval force thus formed and reared up for the support of our common rights. Our manufactures find a generous encouragement by the policy which patronizes domestic industry, and the surplus of our produce a steady and profitable market by local wants in less-favored parts at home.

Such, then, being the highly favored condition of our country, it is the interest

詹姆斯·门罗
James Monroe

　　这就是我们所拥有的美好政府,它符合社会契约论的所有要求。政府各部门都是民选的,而且任何人都可凭自己的功绩取得宪法所认可的最大信任。在这种情况下,就不会再出现不和谐的情形,而且也不会对各个不同地区存在任何偏见。政府保障每个公民完全享有他的权利,同时也可以保卫国家免受外国的侵害。

　　其他诸多至关重要的因素也告诫我们:要珍爱这个联邦并衷心支持联邦政府。我们如此幸运地生活在这个政体之下,所以在繁荣和幸福所依赖的其他因素方面,我们同样是幸运的。美国地处温带,并且沿着大西洋跨越了许多纬度,享受着如此多样的气候及这些地域带来的各种物产。我国内部贯穿着五大湖区,其资源丰富,且联络全国内地的各大河川,再也没有任何一个国家对其地域能如此自豪。由于土地肥沃,我们的收成总是极为丰足,即使在最恶劣的年景,也有余粮输往其他缺粮国家,以解决其人民的需要。联邦里的每个公民都拥护这个国家,这就是我们的幸福所在。在这种保护之下,国家庞大的农业因此繁荣,地域性的利益也受到扶植。从事航海运输业的北部同胞受到鼓励,而成为美国其他地区大宗货物的运载者,而且这些地区的居民也因为对海员及为维护我们共同利益而组建的海军的抚育得到足够的报偿。由于保护民族工业的政策,剩余产品靠国内不发达地区的需要而找到了稳定有利的市场,我国的制造业受到了巨大的推动。

　　我们的国家既然处在这样一个极为有利的状况下,那么每个公民努力维

of every citizen to maintain it. What are the dangers which menace us? If any exist they ought to be ascertained and guarded against.

In explaining my sentiments on this subject it may be asked, What raised us to the present happy state? How did we accomplish the Revolution? How remedy the defects of the first instrument of our Union, by infusing into the National Government sufficient power for national purposes, without impairing the just rights of the States or affecting those of individuals? How sustain and pass with glory through the late war? The Government has been in the hands of the people. To the people, therefore, and to the faithful and able depositaries of their trust is the credit due. Had the people of the United States been educated in different principles, had they been less intelligent, less independent, or less virtuous, can it be believed that we should have maintained the same steady and consistent career or been blessed with the same success? While, then, the constituent body retains its present sound and healthful state everything will be safe. They will choose competent and faithful representatives for every department. It is only when the people become ignorant and corrupt, when they degenerate into a populace, that they are incapable of exercising the sovereignty. Usurpation is then an easy attainment, and a usurper soon found. The people themselves become the willing instruments of their own debasement and ruin. Let us, then, look to the great cause, and endeavor to preserve it in full force. Let us by all wise and constitutional measures promote intelligence among the people as the best means of preserving our liberties.

Dangers from abroad are not less deserving of attention. Experiencing the fortune of other nations, the United States may be again involved in war, and it may in that event be the object of the adverse party to overset our Government, to break our Union, and demolish us as a nation. Our distance from Europe and the just, moderate, and pacific policy of our Government may form some security against these dangers, but they ought to be anticipated and guarded against. Many of our citizens are engaged in commerce and navigation, and all of them are in a certain degree dependent on their prosperous state. Many are engaged in the fisheries. These interests are exposed to invasion in the wars between other powers, and we should disregard the faithful admonition

詹姆斯·门罗
James Monroe

护它也符合其自身的利益。是否有危险威胁着我们?如果有的话,我们就必须找出它,然后加以预防。

为了表达我对这个问题的看法,我们不妨试问:是什么力量将我们推到目前的顺境呢?我们是怎样完成独立战争的?为了国家的需要,要给予联邦政府足够的力量,却又不能损害各州及个人的权利,到底是什么纠正了我们联邦政府最初体制上的不足呢?我们是如何不屈不挠而又勇敢地度过了最近的战争?这是因为:政府一直都是人民的政府。因此,对人民而言,将他们的信任交付给忠实而又有能力的受托者,是件值得的事。试想,要是美国人民被不同的主义所教育,要是他们不明智、缺乏独立性和理智,我们还能拥有像目前这样稳定持续的事业或享有如此成功的幸福吗?因此,只要将选举制度维持在目前合理、健全的状态,一切都会安全。他们将为每一部门选出能干而忠诚的代表。只有当选民变得无知愚昧,堕落退化成乌合之众时,才无法行使他们的主权。如果这样,就容易发生篡权的现象,篡夺者就会随即出现,人民本身将变成自甘堕落的工具。因此,让我们精心维护这个伟大的事业,并全力以赴去保护它。让我们依靠理智和合乎宪法的办法,来提高人民的才智,以此作为保障我们自由的最佳方法。

我们同样不能对来自国外的危险掉以轻心。就其他国家的经验而言,美国可能会重新卷入战争,而在战争中,反对党可能借机利用它来颠覆政府、解散联邦和破坏我们的国家。虽然我们远离欧洲,虽然我们政府的公正温和、主张和平的政策会防御这些外来的危险,但我们必须事先做好准备以阻止其发生。我们的人民大多都从事商业及航海业,在某种程度上,他们都依靠目前的繁荣状态。还有许多人从事渔业。这些人的利益,将会由于其他列强之间的战争而受到损害。如果我们不希望战争发生,那么我们就应重视经验所给予我们的忠告。我们必须维护我们的权利,不然就会失去我们的尊严,甚至自由也可能因此而丧失。一个国家的人民若无法做到这一点,那么它在自由独立的国家中,就很难占据应有的地位。国家的

of experience if we did not expect it. We must support our rights or lose our character, and with it, perhaps, our liberties. A people who fail to do it can scarcely be said to hold a place among independent nations. National honor is national property of the highest value. The sentiment in the mind of every citizen is national strength. It ought therefore to be cherished.

To secure us against these dangers our coast and inland frontiers should be fortified, our Army and Navy, regulated upon just principles as to the force of each, be kept in perfect order, and our militia be placed on the best practicable footing. To put our extensive coast in such a state of defense as to secure our cities and interior from invasion will be attended with expense, but the work when finished will be permanent, and it is fair to presume that a single campaign of invasion by a naval force superior to our own, aided by a few thousand land troops, would expose us to greater expense, without taking into the estimate the loss of property and distress of our citizens, than would be sufficient for this great work. Our land and naval forces should be moderate, but adequate to the necessary purposes — the former to garrison and preserve our fortifications and to meet the first invasions of a foreign foe, and, while constituting the elements of a greater force, to preserve the science as well as all the necessary implements of war in a state to be brought into activity in the event of war; the latter, retained within the limits proper in a state of peace, might aid in maintaining the neutrality of the United States with dignity in the wars of other powers and in saving the property of their citizens from spoliation. In time of war, with the enlargement of which the great naval resources of the country render it susceptible, and which should be duly fostered in time of peace, it would contribute essentially, both as an auxiliary of defense and as a powerful engine of annoyance, to diminish the calamities of war and to bring the war to a speedy and honorable termination.

But it ought always to be held prominently in view that the safety of these States and of everything dear to a free people must depend in an eminent degree on the militia. Invasions may be made too formidable to be resisted by any land and naval force which it would comport either with the principles

荣誉,是国家最宝贵的财产,每位公民的情操都是国家的力量,因此应该珍惜与爱护。

为了防御外来的侵略,我们的海岸及内陆边疆应该设有堡垒;我们的陆海军,也必须各自依适当的原则加以管理,使之名副其实、军纪整齐;我们的国民军必须训练有素;为了保卫城市及内地免遭侵略,必须在我们广阔的海岸建筑防御工事,显然这将耗费巨大。不过一旦这一工程完成,其作用将是永久的,我们不妨这样假设,一旦和一个优于我们的海军再加上数千名地面部队士兵交战时,且不估计财产及人民所受的损失,其花费也远比建造这样的防御工事要多得多。我们的陆军及海军规模要保持适中,但应足以达到必要的目标——前者得戍守、保卫要塞,并对付最先入侵的外敌,而且当它成为构成巨大战斗力要素时,在战时还要把科学和其他战争要素保持在应用的状态;而后者在和平时期应保持在适当的范围内,这样可能有助于在其他国家的战争中保持中立而又不损失尊严,并维护我国公民的财产不被他国船只掠夺。由于我们有一支强大的海军力量,在战争期间,即使战争不断扩大,也不致对我们构成威胁,所以在平时就应加以适当培养和训练。实际上,海军既是国防的辅助力量,同时也是消除战争及结束战争的有力手段。

然而,我们应始终相信:各州及自由人民的安危在很大程度上也须依靠民兵。外敌进攻可能过于强大,在这种状况下,要坚持政府的原则及维护美国的现状,只凭陆军和海军的力量,恐怕是不够的。所以,我们必须在能产生最大效果的方式下,依靠广大民众的援助。因此,当务之急就是组织和训

of our Government or the circumstances of the United States to maintain. In such cases recourse must be had to the great body of the people, and in a manner to produce the best effect. It is of the highest importance, therefore, that they be so organized and trained as to be prepared for any emergency. The arrangement should be such as to put at the command of the Government the ardent patriotism and youthful vigor of the country. If formed on equal and just principles, it can not be oppressive. It is the crisis which makes the pressure, and not the laws which provide a remedy for it. This arrangement should be formed, too, in time of peace, to be the better prepared for war. With such an organization of such a people the United States have nothing to dread from foreign invasion. At its approach an overwhelming force of gallant men might always be put in motion.

Other interests of high importance will claim attention, among which the improvement of our country by roads and canals, proceeding always with a constitutional sanction, holds a distinguished place. By thus facilitating the intercourse between the States we shall add much to the convenience and comfort of our fellow-citizens, much to the ornament of the country, and, what is of greater importance, we shall shorten distances, and, by making each part more accessible to and dependent on the other, we shall bind the Union more closely together. Nature has done so much for us by intersecting the country with so many great rivers, bays, and lakes, approaching from distant points so near to each other, that the inducement to complete the work seems to be peculiarly strong. A more interesting spectacle was perhaps never seen than is exhibited within the limits of the United States — a territory so vast and advantageously situated, containing objects so grand, so useful, so happily connected in all their parts!

Our manufacturers will likewise require the systematic and fostering care of the Government. Possessing as we do all the raw materials, the fruit of our own soil and industry, we ought not to depend in the degree we have done on supplies from other countries. While we are thus dependent the sudden event of war, unsought and unexpected, can not fail to plunge us into the most serious difficulties. It is important, too, that the capital which nourishes

詹姆斯·门罗
James Monroe

练民众以适应任何紧急状况。[1]这一安排,应交给政府指挥,当然还必须依靠同胞们诚挚的爱国心及国家中青年人的活力。只要将其建立在平等和公正的原则之上,就不会带来压制性的后果。压力来自危机,而不是来自对付危机的法律。为了更好地应付战争,这种组织在平时就应形成。有了这样的民众组织的力量,美国将无畏于任何外来的威胁。在这种组织方式下,勇敢的民众的巨大力量将脱颖而出,并可随时发挥作用。

其他有关国计民生的利益,我们也必须加以重视,如改进国内道路交通及运河等,都必须经常依宪法所允许的方式来进行。为了州际交往的便利,我们将尽量使人民的生活便利、舒适,把国家装点得更秀丽,更重要的是缩小彼此间的差距,并且为使各个不同地区更容易沟通、彼此依赖,我们的联盟更应该紧密结合在一起。大自然已经赐予我们如此众多的河流、海湾及湖泊,使得远离的两地变得接近。因此,完成这项工作的愿望似乎更为强烈。在美国疆域内,有一种前所未见而令人振奋的景观——在一个拥有广大领土的地域上,蕴藏着如此丰富的资源,而各部分却又那么巧妙地相互接壤。

我们的制造业也同样需要政府有计划的扶植。依照我们拥有的,由我国土地和基础工业提供原材料,我们不应像过去那样依赖国外的供给。由于我们过去依赖国外,在面临不期而遇的战争时,它总是使我们卷入极为

---

[1]1812年之战,美国之所以屡次受挫于英军,主要原因之一是美军多系民众仓促组织而成,既缺乏训练,又无士气,门罗想改进这一状况,乃出此语。

our manufacturers should be domestic, as its influence in that case instead of exhausting, as it may do in foreign hands, would be felt advantageously on agriculture and every other branch of industry. Equally important is it to provide at home a market for our raw materials, as by extending the competition it will enhance the price and protect the cultivator against the casualty's incident to foreign markets.

With the Indian tribes it is our duty to cultivate friendly relations and to act with kindness and liberality in all our transactions. Equally proper is it to persevere in our efforts to extend to them the advantages of civilization.

The great amount of our revenue and the flourishing state of the Treasury are a full proof of the competency of the national resources for any emergency, as they are of the willingness of our fellow-citizens to bear the burdens which the public necessities require. The vast amount of vacant lands, the value of which daily augments, forms an additional resource of great extent and duration. These resources, besides accomplishing every other necessary purpose, put it completely in the power of the United States to discharge the national debt at an early period. Peace is the best time for improvement and preparation of every kind; it is in peace that our commerce flourishes most, that taxes are most easily paid, and that the revenue is most productive.

The Executive is charged officially in the Departments under it with the disbursement of the public money, and is responsible for the faithful application of it to the purposes for which it is raised. The Legislature is the watchful guardian over the public purse. It is its duty to see that the disbursement has been honestly made. To meet the requisite responsibility every facility should be afforded to the Executive to enable it to bring the public agents entrusted with the public money strictly and promptly to account. Nothing should be presumed against them; but if, with the requisite facilities, the public money is suffered to lie long and uselessly in their hands, they will not be the only defaulters, nor will the demoralizing effect be confined to them. It will evince a relaxation and want of tone in the Administration which will be felt by the whole community. I shall do all I can to secure economy and fidelity in this important branch of the Administration, and I doubt not that the Legislature

詹姆斯·门罗
James Monroe

严重的困窘之中。另外有一点也是很重要的，即用以扶植制造业的资金应来自国内，因为它对农业和工业的其他部门的影响是显而易见的。资金依赖外国，它就可能枯竭。[1]同样重要的是，我们也应将我们的原料提供给国内的市场，这是因为，扩大竞争不仅可降低价格，并可保护种植者的利益，以对抗因国外市场偶发的不景气所造成的损失。

对于印第安部族，我们的职责在于建立友好的关系，而且在交往的过程中，要以诚相待。同样地，我们要以不懈的努力向他们传播文明的福音。

我们可观的岁收和充盈的国库，是使我们国家的资源有能力去应付任何紧急状况的充分保证。充盈的国库和岁收，正是我们的同胞愿意去承担社会公共需要的表现。大量未开垦的土地及其与日俱增的价值，形成了大量、持久的额外资源。这些资源除了用来完成其他必需的项目外，则完全属国家所有，使国家有能力早日偿清国债。和平时期是改进和做各项准备的最佳时机；正是在和平时期，我们的商业才能很快地繁荣起来，税金也最容易征收，因此收入最为可观。

就职能而言，行政部门是正式负责支付运用公款的部门，但必须完全根据其所征收的目的不折不扣地使用这些公款。立法部门则是公款的实际监管者，其职责在于监督公款是否被适当地运用和支付。为完成必要的职责起见，立法部门应给予行政部门各种便利条件，这样就可以使那些与公款打交道的政府机关能够严格而及时地负起责任。对它们，我们不该存有偏见，但如果它们利用手中之便滥用和浪费公款，那么，它们不仅是亵渎公职者，而且这一现象不仅是它们自身道德败坏的表现，同时，也是行政机构散漫与缺乏条理的表现，而这种情况一定也会为整个社会所察觉。我将尽我最大的努力去促进政府各个部门节约开支，恪尽职守。我也相信，立法机关将以同样的热诚去履行其职责。全面检查必须定期进行，对此我

---

[1]1812年之前，欧洲的资金是美国工商业赖以发展的基础，1812年战争发生后，国外资金纷纷撤出，美国工商业受到巨大损失。

will perform its duty with equal zeal. A thorough examination should be regularly made, and I will promote it.

It is particularly gratifying to me to enter on the discharge of these duties at a time when the United States are blessed with peace. It is a state most consistent with their prosperity and happiness. It will be my sincere desire to preserve it, so far as depends on the Executive, on just principles with all nations, claiming nothing unreasonable of any and rendering to each what is its due.

Equally gratifying is it to witness the increased harmony of opinion which pervades our Union. Discord does not belong to our system. Union is recommended as well by the free and benign principles of our Government, extending its blessings to every individual, as by the other eminent advantages attending it. The American people have encountered together great dangers and sustained severe trials with success. They constitute one great family with a common interest. Experience has enlightened us on some questions of essential importance to the country. The progress has been slow, dictated by a just reflection and a faithful regard to every interest connected with it. To promote this harmony in accord with the principles of our republican Government and in a manner to give them the most complete effect, and to advance in all other respects the best interests of our Union, will be the object of my constant and zealous exertions.

Never did a government commence under auspices so favorable, nor ever was success so complete. If we look to the history of other nations, ancient or modern, we find no example of a growth so rapid, so gigantic, of a people so prosperous and happy. In contemplating what we have still to perform, the heart of every citizen must expand with joy when he reflects how near our Government has approached to perfection; that in respect to it we have no essential improvement to make; that the great object is to preserve it in the essential principles and features which characterize it, and that is to be done by preserving the virtue and enlightening the minds of the people; and as a security against foreign dangers to adopt such arrangements as are indispensable to the support of our independence, our rights and liberties. If we persevere in the career in which we have advanced so far and in the path already traced,

将全力促成。

使我感到特别欣慰的是,在美国享受和平的日子里,我开始履行这些职责。这种和平状态有利于美国的繁荣和幸福。我真诚地愿意去维持这种幸福、繁荣,依靠行政部门的努力,以公正的原则和各国交往,不提任何不合理的要求并对各国区别对待。

同样使我感到欣慰的是,能亲眼看到我们的联邦民意日趋一致,倾轧与不和为我们的制度所不容,我们的联邦是由一个将自由及慈爱政策施惠于人民的政府和其他重要优势因素促成的。美国人民曾共同面对重大危机而且成功地经受了严峻的考验;他们因共同的利益组成了这个大家庭,经验使我们认识到那些对国家至关重要的问题。例如,我们在合理、忠实地反映和照顾各方的利益方面,进展一直很慢。根据我们共和政府的原则,以一种可达到圆满效果的方式,来增进和谐及联邦其他方面的最佳利益,是我继续热诚努力追求的目标。

以前没有任何一个政府能在如此顺利的情况下开始自己的工作,也没有任何一个政府能如此完全地获得成功。如果翻开其他国家的历史,古代的也好,现代的也好,我们找不到一个像我们这样发展迅速、伟大繁荣和人民幸福的例子,展望前程,每个公民都会因其所见而满心欢喜,我们的政府已臻完美。就此而言,我们基本上不需要大的改革,而重要的是如何保持,使它保持住原来那些基本原则和特征。为达到这个目的,就必须保持人民的道德心并启发人民的智慧,只有这样做,才能遏止外来的威胁,而且也是支持我们的独立、权利及自由所不可缺少的必要措施。如果我们能继续坚持目前已经完成的事业,而且坚定地走已经开辟的道路,我们一定会胜利,在万能的神灵的关照下,属于我们的伟大前程正在等待着我们。

we can not fail, under the favor of a gracious Providence, to attain the high destiny which seems to await us.

In the Administrations of the illustrious men who have preceded me in this high station, with some of whom I have been connected by the closest ties from early life, examples are presented which will always be found highly instructive and useful to their successors. From these I shall endeavor to derive all the advantages which they may afford. Of my immediate predecessor, under whom so important a portion of this great and successful experiment has been made, I shall be pardoned for expressing my earnest wishes that he may long enjoy in his retirement the affections of a grateful country, the best reward of exalted talents and the most faithful and meritorious service. Relying on the aid to be derived from the other departments of the Government, I enter on the trust to which I have been called by the suffrages of my fellow-citizens with my fervent prayers to the Almighty that He will be graciously pleased to continue to us that protection which He has already so conspicuously displayed in our favor.

詹姆斯·门罗
James Monroe

  在历任著名总统中,某些总统在我年轻时,我们彼此间就有了亲密的联系,他们所树立的典范,将给继任者有益的启示。在这些典范中,我将尽力从中获取一切可能的长处。上任总统,由于他在我们这个伟大而成功的事业中的卓越贡献,我不胜荣幸地在此向他致以热烈的祝福,希望他退休之后,永远享有国家对他的感激之情。这也是对他卓越的才能、忠诚及功绩卓著的服务的最好报答。依靠政府其他部门的协助,我开始肩负起由公民通过投票所交给我的重托,并诚挚热切地祈求全能的上帝,希望他将乐于继续一如既往地保佑我们。

约翰·昆西·亚当斯
John Quincy Adams

约翰·昆西·亚当斯（John Quincy Adams）

生平简介 >>

约翰·昆西·亚当斯是美国第六任总统。他于1767年6月11日出生在马萨诸塞州。他是一位天才，14岁时赴俄国担任美国公使的书记员，21岁时获哈佛大学学士学位。

大学毕业后，亚当斯成了律师。26岁时，被华盛顿任命为驻海牙公使。1802年，亚当斯回国后即当选为国会参议员。1812年美英战争爆发时，他被派往英国，签订《根特条约》。1815—1817年，任驻英公使。1817年，门罗总统召回亚当斯，他改任国务卿，直到1825年门罗两任总统期满。他是"门罗主义"的主要缔造者；他成功地与西班牙签订条约，使美国轻易得到佛罗里达。

1824年，亚当斯当选总统。但由于众议院投票中克莱支持他，而他任命克莱为国务卿，他的对手杰克逊的势力称这件事为"腐败的交易"，这种指责使亚当斯在1828年连任竞选中失败。

离开白宫后，他回到故乡，想安度晚年，但1830年又被选入众议院，成为一位雄辩的议员。他积极反对奴隶制度，为后来解放黑奴贡献了力量。

1848年2月21日，他因中风倒在议会的地板上，两天后逝世。

美国历届总统就职演说
THE INAUGURAL ADDRESSES OF THE U.S. PRESIDENTS

John Quincy Adams
Inaugural Address

March 4, 1825

In compliance with an usage coeval with the existence of our Federal Constitution, and sanctioned by the example of my predecessors in the career upon which I am about to enter, I appear, my fellow-citizens, in your presence and in that of Heaven to bind myself by the solemnities of religious obligation to the faithful performance of the duties allotted to me in the station to which I have been called.

In unfolding to my countrymen the principles by which I shall be governed in the fulfillment of those duties my first resort will be to that Constitution which I shall swear to the best of my ability to preserve, protect, and defend. That revered instrument enumerates the powers and prescribes the duties of the Executive Magistrate, and in its first words declares the purposes to which these and the whole action of the Government instituted by it should be invariably and sacredly devoted — to form a more perfect union, establish justice, insure domestic tranquility, provide for the common defense, promote the general welfare, and secure the blessings of liberty to the people of this Union in their successive generations. Since the adoption of this social compact one of these generations has passed away. It is the work of our forefathers. Administered by some of the most eminent men who contributed to its formation, through a most eventful period in the annals of the world, and through all the vicissitudes of peace and war incidental to the condition of associated man, it has not disappointed the hopes and aspirations of those illustrious benefactors of their age and nation. It has promoted the lasting welfare of that country so dear to us all; it has to an extent far beyond the ordinary lot of humanity secured the freedom and happiness of this people. We now receive it as a precious inheritance from those to whom we are indebted for its establishment, doubly bound by the examples which they have left us and by the blessings which we

约翰·昆西·亚当斯
John Quincy Adams

亚当斯总统就职演说

1825年3月4日

一方面为遵从这一与联邦宪法同样长久的惯例，一方面以历任总统为榜样，同胞们，在你们和上帝的面前，在宗教仪式的肃穆庄严之下，我宣誓忠实执行托付于我的职责。

在此，我要向你们宣布我履行职责所遵循的原则。我首先要实行的是我将宣誓尽我最大力量去维护、保护及捍卫宪法。在这部神圣的文献中，列举了行政元首的权力及其职责，并在篇首的第一句话，就说明了政府机构的所有行动目标，它们应是宪法所设定的所有政府机构始终不渝和神圣献身的目标：组成一个更完美的联邦，主持正义，保障国内安定，提供国防力量，促进大众福利，确保这个联邦后代子孙的自由。自这个社会契约实行以来，一代人已经过世了。这个宪法是我们祖先的杰作。靠着这些立宪有功的杰出人物的管理，我们度过了世界历史上最重要的阶段，也经历了人类社会中难免的战争与和平的变迁。这些考验并没有辜负开国元勋所代表的时代及国家。事实上，它反而增进了我们所热爱的国家的永恒幸福。该宪法以远超出一般人本主义范围的程度确保了我们人民的自由和幸福。我们要继承祖先遗留下来的宝贵遗产，对于他们为我们树立的榜样及由他们的辛勤耕耘所带来的幸福，我们应加倍地珍惜保护，并将它完整无缺地传给下一代。

have enjoyed as the fruits of their labors to transmit the same unimpaired to the succeeding generation.

In the compass of thirty-six years since this great national covenant was instituted a body of laws enacted under its authority and in conformity with its provisions has unfolded its powers and carried into practical operation its effective energies. Subordinate departments have distributed the executive functions in their various relations to foreign affairs, to the revenue and expenditures, and to the military force of the Union by land and sea. A coordinate department of the judiciary has expounded the Constitution and the laws, settling in harmonious coincidence with the legislative will numerous weighty questions of construction which the imperfection of human language had rendered unavoidable. The year of jubilee since the first formation of our Union has just elapsed; that of the declaration of our independence is at hand. The consummation of both was effected by this Constitution.

Since that period a population of four millions has multiplied to twelve. A territory bounded by the Mississippi has been extended from sea to sea. New States have been admitted to the Union in numbers nearly equal to those of the first Confederation. Treaties of peace, amity, and commerce have been concluded with the principal dominions of the earth. The people of other nations, inhabitants of regions acquired not by conquest, but by compact, have been united with us in the participation of our rights and duties, of our burdens and blessings. The forest has fallen by the ax of our woodsmen; the soil has been made to teem by the tillage of our farmers; our commerce has whitened every ocean. The dominion of man over physical nature has been extended by the invention of our artists. Liberty and law have marched hand in hand. All the purposes of human association have been accomplished as effectively as under any other government on the globe, and at a cost little exceeding in a whole generation the expenditure of other nations in a single year.

Such is the unexaggerated picture of our condition under a Constitution founded upon the republican principle of equal rights. To admit that this picture has its shades is but to say that it is still the condition of men upon earth. From evil — physical, moral, and political — it is not our claim to be exempt. We

约翰·昆西·亚当斯
John Quincy Adams

自这部宪法施行以来,已有36年了,我们都尽力根据宪法条款发挥其作用,并使之能有效地应用于实际操作中。附属的各部门已将其特有的行政功能如外交事务、岁收和支出、联邦海军和陆军等不同事项进行了划分,以各负其责。另外,对等平行的司法部门也根据宪法和法律[1],解决了由于人类语言的不完善所导致的许多重大且不可避免的争论。联邦成立至今已50年,独立宣言的发表至今也快到50年,此二者都是通过这部宪法而产生巨大影响的。

自那时起,人口已由400万增至1200万;疆界也由密西西比河拓展到两大洋;允许加入联邦的新州数目已接近联邦最初成立时的成员数目。我们还和地球上其他主要国家缔结了和平、友好及商务条约。那些其住地并非由征服,而是由契约得到的其他民族和人民,已和我们相结合以分享我们的权利,共同承担我们的责任和义务,共同追求我们的幸福。经伐木工人之斧,森林得以开采;经农夫之耕作,土地开始生产;我们的商业也已拓展到每个海洋。人类对大自然的驾驭,由于技术的发展而扩大;自由与法治携手并进。我们的政府与其他任何政府一样均实现了人类合作的各项目标,而且我们整整一代人为此所付出的代价仅仅略超过其他国家一年的花费。

这就是我们在一部根据平等权利的共和原则所建立的宪法之上,真实而不夸张的画面。当然,我们承认在这幅画面中也有其晦暗之处,但我们

---

[1]指约翰·马歇尔任最高法院首席大法官时所树立的诠释宪法及一般法律的权威。

have suffered sometimes by the visitation of Heaven through disease; often by the wrongs and injustice of other nations, even to the extremities of war; and, lastly, by dissensions among ourselves—dissensions perhaps inseparable from the enjoyment of freedom, but which have more than once appeared to threaten the dissolution of the Union, and with it the overthrow of all the enjoyments of our present lot and all our earthly hopes of the future. The causes of these dissensions have been various, founded upon differences of speculation in the theory of republican government; upon conflicting views of policy in our relations with foreign nations; upon jealousies of partial and sectional interests, aggravated by prejudices and prepossessions which strangers to each other are ever apt to entertain.

It is a source of gratification and of encouragement to me to observe that the great result of this experiment upon the theory of human rights has at the close of that generation by which it was formed been crowned with success equal to the most sanguine expectations of its founders. Union, justice, tranquility, the common defense, the general welfare, and the blessings of liberty — all have been promoted by the Government under which we have lived. Standing at this point of time, looking back to that generation which has gone by and forward to that which is advancing, we may at once indulge in grateful exultation and in cheering hope. From the experience of the past we derive instructive lessons for the future. Of the two great political parties which have divided the opinions and feelings of our country, the candid and the just will now admit that both have contributed splendid talents, spotless integrity, ardent patriotism, and disinterested sacrifices to the formation and administration of this Government, and that both have required a liberal indulgence for a portion of human infirmity and error. The revolutionary wars of Europe, commencing precisely at the moment when the Government of the United States first went into operation under this Constitution, excited a collision of sentiments and of sympathies which kindled all the passions and embittered the conflict of parties till the nation was involved in war and the Union was shaken to its center. This time of trial embraced a period of five and twenty years, during which the policy of the Union in its relations with Europe

约翰·昆西·亚当斯
John Quincy Adams

也必须指出那是地球上的人类所共有的情况。来自生理上、道德上、政治上的不幸很难免除。我们有时遭受天灾与疾病的祸害；还得承受来自其他国家的错误及不公平待遇，甚至非常残酷的战争；我们有时也为自身内部意见冲突所牵制，也许这种意见冲突与享受自由是密不可分的，但它却不止一次地威胁联邦的瓦解；而联邦的瓦解，必然会使我们失去现有的一切幸福及对未来的期望。造成意见冲突的原因很多，有的是基于对共和政府原则信念的差异；有的是基于在对外关系政策上意见的争吵；也有的是基于对区域性利益的猜忌；最终这些成见与歧视的加重更使人人都心怀疑虑。

上一代即将结束时所形成的人权理论，根据实践结果所显示出的辉煌成果，就如同其创建者所热切期望的那样成功，这就是鼓舞并令我感激的源泉。联邦、正义、稳定、国防、大众福利和自由都已在我们政府中得到全面促进。站在现在这个时间点上，回顾前人，展望未来，我们可能会一下子沉浸在极度的狂欢和愉快的希望中。从过去的经验我们可以得到未来的启示。对于使我们国家意志和信念一分为二的两大主要政党，一切正直公正的人们，都会承认这两党为我们政府的组成和发挥作用贡献出了优异的才能、绝对的诚实和热诚的爱国心，并做出了大公无私的牺牲。[1]此外，两党都曾要求对人类固有的弱点和不足加以宽容。正当美国政府在宪法下开始进行工作时，欧洲革命战争爆发了，这次战争必然激起我们对敌对双方不同的态度和感情，因而引起摩擦和冲突；此种摩擦和冲突一直持续到我国介入战争，以致联邦基础都为之动摇。这段艰苦的考验期长达25年。在这段时间里，联邦对欧洲采取的政策，造成我国政治上的分裂，也构成了联邦政府决策行动最困难的部分。由于法国革命战争带来的巨大灾难，以及我们后来与大英帝国所达成的和平，政党争斗的险恶灾难才得以根除。从那时起，无论在政府理论还是对外关系上，再也不存在任何原则上的差异，而是有足够的力量去维护党派的团结。当然，也没有因公共舆论或过度对立法争辩所产生的刺激。根据民众的声音，我们的政治信条是：民意是地球上所有合法政府的根源，而人民的幸福是其目的。自由且经常性的公众选举是保证权力不遭滥用的最佳手段。联邦政府及其他州政府在其权限范围

---

[1]实际上，联邦党此时已趋没落，1820年后，它已无力推举总统候选人。

constituted the principal basis of our political divisions and the most arduous part of the action of our Federal Government. With the catastrophe in which the wars of the French Revolution terminated, and our own subsequent peace with Great Britain, this baneful weed of party strife was uprooted. From that time no difference of principle, connected either with the theory of government or with our intercourse with foreign nations, has existed or been called forth in force sufficient to sustain a continued combination of parties or to give more than wholesome animation to public sentiment or legislative debate. Our political creed is, without a dissenting voice that can be heard, that the will of the people is the source and the happiness of the people the end of all legitimate government upon earth; that the best security for the beneficence and the best guaranty against the abuse of power consists in the freedom, the purity, and the frequency of popular elections; that the General Government of the Union and the separate governments of the States are all sovereignties of limited powers, fellow-servants of the same masters, uncontrolled within their respective spheres, uncontrollable by encroachments upon each other; that the firmest security of peace is the preparation during peace of the defenses of war; that a rigorous economy and accountability of public expenditures should guard against the aggravation and alleviate when possible the burden of taxation; that the military should be kept in strict subordination to the civil power; that the freedom of the press and of religious opinion should be inviolate; that the policy of our country is peace and the ark of our salvation union are articles of faith upon which we are all now agreed.

If there have been those who doubted whether a confederated representative democracy were a government competent to the wise and orderly management of the common concerns of a mighty nation, those doubts have been dispelled; if there have been projects of partial confederacies to be erected upon the ruins of the Union, they have been scattered to the winds; if there have been dangerous attachments to one foreign nation and antipathies against another, they have been extinguished. Ten years of peace, at home and abroad, have assuaged the animosities of political contention and blended into harmony the most discordant elements of public opinion. There still remains one effort

内拥有自主权,同一主管下的公务员们在各自的工作范围内不受干预,彼此间也不受干扰。就和平而言,最强有力的屏障即是平时做好对战争的防卫;在稳健且充满活力的经济发展中,不要刻意加重公共开支,注意减轻税负。军队应严格隶属于文官权力;出版及宗教信仰上的自由不容侵犯;我国的政策是和平,拯救我们联邦的方舟是我们大家都同意的信任条款。

如果说曾有人怀疑实行联邦式的代议制民主的政府是否有能力以开明有序的方法处理一个大国的共同利益,那么,这种疑虑已经消失了;如果曾有过以瓦解联邦为目的的局部联盟计划,现在这种计划也消失得无影无踪了;如果说曾经冒过险去依附某一国家,而反对另一国家,那种情形亦不存在了。国内外十年来的和平已缓和了政治上的纠纷,并且也把民意上的最尖锐的分歧因素调和了。目前还有两件事必须依靠全国一直追随政党准则的人们去完成。一是努力表现出各自的宽宏大量,二是放弃偏见和冲动,也就是抛弃相互间心中残存的怨恨,彼此视为同胞兄弟,并且在维护原则的斗争中必须坚守道德和才能。这些努力所显示的信心,正是达成党

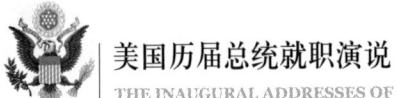

of magnanimity, one sacrifice of prejudice and passion, to be made by the individuals throughout the nation who have heretofore followed the standards of political party. It is that of discarding every remnant of rancor against each other, of embracing as countrymen and friends, and of yielding to talents and virtue alone that confidence which in times of contention for principle was bestowed only upon those who bore the badge of party communion.

The collisions of party spirit which originate in speculative opinions or in different views of administrative policy are in their nature transitory. Those which are founded on geographical divisions, adverse interests of soil, climate, and modes of domestic life are more permanent, and therefore, perhaps, more dangerous. It is this which gives inestimable value to the character of our Government, at once federal and national. It holds out to us a perpetual admonition to preserve alike and with equal anxiety the rights of each individual State in its own government and the rights of the whole nation in that of the Union. Whatsoever is of domestic concernment, unconnected with the other members of the Union or with foreign lands, belongs exclusively to the administration of the State governments. Whatsoever directly involves the rights and interests of the federative fraternity or of foreign powers is of the resort of this General Government. The duties of both are obvious in the general principle, though sometimes perplexed with difficulties in the detail. To respect the rights of the State governments is the inviolable duty of that of the Union; the government of every State will feel its own obligation to respect and preserve the rights of the whole. The prejudices everywhere too commonly entertained against distant strangers are worn away, and the jealousies of jarring interests are allayed by the composition and functions of the great national councils annually assembled from all quarters of the Union at this place. Here the distinguished men from every section of our country, while meeting to deliberate upon the great interests of those, by whom they are deputed, learn to estimate the talents and do justice to the virtues of each other. The harmony of the nation is promoted and the whole Union is knit together by the sentiments of mutual respect, the habits of social intercourse, and the ties of personal friendship formed between the representatives of its

派联盟的象征。

    从本质上说，由行政政策上不同理论的理解所产生的分歧是暂时的。那些因地理上的差异、土壤的贫瘠、气候及国内生活方式的不同而产生的冲突无疑是长期的，也是最危险的。因此，我们联邦政府及州政府的地位就具有无可估量的价值。从宪法中我们得到的永久教训，便是各州及其政府权利应和联邦政府权利受到同等的保护。就内政而言，无论何事，只要与联邦内其他成员州及他国无关，就完全归州政府处理，但是凡与联邦各州间或与他国权利有关的事务，则归联邦政府处理。这二者职责的划分总的来看是很明显的，虽然有时在细节上划分也有困难。尊重州政府政策的权利，是联邦不可违犯的原则；每个州政府也必须认识到尊重及确保整个国家的权利是其职责所在。一度曾流行的各地对待他乡人的偏见正在消失。此外，对于利益冲突的愤怒情绪也随着一年一度全国各地代表在此参加国会而得以缓和。这些来自四面八方的杰出人物在聚会之际，除了代表其所属地区的重大利益外，也懂得了互相尊重和欣赏对方的才能和贤德。国家的和谐及整个联邦的团结显然是靠彼此的尊重、社交惯例以及在首都内各区代表在公务往来上所建立的友谊才得以促进和巩固的。

several parts in the performance of their service at this metropolis.

Passing from this general review of the purposes and injunctions of the Federal Constitution and their results as indicating the first traces of the path of duty in the discharge of my public trust, I turn to the Administration of my immediate predecessor as the second. It has passed away in a period of profound peace, how much to the satisfaction of our country and to the honor of our country's name is known to you all. The great features of its policy, in general concurrence with the will of the Legislature, have been to cherish peace while preparing for defensive war; to yield exact justice to other nations and maintain the rights of our own; to cherish the principles of freedom and of equal rights wherever they were proclaimed; to discharge with all possible promptitude the national debt; to reduce within the narrowest limits of efficiency the military force; to improve the organization and discipline of the Army; to provide and sustain a school of military science; to extend equal protection to all the great interests of the nation; to promote the civilization of the Indian tribes, and to proceed in the great system of internal improvements within the limits of the constitutional power of the Union. Under the pledge of these promises, made by that eminent citizen at the time of his first induction to this office, in his career of eight years the internal taxes have been repealed; sixty millions of the public debt have been discharged; provision has been made for the comfort and relief of the aged and indigent among the surviving warriors of the Revolution; the regular armed force has been reduced and its constitution revised and perfected; the accountability for the expenditure of public moneys has been made more effective; the Floridas have been peaceably acquired, and our boundary has been extended to the Pacific Ocean; the independence of the southern nations of this hemisphere has been recognized, and recommended by example and by counsel to the potentates of Europe; progress has been made in the defense of the country by fortifications and the increase of the Navy, toward the effectual suppression of the African traffic in slaves; in alluring the aboriginal hunters of our land to the cultivation of the soil and of the mind, in exploring the interior regions of the Union, and in preparing by scientific researches and surveys for the further application of our national resources to

约翰·昆西·亚当斯
John Quincy Adams

在履行总统职责时，回顾联邦宪法的宗旨及所含的深刻寓意，是指引我的第一条途径。至于第二条途径，乃是参考前任总统的政府。上届政府已在极为和平的状态下度过了，它是怎样促进国家的繁荣及荣耀的，这是我们非常熟悉的。在各项原则与立法机关一致的基础上，上届政府政策的重大特点是保护和平，同时不忘国防建设以防止战争；公正地对待他国，同时维护自己的利益；对各地所呼吁的自由、平等予以支持；并尽可能快地偿还国债、缩减军队编制，改进军队组织、整顿纪律；加强军事学校的建设；扩大对全国各利益集团的保护，促进印第安人的文明；并在联邦宪法的权力范围内，进行国内一系列的重大改革。杰出的上届总统实现了在其第一次就职时所立下的保证，我们看出：八年来国内税已消除；偿还了600万的公债；那些年老贫困、饱经战祸的士兵都得到了充足的食物；正规武装部队已经缩减，其编制也已经过改进而渐趋完善；对公众的开支管理更有效率；而且佛罗里达是以和平方式取得的，国界已拓展到太平洋沿岸；南美各国的独立也已得到普通承认，并通过劝告及商议的方式告诉欧洲列强要尊重它们的独立。另外，我们的国防由于加强了堡垒建设和扩编了海军而得到很大巩固；我们还有效地制止了非洲奴隶的贩卖和运输；对早期居住在这块土地上的猎人，我们也引导他们从事联邦内的土地耕种并对他们进行文化教育；致力于开发联邦内部并发展科学研究及调查，以进一步将我们的资源用于国内的改革上。

the internal improvement of our country.

In this brief outline of the promise and performance of my immediate predecessor the line of duty for his successor is clearly delineated. To pursue to their consummation those purposes of improvement in our common condition instituted or recommended by him will embrace the whole sphere of my obligations. To the topic of internal improvement, emphatically urged by him at his inauguration, I recur with peculiar satisfaction. It is that from which I am convinced that the unborn millions of our posterity who are in future ages to people this continent will derive their most fervent gratitude to the founders of the Union; that in which the beneficent action of its Government will be most deeply felt and acknowledged. The magnificence and splendor of their public works are among the imperishable glories of the ancient republics. The roads and aqueducts of Rome have been the admiration of all after ages, and have survived thousands of years after all her conquests have been swallowed up in despotism or become the spoil of barbarians. Some diversity of opinion has prevailed with regard to the powers of Congress for legislation upon objects of this nature. The most respectful deference is due to doubts originating in pure patriotism and sustained by venerated authority. But nearly twenty years have passed since the construction of the first national road was commenced. The authority for its construction was then unquestioned. To how many thousands of our countrymen has it proved a benefit? To what single individual has it ever proved an injury? Repeated, liberal, and candid discussions in the Legislature have conciliated the sentiments and approximated the opinions of enlightened minds upon the question of constitutional power. I can not but hope that by the same process of friendly, patient, and persevering deliberation all constitutional objections will ultimately be removed. The extent and limitation of the powers of the General Government in relation to this transcendently important interest will be settled and acknowledged to the common satisfaction of all, and every speculative scruple will be solved by a practical public blessing.

Fellow-citizens, you are acquainted with the peculiar circumstances of the recent election, which have resulted in affording me the opportunity of addressing you at this time. You have heard the exposition of the principles

约翰·昆西·亚当斯
John Quincy Adams

通过对前任总统所做的承诺及其实践的简单描述，我们便可清楚地看出下任总统的职责所在。进一步完成上任总统对改善人民日常生活所做的承诺和建议是我职责内的事情。就内部改革而言，在他的就职演说中所再三强调的，我将特别予以重视。据此，我相信后代百万子孙将对联邦创建者报以衷心的感谢并对联邦造福人民的行动有进一步的认识和了解。他们所做的公共工作成绩卓著并与古代共和国的光荣同样不朽。罗马大道及水道，虽历经暴政或野蛮入侵的破坏，依然存在数千年。国会对这方面的立法引起了许多不同的争论。然而所有这些质疑都源于一颗纯粹的爱国心，也因此受到了当局最崇高的敬意。可是自第一条国家道路完成至今已快20年了，授权建造此路在当时确实无可非议。对我们同胞中成千上万的人来说，是否是一项利益呢？它对谁又是一种伤害呢？国会自由而坦诚的讨论协商已经安慰了大众的情绪，而且在宪法赋予的权力问题上，各种有见解的思想基本一致。我竭诚希望在友好、忍耐、不屈不挠的考量后，所有反对宪法的议论最终将销声匿迹。联邦政府会以大多数人都满意的方式来处理这些问题，此外，所有这些不负责任的责难也会因为公众在现实中的幸福生活而消失。

同胞们，你们已经看到了最新的选举结果，使我得以站在你们面前发表演说。你们也已非常了解那些将指导我履行崇高而庄严的职责的原则。由于你们现在对我的信任较之历任总统都少，所以，我深切地感受到将来

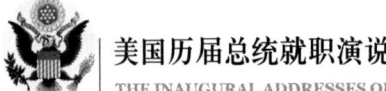

which will direct me in the fulfillment of the high and solemn trust imposed upon me in this station. Less possessed of your confidence in advance than any of my predecessors, I am deeply conscious of the prospect that I shall stand more and oftener in need of your indulgence. Intentions upright and pure, a heart devoted to the welfare of our country, and the unceasing application of all the faculties allotted to me to her service are all the pledges that I can give for the faithful performance of the arduous duties I am to undertake. To the guidance of the legislative councils, to the assistance of the executive and subordinate departments, to the friendly cooperation of the respective State governments, to the candid and liberal support of the people so far as it may be deserved by honest industry and zeal, I shall look for whatever success may attend my public service; and knowing that "except the Lord keep the city the watchman waketh but in vain," with fervent supplications for His favor, to His overruling providence I commit with humble but fearless confidence my own fate and the future destinies of my country.

约翰·昆西·亚当斯
John Quincy Adams

更需要你们的包涵。诚实纯净的动机、为国家福利而奉献的心愿，不断地运用我的全部智慧为国效忠，这些都是我将忠实履行职责的保证。在国会诸位的指导下，在行政及其附属部门的辅助和各州政府诚挚的合作下，在因我的勤勉和热诚而博得人民开诚布公的支持下，我期待在我的任期内将有所成就。而且我知道"除了神以外，无论守城人如何警觉也无法保住城市"，所以，我热切祈求神灵的保佑，并以谦卑无惧的信心，将我的命运和国家未来的前途托付于他。

安德鲁·杰克逊
Andrew Jackson

安德鲁·杰克逊 (Andrew Jackson)

生平简介 >>

安德鲁·杰克逊是美国第七任总统。他于1767年3月15日出生在北卡罗来纳和南卡罗来纳交界地的一个新开拓的边远地区。13岁时就在军队里当通信员。17岁时,他决定学习法律,后来成为律师。

1796年,他成为田纳西州在国会中的一名众议员。后来,又当过六个月的参议员,六年高等法院法官。1812年战争爆发后,杰克逊由于其政治上的名望而在1814年被任命为志愿军少将。1815年1月,新奥尔良一役的胜利,使他名声大振,成为美国在战争中取得最伟大胜利的指挥官。

1828年11月4日,杰克逊当选为总统。1832年11月6日又蝉联总统。任职期间,他大大扩大了总统的权力,并停止设立美国国家银行;在各州拒绝执行国会法令期间,杰克逊的坚定态度阻止了南北卡罗来纳州解散合众国的企图,使内战推迟了30年,在围绕着杰克逊和他的对立面展开全国性的政治斗争的同时,出现了两个政党——追随杰克逊的民主党和反对他的国民共和党,或叫辉格党。

1845年6月8日,杰克逊在田纳西州他的家中去世,终年78岁。

Andrew Jackson
First Inaugural Address

March 4, 1829

Fellow-Citizens:

About to undertake the arduous duties that I have been appointed to perform by the choice of a free people, I avail myself of this customary and solemn occasion to express the gratitude which their confidence inspires and to acknowledge the accountability which my situation enjoins. While the magnitude of their interests convinces me that no thanks can be adequate to the honor they have conferred, it admonishes me that the best return I can make is the zealous dedication of my humble abilities to their service and their good.

As the instrument of the Federal Constitution it will devolve on me for a stated period to execute the laws of the United States, to superintend their foreign and their confederate relations, to manage their revenue, to command their forces, and, by communications to the Legislature, to watch over and to promote their interests generally. And the principles of action by which I shall endeavor to accomplish this circle of duties it is now proper for me briefly to explain.

In administering the laws of Congress I shall keep steadily in view the limitations as well as the extent of the Executive power, trusting thereby to discharge the functions of my office without transcending its authority. With foreign nations it will be my study to preserve peace and to cultivate friendship on fair and honorable terms, and in the adjustment of any differences that may exist or arise to exhibit the forbearance becoming a powerful nation rather than the sensibility belonging to a gallant people.

In such measures as I may be called on to pursue in regard to the rights of the separate States I hope to be animated by a proper respect for those sovereign members of our Union, taking care not to confound the powers they have reserved to themselves with those they have granted to the Confederacy.

安德鲁·杰克逊
Andrew Jackson

杰克逊总统首次就职演说

1829年3月4日

同胞们：

　　根据自由人民的选择，我被委任开始承担一项十分艰巨的职责。依照惯例在这个庄严的仪式中，我要对同胞们的信任，表示深深的感激之情，并认识到我的职位所担负的责任。我相信你们所给予我的荣耀是无法用语言感谢的，我所能做的最好回报，就是为你们服务，为了你们的利益热诚地贡献出敝人的全部力量。

　　身为联邦宪法的执行人，宪法赋予我在任期内执行美国的法律，监督各州对外、对内关系，管理国家的税收和统率武装力量的责任，并且通过与立法机关的沟通，广泛地保护和促进国家利益。现在正是我把如何努力完成这一任期责任的施政纲领，做一简短说明的恰当时机。

　　在实施国会的法律时，我会牢记并恪守我的行政权力范围，在不超越权限的情况下，履行我的职责。在对外关系方面，我将努力争取在公平和体面的条件下，在调解现存的或可能发生的争端和冲突时，表现出一个强国所具有的宽容，而不能以一个英雄民族所固有的感情用事。

　　在处理有关各州的权利时，希望我对联邦各州的敬意，能促使我谨慎行事，不要把那些保留给各州的权力及授予联邦的权力混淆了。

美国历届总统就职演说
THE INAUGURAL ADDRESSES OF THE U.S. PRESIDENTS

The management of the public revenue — that searching operation in all governments — is among the most delicate and important trusts in ours, and it will, of course, demand no inconsiderable share of my official solicitude. Under every aspect in which it can be considered it would appear that advantage must result from the observance of a strict and faithful economy. This I shall aim at the more anxiously both because it will facilitate the extinguishment of the national debt, the unnecessary duration of which is incompatible with real independence, and because it will counteract that tendency to public and private profligacy which a profuse expenditure of money by the Government is but too apt to engender. Powerful auxiliaries to the attainment of this desirable end are to be found in the regulations provided by the wisdom of Congress for the specific appropriation of public money and the prompt accountability of public officers.

With regard to a proper selection of the subjects of impost with a view to revenue, it would seem to me that the spirit of equity, caution, and compromise in which the Constitution was formed requires that the great interests of agriculture, commerce, and manufactures should be equally favored, and that perhaps the only exception to this rule should consist in the peculiar encouragement of any products of either of them that may be found essential to our national independence.

Internal improvement and the diffusion of knowledge, so far as they can be promoted by the constitutional acts of the Federal Government, are of high importance.

Considering standing armies as dangerous to free governments in time of peace, I shall not seek to enlarge our present establishment, nor disregard that salutary lesson of political experience which teaches that the military should be held subordinate to the civil power. The gradual increase of our Navy, whose flag has displayed in distant climes our skill in navigation and our fame in arms; the preservation of our forts, arsenals, and dockyards, and the introduction of progressive improvements in the discipline and science of both branches of our military service are so plainly prescribed by prudence that I should be excused for omitting their mention sooner than for enlarging

安德鲁·杰克逊
Andrew Jackson

公共税收管理，这是所有政府的普遍工作，也是你们托付给政府最重要的职责，无疑，它将成为我任职期间最关切的事务之一。无论从哪个角度看，厉行节约都将大有裨益，在此我将会努力地朝此目标迈进。一是税收将利于偿还国债，因为债务的继续存在与国家的真正独立，是相互矛盾的；二是它可防止政府及个人的恣意浪费趋势，使政府廉洁，不挥霍人民的财产。实现这一理想目标的强有力的辅助手段，可以在国会所规定的关于公共资金的具体拨款和公务费问责条例中找到。

有关因为税收而必须适当选择课税对象这件事，对我而言，宪法赖以制定的精神——平等、谨慎、妥协，就是要求对农业、商业和制造业的重大利益给予同等的重视。[1]然而这项原则的唯一例外，就是对国家独立有其特殊重要性的产品，应给予特殊的鼓励。

国内状况的改善和知识的传播——只要联邦政府依宪法条款就可以推进这两方面的工作——是非常重要的。

鉴于常备军在和平时期对自由政府所构成的潜在危险，我将不寻求扩大我们现有的军队编制，也不会忽视政治经验上有价值的教训，即军队必须置于文官的权力之下。我们的海军日渐扩大，海军的旗帜飘扬四方显示了我们的航海技术及武器的威力；维护我们的堡垒、兵工厂和造船厂，并引导我们的陆海军在纪律和军事研究方面逐渐有所改进和提高，这些工作都必须在如此审慎的规定下进行，恕我不在此赘述其重要性。我们的防御保障是国民

---

[1]1828年国会通过了高达30%的关税税率，严重影响了南方棉花种植者的出口利益，杰克逊竞选时就曾对此税率大加攻击。

on their importance. But the bulwark of our defense is the national militia, which in the present state of our intelligence and population must render us invincible. As long as our Government is administered for the good of the people, and is regulated by their will; as long as it secures to us the rights of person and of property, liberty of conscience and of the press, it will be worth defending; and so long as it is worth defending a patriotic militia will cover it with an impenetrable aegis. Partial injuries and occasional mortifications we may be subjected to, but a million of armed freemen, possessed of the means of war, can never be conquered by a foreign foe. To any just system, therefore, calculated to strengthen this natural safeguard of the country I shall cheerfully lend all the aid in my power.

It will be my sincere and constant desire to observe toward the Indian tribes within our limits a just and liberal policy, and to give that humane and considerate attention to their rights and their wants which is consistent with the habits of our Government and the feelings of our people.

The recent demonstration of public sentiment inscribes on the list of Executive duties, in characters too legible to be overlooked, the task of reform, which will require particularly the correction of those abuses that have brought the patronage of the Federal Government into conflict with the freedom of elections, and the counteraction of those causes which have disturbed the rightful course of appointment and have placed or continued power in unfaithful or incompetent hands.

In the performance of a task thus generally delineated I shall endeavor to select men whose diligence and talents will insure in their respective stations able and faithful cooperation, depending for the advancement of the public service more on the integrity and zeal of the public officers than on their numbers.

A diffidence, perhaps too just, in my own qualifications will teach me to look with reverence to the examples of public virtue left by my illustrious predecessors, and with veneration to the lights that flow from the mind that founded and the mind that reformed our system. The same diffidence induces me to hope for instruction and aid from the coordinate branches of

安德鲁·杰克逊
Andrew Jackson

军,以我们现有的能力和数量,国民军一定能使我们所向无敌。只要我们的政府是为人民的利益着想,并且按其意志进行管理,只要能保障我们的人权和财产权、意志自由和出版自由,它就值得我们去保卫。正是因为它值得我们去保卫,所以爱国的国民军才以其坚固的盾牌去保护它。我们可能会遭到局部的伤害和偶发的屈辱,可是成千上万持有武装的自由人民是永远不会被外国侵略者所征服的。因此,对于将被用来加强我们国家自然屏障的任何适当措施,我都将乐意在权力所及的范围内提供我所有的帮助。

对于国内的印第安部落,我有一个诚挚不变的愿望,在我们力所能及的范围内,奉行公正和宽容的政策,并且以人道主义的和周到的态度关心他们的权利与需要。这与我们政府的习惯和人民的情感都是相符的。

最近在政府职责问题上所反映出的公众情绪不容忽视。改革将纠正那些造成联邦政府滥用任命权和选举自由相互冲突的弊端,并且消除那些干扰正确的任命并把权力置于不忠诚和无能之辈手中的情况。

在执行上述工作时,我将尽力选择适当的人选,以他们的勤奋和智慧来确保在各自的岗位上提供称职的和忠诚的合作。为了推进这项公职,我将更多地依赖政府官员的廉正和热忱,而不是他们的数量。

也许是过于严格,我总是对自己的资格缺乏自信,但也因此导致我参考前几任杰出总统所留传下来的共同典范之时,对他们为创建及改革我们体制所花费的心血,充满无比崇敬之情。同时,这种不太自信的态度,也使我希望能得到政府其他联合部门的帮助和支持,并广泛地得到同胞们的参与和指导。我坚定信赖神的恩典,他的保佑曾使我们国家度过了初创时

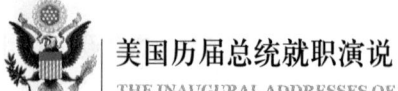

the Government, and for the indulgence and support of my fellow-citizens generally. And a firm reliance on the goodness of that Power whose providence mercifully protected our national infancy, and has since upheld our liberties in various vicissitudes, encourages me to offer up my ardent supplications that He will continue to make our beloved country the object of His divine care and gracious benediction.

期,并且在许多盛衰兴败时期确保了我们的自由,这将激励我奉上热忱的祈祷,祈求他会继续赐给我们可爱的国家以关切及美好的祝福。

扎卡里·泰勒
Zachary Taylor

扎卡里·泰勒（Zachary Taylor）

生平简介 >>

扎卡里·泰勒是美国第十二任总统。他于1784年11月24日出生在弗吉尼亚，后移居肯塔基，在一个农场里长大。他所受的正规教育很少。1808年任中尉，1812年9月在与印第安人交战的哈里逊堡战役中，因表现英勇而崭露头角，荣升少校。1838年荣升将军，统率所有佛罗里达的部队。1846年美墨冲突趋于激烈，泰勒奉命与墨西哥军队交战，经过鏖战，终使墨西哥政府屈服，泰勒因此成为国家英雄，声望大增。1849年，泰勒击败对手盖斯及范布伦，荣登总统宝座。

身为总统，泰勒反对新加盟的州蓄奴；秉承杰克逊的理想及观念，矢志运用他的权力以压制任何形式的叛乱。在任期内曾与英国订立了克雷登暨巴尔威条约，此约使美国得以控制未来横跨中美洲的运河和其他通道。

1850年7月4日，他参加华盛顿纪念碑典礼仪式之后病倒，五天后逝世。他是在任期内逝世的第二位总统。

美国历届总统就职演说

THE INAUGURAL ADDRESSES OF THE U.S. PRESIDENTS

Zachary Taylor
Inaugural Address

March 5, 1849

Elected by the American people to the highest office known to our laws, I appear here to take the oath prescribed by the Constitution, and, in compliance with a time-honored custom, to address those who are now assembled.

The confidence and respect shown by my countrymen in calling me to be the Chief Magistrate of a Republic holding a high rank among the nations of the earth have inspired me with feelings of the most profound gratitude; but when I reflect that the acceptance of the office which their partiality has bestowed imposes the discharge of the most arduous duties and involves the weightiest obligations, I am conscious that the position which I have been called to fill, though sufficient to satisfy the loftiest ambition, is surrounded by fearful responsibilities. Happily, however, in the performance of my new duties I shall not be without able cooperation. The legislative and judicial branches of the Government present prominent examples of distinguished civil attainments and matured experience, and it shall be my endeavor to call to my assistance in the Executive Departments individuals whose talents, integrity, and purity of character will furnish ample guarantees for the faithful and honorable performance of the trusts to be committed to their charge. With such aids and an honest purpose to do whatever is right, I hope to execute diligently, impartially, and for the best interests of the country the manifold duties devolved upon me.

In the discharge of these duties my guide will be the Constitution, which I this day swear to "preserve, protect, and defend." For the interpretation of that instrument I shall look to the decisions of the judicial tribunals established by its authority and to the practice of the Government under the earlier Presidents, who had so large a share in its formation. To the example of those illustrious patriots I shall always defer with reverence, and especially to his example who

扎卡里·泰勒
Zachary Taylor

泰勒总统就职演说

1849年3月5日

美国人民选举我担任我国法定的最高职务，我遵照宪法规定就此宣誓就职，并遵循一项历史悠久的惯例，向聚会在此的诸位发表演说。

同胞们对我如此的信任和敬重，要我出任这个立于世界强国之林的共和国的总统，实在让我感激不尽。每想到有幸得到人民爱戴，而任职后所要履行及可能接触到的任务又是那么艰巨沉重，我便意识到这一职位虽然可满足我崇高的理想，但它所赋予的责任却是可畏的。令人欣慰的是，无论如何，在我履行新的职务之后，我将得到各方有力的辅佐和帮助。政府的立法及司法部门人才济济，知识丰富，经验充足。所以，我必须努力召集一批有才干、诚实又廉洁的人，到行政部门来辅佐我。因为，只有这样的人才能将交给他们的事情认真而又圆满地完成。有了这些帮助，再加上诚实可行的目标，我愿意以勤勉、大公无私的精神，并以国家的最高利益为重，去完成交付于我的各种任务。

在履行这些职责时，我立誓要以"维护、保护和捍卫"宪法为指导原则。我也将根据司法裁判所做的决定以及前几任总统处理事务的惯例来解释宪法。前几位总统在宪法的形成过程中做出了巨大的贡献，我也将永远虔诚地尊崇那些杰出的爱国者，尤其是被尊为"国父"的华盛顿所立下的典范。

was by so many titles "the Father of his Country."

To command the Army and Navy of the United States; with the advice and consent of the Senate, to make treaties and to appoint ambassadors and other officers; to give to Congress information of the state of the Union and recommend such measures as he shall judge to be necessary; and to take care that the laws shall be faithfully executed — these are the most important functions entrusted to the President by the Constitution, and it may be expected that I shall briefly indicate the principles which will control me in their execution.

Chosen by the body of the people under the assurance that my Administration would be devoted to the welfare of the whole country, and not to the support of any particular section or merely local interest, I this day renew the declarations I have heretofore made and proclaim my fixed determination to maintain to the extent of my ability the Government in its original purity and to adopt as the basis of my public policy those great republican doctrines which constitute the strength of our national existence.

In reference to the Army and Navy, lately employed with so much distinction on active service, care shall be taken to insure the highest condition of efficiency, and in furtherance of that object the military and naval schools, sustained by the liberality of Congress, shall receive the special attention of the Executive.

As American freemen we can not but sympathize in all efforts to extend the blessings of civil and political liberty, but at the same time we are warned by the admonitions of history and the voice of our own beloved Washington to abstain from entangling alliances with foreign nations. In all disputes between conflicting governments it is our interest not less than our duty to remain strictly neutral, while our geographical position, the genius of our institutions and our people, the advancing spirit of civilization, and, above all, the dictates of religion direct us to the cultivation of peaceful and friendly relations with all other powers. It is to be hoped that no international question can now arise which a government confident in its own strength and resolved to protect its own just rights may not settle by wise negotiation; and it eminently becomes a government like our own, founded on the morality and intelligence of its citizens and upheld by their affections, to exhaust every resort of honorable

扎卡里·泰勒
Zachary Taylor

宪法赋予总统多项重任：统率美国陆、海军；经参议院的讨论及认可，签订条约并委派大使及其他官吏；将联邦情况向国会报告，并向国会提出必要的建议；关心法律是否被忠实执行。现在大家可能正等着我把履行这些职责时所要遵循的指导原则简略说明一下。

人民选择了我，因为他们相信我的这届政府将致力于为全国谋福利，而不是只支持某一特定地区或地方的利益。今天我要重申我过去所做的声明，表明我坚定的决心，我将尽我最大努力去维护政府的廉洁，并采取伟大的共和主义信条作为我们公共行政的基石，因为它一直是我们国家生存的力量所在。

提到最近做出许多重大贡献的陆军及海军，我们也应该注意必须确保其维持高水平的战斗力，为达此目的，行政部门也应对陆、海军训练学校给以特别的关切，国会一向都很支持这项训练。

身为美国的自由公民，我们必须赞同尽各种努力去扩大公民自由及政治自由所带来的幸福。但同时，我们也必须牢记历史的教训，并且恪守敬爱的华盛顿总统给我们的忠告，决不与他国有任何联盟或瓜葛。对于冲突国之间的所有争端，基于本身的利益及义务，我们必须严守中立；但在另一方面，我国的地理位置、我国的政治体制及人民的特质、人类文明的进步精神，以及宗教的诫令等，都要求我们必须与其他国家建立和平友好的关系。只要政府对自身的力量充满信心，并决心保卫自己正当的权利，那么目前出现的一切国际问题都有望通过明智的谈判来解决，就如同我们的政府一样，都必须是建立在人民的道德、智慧及对国家的热爱之上。在诉诸武力之前，必先用一切可能的外交手段进行调解。在处理我国的外交关系时，我会坚持这些观点，因为我把它们视为国家利益及国家荣誉的根本。

diplomacy before appealing to arms. In the conduct of our foreign relations I shall conform to these views, as I believe them essential to the best interests and the true honor of the country.

The appointing power vested in the President imposes delicate and onerous duties. So far as it is possible to be informed, I shall make honesty, capacity, and fidelity indispensable prerequisites to the bestowal of office, and the absence of either of these qualities shall be deemed sufficient cause for removal.

It shall be my study to recommend such constitutional measures to Congress as may be necessary and proper to secure encouragement and protection to the great interests of agriculture, commerce, and manufactures, to improve our rivers and harbors, to provide for the speedy extinguishment of the public debt, to enforce a strict accountability on the part of all officers of the Government and the utmost economy in all public expenditures; but it is for the wisdom of Congress itself, in which all legislative powers are vested by the Constitution, to regulate these and other matters of domestic policy. I shall look with confidence to the enlightened patriotism of that body to adopt such measures of conciliation as may harmonize conflicting interests and tend to perpetuate that Union which should be the paramount object of our hopes and affections. In any action calculated to promote an object so near the heart of everyone who truly loves his country I will zealously unite with the coordinate branches of the Government.

In conclusion I congratulate you, my fellow-citizens, upon the high state of prosperity to which the goodness of Divine Providence has conducted our common country. Let us invoke a continuance of the same protecting care which has led us from small beginnings to the eminence we this day occupy, and let us seek to deserve that continuance by prudence and moderation in our councils, by well-directed attempts to assuage the bitterness which too often marks unavoidable differences of opinion, by the promulgation and practice of just and liberal principles, and by an enlarged patriotism, which shall acknowledge no limits but those of our own widespread Republic.

扎卡里·泰勒
Zachary Taylor

总统手中掌握官职任命权的同时，也面临着艰巨的责任。我只能告诉各位，诚实、能干及忠贞将是我任命官吏的先决条件，一旦缺乏上述任何一项条件，我便有足够的理由将其免职。

向国会推荐某些必要、适当而又合乎宪法原则的议案，以鼓励保护农业、贸易、制造业的重大利益，改进河流及港口，尽快偿还公债，敦促政府所有的官员忠于职守并尽力节约公款的花费，这是我的职责所在。但是，制定管理这些项目及国家内政上其他问题的规定，则就有赖于国会的智慧了。宪法赋予国会所有的立法权，我对具有开明的爱国精神的国会相当信任，因为只有这样的国会才会采取调解的方式去调和相互冲突的利益，并使联邦永世长存，而这正是我们的希望及感情所追求的最高目标，我将积极地与政府有关部门联合采取行动，以达到真正爱国者内心的理想和向往的目标。

最后，我要恭祝各位同胞的是，在上帝的指引下，我们享有了高度的繁荣。让我们祈求他能继续保护、关怀我们，就像过去他把我们从起初的狭小之邦带到繁荣的今天一样。为赢得仁慈的神继续保佑，愿我们的施政采取谨慎与温和的方式；愿根据妥善的措施减轻因意见分歧所带来的痛苦；根据公正自由的原则从事行政；发扬爱国主义精神，使这种爱国情绪在我们广袤的共和国土地上四处传扬，并渗入每个人的心田。

詹姆斯·布坎南
James Buchanan

詹姆斯·布坎南（James Buchanan）

生平简介 >>

詹姆斯·布坎南是美国第十五任总统。他于1791年4月23日出生在宾夕法尼亚州。他毕业于迪金森学院，精通法律。

1814年，他被选为宾州议会议员；1820年任国会议员；1831年至1833年由杰克逊总统派至俄国担任大使；1834年当选为参议员；1845年任波尔克总统的国务卿；1853年任驻英国大使。1856年获民主党提名，竞选总统获胜。

布坎南是宪法的坚定捍卫者，坚决维护联邦的统一。他认为只要坚定不移地信奉宪法条文，就能弥合正在加剧的分裂。关于奴隶制问题，他赞成由大众决定，并经由各州立法加以选择，后来他接受了联邦最高法院关于奴隶斯科特的判决，认为联邦政府无权在其领地内禁止奴隶制度的存在。他的这种态度遭到北方共和党人的强烈谴责。作为一个民主党人，他无法解决南北的剧烈冲突，只能把这个非常棘手的问题留给继任者解决。

1868年6月1日，他在宾州兰开斯特附近自己的宅邸去世。

布坎南是美国唯一一位未婚总统。早年因未婚妻与其解除婚约，他决意终身不娶。

James Buchanan
Inaugural Address

March 4, 1857

Fellow-Citizens:

I appear before you this day to take the solemn oath "that I will faithfully execute the office of President of the United States and will to the best of my ability preserve, protect, and defend the Constitution of the United States."

In entering upon this great office I must humbly invoke the God of our fathers for wisdom and firmness to execute its high and responsible duties in such a manner as to restore harmony and ancient friendship among the people of the several States and to preserve our free institutions throughout many generations. Convinced that I owe my election to the inherent love for the Constitution and the Union which still animates the hearts of the American people, let me earnestly ask their powerful support in sustaining all just measures calculated to perpetuate these, the richest political blessings which Heaven has ever bestowed upon any nation. Having determined not to become a candidate for reelection, I shall have no motive to influence my conduct in administering the Government except the desire ably and faithfully to serve my country and to live in grateful memory of my countrymen.

We have recently passed through a Presidential contest in which the passions of our fellow-citizens were excited to the highest degree by questions of deep and vital importance; but when the people proclaimed their will the tempest at once subsided and all was calm.

The voice of the majority, speaking in the manner prescribed by the Constitution, was heard, and instant submission followed. Our own country could alone have exhibited so grand and striking a spectacle of the capacity of man for self-government.

詹姆斯·布坎南
James Buchanan

布坎南总统就职演说

1857年3月4日

同胞们：

今天我在你们面前郑重地宣誓："我将忠实地履行美国总统的职务，并尽全力维护、保护和捍卫美国宪法。"

在即将担负这一重大职务的此刻，我必须谦卑地祈求上帝赋予我智慧和意志，以恢复几个州人民长久以来的和谐与情谊，并维护我们的子孙享有自由制度这个历史交给我的伟大使命。我深信我之所以当选，是因为同胞们对于宪法和联邦的固有热爱的结果，它们深深地铭刻在美国人民的心中。此刻，我恳切地请求你们给予我全力的支持，用各种公正合法的方式，捍卫上帝赐给我们的这个最丰富的政治产物，使它永世长存。由于我已经决定不再竞选连任，所以我将不会使政府政务的执行受到个人行为的左右，我将忠实地全力服务于我们的国家，以感谢人民对我的重托。

总统竞选刚刚结束，在这次竞选期间，我们的公民、同胞们所讨论的深刻、重要的问题，激起了空前热烈的情绪[1]，但是结果一揭晓，热烈的气氛马上平息下来，一切又恢复了平静。

大多数公民的心声，通过宪法规定的方式表达出来，均能被倾听与执行。只有我们的国家，才可能充分表现出人类有如此巨大、惊人的能力去进行自治。

[1]废奴或蓄奴的争执，此时已成为关键问题。

What a happy conception, then, was it for Congress to apply this simple rule, that the will of the majority shall govern, to the settlement of the question of domestic slavery in the Territories. Congress is neither "to legislate slavery into any Territory or State nor to exclude it therefrom, but to leave the people thereof perfectly free to form and regulate their domestic institutions in their own way, subject only to the Constitution of the United States."

As a natural consequence, Congress has also prescribed that when the Territory of Kansas shall be admitted as a State it "shall be received into the Union with or without slavery, as their constitution may prescribe at the time of their admission."

A difference of opinion has arisen in regard to the point of time when the people of a Territory shall decide this question for themselves.

This is, happily, a matter of but little practical importance. Besides, it is a judicial question, which legitimately belongs to the Supreme Court of the United States, before whom it is now pending, and will, it is understood, be speedily and finally settled. To their decision, in common with all good citizens, I shall cheerfully submit, whatever this may be, though it has ever been my individual opinion that under the Nebraska-Kansas act the appropriate period will be when the number of actual residents in the Territory shall justify the formation of a constitution with a view to its admission as a State into the Union. But be this as it may, it is the imperative and indispensable duty of the Government of the United States to secure to every resident inhabitant the free and independent expression of his opinion by his vote. This sacred right of each individual must be preserved. That being accomplished, nothing can be fairer than to leave the people of a Territory free from all foreign interference to decide their own destiny for themselves, subject only to the Constitution of the United States.

The whole Territorial question being thus settled upon the principle of popular sovereignty — a principle as ancient as free government itself — everything of a practical nature has been decided. No other question remains for adjustment, because all agree that under the Constitution slavery in the States is beyond the reach of any human power except that of the respective

詹姆斯·布坎南
James Buchanan

国会要是能将这个简单的法则，即服从大多数人的意志，应用于解决领土内部奴隶制问题，那将是多么令人欢欣的啊！国会不应该通过立法"将奴隶制度扩展至任何准州或州内，也不应该排除奴隶制度存在的事实。只能根据美国宪法，将此问题留给人民，以他们自己的方法去组织或规定其内部制度"[1]。

因此，国会很自然地规定，将来堪萨斯准州被批准成为一州时，它将是"根据获准加入联邦时该州宪章所规定之原则，成为蓄奴州或非蓄奴州"[2]。

关于领地内的人民应在何时自行决定蓄奴或不蓄奴这一点，又引起了各种不同意见的争论。

幸好，这个问题在实际上并不那么重要。此外，它属于司法上的问题，根据法律应由联邦最高法院所管辖。这个问题正在处理中，据了解将迅速和最终地获得解决。我自己认为，在《内布拉斯加—堪萨斯法案》下，最适当的时机应该是，当住在该准州内的全部居民想以州的地位加入联邦，而着手制定州宪之时。这时，不管他们的决定怎样，只要是所有公民的决定，我都会欣然赞同。显然，保证每个居民能通过投票方式，自由独立地表达自己的意愿，是美国政府不可推卸的责任。每个人所拥有的神圣权利都必须予以维护。领地内人民不必受到外在的干涉，而能在美国宪法范围内，自由决定他们自己的命运，再也没有比这更公平的事了。

多数主权这项原则的渊源与自由政府的历史同样悠久，所有有关领地的问题都可以根据其顺利解决。没有任何其他问题需要调整，因为大家都同意：在宪法之下，除了居住在该州的人民外，各州的奴隶制度是他人无法改变的，但愿长期以来这个问题所引起的争论能很快结束，并且使开国

[1][2]引自1854年通过的《内布拉斯加—堪萨斯法案》。

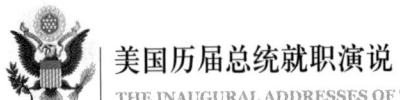

States themselves wherein it exists. May we not, then, hope that the long agitation on this subject is approaching its end, and that the geographical parties to which it has given birth, so much dreaded by the Father of his Country, will speedily become extinct? Most happy will it be for the country when the public mind shall be diverted from this question to others of more pressing and practical importance. Throughout the whole progress of this agitation, which has scarcely known any intermission for more than twenty years, whilst it has been productive of no positive good to any human being it has been the prolific source of great evils to the master, to the slave, and to the whole country. It has alienated and estranged the people of the sister States from each other, and has even seriously endangered the very existence of the Union. Nor has the danger yet entirely ceased. Under our system there is a remedy for all mere political evils in the sound sense and sober judgment of the people. Time is a great corrective. Political subjects which but a few years ago excited and exasperated the public mind have passed away and are now nearly forgotten. But this question of domestic slavery is of far graver importance than any mere political question, because should the agitation continue it may eventually endanger the personal safety of a large portion of our countrymen where the institution exists. In that event no form of government, however admirable in itself and however productive of material benefits, can compensate for the loss of peace and domestic security around the family altar. Let every Union-loving man, therefore, exert his best influence to suppress this agitation, which since the recent legislation of Congress is without any legitimate object.

It is an evil omen of the times that men have undertaken to calculate the mere material value of the Union. Reasoned estimates have been presented of the pecuniary profits and local advantages which would result to different States and sections from its dissolution and of the comparative injuries which such an event would inflict on other States and sections. Even descending to this low and narrow view of the mighty question, all such calculations are at fault. The bare reference to a single consideration will be conclusive on this point. We at present enjoy a free trade throughout our extensive and expanding country such as the world has never witnessed. This trade is conducted on railroads and

詹姆斯·布坎南
James Buchanan

元勋们所担忧的问题——因奴隶制度而引起的地区性党派活动能迅速地销声匿迹。公众注意力若能从这个问题转向其他更紧迫、更切实的重要问题，便是国家之大幸。综观20余年来连续动乱的整个过程，它对任何人都没有好处，对奴隶主、奴隶、对整个国家都已成为灾难的根源。它不仅离间各州人民之间的关系，甚至危及联邦的生存，至今这种危险仍未完全消除。在我们的制度下，通过人民公正、冷静的判断，所有政治上的问题都可找到解决的办法。时间就是一种良方，数年前曾煽动、分化大众的政治问题，如今已经消失，甚至几乎被人所忘记。但是一个国家内奴隶制度的问题比任何单纯的政治问题都重要得多。如果由于这个问题造成的动乱持续不断，最终将危及生存在这个制度下大部分同胞的人身安全。如果不幸真的发生，那么任何政府，不论其本身多么为人所称赞，物质利益是多么的丰厚，都无法弥补同胞们所丧失的和平与内部的安定。因此，我呼吁每位热爱联邦的人，尽自己的最大努力制止这种使国会最近的立法达不到法律目的的煽动和骚乱。

在这个时候人们都来推测联邦的财富的价值，这的确是时代的不祥之兆。大家都以理性的估计评价金钱利益与地域利益，然而各州各区利益皆不相同，对某州或某地有利的，却相对地对他州或他区造成损害。即使从这种浅薄的和狭隘的观点认识这个问题，所有这些算计也都是错误的。这里仅提一个事实对这个问题就能有个结论了。目前我们享有前所未有的、遍及全国广大区域的自由贸易。这些贸易在铁路与运河、壮丽的河川与广阔的海洋上到处都可显现，它将我们联邦的东、西、南、北紧紧地联系在一起。这种贸易若不幸被相互嫉妒、敌意和州际间的地域偏见所扼杀，则必然会毁掉我们的繁荣，并使我们陷入共同的灾难。尽管这些考虑非常重

canals, on noble rivers and arms of the sea, which bind together the North and the South, the East and the West, of our Confederacy. Annihilate this trade, arrest its free progress by the geographical lines of jealous and hostile States, and you destroy the prosperity and onward march of the whole and every part and involve all in one common ruin. But such considerations, important as they are in themselves, sink into insignificance when we reflect on the terrific evils which would result from disunion to every portion of the Confederacy — to the North, not more than to the South, to the East not more than to the West. These I shall not attempt to portray, because I feel an humble confidence that the kind Providence which inspired our fathers with wisdom to frame the most perfect form of government and union ever devised by man will not suffer it to perish until it shall have been peacefully instrumental by its example in the extension of civil and religious liberty throughout the world.

Next in importance to the maintenance of the Constitution and the Union is the duty of preserving the Government free from the taint or even the suspicion of corruption. Public virtue is the vital spirit of republics, and history proves that when this has decayed and the love of money has usurped its place, although the forms of free government may remain for a season, the substance has departed forever.

Our present financial condition is without a parallel in history. No nation has ever before been embarrassed from too large a surplus in its treasury. This almost necessarily gives birth to extravagant legislation. It produces wild schemes of expenditure and begets a race of speculators and jobbers, whose ingenuity is exerted in contriving and promoting expedients to obtain public money. The purity of official agents, whether rightfully or wrongfully, is suspected, and the character of the government suffers in the estimation of the people. This is in itself a very great evil.

The natural mode of relief from this embarrassment is to appropriate the surplus in the Treasury to great national objects for which a clear warrant can be found in the Constitution. Among these I might mention the extinguishment of the public debt, a reasonable increase of the Navy, which is at present inadequate to the protection of our vast tonnage afloat, now greater than that

詹姆斯·布坎南
James Buchanan

要，但如果联邦各地造成分裂，那么这些考虑就毫无意义。对此我不再叙述，因为我确信那激发了我们先辈的智慧，造就空前完美政府与联邦形式的仁慈的上帝，是一定会将我们人民所享有的文明和宗教自由以和平方式宣扬于全世界的。

次于维护宪法与联邦工作的是使政府免于贪污和腐败。公众的美德是共和国的精髓所在，历史证明，这种美德如果消失，而代之以钱财与贪婪，那么自由政府的形式虽可幸存于一时，但其本质却永逝不复存在！

我们现在的财政状况之好，是历史上前所未有的。过去从没有一个国家因国库盈余太多而不安，但这几乎必然导致挥霍无度的立法，因而就产生了疯狂无节制的支出计划，而且还产生了一批投机分子和假公济私者，绞尽脑汁设法用不当的手段谋取公款。因此，政府官员不管好坏都受到怀疑，政府品格也受到人民的不信任。这种事本身就是一大罪恶。

要自然消除这种情况，我们可以从宪法条文中寻得解决的办法，即拨出国库盈余作为国家的长远目标建设之用。对此我想列出如下几项，如清偿国债；合理地增加海军预算，目前海军规模不足以保护我们的那支比任何其他国家都庞大的海上运输船队，也不足以防卫我国已经扩展的海岸线。

of any other nation, as well as to the defense of our extended seacoast.

It is beyond all questions the true principle that no more revenue ought to be collected from the people than the amount necessary to defray the expenses of a wise, economical, and efficient administration of the Government. To reach this point it was necessary to resort to a modification of the tariff, and this has, I trust, been accomplished in such a manner as to do as little injury as may have been practicable to our domestic manufactures, especially those necessary for the defense of the country. Any discrimination against a particular branch for the purpose of benefiting favored corporations, individuals, or interests would have been unjust to the rest of the community and inconsistent with that spirit of fairness and equality which ought to govern in the adjustment of a revenue tariff.

But the squandering of the public money sinks into comparative insignificance as a temptation to corruption when compared with the squandering of the public lands.

No nation in the tide of time has ever been blessed with so rich and noble an inheritance as we enjoy in the public lands. In administering this important trust, whilst it may be wise to grant portions of them for the improvement of the remainder, yet we should never forget that it is our cardinal policy to reserve these lands, as much as may be, for actual settlers, and this at moderate prices. We shall thus not only best promote the prosperity of the new States and Territories, by furnishing them a hardy and independent race of honest and industrious citizens, but shall secure homes for our children and our children's children, as well as for those exiles from foreign shores who may seek in this country to improve their condition and to enjoy the blessings of civil and religious liberty. Such emigrants have done much to promote the growth and prosperity of the country. They have proved faithful both in peace and in war. After becoming citizens they are entitled, under the Constitution and laws, to be placed on a perfect equality with native-born citizens, and in this character they should ever be kindly recognized.

The Federal Constitution is a grant from the States to Congress of certain specific powers, and the question whether this grant should be liberally or

詹姆斯·布坎南
James Buchanan

毫无疑问，真正的原则在于除了支付一笔明智的、节约又具效率的政府费用外，不该多征人民的税赋。为达到此目标，调整关税迫在眉睫。对此，我认为应尽量减少对国内制造业的损害，特别是国防工业。任何偏袒某个公司、个人企业而歧视其他部门的做法，都是不平等的，也不符合税赋调整所依据的公平和公正精神。

但是，比较而言，公款的挥霍对政府的侵蚀，比起公共土地的浪费来说，就显得次要了。

在历史上，没有任何国家，在享用土地方面能像我们一样，幸运地拥有如此丰富、宝贵的遗产。在管理这项重要的财产上，虽然租售其中一部分以备其他建设之用，也是应该的，但我们不应忘记，尽量保存这些土地，以合理价格提供给实际垦拓者之用，乃是我们的基本国策。我们不仅应将它提供给新州及准州的那些勤劳的公民，以全力促进其繁荣，而且还需帮助我们的子孙和外国移居到我国寻求改善生活状况、追求享受民权和宗教自由的人，使他们能有安身立命之处。这些移民对促进国家成长和繁荣做出了很大的贡献。不论平时还是战时，他们都是忠心耿耿的，成为美国公民后，他们即在宪法保护下，享有与本国出生的公民同样完全平等的权利，而且他们也应该受到善待。

联邦宪法是各州授予国会某些特定权力的标志。从一开始，各党派对这项授权的解释应该从宽还是从严，就争论不休。我的政府即将执政之际，在

strictly construed has more or less divided political parties from the beginning. Without entering into the argument, I desire to state at the commencement of my Administration that long experience and observation have convinced me that a strict construction of the powers of the Government is the only true, as well as the only safe, theory of the Constitution. Whenever in our past history doubtful powers have been exercised by Congress, these have never failed to produce injurious and unhappy consequences. Many such instances might be adduced if this were the proper occasion. Neither is it necessary for the public service to strain the language of the Constitution, because all the great and useful powers required for a successful administration of the Government, both in peace and in war, have been granted, either in express terms or by the plainest implication.

Whilst deeply convinced of these truths, I yet consider it clear that under the war-making power Congress may appropriate money toward the construction of a military road when this is absolutely necessary for the defense of any State or Territory of the Union against foreign invasion. Under the Constitution Congress has power "to declare war," "to raise and support armies," "to provide and maintain a navy," and to call forth the militia to "repel invasions." Thus endowed, in an ample manner, with the war-making power, the corresponding duty is required that "the United States shall protect each of them [the States] against invasion." Now, how is it possible to afford this protection to California and our Pacific possessions except by means of a military road through the Territories of the United States, over which men and munitions of war may be speedily transported from the Atlantic States to meet and to repel the invader? In the event of a war with a naval power much stronger than our own we should then have no other available access to the Pacific Coast, because such a power would instantly close the route across the isthmus of Central America. It is impossible to conceive that whilst the Constitution has expressly required Congress to defend all the States it should yet deny to them, by any fair construction, the only possible means by which one of these States can be defended. Besides, the Government, ever since its origin, has been in the constant practice of constructing military roads. It might also be wise

詹姆斯·布坎南
James Buchanan

不涉及这些争论的情况下，我想告诉大家，基于长期以来的经验和观察，我确信对于政策权力加以严格解释，是唯一真实且安全的宪法理论。历史表明，每次国会若是运用引起争论的权力，则必定产生有害或不愉快的结果。今天，如果场合允许，我可以举出很多类似的例子。公务人员亦不必故意曲解宪法条文，因为所有平时或战时维持一个成功的政府所需的巨大权力，都以宪法条款或以最明确的暗示授予了。

尽管我明白这些真理，在国会的宣战权下，国会可以拨款建造军用道路，只要这是防卫联邦的州或领地，以抵抗外国侵略所绝对需要的，但我认为这一点还不够清楚。宪法规定：国会有权"宣战"、"集结和维持军队"、"装备给养海军"、号召国民军以"驱逐侵略者"等，这么多的权力都是附属于战争权之下的。因此，相应的责任便是"联邦需保护各州以抵抗侵略"。所以，除非建造一条军用道路横穿美国各地，以便快速从大西洋沿岸诸州输送人员和军用物资以对抗及驱逐侵略者，否则我们怎能保护加利福尼亚和太平洋沿岸地区呢？假设我国与某一海军强国作战，我们就无法寻找一条通往太平洋沿岸的通道，因为他们会立即封锁通往中美洲的海峡。宪法明文规定国会必须保护所有各州，但是国会却因此而拒绝各州从事应有的建设——各州自卫的最好方法——这是极为不当的。此外，从建国之初，政府就不断建设军用道路，因此我们必须考虑现在怎样才能激发起太平洋沿岸的同胞们对联邦的热爱，而不应因其偏远、孤立，而忽视或不援助他们，以致未能及时"保护"他们，并"抵抗侵略"。对于政府到底应以哪种最明智、最经济的方法对此项重大而必需的工程提供援助，我现在不宜表示意见。我相信现在看似可怕的种种困难，只要距离最近又最好的设计路线使得各方满意后，一切也就迎刃而解了。

to consider whether the love for the Union which now animates our fellow-citizens on the Pacific Coast may not be impaired by our neglect or refusal to provide for them, in their remote and isolated condition, the only means by which the power of the States on this side of the Rocky Mountains can reach them in sufficient time to "protect" them "against invasion." I forbear for the present from expressing an opinion as to the wisest and most economical mode in which the Government can lend its aid in accomplishing this great and necessary work. I believe that many of the difficulties in the way, which now appear formidable, will in a great degree vanish as soon as the nearest and best route shall have been satisfactorily ascertained.

It may be proper that on this occasion I should make some brief remarks in regard to our rights and duties as a member of the great family of nations. In our intercourse with them there are some plain principles, approved by our own experience, from which we should never depart. We ought to cultivate peace, commerce, and friendship with all nations, and this not merely as the best means of promoting our own material interests, but in a spirit of Christian benevolence toward our fellow-men, wherever their lot may be cast. Our diplomacy should be direct and frank, neither seeking to obtain more nor accepting less than is our due. We ought to cherish a sacred regard for the independence of all nations, and never attempt to interfere in the domestic concerns of any unless this shall be imperatively required by the great law of self-preservation. To avoid entangling alliances has been a maxim of our policy ever since the days of Washington, and its wisdom's no one will attempt to dispute. In short, we ought to do justice in a kindly spirit to all nations and require justice from them in return.

It is our glory that whilst other nations have extended their dominions by the sword we have never acquired any territory except by fair purchase or, as in the case of Texas, by the voluntary determination of a brave, kindred, and independent people to blend their destinies with our own. Even our acquisitions from Mexico form no exception. Unwilling to take advantage of the fortune of war against a sister republic, we purchased these possessions under the treaty of peace for a sum which was considered at the time a fair equivalent. Our

詹姆斯·布坎南
James Buchanan

在今天这个场合,我想应该提一提身为世界各国大家庭一分子的我们所应有的权利和义务。我们和其他国家交往,从经验中获得了某些必须遵守的明确原则。我们必须与所有的国家建立和平、商业和友谊等关系,这不仅是同胞们为获得与己有关的利益的最好方法,而且也是在基督教慈悲的精神下,对待我们那些患难与共的同胞的最佳方法。我们的外交方针必须直接坦白,当取则取,不可过分也不可不及。更应该遵守独立自主的原则,并珍惜和爱护所有其他国家的独立和主权,除非万不得已,绝不卷入任何国家内部的纷争。自华盛顿时代起,避免与盟国纠缠不清,一直是我国所奉行的总政策和行动准则,这种明智的做法是毋庸置疑的。简而言之,我们必须以公正的态度对待所有国家,也要求它们以相同的态度对待我们。

我们感到光荣的是,当其他国家用剑扩展它们的领域之际,我们除以公平的购买,或像得克萨斯州那样通过勇敢、友好、独立的人民自行决定与我国的命运结合在一起以外,没有获取任何土地。甚至我们取得墨西哥领土也不例外。因为我们不愿利用战争胜利之机做出不利邻邦的事情,我们根据所签订的和平条约,以当时颇为合理的价钱购买这些土地。我们过去的历史禁止我们非法取得领土,除非我们用公正光荣的法则来获取土地。基于这个原则,未来我国领土随着时机的发展如再扩展,他国是无权干涉

past history forbids that we shall in the future acquire territory unless this is sanctioned by the laws of justice and honor. Acting on this principle, no nation will have a right to interfere or to complain if in the progress of events we shall still further extend our possessions. Hitherto in all our acquisitions the people, under the protection of the American flag, have enjoyed civil and religious liberty, as well as equal and just laws, and have been contented, prosperous, and happy. Their trade with the rest of the world has rapidly increased, and thus every commercial nation has shared largely in their successful progress.

I shall now proceed to take the oath prescribed by the Constitution, whilst humbly invoking the blessing of Divine Providence on this great people.

或埋怨的。迄今为止,在美国旗帜的保护下,所有领土上的人民,不仅享有民权和宗教自由,受平等、公正的法律保护,而且一直都过着美满、繁荣和幸福的生活。他们与世界其他国家的贸易迅速发展,因此给每个商业国家带来巨大的成功和进步。

现在我谨根据宪法的规定郑重宣誓,并虔诚地恳求全能的神保佑我们伟大的人民。

亚伯拉罕·林肯
Abraham Lincoln

亚伯拉罕·林肯 (Abraham Lincoln)

生平简介 >>

亚伯拉罕·林肯是美国第十六任总统。他于1809年2月12日出生在肯塔基州，未曾受过任何正规教育。1832年4月，印第安人发动黑鹰战争，林肯自愿从军，被任命为上尉。

1860年林肯获共和党的总统提名，并顺利当选。林肯1862年发表的《解放黑奴宣言》时机选择得非常好，且文笔出色，促进了北方人民的团结，阻止了欧洲承认南方联邦。由于林肯不懈的努力，国会终于于1865年底批准了《第十三号修正案》，使奴隶制最终在美国消亡。1864年，林肯再次当选为总统。

1865年4月14日，林肯在华盛顿一家剧院被一位叫布思的演员刺杀。林肯是美国历史上第一位遇刺的总统。

Abraham Lincoln
First Inaugural Address

March 4, 1861

Fellow-Citizens of the United States:

In compliance with a custom as old as the Government itself, I appear before you to address you briefly and to take in your presence the oath prescribed by the Constitution of the United States to be taken by the President "before he enters on the execution of this office."

I do not consider it necessary at present for me to discuss those matters of administration about which there is no special anxiety or excitement.

Apprehension seems to exist among the people of the Southern States that by the accession of a Republican Administration their property and their peace and personal security are to be endangered. There has never been any reasonable cause for such apprehension. Indeed, the most ample evidence to the contrary has all the while existed and been open to their inspection. It is found in nearly all the published speeches of him who now addresses you. I do but quote from one of those speeches when I declare that—

I have no purpose, directly or indirectly, to interfere with the institution of slavery in the States where it exists. I believe I have no lawful right to do so, and I have no inclination to do so.

Those who nominated and elected me did so with full knowledge that I had made this and many similar declarations and had never recanted them; and more than this, they placed in the platform for my acceptance, and as a law to themselves and to me, the clear and emphatic resolution which I now read:

Resolved, That the maintenance inviolate of the rights of the States, and especially the right of each State to order and control its own domestic institutions according to its own judgment exclusively, is essential to that balance of power on which the perfection and endurance of our political fabric depend; and we denounce the lawless invasion by armed force of the soil of

亚伯拉罕·林肯
Abraham Lincoln

林肯总统首次就职演说

1861年3月4日

美国公民们：

遵循这个与政府同样悠久的习惯，我在你们面前做简单的演说，并根据美国宪法宣读"总统在行使其职权之前"的必读誓言。

我认为，我现在不该谈论那些不是令人特别担忧或兴奋的行政事务。

南部各州的人民似乎已有一种担心：共和党一旦执政，他们的财产、和平及个人生命都会岌岌可危。这种担心是没有任何合理根据的。事实上，与上述看法完全相反的证据却一直存在着，也可以随时公开查证，而且几乎在我所有已出版的演讲中都可以找到。现在仅选录一段：

"我从未蓄意直接或间接干涉奴隶州的奴隶制度，我深信在法律上，我无权干涉，也无意去干涉。"

提名并选举我的人都深深地了解，我曾经做了类似的声明，并且从未出尔反尔；更进一步地说，为表示对我的支持，他们将这种原则视为我们共同的规范，并将下列鲜明、强而有力的决议列入竞选政纲。

我们决议坚决维持各州的权利不受侵犯，尤其是各州完全凭自己的决断来安排和控制本州内部各种制度的权利不受侵犯，乃是我们的政治结构赖以完善和得以持久的权力均衡的至为重要的因素；我们谴责那种目无法纪、以武力侵害任何一州或准州的土地的行为，不论基于何种借口，都是

any State or Territory, no matter what pretext, as among the gravest of crimes.

I now reiterate these sentiments, and in doing so I only press upon the public attention the most conclusive evidence of which the case is susceptible that the property, peace, and security of no section are to be in any wise endangered by the now incoming Administration. I add, too, that all the protection which, consistently with the Constitution and the laws, can be given will be cheerfully given to all the States when lawfully demanded, for whatever cause — as cheerfully to one section as to another.

There is much controversy about the delivering up of fugitives from service or labor. The clause I now read is as plainly written in the Constitution as any other of its provisions:

No person held to service or labor in one State, under the laws thereof, escaping into another, shall in consequence of any law or regulation therein be discharged from such service or labor, but shall be delivered up on claim of the party to whom such service or labor may be due.

It is scarcely questioned that this provision was intended by those who made it for the reclaiming of what we call fugitive slaves; and the intention of the lawgiver is the law. All members of Congress swear their support to the whole Constitution — to this provision as much as to any other. To the proposition, then, that slaves whose cases come within the terms of this clause "shall be delivered up" their oaths are unanimous. Now, if they would make the effort in good temper, could they not with nearly equal unanimity frame and pass a law by means of which to keep good that unanimous oath?

There is some difference of opinion whether this clause should be enforced by national or by State authority, but surely that difference is not a very material one. If the slave is to be surrendered, it can be of but little consequence to him or to others by which authority it is done. And should anyone in any case be content that his oath shall go unkept on a merely unsubstantial controversy as to how it shall be kept?

亚伯拉罕·林肯
Abraham Lincoln

万恶不赦的罪行。[1]

现在，我重申我的看法，并让大家注意到这项最有力的证明——证明这个将要上任的政府，无论如何都不会让人民的财产、和平及安全受到侵害。同时，我要附带说明的是，只要各州的要求合法提出，政府将乐意提供所有合于宪法及法律的保护措施，而不管是出于什么原因，各州一律平等。[2]

如何遣送逃跑的奴隶一事，曾引起了许多争论，下面我宣读一条载于宪法的条文：

"被约束依附于某州的劳役或劳工，如果逃亡到另一州，根据宪法规定，应将其遣返于原来之州，而不能根据另一州的法律撤销其原来奴工的身份地位。"[3]

很少有人怀疑这项条款是那些想召回逃奴的人所设定的。而立法者心里所想的往往就形成了法律，国会议员都曾立誓维护整个宪法，包括该项条款及其他条款。对于把合于该宪法条款条件的奴隶予以遣回的提议，他们的誓言是一致的。现在他们如果能心平气和的话，难道不能以几乎同样的心情，起草并通过一条法律，使他们的那项誓言得以实现吗？

上面"将其遣回"的条款应由联邦还是由各州来执行，目前有些不同的意见。但这些意见并不十分重要。如果奴隶将被遣回，那么对他或其他人而言，到底是由州还是由联邦来执行，并没有什么差别。如果一个人的誓言因诸如怎样去遵守这类不太重要的争执而没有去遵守，他怎么能满意呢？

---

[1]共和党1860年全国代表大会所通过的17项政纲中的第四项。
[2]1859年威斯康辛州最高法院将1850年通过的《逃奴法案》判为违宪，使得各州政府、法院无法再将由南方逃至北方的黑奴遣回原地，是年经联邦最高法院更改，判为并不违宪。
[3]联邦宪法第四条第二款。

Again: In any law upon this subject ought not all the safeguards of liberty known in civilized and humane jurisprudence to be introduced, so that a free man be not in any case surrendered as a slave? And might it not be well at the same time to provide by law for the enforcement of that clause in the Constitution which guarantees that "the citizens of each State shall be entitled to all privileges and immunities of citizens in the several States"?

I take the official oath to-day with no mental reservations and with no purpose to construe the Constitution or laws by any hypercritical rules; and while I do not choose now to specify particular acts of Congress as proper to be enforced, I do suggest that it will be much safer for all, both in official and private stations, to conform to and abide by all those acts which stand unrepealed than to violate any of them trusting to find impunity in having them held to be unconstitutional.

It is seventy-two years since the first inauguration of a President under our National Constitution. During that period fifteen different and greatly distinguished citizens have in succession administered the executive branch of the Government. They have conducted it through many perils, and generally with great success. Yet, with all this scope of precedent, I now enter upon the same task for the brief constitutional term of four years under great and peculiar difficulty. A disruption of the Federal Union, heretofore only menaced, is now formidably attempted.

I hold that in contemplation of universal law and of the Constitution the Union of these States is perpetual. Perpetuity is implied, if not expressed, in the fundamental law of all national governments. It is safe to assert that no government proper ever had a provision in its organic law for its own termination. Continue to execute all the express provisions of our National Constitution, and the Union will endure forever, it being impossible to destroy it except by some action not provided for in the instrument itself.

Again: If the United States be not a government proper, but an association of States in the nature of contract merely, can it, as a contract, be peaceably unmade by less than all the parties who made it? One party to a contract may

亚伯拉罕·林肯
Abraham Lincoln

再者，就法律而言，我们应该把在文明人道的法律学中所有护卫自由的规定公之于世。这样一来，每一个自由人无论在什么情况下，都不致沦为奴隶。在这种情况下，我们也就实现了宪法所保证的"每州公民皆有资格享有其他州公民所享有的权利，及免予被迫害的权利"[1]。

今天，我以赤诚的心在此宣誓，无意用过分苛刻的原则解析宪法或法律。现在我不想特别指明国会通过的法案中哪些适于执行，但我的建议是，不管是在官方还是个人位置上，遵守尚未废止的法案，要比认为它是违宪的而去触犯它，更要稳当得多。

第一任总统依宪法就职以来，已经72年了。在这段时期，先后有15位非常杰出的公民担任总统，他们在许多艰难坎坷的情况下履行职责，大致说来，都相当成功。在今后依据宪法规定的短暂的四年任期里，我在特别困难的情况下承担起同样的重任，因为现在(过去仅是威胁)有人正处心积虑地要瓦解联邦。

从普通法及宪法的观点来看，我相信由州组成的联邦是永久的。所有管理国家的根本大法都隐含永久性，即使没有明确表达，我们也可以明确地指出，从没有一个政府会准备将该政府的执政期限列入其基本法中。只要切实执行宪法所规定的条款，联邦就可以永世长存，除非联邦本身自毁前程，要不然它绝不会垮台。

同样，就算美国不是一个正规的政府，而仅仅是契约性质的州联盟的话，那么就如同契约一样，它可以被缔约的任何一方随意撤销吗？尽管缔

---

[1]联邦宪法第四条第二款。

violate it — break it, so to speak — but does it not require all to lawfully rescind it?

Descending from these general principles, we find the proposition that in legal contemplation the Union is perpetual confirmed by the history of the Union itself. The Union is much older than the Constitution. It was formed, in fact, by the Articles of Association in 1774. It was matured and continued by the Declaration of Independence in 1776. It was further matured, and the faith of all the then thirteen States expressly plighted and engaged that it should be perpetual, by the Articles of Confederation in 1778. And finally, in 1787, one of the declared objects for ordaining and establishing the Constitution was "to form a more perfect Union."

But if destruction of the Union by one or by a part only of the States be lawfully possible, the Union is less perfect than before the Constitution, having lost the vital element of perpetuity.

It follows from these views that no State upon its own mere motion can lawfully get out of the Union; that resolves and ordinances to that effect are legally void, and that acts of violence within any State or States against the authority of the United States are insurrectionary or revolutionary, according to circumstances.

I therefore consider that in view of the Constitution and the laws the Union is unbroken, and to the extent of my ability, I shall take care, as the Constitution itself expressly enjoins upon me, that the laws of the Union be faithfully executed in all the States. Doing this I deem to be only a simple duty on my part, and I shall perform it so far as practicable unless my rightful masters, the American people, shall withhold the requisite means or in some authoritative manner direct the contrary. I trust this will not be regarded as a menace, but only as the declared purpose of the Union that it will constitutionally defend and maintain itself.

In doing this there needs to be no bloodshed or violence, and there shall be none unless it be forced upon the national authority. The power confided to me will be used to hold, occupy, and possess the property and places belonging to the Government and to collect the duties and imposts; but beyond what

亚伯拉罕·林肯
Abraham Lincoln

约的某一方可以违约甚至毁约，但它难道不需要所有订约者通过合法的途径废止吗？

以此类推，按法理我们发现联邦的永久性已被联邦本身的历史证明。联邦本身的历史要比宪法更早。事实上，早在1774年的联盟条款下，州联盟就形成了。1776年的《独立宣言》使其持续并发展成熟。1778年的联邦条款使其日臻完善。当时，13个州都表明信守联邦的永久性。最后，1787年，宣布制定的宪法目的之一就是"组织一个更完美的联邦"。

如果联邦可以被某一州或某些州依法摧毁的话，那么这个联邦就远不如制宪前的联邦完美，因为它已丧失了永久性这一重要的因素。

根据这些观点，任何一州如果仅依其意愿就脱离联邦便是违法的，那些为了脱离联邦而做出的决议及法令是无效的，在一州或数州内反抗美国政府的任何暴动，将依情形被定为叛乱或革命。[1]

因此，从宪法及法律的观点看，联邦是不可分裂的，并且就能力所及，让联邦法律在我国国土上切实地执行，这是宪法明确赋予我的职责。以可行的方法执行我分内的职责，除非我的合法的主人——美国人民拒绝我所采取的措施，或是以权威的方式指示我相反的做法。我深信大家不会将它视为一种威胁，而应该将它看成是联邦确定的目标，即为依据宪法维护和捍卫联邦。

进行这项工作，流血及暴力是没有必要的，绝对不会有这种事情，除非它们被强加在联邦当局头上。我会运用我的权力去维护、巩固和捍卫属于政

[1]南方诸领袖认为联邦政府无权辖治各州，而各州随时可以退出联邦。

may be necessary for these objects, there will be no invasion, no using of force against or among the people anywhere. Where hostility to the United States in any interior locality shall be so great and universal as to prevent competent resident citizens from holding the Federal offices, there will be no attempt to force obnoxious strangers among the people for that object. While the strict legal right may exist in the Government to enforce the exercise of these offices, the attempt to do so would be so irritating and so nearly impracticable withal that I deem it better to forego for the time the uses of such offices.

The mails, unless repelled, will continue to be furnished in all parts of the Union. So far as possible the people everywhere shall have that sense of perfect security which is most favorable to calm thought and reflection. The course here indicated will be followed unless current events and experience shall show a modification or change to be proper, and in every case and exigency my best discretion will be exercised, according to circumstances actually existing and with a view and a hope of a peaceful solution of the national troubles and the restoration of fraternal sympathies and affections.

That there are persons in one section or another who seek to destroy the Union at all events and are glad of any pretext to do it I will neither affirm nor deny; but if there be such, I need address no word to them. To those, however, who really love the Union may I not speak?

Before entering upon so grave a matter as the destruction of our national fabric, with all its benefits, its memories, and its hopes, would it not be wise to ascertain precisely why we do it? Will you hazard so desperate a step while there is any possibility that any portion of the ills you fly from have no real existence? Will you, while the certain ills you fly to are greater than all the real ones you fly from, will you risk the commission of so fearful a mistake?

All profess to be content in the Union if all constitutional rights can be maintained. Is it true, then, that any right plainly written in the Constitution has been denied? I think not. Happily, the human mind is so constituted that no party can reach to the audacity of doing this. Think, if you can, of a single instance in which a plainly written provision of the Constitution has ever been denied. If by the mere force of numbers a majority should deprive a minority

亚伯拉罕·林肯
Abraham Lincoln

府的财产和地位,并征收普通税及关税。为达到目标,除做好有必要的措施和准备之外,我们必须禁止下列的行为:侵略及运用武力或将武力加诸任何地区的人民。在国内任何地方,如果当地内部对美国联邦的敌意相当强烈而又普遍的话,就会阻碍当地有才能的公民担任联邦职务,在这种地方当然也就不会强迫不受欢迎的外来人去担任那些职位。虽然政府握有绝对合法的权力去强制这些公职的行使,但若真的这样做的话,将会激怒大众,同时又难以执行。所以,我认为目前最好还是放弃这些职位的行使。

邮件除非是被退回的,否则它将继续流通于联邦各地,只有这样,各地的居民才会有相当的安全感,这有利于冷静的思考及反省。除非最近的事件及经验显示出某些修正或改变的必要,否则大家都应该共同遵循联邦所制定的政策。而且无论在任何情况或危难之下,我都会根据实际情况,坚持和平解决国家困难的态度和愿望,再加上对同胞固有的同情和热爱,以最谨慎的态度处理一切事情。

对于一些地区某些人喜欢利用各种借口及不惜任何代价破坏联邦这件事,我不打算肯定或否定。但如果真有此事,我也不必对此说些什么,但对那些真正热爱联邦者,我能不说些什么吗?

在开始讨论那些如破坏联邦体制、它所带来的利益、它的名声及它的意愿等这些重大问题之前,先确定我们为什么这样做不是很明智吗?如果你所要逃避的实际上却并不存在的话,你会冒险而不顾死活向前跨出一步吗?而当你所要承受的不幸远比所要逃离的更惨重时,你又是否愿意冒着危险犯下这样可怕的错误呢?

大家都声称,只要宪法所赋予的各种权利都能加以维护,全国上下在联邦的体制下就能生活得很愉快。那么,宪法内所规定的任何一种权利都可以被否定,这种说法能行吗?我实在不以为然。所幸的是,还没有任何党派厚颜无耻到了这种地步。大家不妨想一想过去宪法中规定的哪一条曾被否定过?如果多数人凭数量上的优势去剥夺少数人应该享有的宪法规定的权利,就道德观点来看,这种情况也许就构成革命的理由。如果这项被

of any clearly written constitutional right, it might in a moral point of view justify revolution; certainly would if such right were a vital one. But such is not our case. All the vital rights of minorities and of individuals are so plainly assured to them by affirmations and negations, guaranties and prohibitions, in the Constitution that controversies never arise concerning them. But no organic law can ever be framed with a provision specifically applicable to every question which may occur in practical administration. No foresight can anticipate nor any document of reasonable length contain express provisions for all possible questions. Shall fugitives from labor be surrendered by national or by State authority? The Constitution does not expressly say. May Congress prohibit slavery in the Territories? The Constitution does not expressly say. Must Congress protect slavery in the Territories? The Constitution does not expressly say.

From questions of this class spring all our constitutional controversies, and we divide upon them into majorities and minorities. If the minority will not acquiesce, the majority must, or the Government must cease. There is no other alternative, for continuing the Government is acquiescence on one side or the other. If a minority in such case will secede rather than acquiesce, they make a precedent which in turn will divide and ruin them, for a minority of their own will secede from them whenever a majority refuses to be controlled by such minority. For instance, why may not any portion of a new confederacy a year or two hence arbitrarily secede again, precisely as portions of the present Union now claim to secede from it? All who cherish disunion sentiments are now being educated to the exact temper of doing this.

Is there such perfect identity of interests among the States to compose a new union as to produce harmony only and prevent renewed secession?

Plainly the central idea of secession is the essence of anarchy. A majority held in restraint by constitutional checks and limitations, and always changing easily with deliberate changes of popular opinions and sentiments, is the only true sovereign of a free people. Whoever rejects it does of necessity fly to anarchy or to despotism. Unanimity is impossible. The rule of a minority, as a permanent arrangement, is wholly inadmissible; so that, rejecting the majority

亚伯拉罕·林肯
Abraham Lincoln

剥夺的权利非常重大的话,那肯定会引发一场革命。但我们的情形并非如此。我们宪法运用肯定及否定、保证及禁止各种条文方式,标明少数人及个人的种种重要的权利,所以有关这方面的争议也就从未出现过。但是从没有一部基本法能完备到设计出一项条文,以解决实际行政工作上所产生的各种问题。谁也没有先见之明,更没有一部宪法足以制定出解决各种可能出现的情况的所有条文。所以,逃奴该由州政府还是联邦政府遣返?宪法并未明确指出。国会可否禁止奴隶制度?宪法也没有载明。那么,国会应该保护奴隶制度吗?宪法也未提及。

由于这类问题衍生出人们对这部宪法的争议,我们将之分为多数派与少数派两类。如果少数团体不愿默从,那么多数团体或联邦政府必须默从。除此之外,别无选择。因为若要政府继续存在,就必须有一方愿意默许。在这种情况下,如果少数团体不愿顺从,反而要脱离联邦的话,他们就会造成脱离联邦的先例,并最终也将分化和毁灭自己。因为退出联盟后,在他们当中的多数人不愿被少数人控制时,这批少数人也就会酝酿脱离。例如:像目前联邦中某些成员可以宣布要退盟,那么将来新加盟的成员在一两年后为何不可以随意退盟呢?因为所有怀着分裂主义情绪的人,目前都受到这种气氛的熏染。

目前能否在各州间找出相当周全的一致的利益来组织新联盟,使今后全国和谐一致,不再发生退盟的现象呢?

很显然,脱离联邦的中心实质上就是无政府主义。一个受着宪法的检查和限制的约束,又能根据舆论、民意做适当调整的多数派,是自由人民的唯一真正的统治者。拒绝接受或否认它的人,必然会走向无政府或专制。意见完全一致是不可能的。把少数派的统治作为一种长久的政治方案是根本行不通的;所以一旦不同意少数服从多数这项原则,那么剩下的就是某种形式的无政府主义或专制暴政了。

principle, anarchy or despotism in some form is all that is left.

I do not forget the position assumed by some that constitutional questions are to be decided by the Supreme Court, nor do I deny that such decisions must be binding in any case upon the parties to a suit as to the object of that suit, while they are also entitled to very high respect and consideration in all parallel cases by all other departments of the Government. And while it is obviously possible that such decision may be erroneous in any given case, still the evil effect following it, being limited to that particular case, with the chance that it may be overruled and never become a precedent for other cases, can better be borne than could the evils of a different practice. At the same time, the candid citizen must confess that if the policy of the Government upon vital questions affecting the whole people is to be irrevocably fixed by decisions of the Supreme Court, the instant they are made in ordinary litigation between parties in personal actions the people will have ceased to be their own rulers, having to that extent practically resigned their Government into the hands of that eminent tribunal. Nor is there in this view any assault upon the court or the judges. It is a duty from which they may not shrink to decide cases properly brought before them, and it is no fault of theirs if others seek to turn their decisions to political purposes.

One section of our country believes slavery is right and ought to be extended, while the other believes it is wrong and ought not to be extended. This is the only substantial dispute. The fugitive-slave clause of the Constitution and the law for the suppression of the foreign slave trade are each as well enforced, perhaps, as any law can ever be in a community where the moral sense of the people imperfectly supports the law itself. The great body of the people abide by the dry legal obligation in both cases, and a few break over in each. This, I think, can not be perfectly cured, and it would be worse in both cases after the separation of the sections than before. The foreign slave trade, now imperfectly suppressed, would be ultimately revived without restriction in one section, while fugitive slaves, now only partially surrendered, would not be surrendered at all by the other.

亚伯拉罕·林肯
Abraham Lincoln

我没有忘记某些人主张宪法问题应由最高法院裁决的观点，我也不否认这类的裁决在任何案例中都得约束诉讼的双方及诉讼的对象，同时政府其他部门，也必须以此作为将来遇到类似案例时的衡量标准。虽然针对某一特定案例，法院的裁决很可能有错误，但是它可能被否决或驳回，而不致成为其他案件的先例。所以这种措施所带来的恶果也仅限于原有的案件，较之其他措施的恶果，它还是可以让人忍受的。同时，诚实的公民会承认，如果影响到人民的重大的政府政策受制于最高法院的裁决，那么一旦一般诉讼中的裁决被裁定以后，人民便等于失去自主权。因为，如果到了那种程度，人民实际已经把政府交到最高法院的手中了。上述说法并没有攻击法院或法官的意思。正确地裁决案件是法官不可推卸的责任，而且，如果他人欲将他们的裁决转为政治目的的话，那么，错误也不在他们。[1]

国内有些地区认为奴隶制度是合理的，并应加以推广；而另一地区则认为它是错误的，不容其扩大。这是唯一比较重要的争论。宪法中有关逃奴的条款和抵制买卖外国奴隶的法律，已得到很好的执行，或者说在人民道德感并未完全支持它们的地方已经执行得不错了。大多数人民都还遵守着这两项枯燥的法律条款，只是少数人不予理会。这一点我承认很难完全加以纠正，而且在各个地区的分界都划清后，这两种情况就会更加严重。外奴买卖还没有完全禁止，并将再次公开流行，在某些地区已没有什么限制了。至于逃奴(目前只有一部分交回原主)，在另外一些地区则完全受到保护。

---

[1]当时的最高法院的法官多数倾向赞同奴隶制度，与林肯所属的共和党的立场相左，故林肯有此语。

Physically speaking, we can not separate. We can not remove our respective sections from each other nor build an impassable wall between them. A husband and wife may be divorced and go out of the presence and beyond the reach of each other, but the different parts of our country can not do this. They can not but remain face to face, and intercourse, either amicable or hostile, must continue between them. Is it possible, then, to make that intercourse more advantageous or more satisfactory after separation than before? Can aliens make treaties easier than friends can make laws? Can treaties be more faithfully enforced between aliens than laws can among friends? Suppose you go to war, you can not fight always; and when, after much loss on both sides and no gain on either, you cease fighting, the identical old questions, as to terms of intercourse, are again upon you.

This country, with its institutions, belongs to the people who inhabit it. Whenever they shall grow weary of the existing Government, they can exercise their constitutional right of amending it or their revolutionary right to dismember or overthrow it. I can not be ignorant of the fact that many worthy and patriotic citizens are desirous of having the National Constitution amended. While I make no recommendation of amendments, I fully recognize the rightful authority of the people over the whole subject, to be exercised in either of the modes prescribed in the instrument itself; and I should, under existing circumstances, favor rather than oppose a fair opportunity being afforded the people to act upon it. I will venture to add that to me the convention mode seems preferable, in that it allows amendments to originate with the people themselves, instead of only permitting them to take or reject propositions originated by others, not especially chosen for the purpose, and which might not be precisely such as they would wish to either accept or refuse. I understand a proposed amendment to the Constitution — which amendment, however, I have not seen — have passed Congress, to the effect that the Federal Government shall never interfere with the domestic institutions of the States, including that of persons held to service. To avoid misconstruction of what I have said, I depart from my purpose not to speak of particular amendments so far as to say that, holding such a provision to now be implied constitutional

亚伯拉罕·林肯
Abraham Lincoln

就地理及外在形式而言，我们不可以分离。我们不可以任随各个地区彼此分离，当然也不可以在其间造成一条无法逾越的鸿沟。夫妻可以离婚，从此不再见面，彼此互不相干；但国内各个地区就不能如此。它们还得互相交往，不管是友好还是敌对，彼此间的往来，一定要继续下去。那么，分离后彼此间的往来，难道能比以前更方便、更令人满意吗？与他人订约难道会比与朋友订约更容易吗？难道在外人之间履约，比在朋友之间按法律办事还更忠实吗？如果参与战争，你不可能长期打下去，一旦双方损失惨重且又毫无所获，你就得停战，到那时，你又会再度碰到相同的老问题——恢复沟通的条件。

这个国家及其制度，是属于居住在这里的人民的。一旦对现存政府感到厌倦，他们可利用宪法所赋予的权利去修宪，或者以独立战争时的精神去推翻它。我知道许多具有道德心的爱国公民希望修改宪法，虽然我未提出任何修宪的建议，但我完全承认人民对这个问题的合法权利，他们可依宪法上所规定的方式行使修宪的权利。在目前情况下，我是赞同而不反对人民在适当的时机去行使它。关于修宪的权利我还要补充说明的是，集会是最可行的方式，通过这种方式人民自己可以制定修正案，而不只是表决赞成或反对已经制定的条款。尤其是有些条款根本不切实际，而且也不是人民真正想要接受或拒绝的条款。我知道，国会已经通过一项宪法修正案[1]，虽未亲眼看见是哪一个修正案，不过大意是说联邦政府不可以干涉各州的内政制度，包括蓄奴制。为了避免有人对我刚刚所说的话产生误解，我背离了不谈某个特定修正案的原则，但我要指出，我并不反对把目前宪法中隐含的条款做一个补充，并制定得明白无误。

---

[1]联邦宪法第十三号修正案于1865年2月1日经国会通过。

law, I have no objection to its being made express and irrevocable.

The Chief Magistrate derives all his authority from the people, and they have referred none upon him to fix terms for the separation of the States. The people themselves can do this if also they choose, but the Executive as such has nothing to do with it. His duty is to administer the present Government as it came to his hands and to transmit it unimpaired by him to his successor.

Why should there not be a patient confidence in the ultimate justice of the people? Is there any better or equal hope in the world? In our present differences, is either party without faith of being in the right? If the Almighty Ruler of Nations, with His eternal truth and justice, be on your side of the North, or on yours of the South, that truth and that justice will surely prevail by the judgment of this great tribunal of the American people.

By the frame of the Government under which we live this same people have wisely given their public servants but little power for mischief, and have with equal wisdom provided for the return of that little to their own hands at very short intervals. While the people retain their virtue and vigilance no Administration by any extreme of wickedness or folly can very seriously injure the Government in the short space of four years.

My countrymen, one and all, think calmly and well upon this whole subject. Nothing valuable can be lost by taking time. If there be an object to hurry any of you in hot haste to a step which you would never take deliberately, that object will be frustrated by taking time; but no good object can be frustrated by it. Such of you as are now dissatisfied still have the old Constitution unimpaired, and, on the sensitive point, the laws of your own framing under it; while the new Administration will have no immediate power, if it would, to change either. If it were admitted that you who are dissatisfied hold the right side in the dispute, there still is no single good reason for precipitate action. Intelligence, patriotism, Christianity, and a firm reliance on Him who has never yet forsaken this favored land are still competent to adjust in the best way all our present difficulty.

In your hands, my dissatisfied fellow-countrymen, and not in mine, is the momentous issue of civil war. The Government will not assail you. You can

亚伯拉罕·林肯
Abraham Lincoln

总统的权力来自人民，但人民并未授权他去安排州的分离任务。如果人民这样选择，那就听其自然，总统与此无关，因为他的职责是管理，人民交到他手中的现任政府必须完整无损地传给他的继任者。

那么对人民的最后裁决始终保持信心又有何不可呢？在这个世界上有比这更好或相同的希望吗？在目前的分歧下，难道双方不都是认为自己正确吗？只要全能的上帝，以它不朽的真理及正义支持一方，不管是北方还是南方，它的正义及真理都会经由美国人民这个最高法庭的裁定，而飘扬四方。

在我们的政治体制下，人民十分明智，授予他们的公仆胡作非为的权力的可能性是微乎其微的，而且也可同样地在极短的时间内将其权力收回。因为只要人民仍保有自己的权力及警惕性，不管多么作恶多端或愚蠢的政权，在短短四年内，也不可能严重地伤害联邦。

同胞们，大家都应该从整体上冷静地好好思考这个问题，费点时间想想就不会丢掉什么重要的东西。一个未仔细考虑就要草率从事的目标，时间久了，自然就会错误百出，但是任何一个好的目标，也不会因费时长久而挫败。虽然你们有人对现状不满，仍然必须遵守原封不动的老宪法，而且在敏感的问题上，你们仍然有根据宪法制定的法律。这样，新成立的政府即使有意，也没有立即可行的力量去进行任何改变。即使在这场争论中，你们这些不满现状的人恰好站在正确的一方，你们也没有任何理由采取过激的行动。理智、爱国精神、基督教义，以及对从未遗弃美国这块幸运的土地的上帝的依赖，都能以最圆满的方式摆脱我国目前的困境。

不满现状的同胞们！内战这个重大问题掌握在你们的手中，而不在我的手里，政府不会去侵犯你们，只要你们不做侵犯者，也就不会发生任何

have no conflict without being yourselves the aggressors. You have no oath registered in heaven to destroy the Government, while I shall have the most solemn one to "preserve, protect, and defend it."

I am loath to close. We are not enemies, but friends. We must not be enemies. Though passion may have strained it must not break our bonds of affection. The mystic chords of memory, stretching from every battlefield and patriot grave to every living heart and hearthstone all over this broad land, will yet swell the chorus of the Union, when again touched, as surely they will be, by the better angels of our nature.

Abraham Lincoln
Second Inaugural Address

March 4, 1865

Fellow-Countrymen:

At this second appearing to take the oath of the Presidential office there is fewer occasions for an extended address than there was at the first. Then a statement somewhat in detail of a course to be pursued seemed fitting and proper. Now, at the expiration of four years, during which public declarations have been constantly called forth on every point and phase of the great contest which still absorbs the attention and engrosses the energies of the nation, little that is new could be presented. The progress of our arms, upon which all else chiefly depends, is as well known to the public as to myself, and it is, I trust, reasonably satisfactory and encouraging to all. With high hope for the future, no prediction in regard to it is ventured.

On the occasion corresponding to these four years ago all thoughts were anxiously directed to an impending civil war. All dreaded it, all sought to avert it. While the inaugural address was being delivered from this place, devoted altogether to saving the Union without war, urgent agents were in the city

亚伯拉罕·林肯
Abraham Lincoln

冲突。你们不可能要毁灭这个国家,而我已立下最庄严神圣的誓言,要"维护、保护及捍卫它"。

我不愿就此结束演说。我们并非敌人,而是朋友,我们决不要成为敌人。虽然情绪已经很紧张了,但它绝无法割断我们之间的友情。把在这块土地上的每一个战场、每个爱国者的坟墓到每个活着的人的心、每一个家庭联结起来的那奇妙的记忆之弦,一旦重新为我们天性里的善良天使所拨动,将仍然会使联邦的合唱歌声雄壮嘹亮起来。这琴弦一定会被重新拨动的!

林肯总统第二次就职演说

1865年3月4日

同胞们:

在第二次就职典礼上,我不必像第一次就职时那样发表长篇大论。当时,我有必要将政府所要采取的方针做一番详尽的说明。现在,四年任期已满,其间南北方战争(它现在仍吸引着人民的注意力,并牵扯着整个国家的精力)的每一重要时刻及每一阶段的情况,在公告上都可以看到,所以现在几乎没有新的情况可以报告大家。军队的进展情况,大家也都非常清楚。而我相信目前进展的情况,大家也相当满意,并对所有的人都能起到极大的鼓舞作用。所以,既然对未来充满希望,那么在这里也就无意冒昧做出预测了。

四年前的这个时刻,全国上下都为着一场即将爆发的内战焦虑不安。大家都害怕它,也都想逃避它。当时我就在此发表就职演说,竭尽全力要大家避免战争,拯救联邦。与此同时,叛乱分子却在城市中企图以非战争的手段毁灭联邦——以谈判方式使联邦解散分裂。双方虽然都同声反对战

seeking to destroy it without war — seeking to dissolve the Union and divide effects by negotiation. Both parties deprecated war, but one of them would make war rather than let the nation survive, and the other would accept war rather than let it perish, and the war came.

One-eighth of the whole population were colored slaves, not distributed generally over the Union, but localized in the southern part of it. These slaves constituted a peculiar and powerful interest. All knew that this interest was somehow the cause of the war. To strengthen, perpetuate, and extend this interest was the object for which the insurgents would rend the Union even by war, while the Government claimed no right to do more than to restrict the territorial enlargement of it. Neither party expected for the war the magnitude or the duration which it has already attained. Neither anticipated that the cause of the conflict might cease with or even before the conflict itself should cease. Each looked for an easier triumph, and a result less fundamental and astounding. Both read the same Bible and pray to the same God, and each invokes His aid against the other. It may seem strange that any men should dare to ask a just God's assistance in wringing their bread from the sweat of other men's faces, but let us judge not, that we be not judged. The prayers of both could not be answered. That of neither has been answered fully. The Almighty has His own purposes. "Woe unto the world because of offenses; for it must needs be that offenses come, but woe to that man by whom the offense cometh." If we shall suppose that American slavery is one of those offenses which, in the providence of God, must needs come, but which, having continued through His appointed time, He now wills to remove, and that He gives to both North and South this terrible war as the woe due to those by whom the offense came, shall we discern therein any departure from those divine attributes which the believers in a living God always ascribe to Him? Fondly do we hope, fervently do we pray, that this mighty scourge of war may speedily pass away. Yet, if God wills that it continue until all the wealth piled by the bondsman's two hundred and fifty years of unrequited toil shall be sunk, and until every drop of blood drawn with the lash shall be paid by another drawn with the sword, as was said three thousand years ago, so still it must be said "the judgments of

亚伯拉罕·林肯
Abraham Lincoln

争,可是有一方却不惜牺牲国家而宁愿一战;另一方则宁可一战也不愿国家灭亡,于是战争就爆发了。

黑奴占全国总人口的八分之一,但他们并不是平均分散于全国各地,而是集中于南方。这些黑奴本身就构成(对种植园主)一种特殊强大的利益。大家明白,这项利益也就是战争的肇因。为了达到加强、继续、扩大这项利益的目的,叛乱分子不惜通过战争来分裂联邦,而政府当即声明要限制战争扩大范围。双方都未曾料到冲突的原因会随冲突本身的终止而终止,甚至在冲突以前就已终止。每一方都希望能比较轻易地获得胜利,战争的结果也不那么重要和惊人。有趣的是,双方拜读同一部圣经,向同一位上帝祈祷,而且还向它求助来反对另一方。真是有些奇怪,有人竟敢妄求上帝的帮助,夺取他人血汗得来的成果。我们不要评断别人,以免遭别人评断。双方的祷告不可能都应验,而且也都没能应验。上帝自有它的旨——"这世界有祸了!因为将人绊倒,绊倒人的事是免不了的,但那绊倒人的有祸了!"[1]如果我们假设美国的奴隶制度是其中一种罪恶,而这一罪恶又是上帝的旨意,但到了它所指定的时限,上帝就要除去这罪恶。同时,上帝要南北双方苦战一场,以作为对那些犯这种罪者的惩罚。这样一来,我们是否会发现,信奉上帝者经常把一切都归于上帝,这中间可能没有什么差异。我们热切地希望,虔诚地祈祷,愿战争的惩罚能迅速结束。可是如果上帝有意延续这场战争,直到250年来那些无报酬的劳动所累积的财富化为乌有,或者像3000年前的人所说的,直到被鞭笞的每滴血都用刀剑来报复为止,即使如此,我们也要说"耶和华的典章真实,全然公义"[2]。

---

[1]《圣经·新约》马太福音第十八章第七节。
[2]《圣经·旧约》诗篇第十九篇第九节。

the Lord are true and righteous altogether."

With malice toward none, with charity for all, with firmness in the right as God gives us to see the right, let us strive on to finish the work we are in, to bind up the nation's wounds, to care for him who shall have borne the battle and for his widow and his orphan, to do all which may achieve and cherish a just and lasting peace among ourselves and with all nations.

亚伯拉罕·林肯
Abraham Lincoln

愿我们的人民不要怀恶意对人,而要以善意待人,按上帝给我们指引的方向坚定向前,继续奋斗,以完成我们正在进行的工作,医治国家战争的创伤,照顾战士及他们的遗孀和孤儿,努力在国内和国际缔造并珍惜公正而持久的和平。

尤利西斯·辛普森·格兰特
Ulysses Simpson Grant

尤利西斯·辛普森·格兰特 （Ulysses Simpson Grant）

生平简介>>

尤利西斯·辛普森·格兰特是美国第十八任总统。他于1822年4月27日出生在俄亥俄州。他不情愿地被送进西点军校，毕业时成绩颇差。在军队服役数年后，他过了几年平民生活，先是务农，后是搞不动产投机，但都不大成功。

南北战争爆发后，他被伊利诺伊州政府任命为志愿团的上校。1861年9月，他成了伊利诺伊州凯罗指挥的部队的一名陆军准将。由于受到林肯的赏识，三年后就成了联邦的陆军司令。

1868年，这位驰骋疆场的战斗英雄轻而易举地击败了民主党人霍雷肖·摩西，荣登总统宝座。四年后，尽管他的政府里出了丑闻以及共和党内发生分裂，他仍以绝对优势的票数获得连任。格兰特赞成东部共和党人所主张的保守的稳妥的货币政策和高额的保护关税政策。这些政策对抑制1873年的经济大萧条起了重要作用，使通货膨胀停止，国家信誉恢复。

1872年，他建立了美国第一个国家公园——黄石公园。

1885年7月23日，他在纽约州去世。

Ulysses Simpson Grant
First Inaugural Address

March 4, 1869

Citizens of the United States:

Your suffrages having elected me to the office of President of the United States, I have, in conformity to the Constitution of our country, taken the oath of office prescribed therein. I have taken this oath without mental reservation and with the determination to do to the best of my ability all that is required of me. The responsibilities of the position I feel, but accept them without fear. The office has come to me unsought; I commence its duties untrammeled. I bring to it a conscious desire and determination to fill it to the best of my ability to the satisfaction of the people.

On all leading questions agitating the public mind I will always express my views to Congress and urge them according to my judgment, and when I think it advisable will exercise the constitutional privilege of interposing a veto to defeat measures which I oppose; but all laws will be faithfully executed, whether they meet my approval or not.

I shall on all subjects have a policy to recommend, but none to enforce against the will of the people. Laws are to govern all alike — those opposed as well as those who favor them. I know no method to secure the repeal of bad or obnoxious laws so effective as their stringent execution.

The country having just emerged from a great rebellion, many questions will come before it for settlement in the next four years which preceding Administrations have never had to deal with. In meeting these it is desirable that they should be approached calmly, without prejudice, hate, or sectional pride, remembering that the greatest good to the greatest number is the object to be attained.

This requires security of person, property, and free religious and political opinion in every part of our common country, without regard to local prejudice.

尤利西斯·辛普森·格兰特
Ulysses Simpson Grant

格兰特总统首次就职演说

1869年3月4日

美国公民们：

你们选举我担任美国总统，依照我国宪法规定，我在这里宣誓就职。我将毫无保留地、全力以赴地履行我的职责。虽然感觉到责任重大，但我并不畏惧。我并不刻意谋取这个职位，我会放开手脚履行职责，我决心尽力去满足人民的需要。

在困扰大众的诸多重要问题中，我会将我的看法转达国会，并依我的判断来督促国会。而且，在适当的时机，我会运用宪法赋予我的特权——总统否决权，去制止我所反对的事情。无论赞同与否，我都会忠实地执行所有的法律。

我将对每一事宜制定可行的政策，但所有政策都不会违反人民的意愿。法律约束所有的人——包括反对者和赞成者。我知道，法律一旦被有效地严格执行，即使是很糟糕的法律也很难被废除。

我国刚刚经历了一场大动乱，许多问题会接踵而至，这就希望政府在未来的四年里解决它们。这些问题是以前的政府所没有遇到的，而面对当前的处境，我们一定要冷静对付，排除偏见与怨恨，更不该有地域的偏见和歧视。随时都要记住我们的目标是谋求大多数人的最大利益。

要达到这个目标，就必须清除地域观念的束缚，使人身安全、财产保障、自由的宗教信仰及政治意见的表达，遍及国家的每一个角落。一切有

All laws to secure these ends will receive my best efforts for their enforcement.

A great debt has been contracted in securing to us and our posterity the Union. The payment of this, principal and interest, as well as the return to a specie basis as soon as it can be accomplished without material detriment to the debtor class or to the country at large, must be provided for. To protect the national honor, every dollar of Government indebtedness should be paid in gold, unless otherwise expressly stipulated in the contract. Let it be understood that no repudiator of one farthing of our public debt will be trusted in public place, and it will go far toward strengthening a credit which ought to be the best in the world, and will ultimately enable us to replace the debt with bonds bearing less interest than we now pay. To this should be added a faithful collection of the revenue, a strict accountability to the Treasury for every dollar collected, and the greatest practicable retrenchment in expenditure in every department of Government.

When we compare the paying capacity of the country now, with the ten States in poverty from the effects of war, but soon to emerge, I trust, into greater prosperity than ever before, with its paying capacity twenty-five years ago, and calculate what it probably will be twenty-five years hence, who can doubt the feasibility of paying every dollar then with more ease than we now pay for useless luxuries? Why, it looks as though Providence had bestowed upon us a strong box in the precious metals locked up in the sterile mountains of the far West, and which we are now forging the key to unlock, to meet the very contingency that is now upon us.

Ultimately it may be necessary to insure the facilities to reach these riches and it may be necessary also that the General Government should give its aid to secure this access; but that should only be when a dollar of obligation to pay secures precisely the same sort of dollar to use now, and not before. Whilst the question of specie payments is in abeyance the prudent business man is careful about contracting debts payable in the distant future. The nation should follow the same rule. A prostrate commerce is to be rebuilt and all industries encouraged.

The young men of the country — those who from their age must be its rulers

尤利西斯·辛普森·格兰特
Ulysses Simpson Grant

利于实现上述目标的法律，我都尽最大努力施行之。

为了保护联邦的完整，国家背负了一笔庞大的债务。偿还本金和利息以及重建硬币制度必须妥善地安排，而且要避免债务人和大多数人民受到物质上的损害。为了保护国家荣誉，除非有明文规定，否则政府所欠的每一美元的公债都将用黄金来偿付。我们必须明白，如果拒绝偿还公债，即使是一毛钱，政府也会失去公众的信任。因此，我们必须健全我们的信用制度，而且使其成为世界上最令人信得过的制度，这样就能以发行债券偿还债务，从而承担较低的利息。当然，我们还必须有切实的税收收入，国库对每一元钱的使用都要认真计算，而且都要最大限度地削减政府各部门的开支。

由于战争的影响，有10个州还非常贫困，但是，我相信它们的经济很快会繁荣起来。将我们现在的偿还能力和25年前相比，并计算25年后的偿还能力，有谁会去怀疑那时得到的每一元钱，不比我们现在拿来购买无用奢侈品的钱来得更容易呢？那是当然的，这就好比上帝赋予我们一个用金子做成的盒子，此刻被埋在遥远的西部群山中，而现在我们正在铸造一把开启它的钥匙，试图发掘埋藏在其中的财富，以对付我们当前的困境。

无疑，为了获得财富我们必须保证还债没有困难。同时，必须获得政府的帮助才能达到目的。但是我们要遵守一个原则：偿还的每一元钱必须等于今天的一元钱价值而不是以前的价值。目前以硬币付款的方法仍在商议中，谨慎的商人必须小心处理未来应偿付的债务，政府也应本着同样的态度，致力于重建不景气的商业，并振兴所有的工业。

美国青年——国家未来的管理者——在维护国家荣誉上有极大的热情。

twenty-five years hence — have a peculiar interest in maintaining the national honor. A moment's reflection as to what will be our commanding influence among the nations of the earth in their day, if they are only true to themselves, should inspire them with national pride. All divisions — geographical, political, and religious — can join in this common sentiment. How the public debt is to be paid or specie payments resumed is not so important as that a plan should be adopted and acquiesced in. A united determination to do is worth more than divided counsels upon the method of doing. Legislation upon this subject may not be necessary now, or even advisable, but it will be when the civil law is more fully restored in all parts of the country and trade resumes its wonted channels.

It will be my endeavor to execute all laws in good faith, to collect all revenues assessed, and to have them properly accounted for and economically disbursed. I will to the best of my ability appoint to office those only who will carry out this design.

In regard to foreign policy, I would deal with nations as equitable law requires individuals to deal with each other, and I would protect the law-abiding citizen, whether of native or foreign birth, wherever his rights are jeopardized or the flag of our country floats. I would respect the rights of all nations, demanding equal respect for our own. If others depart from this rule in their dealings with us, we may be compelled to follow their precedent.

The proper treatment of the original occupants of this land — the Indians one deserving of careful study. I will favor any course toward them which tends to their civilization and ultimate citizenship.

The question of suffrage is one which is likely to agitate the public so long as a portion of the citizens of the nation are excluded from its privileges in any State. It seems to me very desirable that this question should be settled now, and I entertain the hope and express the desire that it may be by the ratification of the fifteenth article of amendment to the Constitution.

In conclusion I ask patient forbearance one toward another throughout the land, and a determined effort on the part of every citizen to do his share toward cementing a happy union; and I ask the prayers of the nation to Almighty God in behalf of this consummation.

尤利西斯·辛普森·格兰特
Ulysses Simpson Grant

如果他们只对自己真诚，那么稍许考虑一下我们对世界各国的重大影响，也应该激起他们的民族自豪感，所有的方面——地理的、政治的、宗教的等都可汇集到这种共同的感情中来。政府公债如何偿还，实物支付制度如何建立，都比不上这个问题重要，因为一个整体方案需要以共同的决心有效地实行，复杂的意见只会增加困难和阻力。也许我们现在并不需要也不适合以立法来完成这项计划；但是，当每一地区的民法完全建立，商业也走上正轨时，就是执行这项计划的适当时机了。

我将忠实地致力于执行所有法律、税收，公开账目和节省开支，而且我会尽力选择那些能胜任这些工作的人担任公职。

至于外交政策，我将公正地与其他各国友好相处，像平等地对待个人一样。我会保护奉公守法的公民，不论他是在本地还是在外国出生的；当他的权利或我们国家飘扬着的旗帜受到威胁时，我都会予以保护。我将尊重所有国家的权利，也要求其他国家尊重我们的权利。如果违背这项原则，我们也将被迫做同样的回击。

如何妥善处置印第安人——早期美国的居民，这是一个急需认真研究的问题，我将赞成一切维护印第安人文化与基本公民权的做法。

有关选举权的问题，是公众颇为关注的，在任何一州，只要部分公民的选举权被剥夺，必然会引起民众的骚动和不满。我觉得这个问题非解决不可。我把一切希望都寄托在第十五号宪法修正案[1]上，望其能获得通过。

最后，我希望全国上下温良俭让，凝心聚力，为建立一个幸福联邦贡献力量，并祈求上帝保佑得偿所愿。

---

[1]在格兰特就职前，2月27日国会已通过这项修正案，1780年3月获各州批准，正式执行。

格罗弗·克利夫兰
Grover Cleveland

格罗弗·克利夫兰（Grover Cleveland）

生平简介 >>

格罗弗·克利夫兰是美国第二十二任和第二十四任总统。1837年3月18日他生于新泽西州。1881年，他被选为布法罗市市长，一年后又被选为纽约州州长。

1884年，他作为民主党的总统候选人，在选举中获胜。在1888年的大选中，他败给了本杰明·哈里森，但1892年再次与哈里森在竞选中相遇时，终于东山再起，第二次入主白宫。他认为政府对任何经济团体，不管其强弱，都不能给予特别的优惠。因此，无论是对大型企业进行关税保护，对参加过内战的军人发放津贴，还是对遭受自然灾害的农民提供救济，都被他称为政府"家长制作风的弊病"，并对此进行了不懈的斗争。

他离开白宫后在新泽西的普林斯顿过退休生活，1908年6月24日去世。临终的遗言是："我已尽我所能力图把事情做好。"

在美国总统中，克利夫兰占据了三个第一：他是内战结束后第一个当选为总统的民主党人；他是唯一在离任四年后又再度当选的总统；他是第一位在白宫举行婚礼的总统。

Grover Cleveland
First Inaugural Address

March 4, 1885

Fellow-Citizens:

In the presence of this vast assemblage of my countrymen I am about to supplement and seal by the oath which I shall take the manifestation of the will of a great and free people. In the exercise of their power and right of self-government they have committed to one of their fellow-citizens a supreme and sacred trust, and he here consecrates himself to their service.

This impressive ceremony adds little to the solemn sense of responsibility with which I contemplate the duty I owe to all the people of the land. Nothing can relieve me from anxiety lest by any act of mine their interests may suffer, and nothing is needed to strengthen my resolution to engage every faculty and effort in the promotion of their welfare.

Amid the din of party strife the people's choice was made, but its attendant circumstances have demonstrated anew the strength and safety of a government by the people. In each succeeding year it more clearly appears that our democratic principle needs no apology, and that in its fearless and faithful application is to be found the surest guaranty of good government.

But the best results in the operation of a government wherein every citizen has a share largely depend upon a proper limitation of purely partisan zeal and effort and a correct appreciation of the time when the heat of the partisan should be merged in the patriotism of the citizen.

To-day the executive branch of the Government is transferred to new keeping. But this is still the Government of all the people, and it should be none the less an object of their affectionate solicitude. At this hour the animosities of political strife, the bitterness of partisan defeat, and the exultation of partisan triumph should be supplanted by an ungrudging acquiescence in the

格罗弗·克利夫兰
Grover Cleveland

克利夫兰总统首次就职演说

1885年3月4日

同胞们：

值此盛会之际，我将以所要宣读的誓言来接受一个伟大的自由民族所表明的意愿。人民在行使其自治权力和权利之时，将至高而神圣的信任托付于其中的一位同胞身上，在此，他也将为人民的事业奉献自己。

这令人难忘的典礼不会影响我神圣的使命感和我对这块土地上的所有人民应尽的职责。没有什么能够使我从担心人民的利益会因我的任何行为而蒙受损失的忧虑中解脱出来。我也不需要借助任何东西来强化自己要尽全部能力和努力去增进人民利益的决心。

在党派竞争中，人民做了选择，随之而来的局势再度显示出民治政府的力量和安定。年复一年，我们的民主原则更清楚地显示出它的正确性，并在忠实无畏的执行中，有了成为卓越政府的最可靠保证。

但是，使这一人人有责的政府在运作中达到最好的效果，却主要依赖于适当地限制纯粹的党派热情和行为，并能抓住这种党派的热情与公民的爱国精神融合的时机。

今天，政府的行政部门虽然全交给新人管理，但它仍是全体人民的政府，这一政府也应是人民继续深切关注的对象。此时此刻，无论是政治争斗的敌意，党派挫败的痛苦，还是党派胜利的喜悦，都应被由衷地默许大众的意愿以及冷静认真地关心社会福利所取代。更重要的是，如果从今以后，我们真心实意地摒弃所有区域性的偏见和猜疑，并决意以坦率的相互

popular will and a sober, conscientious concern for the general weal. Moreover, if from this hour we cheerfully and honestly abandon all sectional prejudice and distrust, and determine, with manly confidence in one another, to work out harmoniously the achievements of our national destiny, we shall deserve to realize all the benefits which our happy form of government can bestow.

On this auspicious occasion we may well renew the pledge of our devotion to the Constitution, which, launched by the founders of the Republic and consecrated by their prayers and patriotic devotion, has for almost a century borne the hopes and the aspirations of a great people through prosperity and peace and through the shock of foreign conflicts and the perils of domestic strife and vicissitudes.

By the Father of his Country our Constitution was commended for adoption as "the result of a spirit of amity and mutual concession." In that same spirit it should be administered, in order to promote the lasting welfare of the country and to secure the full measure of its priceless benefits to us and to those who will succeed to the blessings of our national life. The large variety of diverse and competing interests subject to Federal control, persistently seeking the recognition of their claims, need give us no fear that "the greatest good to the greatest number" will fail to be accomplished if in the halls of national legislation that spirit of amity and mutual concession shall prevail in which the Constitution had its birth. If this involves the surrender or postponement of private interests and the abandonment of local advantages, compensation will be found in the assurance that the common interest is subserved and the general welfare advanced.

In the discharge of my official duty I shall endeavor to be guided by a just and unstrained construction of the Constitution, a careful observance of the distinction between the powers granted to the Federal Government and those reserved to the States or to the people, and by a cautious appreciation of those functions which by the Constitution and laws have been especially assigned to the executive branch of the Government.

But he who takes the oath today to preserve, protect, and defend the Constitution of the United States only assumes the solemn obligation which

格罗弗·克利夫兰
Grover Cleveland

信任协力实现我们国家的愿望,那么,就一定能使我们完美的政府形式所赐予的全部裨益成为现实。

在这良辰吉日,我们不妨对宪法重申效忠的誓言。由共和国的奠基者们所创立的,并通过他们的祈求和爱国热忱所奉献出的宪法,在近一个世纪以来,无论是在和平与繁荣时期,还是在国外冲突的震撼与国内战争和社会变迁的危机时期,都一直肩负着人民的希望与抱负。

我国的宪法,作为"友好互让精神的成果",在美国国父的推荐下被采用。为了促进国家持久的福利,并充分确保我们自身无法估量的各种利益,以及那些愿为我们民族的生活而继续祈祷的人们,宪法应在同样的精神下被奉行。那些一直寻求得到承认的、数目庞大、种类繁多而又具有竞争性的利益问题,都处于联邦的控制之下。如果作为宪法诞生地的全国各立法机关都能普及那种和睦互让的精神的话,那么,我们就不必担心"为大多数人谋取最大幸福"的目标不能实现;因为如果这意味着摒弃或延缓个人利益和放弃地区利益的话,那么我们必定能够以促进共同利益和提高共同福利来作为补偿。

在我履行职责之时,我将努力以公正正确的宪法解释为指导,小心遵守赋予联邦政府和保留给各州或人民的权利之间的区别,并且谨慎地重视宪法和法律特别授予政府部门的功能。

但是,今天在此宣誓要维护、保护和捍卫美国宪法的这一个人所承担的神圣职责,也是每个爱国公民——农、工、商及各界人士所应共同承担的。

every patriotic citizen — on the farm, in the workshop, in the busy marts of trade, and everywhere — should share with him. The Constitution which prescribes his oath, my countrymen, is yours; the Government you have chosen him to administer for a time is yours; the suffrage which executes the will of freemen is yours; the laws and the entire scheme of our civil rule, from the town meeting to the State capitals and the national capital, is yours. Your every voter, as surely as your Chief Magistrate, under the same high sanction, though in a different sphere, exercises a public trust. Nor is this all. Every citizen owes to the country a vigilant watch and close scrutiny of its public servants and a fair and reasonable estimate of their fidelity and usefulness. Thus is the people's will impressed upon the whole framework of our civil polity — municipal, State, and Federal; and this is the price of our liberty and the inspiration of our faith in the Republic.

It is the duty of those serving the people in public place to closely limit public expenditures to the actual needs of the Government economically administered, because this bounds the right of the Government to exact tribute from the earnings of labor or the property of the citizen, and because public extravagance begets extravagance among the people. We should never be ashamed of the simplicity and prudential economies which are best suited to the operation of a republican form of government and most compatible with the mission of the American people. Those who are selected for a limited time to manage public affairs are still of the people, and may do much by their example to encourage, consistently with the dignity of their official functions, that plain way of life which among their fellow-citizens aids integrity and promotes thrift and prosperity.

The genius of our institutions, the needs of our people in their home life, and the attention which is demanded for the settlement and development of the resources of our vast territory dictate the scrupulous avoidance of any departure from that foreign policy commended by the history, the traditions, and the prosperity of our Republic. It is the policy of independence, favored by our position and defended by our known love of justice and by our power. It is the policy of peace suitable to our interests. It is the policy of neutrality,

格罗弗·克利夫兰
Grover Cleveland

同胞们，规定他宣誓的宪法是你们的，选择他代为管理的政府是你们的，履行自由人意志的投票权是你们的，所有法律和民权设计，从城镇会议到州政府以及国家首都，也都是你们的。虽然各自的领域不同，但每位选民和你们的行政首长一样，都在同样崇高的法律之下，履行着公共职责。不仅如此，每位公民对国家公仆应严密注视和监督，并且公正合理地评价他们的忠诚和能力。这样，人民的意愿将深深影响我们国民的政治结构——市、州和联邦政府。这就是我们自由的价值和我们对共和国信念的所在。

依据节约原则管理政府的实际需要，严格限制公共开支是担任公职者的责任，因为这会限制政府从公民的劳动和财产所得中强求纳税的权力，同时也因为政府部门的浪费会引发群众的挥霍无度。我们永远不应因简朴和谨慎的节约而感到羞愧；它们二者最适于共和制政府的运行，而且也与美国人民的使命相一致。那些被挑选出来在一定时期处理公共事务的人，仍是人民的一分子，在与其官职尊严不矛盾的情况下，可以用自身的榜样来鼓励同胞们认识到，朴素的生活方式有助于培养正直的品质，形成节俭的风气，促进经济繁荣。

我国的制度特征，人民生活所需以及对解决和发展我国国土资源要求的关注，都要求我们审慎地避免背离符合我国历史、传统以及繁荣的外交政策。那就是由于我们的位置而受到偏爱，由于我们的力量和对正义的热爱而得到捍卫的独立的政策；那就是符合我们利益的和平政策；那就是拒绝参与国外争端和对其他大陆的野心以及抵制别国入侵的中立政策；那就是门罗、华盛顿和杰斐逊的政策："与所有国家保持和平、贸易和诚实的友谊，不与任何国家结盟。"

rejecting any share in foreign broils and ambitions upon other continents and repelling their intrusion here. It is the policy of Monroe and of Washington and Jefferson — "Peace, commerce, and honest friendship with all nations; entangling alliance with none."

A due regard for the interests and prosperity of all the people demands that our finances shall be established upon such a sound and sensible basis as shall secure the safety and confidence of business interests and make the wage of labor sure and steady, and that our system of revenue shall be so adjusted as to relieve the people of unnecessary taxation, having a due regard to the interests of capital invested and workingmen employed in American industries, and preventing the accumulation of a surplus in the Treasury to tempt extravagance and waste.

Care for the property of the nation and for the needs of future settlers requires that the public domain should be protected from purloining schemes and unlawful occupation.

The conscience of the people demands that the Indians within our boundaries shall be fairly and honestly treated as wards of the Government and their education and civilization promoted with a view to their ultimate citizenship, and that polygamy in the Territories, destructive of the family relation and offensive to the moral sense of the civilized world, shall be repressed.

The laws should be rigidly enforced which prohibit the immigration of a servile class to compete with American labor, with no intention of acquiring citizenship, and bringing with them and retaining habits and customs repugnant to our civilization.

The people demand reform in the administration of the Government and the application of business principles to public affairs. As a means to this end, civil-service reform should be in good faith enforced. Our citizens have the right to protection from the incompetence of public employees who hold their places solely as the reward of partisan service, and from the corrupting influence of those who promise and the vicious methods of those who expect such rewards; and those who worthily seek public employment have the right to insist that

格罗弗·克利夫兰
Grover Cleveland

关注全体人民的利益和富裕要求我们的财政就得迅速建立在一个健全的和明智的基础之上，它将保证商业利益的安全和信心，确保劳动工资的稳定；我们的税收体制必须调整，以减轻人民不必要的税赋；应当关心投资者和美国工人的利益；应当防止因国库积累过多而造成的奢侈和浪费。

考虑到国家财产和未来移民的需要，要求国土必须受到保护，以防各种偷窃阴谋和非法的侵占。

人民的良知要求我们境内的印第安人应被视为受政府保护的人，而受到公平坦诚的对待。为了使其具有基本的公民资格，他们的教育和文明也应得到提高，那种破坏家庭关系并触犯文明世界道德观念的一夫多妻制，应该受到抑制。[1]

有关禁止与美国劳工竞争的劳务阶层移民的法律，必须严格执行。这些移民虽无意于获得公民资格，但他们带来并留下的风俗习惯却与我们的文明相抵触。

人民要求政府在管理方面应有所改革，并要求将商业原则[2]运用到公共事务上，为此，文官制度的改革应得到切实地实行。人民有权防范那些服务于政党而获得官职作为报偿的不合格官员，避免随意许诺者的腐败影响和为得到这种报酬而使用的卑鄙手段。同时，有权坚持以才干和任职能力为标准，而不是屈从党派，放弃诚实的政治信仰。

---

[1]指聚居于犹他州的摩门教徒。
[2]所谓商业原则是指精简开支、核算成本、消除赤字等。

merit and competency shall be recognized instead of party subservience or the surrender of honest political belief.

In the administration of a government pledged to do equal and exact justice to all men there should be no pretext for anxiety touching the protection of the freedmen in their rights or their security in the enjoyment of their privileges under the Constitution and its amendments. All discussion as to their fitness for the place accorded to them as American citizens are idle and unprofitable except as it suggests the necessity for their improvement. The fact that they are citizens entitles them to all the rights due to that relation and charges them with all its duties, obligations, and responsibilities.

These topics and the constant and ever-varying wants of an active and enterprising population may well receive the attention and the patriotic endeavor of all who make and execute the Federal law. Our duties are practical and call for industrious application, an intelligent perception of the claims of public office, and, above all, a firm determination, by united action, to secure to all the people of the land the full benefits of the best form of government ever vouchsafed to man. And let us not trust to human effort alone, but humbly acknowledging the power and goodness of Almighty God, who presides over the destiny of nations, and who has at all times been revealed in our country's history, let us invoke His aid and His blessings upon our labors.

格罗弗·克利夫兰
Grover Cleveland

　　管理一个保证行事公平、待民公正的政府时，不应有任何借口触犯在宪法和宪法修正案保护下自由人享有的权利或安全保证。所有关于美国公民的名不副实的讨论都是无意义的，除非那是一种必要的改进意见。他们是美国公民这一事实，赋予了他们所有应得的权利。与此同时，也使之承担起所有应尽的职责、义务和责任。

　　上述这些话题与积极向上的民众千变万化的需求，应该受到联邦法律制定者和执行者关注。我们的职责是讲究实际，勤奋地贯彻，明智地理解公职的要求。更为重要的是，要通过联合的行动，确保我国人民享有人类历史上最好的政府能给予人民的全部裨益。但是，我们不要只依赖人类的努力，还应谦卑地承认上帝的力量和慈善，他主宰所有国家的命运，他也一直在我们的历史中显现。让我们祈求它的帮助，保佑我们的努力。

威廉·麦金莱
William McKinley

威廉·麦金莱（William Mckinley）

生平简介 >>

威廉·麦金莱是美国第二十五任总统。他于1843年1月29日出生在俄亥俄州。他在34岁时进入众议院，不久就担任了赋税委员会的主席。他在众议院的14年期间，成为共和党主要的关税专家。1890年所制定的一项法案被称为《麦金莱法案》。后来他被选为俄亥俄州州长，并任满两届。

1896年，坚决主张金本位制度的麦金莱，在选举中击败对手而当选为总统。在任期间，他召开国会特别会议，批准了《丁利关税法案》，使作为工业联合企业的托拉斯以空前的速度发展起来。

1900年，麦金莱因坚持共和党深得人心的"吃饱吃好"的主张，顺利地赢得了第二届任期。但是，第二届任期未及一年，他就遭到一名无政府主义者的枪击，于1901年9月14日去世。

William McKinley
First Inaugural Address

March 4, 1897

Fellow-Citizens:

In obedience to the will of the people, and in their presence, by the authority vested in me by this oath, I assume the arduous and responsible duties of President of the United States, relying upon the support of my countrymen and invoking the guidance of Almighty God. Our faith teaches that there is no safer reliance than upon the God of our fathers, who has so singularly favored the American people in every national trial, and who will not forsake us so long as we obey His commandments and walk humbly in His footsteps.

The responsibilities of the high trust to which I have been called — always of grave importance — are augmented by the prevailing business conditions entailing idleness upon willing labor and loss to useful enterprises. The country is suffering from industrial disturbances from which speedy relief must be had. Our financial system needs some revision; our money is all good now, but its value must not further be threatened. It should all be put upon an enduring basis, not subject to easy attack, nor its stability to doubt or dispute. Our currency should continue under the supervision of the Government. The several forms of our paper money offer, in my judgment, a constant embarrassment to the Government and a safe balance in the Treasury. Therefore I believe it necessary to devise a system which, without diminishing the circulating medium or offering a premium for its contraction, will present a remedy for those arrangements which, temporary in their nature, might well in the years of our prosperity have been displaced by wiser provisions. With adequate revenue secured, but not until then, we can enter upon such changes in our fiscal laws as will, while insuring safety and volume to our money, no longer impose upon the Government the necessity of maintaining so large a gold reserve, with its

威廉·麦金莱
William McKinley

麦金莱总统首次就职演说

1897年3月4日

同胞们：

　　顺应人民的意愿并站在人民面前，借誓约所赋予的权力，我肩负起美国总统之职。承担这一重大使命，仰赖于全民的支持和上帝的指引。我们忠实于先辈的教诲，唯有上帝是最值得依赖的，它在各种考验中，都给予了美国人民以得天独厚的恩赐。因此，只要我们恪守其训令，虚心追随其脚步，它仍不会将我们遗弃。

　　人民托付于我的责任，本来已非常重要，再加上目前商业情况造成的劳力浪费和有益企业的亏损，使这一责任的分量大为增加。工业的混乱局面需迅速扭转；财政制度有待改善；货币情况目前尚好，但币值不容再受到威胁。一国的金融应建立在一个持久的基础上，才不致轻易遭受打击；而保持它的稳定，更是不容置疑和不容争辩的，因此，货币流通应继续由政府来监督。就我看来，我们的几种纸币，不断给政府带来困扰，却为财政提供了安全的平衡。所以我认为，有必要创立一个既不减少流通手段，也不因其紧缩而升值的新的体制，作为对那些临时性措施的一种纠正。那些经济景气时期的措施，现在可由更妥善的规定所取代。一旦经济景气，岁入充裕，我们即可着手改革财政法规，以确保金融稳定和货币发行的数量。现在不必迫使政府预备大量的黄金储备，过多的黄金储备容易产生投机。我国的财政法规大都是经验和实践的成果，除非变革的建议经过了明智的调查和论证，否则就不可轻举妄动。我们应该"保证万无一失"的同时"稍安勿躁"。因此，如果国会能够明智地成立一个委员会作为权宜之计，把修订铸币法、银行法和货币法列为优先考虑的对象，并对它们做一番彻底的、审慎的和无偏见的审查，那么，我将采取积极的配合行动。如果允许总统有这样的权力，我将指定一个由各党知名的专家组成的委员会，

attendant and inevitable temptations to speculation. Most of our financial laws are the outgrowth of experience and trial, and should not be amended without investigation and demonstration of the wisdom of the proposed changes. We must be both "sure we are right" and "make haste slowly." If, therefore, Congress, in its wisdom, shall deem it expedient to create a commission to take under early consideration the revision of our coinage, banking and currency laws, and give them that exhaustive, careful and dispassionate examination that their importance demands, I shall cordially concur in such action. If such power is vested in the President, it is my purpose to appoint a commission of prominent, well-informed citizens of different parties, who will command public confidence, both on account of their ability and special fitness for the work. Business experience and public training may thus be combined, and the patriotic zeal of the friends of the country is so directed that such a report will be made as to receive the support of all parties, and our finances cease to be the subject of mere partisan contention. The experiment is, at all events, worth a trial, and, in my opinion, it can but prove beneficial to the entire country.

The question of international bimetallism will have early and earnest attention. It will be my constant endeavor to secure it by co-operation with the other great commercial powers of the world. Until that condition is realized when the parity between our gold and silver money springs from and is supported by the relative value of the two metals, the value of the silver already coined and of that which may hereafter be coined, must be kept constantly at par with gold by every resource at our command. The credit of the Government, the integrity of its currency, and the inviolability of its obligations must be preserved. This was the commanding verdict of the people, and it will not be unheeded.

Economy is demanded in every branch of the Government at all times, but especially in periods, like the present, of depression in business and distress among the people. The severest economy must be observed in all public expenditures, and extravagance stopped wherever it is found, and prevented wherever in the future it may be developed. If the revenues are to remain as now, the only relief that can come must be from decreased expenditures. But the

威廉·麦金莱
William McKinley

他们将以自己的能力和对这一工作的胜任而深得民心。这样一来，商业经验与公共管理训练结合，爱国人士群情一致，各党纷纷起而支持，那么，财政问题就不会是党派之间争论的一个论题。无论如何，这项试验值得尝试，而且在我看来，它对整个国家是有益的。

国际复本位制问题应及早予以认真的关注。通过与世界上其他商业大国的合作，我将努力不懈地促成此事。[1]一旦金银这两种金属的相对价格带动并促使金币与银币等价的情况出现，我们就得尽力使已铸和待铸的银价与黄金持续地保持平价。对一个国家来说，政府的信誉、通货的完整和神圣的职责，都是必须加以维护的。不论过去还是现在，这都是人民的最高意愿，不容忽视。

节约是政府各部门任何时候都应遵守的原则。在目前工商业萧条、民

---

[1]从1893年起，美国经济发生严重萧条，持续至麦金莱入主白宫时仍未见起色。关于经济不景气的原因，当时被关注的焦点是币值问题。一派主张采取银本位制，降低钱币实值，以减轻政府的债务负担；而麦金莱代表的另一派则主张采取金本位制，使钱币与实值相符，以稳定币制，保护债权，促使工商业稳定发展。由于美国当时国库的黄金储备已将用尽，所以造成金价上涨，而银价相对跌落。

present must not become the permanent condition of the Government. It has been our uniform practice to retire, not increase our outstanding obligations, and this policy must again be resumed and vigorously enforced. Our revenues should always be large enough to meet with ease and promptness not only our current needs and the principal and interest of the public debt, but to make proper and liberal provision for that most deserving body of public creditors, the soldiers and sailors and the widows and orphans who are the pensioners of the United States.

The Government should not be permitted to run behind or increase its debt in times like the present. Suitably to provide against this is the mandate of duty — the certain and easy remedy for most of our financial difficulties. A deficiency is inevitable so long as the expenditures of the Government exceed its receipts. It can only be met by loans or increased revenue. While a large annual surplus of revenue may invite waste and extravagance, inadequate revenue creates distrust and undermines public and private credit. Neither should be encouraged. Between more loans and more revenue there ought to be but one opinion. We should have more revenue and that without delay, hindrance, or postponement. A surplus in the Treasury created by loans is not a permanent or safe reliance. It will suffice while it lasts, but it can not last long while the outlays of the Government are greater than its receipts, as has been the case during the past two years. Nor must it be forgotten that however much such loans may temporarily relieve the situation, the Government is still indebted for the amount of the surplus thus accrued, which it must ultimately pay, while its ability to pay is not strengthened, but weakened by a continued deficit. Loans are imperative in great emergencies to preserve the Government or its credit, but a failure to supply needed revenue in time of peace for the maintenance of either has no justification.

The best way for the Government to maintain its credit is to pay as it goes — not by resorting to loans, but by keeping out of debt — through an adequate income secured by a system of taxation, external or internal, or both. It is the settled policy of the Government, pursued from the beginning and practiced by all parties and Administrations, to raise the bulk of our revenue from taxes

威廉·麦金莱
William McKinley

心沮丧之际，尤其要强调这一原则。只要各种公共支出都遵守最严格的节约原则，浪费挥霍的情形必然会在各处销声匿迹，甚至会从此根绝。如果国家的岁入仍维持在现在的水平上，那么唯一的解救办法就是缩减支出。政府目前的这种入不敷出的状况不容再长久持续下去了。我们都有一个共同的经验，那就是应尽量减少而不是增加未偿清的债务，这一经验应再度受到重视并切实得到执行。国家的岁入不仅应该毫无困难地随时支付现时的花费、公债的本金和利息，还要为最需要帮助的公债债权人，为那些领取美国政府救济的军人和海员及其寡妇、孤儿等提供适当而慷慨的援助。

像目前这种非常时期，不能允许政府入不敷出或增加债务。对付负债的最好办法是要求纳税，这是解决我国财政困难简易而有效的对策。一旦政府的支出超出其收入，赤字就会不可避免，我们也就会面临或者借贷或者增加税收这两条道路。岁入过多，每年巨额的盈余只会造成无用的浪费；岁入不足，则会造成不信任，从而损害公家和私人的信誉。所以岁入过多或过少，均不足取。目前，我们只有在增加贷款和增加税收这两者之间做出选择。我们必须要有更多的岁入，这是不容耽搁或延迟的。但国库盈余赖于借贷，这不是稳妥、长久之计。因为这样一来，国家的开支只有靠不断的借贷才能维持，而值此入不敷出之时，举债之风，实不可长。过去的两年即是证明。人们不应忘记，尽管能用各种方法取得大量的借贷，以解救我们一时的困难，但政府却会因此而负债累累。欠债终必偿还，而国家持续不断的赤字，使得偿债能力非但不能增加，反而会更加减弱。在非常时期，为维持政府或维护国家的信誉，借贷尚情有可原。但在安定时期，却依然无法提供必要的岁入，这无论如何是说不过去的。

能够维持政府的信誉，为其开支提供补偿的最好方式，不是借助于借贷，而是不陷入债务中去。即通过对外或对内，或者两者兼而有之的税收体制，提供充足可靠的收入来源。征税是我国固有的政策，自建国以来，历届政府都向在我国销售和消费的外国产品课税，以筹集国家大部分的岁入。然而除战时以外，多半避免各种形式的直接税。我国向来明确反对增

upon foreign productions entering the United States for sale and consumption, and avoiding, for the most part, every form of direct taxation, except in time of war. The country is clearly opposed to any needless additions to the subject of internal taxation, and is committed by its latest popular utterance to the system of tariff taxation. There can be no misunderstanding, either, about the principle upon which this tariff taxation shall be levied. Nothing has ever been made plainer at a general election than that the controlling principle in the raising of revenue from duties on imports is zealous care for American interests and American labor. The people have declared that such legislation should be had as will give ample protection and encouragement to the industries and the development of our country. It is, therefore, earnestly hoped and expected that Congress will, at the earliest practicable moment, enact revenue legislation that shall be fair, reasonable, conservative, and just, and which, while supplying sufficient revenue for public purposes, will still be signally beneficial and helpful to every section and every enterprise of the people. To this policy we are all, of whatever party, firmly bound by the voice of the people — a power vastly more potent than the expression of any political platform. The paramount duty of Congress is to stop deficiencies by the restoration of that protective legislation which has always been the firmest prop of the Treasury. The passage of such a law or laws would strengthen the credit of the Government both at home and abroad, and go far toward stopping the drain upon the gold reserve held for the redemption of our currency, which has been heavy and well-nigh constant for several years.

In the revision of the tariff especial attention should be given to the re-enactment and extension of the reciprocity principle of the law of 1890, under which so great a stimulus was given to our foreign trade in new and advantageous markets for our surplus agricultural and manufactured products. The brief trial given this legislation amply justifies a further experiment and additional discretionary power in the making of commercial treaties, the end in view always to be the opening up of new markets for the products of our country, by granting concessions to the products of other lands that we need and cannot produce ourselves, and which do not involve any loss of labor to

威廉·麦金莱
William McKinley

加任何不必要的国内税收，最近人民又一致主张政府应全力实行关税制度，但是，对于这一关税制度的原则不应被曲解。在每次普选中，都会由于关心美国利益和美国劳工的热情，而提出明确的有关提高进口税以增加岁入的管理原则。人们主张这些关税法应能充分地保护国内工业，鼓励国家建设。因此，都寄希望于国会尽早采取行动，制定出公平合理、慎重妥切的国税法令，以便为公益事业提供充分的财源，并使各行各业的人们都能蒙利受惠。对这一政策，我们所有的人不分党派，莫不同声赞成。这是人民的声音。其力量远远胜于任何政治纲领。目前，国会最重要的任务，是通过恢复保护性的立法来结束这种入不敷出的状况，这种保护性的立法一直是国库坚实的支柱。这些法律的通过，必将提高政府在国内外的信誉，也将有助于避免耗尽用于货币回笼的黄金储备。在过去的几年里，这种消耗是大量的，几乎是持续不断的。

对于关税的修改，最受关注的应该是重新制定和推行1890年法案中的互惠原则，这一原则极大地促进了我国外贸的发展，使国内剩余的农产品和工业品，在海外获得了新的有利的市场。这一成功尝试，充分证实了互惠原则的正确性，在签订商约时应被更进一步地运用和加强这一原则，其目的一方面在于开辟新的市场，另一方面也允许国内需要但又不能生产的商品输入我国。这不但不会造成本国劳动力的任何损失，反而会增加他们的就业机会。

our own people, but tend to increase their employment.

The depression of the past four years has fallen with especial severity upon the great body of toilers of the country, and upon none more than the holders of small farms. Agriculture has languished and labor suffered. The revival of manufacturing will be a relief to both. No portion of our population is more devoted to the institution of free government nor more loyal in their support, while none bears more cheerfully or fully its proper share in the maintenance of the Government or is better entitled to its wise and liberal care and protection. Legislation helpful to producers is beneficial to all. The depressed condition of industry on the farm and in the mine and factory has lessened the ability of the people to meet the demands upon them, and they rightfully expect that not only a system of revenue shall be established that will secure the largest income with the least burden, but that every means will be taken to decrease, rather than increase, our public expenditures. Business conditions are not the most promising. It will take time to restore the prosperity of former years. If we cannot promptly attain it, we can resolutely turn our faces in that direction and aid its return by friendly legislation. However troublesome the situation may appear, Congress will not, I am sure, be found lacking in disposition or ability to relieve it as far as legislation can do so. The restoration of confidence and the revival of business, which men of all parties so much desire, depend more largely upon the prompt, energetic, and intelligent action of Congress than upon any other single agency affecting the situation.

It is inspiring, too, to remember that no great emergency in the one hundred and eight years of our eventful national life has ever arisen that has not been met with wisdom and courage by the American people, with fidelity to their best interests and highest destiny, and to the honor of the American name. These years of glorious history have exalted mankind and advanced the cause of freedom throughout the world, and immeasurably strengthened the precious free institutions which we enjoy. The people love and will sustain these institutions. The great essential to our happiness and prosperity is that we adhere to the principles upon which the Government was established and insist upon their faithful observance. Equality of rights must prevail, and our

威廉·麦金莱
William McKinley

　　四年来，经济不景气已严重影响了广大的劳动群众，特别是小农场经营者。农业衰萎，劳工饱受其苦，唯有复兴制造业才能解除这两方面的困境。没有哪个国家像我国人民这样热爱和支持自由政府的制度，他们无不全力拥护政府，并慷慨地贡献出自己对政府的关心和爱护。因此，有利于生产者的立法，便是对全国有利的立法。农业、矿业和工业的萧条景象已降低了人们的生产热情，他们有充分的权利要求政府制定负荷最轻、收入最高的税收制度，并且希望政府采取种种办法，以减少而不是增加公共开支。商业的形势也并不理想，恢复旧日繁荣是需要时间的。所以，如果我们不能很快地实现这些目标，至少应朝某个方向努力，借助于立法的帮助，尽早恢复繁荣。不论形势多么麻烦，我相信国会将会尽其全力以立法来解除这些困难。各党派所一致盼望的信心的恢复，商业的振兴，不是单靠个别的机构所能完成的，而更多的是有赖于国会采取迅速、明智而有魄力的行动，才能扭转局势。

　　回顾过去真是件令人鼓舞的事。在我国108年的丰富多彩的历史中，没有哪次危难不是由于人民的智慧和勇气而得到解决的。这是由于人民忠实于他们的最大利益和至高无上的命运以及国家的荣誉。这些辉煌的历史，提高了人类的地位，并促使了自由在世界各地的发展；同时，也更增加了我们宝贵的自由制度的意义，人民热爱并支持这些制度。我们的幸福和繁荣的根基在于我们是否能够坚决遵守政府得以建立的原则，提倡人人平等和普遍地、一贯地遵守法令。身为伟大共和国的公民，我们并没有完全地承担起我们的责任。但值得欣慰的是，今日的美国公民已较过去享有更多的自由，包括言论自由、出版自由、思想自由、教育自由、宗教自由，以及较过去更为普及的自由公正的选举。对这些自由的保障，应得到认真的

laws are always and everywhere respected and obeyed. We may have failed in the discharge of our full duty as citizens of the great Republic, but it is consoling and encouraging to realize that free speech, a free press, free thought, free schools, the free and unmolested right of religious liberty and worship, and free and fair elections are dearer and more universally enjoyed to-day than ever before. These guaranties must be sacredly preserved and wisely strengthened. The constituted authorities must be cheerfully and vigorously upheld. Lynching must not be tolerated in a great and civilized country like the United States; courts, not mobs, must execute the penalties of the law. The preservation of public order, the right of discussion, the integrity of courts, and the orderly administration of justice must continue forever the rock of safety upon which our Government securely rests.

One of the lessons taught by the late election, which all can rejoice in, is that the citizens of the United States are both law-respecting and law-abiding people, not easily swerved from the path of patriotism and honor. This is in entire accord with the genius of our institutions, and but emphasizes the advantages of inculcating even a greater love for law and order in the future. Immunity should be granted to none who violate the laws, whether individuals, corporations, or communities; and as the Constitution imposes upon the President the duty of both its own execution, and of the statutes enacted in pursuance of its provisions, I shall endeavor carefully to carry them into effect. The declaration of the party now restored to power has been in the past that of "opposition to all combinations of capital organized in trusts, or otherwise, to control arbitrarily the condition of trade among our citizens," and it has supported "such legislation as will prevent the execution of all schemes to oppress the people by undue charges on their supplies, or by unjust rates for the transportation of their products to the market." This purpose will be steadily pursued, both by the enforcement of the laws now in existence and the recommendation and support of such new statutes as may be necessary to carry it into effect.

Our naturalization and immigration laws should be further improved to the constant promotion of a safer, a better, and a higher citizenship. A grave peril to

威廉·麦金莱
William McKinley

维护和加强,由此而构成的各项权利,也应得到强有力的支持和赞同。在我们如此文明和伟大的国度里,私刑的存在是不能容许的[1],违法的处罚不应由暴民而应由法庭来执行。对于公共秩序、讨论权、法院的公正和正常的司法管理的维护,应该永远都是政府赖以存在的安全的基石。

从最近的选举中,可以得出一条令所有人都高兴的结论,那就是美国公民是最尊法、最守法的公民,都具有坚定的爱国心和荣誉感,这与美国精神是完全吻合的。这同时也说明了将来进一步加强热爱法律和秩序教育的重要性。无论是个人、公司还是团体,一旦犯法,都必须接受法律的制裁。宪法规定,总统必须执行宪法和成文法令,我会全力以赴完成使命。我党向来反对托拉斯式的资本集中,以及对民间交易的垄断,而非常支持所有杜绝那些通过向产品供应勒索高价和为运输他们的产品到市场制定不合理的价格来压榨人民的现象的法律。为了实现这些目标,不但要使现行法令尽力付诸实施,更要推荐和支持必要的新法规。

我国的国籍法和移民法应该加以改善,使其公民权更可靠、更完备、更

[1]南方的黑人经常被白人种族主义集团滥加杀害。

the Republic would be a citizenship too ignorant to understand or too vicious to appreciate the great value and beneficence of our institutions and laws, and against all who come here to make war upon them our gates must be promptly and tightly closed. Nor must we be unmindful of the need of improvement among our own citizens, but with the zeal of our forefathers encourage the spread of knowledge and free education. Illiteracy must be banished from the land if we shall attain that high destiny as the foremost of the enlightened nations of the world which, under Providence, we ought to achieve.

Reforms in the civil service must go on; but the changes should be real and genuine, not perfunctory, or prompted by zeal in behalf of any party simply because it happens to be in power. As a member of Congress I voted and spoke in favor of the present law, and I shall attempt its enforcement in the spirit in which it was enacted. The purpose in view was to secure the most efficient service of the best men who would accept appointment under the Government, retaining faithful and devoted public servants in office, but shielding none, under the authority of any rule or custom, who are inefficient, incompetent, or unworthy. The best interests of the country demand this, and the people heartily approve the law wherever and whenever it has been thus administered.

Congress should give prompt attention to the restoration of our American merchant marine, once the pride of the seas in all the great ocean highways of commerce. To my mind, few more important subjects so imperatively demand its intelligent consideration. The United States has progressed with marvelous rapidity in every field of enterprise and endeavor until we have become foremost in nearly all the great lines of inland trade, commerce, and industry. Yet, while this is true, our American merchant marine has been steadily declining until it is now lower, both in the percentage of tonnage and the number of vessels employed, than it was prior to the Civil War. Commendable progress has been made of late years in the upbuilding of the American Navy, but we must supplement these efforts by providing as a proper consort for it a merchant marine amply sufficient for our own carrying trade to foreign countries. The question is one that appeals both to our business necessities and the patriotic aspirations of a great people.

威廉·麦金莱
William McKinley

庄重。作为一个公民，如果由于太无知而不能懂得，或太恶劣而不能享用我国制度和法律的巨大价值和恩惠，这对我们的共和国来说是最危险的。对那些前来向我国的法律和制度挑衅的人，我们应该尽快关紧国门。我们也不能忽视那些提高国民素质的必要措施，而应继承先辈的热忱，大力推广科技知识和义务教育。我们若期望在上帝的保佑下，使我国成为世界上最文明的国家，就必须在我国消灭文盲。我们应该做到这一点。

文官制度的改革应继续进行，而且每一项改革都必须是确确实实的，不可敷衍了事或仅仅出于某个执政党的一时热情。身为议会的一员，我赞同现行的法律，我将本着当初制定这一法律时的精神，尽全力去执行。公务员法的目的，在于任命最优秀的人才为人民提供最好的服务。所以，政府应使热心职守的公职人员各得其所。然而，不论在任何规定或惯例之下，都不该偏袒失职无能之人，这是国家最高利益所要求的，人民也应随时随地支持这些法规的执行。

国会应尽快着手重建美国的商船队。过去，它航行在所有大洋的商业干线中，成为我们海上的骄傲。在我看来，目前再也没有比它更值得我们明智地考虑的了。近几年，国内各行各业进步神速，正努力使美国成为内陆贸易和工商业中的佼佼者。然而我国的商船队却逐渐退步衰落。现在的事实是，无论吨位还是征用的船只数量都少于内战前的时期。这些年来，我国在重建海军方面已有长足的进步，但这还不够，我们还应该努力提供一支能与我国海军相称的、足以承担对外贸易的商船队。这个问题相当重要，因为它既符合商业的需要，也符合一个伟大民族爱国抱负的要求。

It has been the policy of the United States since the foundation of the Government to cultivate relations of peace and amity with all the nations of the world, and these accords with my conception of our duty now. We have cherished the policy of non-interference with affairs of foreign governments wisely inaugurated by Washington, keeping ourselves free from entanglement, either as allies or foes, content to leave undisturbed with them the settlement of their own domestic concerns. It will be our aim to pursue a firm and dignified foreign policy, which shall be just, impartial, ever watchful of our national honor, and always insisting upon the enforcement of the lawful rights of American citizens everywhere. Our diplomacy should seek nothing more and accept nothing less than is due us. We want no wars of conquest; we must avoid the temptation of territorial aggression. War should never be entered upon until every agency of peace has failed; peace is preferable to war in almost every contingency. Arbitration is the true method of settlement of international as well as local or individual differences. It was recognized as the best means of adjustment of differences between employers and employees by the Forty-ninth Congress, in 1886, and its application was extended to our diplomatic relations by the unanimous concurrence of the Senate and House of the Fifty-first Congress in 1890. The latter resolution was accepted as the basis of negotiations with us by the British House of Commons in 1893, and upon our invitation a treaty of arbitration between the United States and Great Britain was signed at Washington and transmitted to the Senate for its ratification in January last. Since this treaty is clearly the result of our own initiative; since it has been recognized as the leading feature of our foreign policy throughout our entire national history — the adjustment of difficulties by judicial methods rather than force of arms — and since it presents to the world the glorious example of reason and peace, not passion and war, controlling the relations between two of the greatest nations in the world, an example certain to be followed by others, I respectfully urge the early action of the Senate thereon, not merely as a matter of policy, but as a duty to mankind. The importance and moral influence of the ratification of such a treaty can hardly be overestimated in the cause of advancing civilization. It may well engage the best thought of the

威廉·麦金莱
William McKinley

建国至今，我国政府一贯的外交政策乃是与世界各国维护和平友好的关系，这也是我目前的任务之所在。我们一向推崇华盛顿总统倡导的不干预政策，尽量置身于外国纠纷之外，不论是敌是友，让其自行解决内政问题。稳固而有威望的外交政策，是我们追寻的目标，这一外交政策应是：公正无私，珍视国家荣誉，并能顾及在世界各地的美国公民的合法权益。我国外交政策力求正当合理，既不贪图额外的，也不失去应得的，反对以战争征服他国，反对领土侵略，除非所有的和平手段都已无效，否则无论如何不应诉诸战争。和平在所有可能的情况下，都比战争更为可取。和平仲裁是解决国际间、地区间甚至个人纠纷的有效办法。1886年，第49届国会承认仲裁为调解劳资纠纷的最佳方法。1890年，第51届国会时，参众两院一致通过将和平仲裁扩大运用到外交政策上，这项决议，后来在1893年被英国下议院接受作为与我国谈判的基础。[1]应我国之请，英美仲裁条约在华盛顿签订，去年一月呈送参议院核准。由于这个条约是我国发起的，因此，仲裁被认为是我国开国以来外交政策的主要特征，即用司法而不是用武力来调解纠纷。这一条约也为全世界提供了理性与和平的光辉榜样。在不用意气、不动干戈的前提下，它维系了世界两大强国的关系，这的确值得其他国家仿效。因此，我诚恳地请求参议院尽早批准这个条约，因为这不仅是改变政策问题，而且也是对全人类应尽的责任。在增进人类文明的过程中，批准这类条约的重要性和道德影响是难以衡量的。推进人类文明当然需要各国的人民和政治家的集思广益；然而，我不能不庆幸，我国在这伟大的事业中，一直遥遥领先。

---

[1]1892年，英属加拿大与美国在狩捕海獭问题上发生争执。美国和英国同意将此事交付由法国、荷兰、意大利等国共同组成的仲裁法庭解决。判决结果是美国无权要求英属加拿大停止狩捕美国领海以外的海獭，并须赔偿加拿大被美国以入侵领海之名而扣押的捕猎船只的损失。

美国历届总统就职演说
THE INAUGURAL ADDRESSES OF THE U.S. PRESIDENTS

statesmen and people of every country, and I cannot but consider it fortunate that it was reserved to the United States to have the leadership in so grand a work.

It has been the uniform practice of each President to avoid, as far as possible, the convening of Congress in extraordinary session. It is an example which, under ordinary circumstances and in the absence of a public necessity, is to be commended. But a failure to convene the representatives of the people in Congress in extra session when it involves neglect of a public duty places the responsibility of such neglect upon the Executive himself. The condition of the public Treasury, as has been indicated, demands the immediate consideration of Congress. It alone has the power to provide revenues for the Government. Not to convene it under such circumstances I can view in no other sense than the neglect of a plain duty. I do not sympathize with the sentiment that Congress in session is dangerous to our general business interests. Its members are the agents of the people, and their presence at the seat of Government in the execution of the sovereign will should not operate as an injury, but a benefit. There could be no better time to put the Government upon a sound financial and economic basis than now. The people have only recently voted that this should be done, and nothing is more binding upon the agents of their will than the obligation of immediate action. It has always seemed to me that the postponement of the meeting of Congress until more than a year after it has been chosen deprived Congress too often of the inspiration of the popular will and the country of the corresponding benefits. It is evident, therefore, that to postpone action in the presence of so great a necessity would be unwise on the part of the Executive because unjust to the interests of the people. Our action now will be freer from mere partisan consideration than if the question of tariff revision was postponed until the regular session of Congress. We are nearly two years from a Congressional election, and politics cannot so greatly distract us as if such contest was immediately pending. We can approach the problem calmly and patriotically, without fearing its effect upon an early election.

Our fellow-citizens who may disagree with us upon the character of this legislation prefer to have the question settled now, even against their

威廉·麦金莱
William McKinley

开国至今,尽量避免召开国会特别会议是历任总统的共同经验。这只是在正常情况下,人民没有特殊的要求时才是可能的。但若涉及渎职问题而没能召开代表人民的国会特别会议,这个责任则完全是行政首长一人的过错。国库的情况前已述及,正等着国会立即予以关注,唯有国会才有权提供政府的岁入。如果在目前如此恶劣的情况下,仍不召开特别会议,我认为这实在是明确的失职。有人认为,国会特别会议的召开,将威胁我国一般的商业利益。我并不以为然。国会的成员是民意的代表,他们的责任在于履行至高无上的民意,他们不是伤害而是要保护人民的利益。目前是确立政府健全的财政和经济基础的最佳时机。最近全民投票的表决也证明,这些都是势在必行之事。所以民意代表目前最重要的任务就是立即采取行动。在我看来,国会被选出来一年多才召开会议,这似乎影响了民意的传达和国家相应的利益。面对这么多待办之事,却采取迟缓的行动,这实为不智之举,对人民的利益而言,这也是不妥当的行为。同把改革关税的议案拖延到国会召开定期会议的那个时候相比,我们目前的行动更少些党派顾虑。距下一次国会选举尚有近两年的时间,如果这种竞选活动立即迫近的话,我们就不能为这些问题而如此操心了,眼下我们可以本着爱国心冷静地面对问题的症结所在,而不必担心关税之事会对即将展开的竞选活动产生不良影响。

同胞中或许有人并不赞同关税立法,但为了改变经济不稳定的情况,永不再威胁美国各重大商业利益,即使这项立法违背他们原有的看法,他

preconceived views, and perhaps settled so reasonably, as I trust and believe it will be, as to insure great permanence, than to have further uncertainty menacing the vast and varied business interests of the United States. Again, whatever action Congress may take will be given a fair opportunity for trial before the people are called to pass judgment upon it, and this I consider a great essential to the rightful and lasting settlement of the question. In view of these considerations, I shall deem it my duty as President to convene Congress in extraordinary session on Monday, the 15th day of March, 1897.

In conclusion, I congratulate the country upon the fraternal spirit of the people and the manifestations of good will everywhere so apparent. The recent election not only most fortunately demonstrated the obliteration of sectional or geographical lines, but to some extent also the prejudices which for years have distracted our councils and marred our true greatness as a nation. The triumph of the people, whose verdict is carried into effect today, is not the triumph of one section, nor wholly of one party, but of all sections and all the people. The North and the South no longer divide on the old lines, but upon principles and policies; and in this fact surely every lover of the country can find cause for true felicitation. Let us rejoice in and cultivate this spirit; it is ennobling and will be both a gain and a blessing to our beloved country. It will be my constant aim to do nothing, and permit nothing to be done, that will arrest or disturb this growing sentiment of unity and cooperation, this revival of esteem and affiliation which now animates so many thousands in both the old antagonistic sections, but I shall cheerfully do everything possible to promote and increase it.

Let me again repeat the words of the oath administered by the Chief Justice which, in their respective spheres, so far as applicable, I would have all my countrymen observe: "I will faithfully execute the office of President of the United States, and will, to the best of my ability, preserve, protect, and defend the Constitution of the United States." This is the obligation I have reverently taken before the Lord Most High. To keep it will be my single purpose, my constant prayer; and I shall confidently rely upon the forbearance and assistance of all the people in the discharge of my solemn responsibilities.

们仍然宁可现在就解决这一问题。而且正如我所确信的那样，这一问题或许能够相当快地予以解决。再者，国会不论采取何种行动，都得经过人民的检验，这正是公正而持久地解决问题所不可缺少的。鉴于这些考虑，身为美国总统，我将在今年3月15日召开国会特别会议。

总之，我很高兴在国内到处可见人民的博爱精神和各种善意。在最近的选举中，不但再也见不到以往的地域界限，而且长久以来一直困扰议会，损害我大国风范的偏见也已消失了。这是人民的胜利，他们的裁决现在已经付诸实行。这一胜利既不属于某一地区，也不属于某一党，而要归功于全国所有地区和所有人民的努力。南北的分野不再是依据过去地理上的界线，而是出于政策和原则的不同。从这一事实中，每个爱国的人都不难发现值得庆贺的原因所在。让我们好好享有并精心培育这和谐的爱国精神，它是崇高的，而且对我们所热爱的国家而言，它既是收获，也是恩赐。所以，今后我所立下的持久的目标是：我不做，也不准别人做任何事情去妨碍或干扰这种逐渐扩大的统一与合作的气氛。这种相互尊重和相互交往，正在融解着许许多多旧日敌对的地区。我也将尽我所能去促进和增强这种气氛。

让我再次重述这一由大法官主持宣读的誓词中的几句话，使全国同胞在他们各自的领域中看到："我将忠实执行美国总统之职，并尽全力维护、捍卫和保卫美国宪法。"这是我在至高至尊的上帝面前，虔诚地承担下来的责任。我将一心一意地履行这一责任。凭借同胞们耐心的支持，我将满怀信心去执行我所肩负的庄严使命。

西奥多·罗斯福
Theodore Roosevelt

西奥多·罗斯福（Theodore Roosevelt）

生平简介 >>

西奥多·罗斯福是美国第二十六任总统。1858年10月27日他出生于纽约。他早年体弱多病，因此在家随私人教师学习，一直到18岁进哈佛大学。在大学四年级时，他开始写《一八一二年海战史》一书，这是他后来所写的大约40本书中的第一本。23岁时他被选进州议会，不久便以一个直言不讳的改革者的形象引起人们的关注。他相继担任过美国文官考试委员会委员、纽约市警察局长、海军部长助理和纽约州州长。

1900年，共和党赢得了选举，他成为副总统。一年后，麦金莱总统遇刺身亡，42岁的罗斯福继任总统。三年后，他再度连任总统。他的就职演说只有985个字，并一次也没有使用人称代词"我"。在两任总统期间，他共否决了82项法案，其中只有一项是国会未同意的。在外交方面，他采取以武力为后盾的"大棒政策"，建造了巴拿马运河，于1905年出面调停了日俄战争，从而获得了诺贝尔和平奖。

离开总统职位后，他于1912年成立了一个进步党并参加了竞选。在一次竞选演说中，遭到一名狂热分子的枪击，但他坚持讲完话才让人抬进医院。他最后恢复了健康，却在这次竞选中输给了威尔逊。

1919年1月6日，他死于自己的家中。

Theodore Roosevelt
Inaugural Address

March 4, 1905

My Fellow-Citizens:

No people on earth have more cause to be thankful than ours, and this is said reverently, in no spirit of boastfulness in our own strength, but with gratitude to the Giver of Good who has blessed us with the conditions which have enabled us to achieve so large a measure of well-being and of happiness. To us as a people it has been granted to lay the foundations of our national life in a new continent. We are the heirs of the ages, and yet we have had to pay few of the penalties which in old countries are exacted by the dead hand of a bygone civilization. We have not been obliged to fight for our existence against any alien race; and yet our life has called for the vigor and effort without which the manlier and hardier virtues wither away. Under such conditions it would be our own fault if we failed; and the success which we have had in the past, the success which we confidently believe the future will bring, should cause in us no feeling of vainglory, but rather a deep and abiding realization of all which life has offered us; a full acknowledgment of the responsibility which is ours; and a fixed determination to show that under a free government a mighty people can thrive best, alike as regards the things of the body and the things of the soul.

Much has been given us, and much will rightfully be expected from us. We have duties to others and duties to ourselves; and we can shirk neither. We have become a great nation, forced by the fact of its greatness into relations with the other nations of the earth, and we must behave as beseems a people with such responsibilities. Toward all other nations, large and small, our attitude must be one of cordial and sincere friendship. We must show not only in our words, but in our deeds, that we are earnestly desirous of securing their good will by acting toward them in a spirit of just and generous recognition of all

西奥多·罗斯福
Theodore Roosevelt

罗斯福总统就职演说

1905年3月4日

同胞们：

我们以一种虔诚的态度说，在这个世界上，没有其他民族比我们更有理由感恩。我们无意夸耀我们的强大，而应感谢上帝赐予我们的种种便利条件，使我们能够获得如此巨大的财富和幸福。对我们来说，作为一个民族，在这块新大陆上建立我们国家生活的基础，早已得到了承认。我们是时代的继承者，却不需付出其他古老国家因受到传统文化的牵制所必须花费的代价。我们也不必为了生存而与外邦对抗。在我们的生活中，充满了朝气和活力，使人们果断与勇敢的美德不致衰退。在这样的环境下如若失败，那便是我们自己的过错。过去的成功和对将来成功的自信，都不会引起我们的自傲。相反，这一切都是生活提供给我们的认识，以及对我们所负责任的充分了解，这一切也坚定了我们的决心。在自由政府的领导下，人民的力量无论在物质方面还是精神方面，都应最为壮大。

我们被给予了很多，因此也完全有理由被期望付出很多。无论对别人还是对自己，我们都负有不可逃避的责任。我们已经成为一个大国，由于这个事实，在同其他国家的关系中，我们的举止必须与我们的责任相符合。对于其他国家，不论大小，我们都应以诚相待。对此，我们不仅应表现在言辞上，而且也应表现在行动上。我们公正、宽宏地承认他们的一切权利，用这种精神对待他们，我们热切希望能获得他们的善意。不论是国家还是个人，公正和宽厚都是强者而不是弱者的表现。当我们小心避免伤害别人时，我们也需注意自己不受到伤害。我们希望和平，但这一和平必须是公

their rights. But justice and generosity in a nation, as in an individual, count most when shown not by the weak but by the strong. While ever careful to refrain from wrongdoing others, we must be no less insistent that we are not wronged ourselves. We wish peace, but we wish the peace of justice, the peace of righteousness. We wish it because we think it is right and not because we are afraid. No weak nation that acts manfully and justly should ever have cause to fear us, and no strong power should ever be able to single us out as a subject for insolent aggression.

Our relations with the other powers of the world are important; but still more important are our relations among ourselves. Such growth in wealth, in population, and in power as this nation has seen during the century and a quarter of its national life is inevitably accompanied by a like growth in the problems which are ever before every nation that rises to greatness. Power invariably means both responsibility and danger. Our forefathers faced certain perils which we have outgrown. We now face other perils, the very existence of which it was impossible that they should foresee. Modern life is both complex and intense, and the tremendous changes wrought by the extraordinary industrial development of the last half century are felt in every fiber of our social and political being. Never before have men tried so vast and formidable an experiment as that of administering the affairs of a continent under the forms of a Democratic republic. The conditions which have told for our marvelous material well-being, which have developed to a very high degree our energy, self-reliance, and individual initiative, have also brought the care and anxiety inseparable from the accumulation of great wealth in industrial centers. Upon the success of our experiment much depends, not only as regards our own welfare, but as regards the welfare of mankind. If we fail, the cause of free self-government throughout the world will rock to its foundations, and therefore our responsibility is heavy, to ourselves, to the world as it is to-day, and to the generations yet unborn. There is no good reason why we should fear the future, but there is every reason why we should face it seriously, neither hiding from ourselves the gravity of the problems before us nor fearing to approach these problems with the unbending, unflinching purpose to solve them aright.

西奥多·罗斯福
Theodore Roosevelt

正的和正义的。我们希望和平,是因为我们认为那是正当的,而不是因为我们胆怯。没有一个弱国,会因其富有正义的表现而害怕我们;也没有一个强国,可以把我们当成无理挑衅的目标。

　　我们与其他国家之间的关系是重要的,但我们内部之间的关系更重要。在过去的125年中,随着我国的财富、人口和国力的增强所发生的那些问题,如同每个国家迈向强大时都会发生的问题一样。力量也总是意味着责任和危险,随着我们的强大,我们不再遇到先辈们曾遭遇过的危险,但却正面临先辈们所未能预知的危险。现代生活是紧张而复杂的,过去的50年中,在我们的社会和政治生活中,已可以感觉出工业的惊人发展所引起的巨大变化。过去,人类从没有做过如此巨大而艰难的实验,将这块大陆上的事情,以一个民主共和国的形式来治理。这里拥有丰盛的资源,我们的活力、自信心和创造精神,在此得以充分发挥,但也带来了由于工业中心的巨大财富堆积所造成的焦虑和烦恼。我们实验的成功,不但关系着我们的幸福,也同时关系着全人类的幸福。如果我们失败,必将动摇全世界自由的自治政府的根基。因此,对于我们自己,对于今日的世界,以及对于未出生的一代,我们的责任是沉重的。我们没有理由惧怕未来,却有足够的理由严肃地面对未来。我们无须掩饰我们面前的问题的严重性,反而要以不屈服、不畏惧的决心,使这些问题得以正确地解决。

Yet, after all, though the problems are new, though the tasks set before us differ from the tasks set before our fathers who founded and preserved this Republic, the spirit in which these tasks must be undertaken and these problems faced, if our duty is to be well done, remains essentially unchanged. We know that self-government is difficult. We know that no people needs such high traits of character as that people which seeks to govern its affairs aright through the freely expressed will of the freemen who compose it. But we have faith that we shall not prove false to the memories of the men of the mighty past. They did their work; they left us the splendid heritage we now enjoy. We in our turn have an assured confidence that we shall be able to leave this heritage unwasted and enlarged to our children and our children's children. To do so we must show, not merely in great crises, but in the everyday affairs of life, the qualities of practical intelligence, of courage, of hardihood, and endurance, and above all the power of devotion to a lofty ideal, which made great the men who founded this Republic in the days of Washington, which made great the men who preserved this Republic in the days of Abraham Lincoln.

西奥多·罗斯福
Theodore Roosevelt

  虽然我们今天面对的是一些新的问题，虽然我们目前所肩负的任务，不同于先辈们为建立保卫共和国而承担的任务，但敢于承担重任的精神和解决问题的决心是一样的。我们深知自治是困难的，也知道那种自由的人们所组成的、通过自由表达意愿来正确处理各种事务的统治形式，需要人民具备高尚的情操。但我们有信心，不会错误地理解先辈们的启示，他们完成了他们的使命，使我们今日可以享受这些辉煌成就。今天轮到了我们，我们保证不但不会浪费，而且还将扩大这些遗产，以留给我们的子孙后代。为了实现这些目标，我们不但要在重大的危急时刻，同时也要在日常的生活中，表现出华盛顿总统时代为创建国家和林肯总统时代为保卫国家所拥有的智慧、勇气、刚毅、忍耐，以及为了崇高理想而奉献所有力量的情操。

伍德罗·威尔逊
Woodrow Wilson

伍德罗·威尔逊 （Woodrow Wilson）

生平简介 >>

伍德罗·威尔逊是美国第二十八任总统。1856年12月28日生于弗吉尼亚州，毕业于普林斯顿大学，并上过弗吉尼亚大学法学院。

1912年他被民主党提名为总统候选人，并以"新自由"的政纲展开竞选，由于共和党内部的分裂，他赢得了胜利。1916年他再次当选为总统。在任期间，他通过国会制定了三项重要法律，一项是调低税率的《安德伍德法》，一项是确保国家能更灵活地获得财源的《联邦储备银行法》，另一项是反托拉斯的立法。面对欧洲正在进行的战争，他不顾国会的反对，提出了战备计划，并扩大了陆军和海军。当德国公开对美国进行挑衅以后，他于1917年4月6日发布对德宣战的命令。1918年1月，他提出了以"十四点原则"而著称的和平计划，这是一份具有世界历史意义的文件，其中最重要的是提出了建立"国际联盟"的设想，即建立"一个普遍性的各国的联合组织……不分国家大小，互相保证政治独立和领土完整"。

1919年10月，他在各地巡回演说以寻求对国际联盟的支持时，突然中风。从这以后直到他第二任任期结束的17个月中，他的妻子实际上在代他行使职权，1920年参议院否决了国际联盟成立的条约。1924年2月2日，威尔逊在家中去世。

Woodrow Wilson
First Inaugural Address

March 4, 1913

There has been a change of government. It began two years ago, when the House of Representatives became Democratic by a decisive majority. It has now been completed. The Senate about to assemble will also be Democratic. The offices of President and Vice-President have been put into the hands of Democrats. What does the change mean? That is the question that is uppermost in our minds to-day. That is the question I am going to try to answer, in order, if I may, to interpret the occasion.

It means much more than the mere success of a party. The success of a party means little except when the Nation is using that party for a large and definite purpose. No one can mistake the purpose for which the Nation now seeks to use the Democratic Party. It seeks to use it to interpret a change in its own plans and point of view. Some old things with which we had grown familiar, and which had begun to creep into the very habit of our thought and of our lives, have altered their aspect as we have latterly looked critically upon them, with fresh, awakened eyes; have dropped their disguises and shown themselves alien and sinister. Some new things, as we look frankly upon them, willing to comprehend their real character, have come to assume the aspect of things long believed in and familiar, stuff of our own convictions. We have been refreshed by a new insight into our own life.

We see that in many things that life is very great. It is incomparably great in its material aspects, in its body of wealth, in the diversity and sweep of its energy, in the industries which have been conceived and built up by the genius of individual men and the limitless enterprise of groups of men. It is great, also, very great, in its moral force. Nowhere else in the world have noble men and women exhibited in more striking forms the beauty and the energy of sympathy and helpfulness and counsel in their efforts to rectify wrong, alleviate suffering,

伍德罗·威尔逊
Woodrow Wilson

威尔逊总统首次就职演说

1913年3月4日

我们的政府已经发生了变化，这一变化开始于两年前，当时民主党在众议院中取得了明显的多数支持，现在这一变化已经完成，民主党在参议院中也将占有多数。总统、副总统更为民主党所囊括。这个变化意味着什么？这是我们目前思考的最为重要的一个问题，也是我试图要找出答案的一个问题。如果我能够做到这一点，那么，今天就是回答这一问题的适当场合。

政府这种变化的意义绝不仅仅是政党胜利。除非国家要利用政党来完成更大、更明确的目标，否则这种政党胜利的意义是微不足道的。现在大家都明白，国家要利用民主党来解释其逐渐演变的计划和想法。某些旧的事物已为我们所熟知，并逐渐变成我们的思想和生活习惯，当我们用新的、觉醒的眼光从批判的角度来加以审视时，就会发现它们的样子已经改变；就会揭开它们的伪装，显示出它们自身的矛盾和邪恶。而对一些新的事物，如果我们坦诚地对待它们，愿意了解其真正的本质，它们就会呈现出我们久已熟知的事物的形态，那是我们自己所信奉的东西。我们的重新振作，来自对我们自身生活的新感受。

从许多方面来看，我们的生活都是很充实的。尤其在物质方面，其财力之雄厚、其各方面的能量之巨大，是无与伦比的。通过个人的才能和团体的无限进取精神的发挥，许多产业被孕育和建立起来。在其道德力量方面，也是崇高无比。在这个世界上，没有其他地方会像这里一样拥有如此高尚的男男女女，他们以非常引人注目的方式展示了自己美好而有力的同情心和乐于助人的精神；他们努力提出自己的忠告，以纠正错误，或减轻痛苦；并给弱者指出一条强大和希望之路。同时，我们还建立了一套完整

and set the weak in the way of strength and hope. We have built up, moreover, a great system of government, which has stood through a long age as in many respects a model for those who seek to set liberty upon foundations that will endure against fortuitous change, against storm and accident. Our life contains every great thing, and contains it in rich abundance.

But the evil has come with the good, and much fine gold has been corroded. With riches has come inexcusable waste. We have squandered a great part of what we might have used, and have not stopped to conserve the exceeding bounty of nature, without which our genius for enterprise would have been worthless and impotent, scorning to be careful, shamefully prodigal as well as admirably efficient. We have been proud of our industrial achievements, but we have not hitherto stopped thoughtfully enough to count the human cost, the cost of lives snuffed out, of energies overtaxed and broken, the fearful physical and spiritual cost to the men and women and children upon whom the dead weight and burden of it all has fallen pitilessly the years through. The groans and agony of it all had not yet reached our ears, the solemn, moving undertone of our life, coming up out of the mines and factories, and out of every home where the struggle had its intimate and familiar seat. With the great Government went many deep secret things which we too long delayed to look into and scrutinize with candid, fearless eyes. The great Government we loved has too often been made use of for private and selfish purposes, and those who used it had forgotten the people.

At last a vision has been vouchsafed us of our life as a whole. We see the bad with the good, the debased and decadent with the sound and vital. With this vision we approach new affairs. Our duty is to cleanse, to reconsider, to restore, to correct the evil without impairing the good, to purify and humanize every process of our common life without weakening or sentimentalizing it. There has been something crude and heartless and unfeeling in our haste to succeed and be great. Our thought has been "Let every man look out for himself, let every generation look out for itself," while we reared giant machinery which made it impossible that any but those who stood at the levers of control should have a chance to look out for themselves. We had not forgotten our morals.

伍德罗·威尔逊
Woodrow Wilson

的政府体制，长久以来，这一体制在各方面一直是现代人们所试图建立的自由制度的基础。这一体制能够应付偶然的变故、风暴和灾难。我们的生活包含了各种美好的事物因而是丰富多彩的。

但是，长处总是与短处相伴随的，闪光的金子也在被腐蚀，正如我们的财富正在被不可原谅地浪费一样，我们曾浪费了大部分本应加以利用的东西，我们也不曾认真考虑如何保存那些丰富的自然资源。没有这些资源，我们创业的活力会失去价值而一无所用。因此，浪费是可耻的，而高效率则是令人赞美的。我们一直对自己工业上的成就感到骄傲，但至今为止，却从未冷静地计算一下这一切所花费的社会代价，人的代价，生活被毁灭的代价，以及精力由于负担过重而崩溃的代价。多少年来，男女老少为了承受所有无情的加在其肩上的重负，在精神和肉体上都付出了骇人的代价，那些出自矿山、工厂和每个家庭的严峻而动人的生活低吟，在那些地方挣扎和痛苦常常出现在生活的每个角落。这些至今还没有传到我们的耳朵里。因为，对于我们这个政府发生的许多秘密事情，由于被耽搁得太久而无法去调查，并将它们直率而无畏地揭示出来。我们所爱戴的这个伟大的政府，竟也常常为私人所利用，以达到其谋取私利的目的，而那些利用政府的人早已把人民忘记了。

我们现在终于能够对我们的生活进行一番整体观察了，我们看到了好的与不好的，看到了堕落腐败的一面，也看到了健康蓬勃的一面。在这个观察之后，我们有了新的使命，就是要在不损害我们长处的同时，检讨、修正和改良我们的弊端，使我们日常生活的每一环节都能够纯净而富有人性，而不是令人感到虚弱和伤感。在我们急于追求成功和伟大的过程中，已经存在着某种程度的赤裸裸的冷酷和无情。我们一直主张，让每个人自己照料自己，让每一代人自己照料自己。可是，当我们建造了一部庞大的机器后，除控制它的人以外，不可能任何人都有机会自己照料自己。我们并没有忘记我们的那些道德，我们清楚地记得，我们的政策是对最卑微的人和最强有力的人一视同仁的，并一心一意维护这一正义而公道的标准，

We remembered well enough that we had set up a policy which was meant to serve the humblest as well as the most powerful, with an eye single to the standards of justice and fair play, and remembered it with pride. But we were very heedless and in a hurry to be great.

We have come now to the sober second thought. The scales of heedlessness have fallen from our eyes. We have made up our minds to square every process of our national life again with the standards we so proudly set up at the beginning and have always carried at our hearts. Our work is a work of restoration.

We have itemized with some degree of particularity the things that ought to be altered and here are some of the chief items: A tariff which cuts us off from our proper part in the commerce of the world, violates the just principles of taxation, and makes the Government a facile instrument in the hand of private interests; a banking and currency system based upon the necessity of the Government to sell its bonds fifty years ago and perfectly adapted to concentrating cash and restricting credits; an industrial system which, take it on all its sides, financial as well as administrative, holds capital in leading strings, restricts the liberties and limits the opportunities of labor, and exploits without renewing or conserving the natural resources of the country; a body of agricultural activities never yet given the efficiency of great business undertakings or served as it should be through the instrumentality of science taken directly to the farm, or afforded the facilities of credit best suited to its practical needs; watercourses undeveloped, waste places unreclaimed, forests untended, fast disappearing without plan or prospect of renewal, unregarded waste heaps at every mine. We have studied as perhaps no other nation has the most effective means of production, but we have not studied cost or economy as we should either as organizers of industry, as statesmen, or as individuals.

Nor have we studied and perfected the means by which government may be put at the service of humanity, in safeguarding the health of the Nation, the health of its men and its women and its children, as well as their rights in the struggle for existence. This is no sentimental duty. The firm basis of government is justice, not pity. These are matters of justice. There can be no equality or opportunity, the first essential of justice in the body politic, if

我们为此而感到自豪。但我们对这一政策在实行中的不足之处,却非常粗心大意,而想急于求成。

我们现在冷静下来再考虑一下,疏忽所产生的不良后果已从我们眼前消失。我们已下定决心使我们国家生活的每个环节,都重新符合建国以来所建立起的标准。我们对这些标准感到自豪,并总是由衷地贯彻。我们的任务就是这种恢复工作。

我们已详列了那些应该加以改革的事务,以下就是其中重要的几项:一为关税制度。现有的关税制度切断了我们与世界贸易的联系,违反了正确的赋税原则,并使联邦政府成为私人利益集团手中的便利工具。二为货币银行制度。现在的货币银行制度,是50年前政府为了出售公债而建立的,因而只适合于集中现金和限制信贷的要求。三为工业制度。现有的工业制度,控制着资本,限制着特许权和劳动机会,它只是开采却不能恢复和维护国家的自然资源。四为农业制度。现有的农业体制至今不能提高大规模经营的效率,不能直接把科学技术应用于农场的作业之上,也不能为了实际需要而提供更好的信贷服务。其他还有尚待疏通的水道,尚待开垦的废地,无人管理的森林,以及各矿区由于不能有计划地开采和整修,而正在很快报废等。别的国家也许没有像我们这样研究最有效的生产方式,但是,我们也从来没有钻研过成本与节约问题。这本应是企业家、政治家,甚至每个人都必须关心的问题。

我们也从未研究过如何使政府更好地为多数人服务,如何保障国家的兴旺,保障成年男女及其儿童的健康,以及他们争取生存的权利。这并不是在多愁善感,政府的坚定立场是公正而不是怜悯。而上述这些就是属于公正范畴的事情。在不可改变的、不能控制或独自应付的伟大的工业和社会进程中,如果成年男女和儿童生命与精力得不到保护,那么,作为政治机构中公正的第一要素,平等与机会就无法实现,社会必须注意不能自己

men and women and children be not shielded in their lives, their very vitality, from the consequences of great industrial and social processes which they can not alter, control, or singly cope with. Society must see to it that it does not itself crush or weaken or damage its own constituent parts. The first duty of law is to keep sound the society it serves. Sanitary laws, pure food laws, and laws determining conditions of labor which individuals are powerless to determine for themselves are intimate parts of the very business of justice and legal efficiency. These are some of the things we ought to do, and not leave the others undone, the old-fashioned, never-to-be-neglected, fundamental safeguarding of property and of individual right. This is the high enterprise of the new day: To lift everything that concerns our life as a Nation to the light that shines from the hearthfire of every man's conscience and vision of the right. It is inconceivable that we should do this as partisans; it is inconceivable we should do it in ignorance of the facts as they are or in blind haste. We shall restore, not destroy. We shall deal with our economic system as it is and as it may be modified, not as it might be if we had a clean sheet of paper to write upon; and step by step we shall make it what it should be, in the spirit of those who question their own wisdom and seek counsel and knowledge, not shallow self-satisfaction or the excitement of excursions whither they can not tell. Justice, and only justice, shall always be our motto.

And yet it will be no cool process of mere science. The Nation has been deeply stirred, stirred by a solemn passion, stirred by the knowledge of wrong, of ideals lost, of government too often debauched and made an instrument of evil. The feelings with which we face this new age of right and opportunity sweep across our heartstrings like some air out of God's own presence, where justice and mercy are reconciled and the judge and the brother are one. We know our task to be no mere task of politics but a task which shall search us through and through, whether we be able to understand our time and the need of our people, whether we be indeed their spokesmen and interpreters, whether we have the pure heart to comprehend and the rectified will to choose our high course of action.

This is not a day of triumph; it is a day of dedication. Here muster, not the

伍德罗·威尔逊
Woodrow Wilson

来破坏、削弱或损害其自身所赖以构成的各个部分，法律的首要责任是使其所服务的社会健全、合理。卫生法和食品卫生法，以及决定个人所无力决定的有关劳动环境的法律，都是公正和法律效能的最本质的组成部分。这些都是我们应做的事。但也不可将其他的事置之不理，例如，那些传统的、从不应被忽视的对财产和个人权利的基本保障问题。本着每个人的良知和正确的见识，来评判我们国家生活中的每一件事物，这是新时代高度的进取精神。要求我们从党派立场出发，是不可思议的；要求我们在对事实一无所知的情况下，盲目轻率地行事，这也是不可思议的。我们要复兴而不是破坏。我们所论及的经济体制，应该是现实的和可以被调整的，而不是我们似乎又有一张白纸去随意写画，并且应该以一种虚心求教的态度和不懈的求知欲，而不是浅薄的自满或半瓶醋知识的兴奋，将理想的经济体制一步步建立起来。公正，只有公正，才永远是我们的座右铭。

然而这一过程并不是纯粹科学的一板一眼的过程。全国人民都被激发起来，源自一种冷峻的激情，来自错误的认识和失落的理想，也来自政府由于太经常的腐败而成为邪恶的工具。面对这一权利与机会的新时代，我们心中有一种感觉，就好像上帝出现所带来的微风，吹过我们的心弦，在那里，公正与怜悯相互和谐，法官与兄弟同为一体。我们知道我们的工作不仅是政治活动，而且也是一次对我们的彻底检验。检验我们是否能了解我们的时代和人民的需求，检验我们是否真正是他们的代言人或解说者，检验我们是否具有纯洁的心灵去了解和调整我们将要选择的崇高的行动路线。

今天不是一个凯旋的日子，而是一个献身的日子；聚集在这里的不是

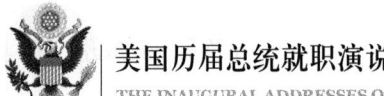

forces of party, but the forces of humanity. Men's hearts wait upon us; men's lives hang in the balance; men's hopes call upon us to say what we will do. Who shall live up to the great trust? Who dares fail to try? I summon all honest men, all patriotic, all forward-looking men, to my side. God helping me, I will not fail them, if they will but counsel and sustain me!

伍德罗·威尔逊
Woodrow Wilson

党派的力量，而是人民的力量。人民正企盼着我们，他们的命运悬而未决。人民希望我们说明我们将做些什么。谁能无愧于这一伟大的托付?谁敢不承受这一伟大的托付?我号召所有正直的人，所有爱国的人，所有有远见的人，站到我这一边来。上帝帮助我，我将不辜负他们，如果他们给予我忠告和支持!

赫伯特·胡佛
Herbert Hoover

赫伯特·胡佛（Herbert Hoover）

生平简介>>

赫伯特·胡佛是美国第三十一任总统。他于1874年8月10日出生在爱荷华州。他是斯坦福大学的首批毕业生，之后当了20年采矿工程师，建立起一个国际性的企业集团，并拥有400万美元的私人财产。第一次世界大战期间，威尔逊总统任命他为食品管理局局长，他也是哈丁和柯立芝政府中的商业部部长。

1928年他接受了共和党总统候选人的提名，并在选举中获胜。1929年美国进入大萧条时期，胡佛试图利用政府的领导，通过自愿的方法刺激经济的复苏，但收效甚微，因而在1932年同富兰克林·罗斯福的竞选中惨败。

他后来分别在杜鲁门和艾森豪威尔的政府中担任行政改革委员会主席的职务。

1964年10月20日，胡佛死于纽约，终年90岁。

Herbert Hoover
Inaugural Address

March 4, 1929

My Countrymen:

This occasion is not alone the administration of the most sacred oath which can be assumed by an American citizen. It is a dedication and consecration under God to the highest office in service of our people. I assume this trust in the humility of knowledge that only through the guidance of Almighty Providence can I hope to discharge its ever-increasing burdens.

It is in keeping with tradition throughout our history that I should express simply and directly the opinions which I hold concerning some of the matters of present importance.

Our Progress

If we survey the situation of our Nation both at home and abroad, we find many satisfactions; we find some causes for concern. We have emerged from the losses of the Great War and the reconstruction following it with increased virility and strength. From this strength we have contributed to the recovery and progress of the world. What America has done has given renewed hope and courage to all who have faith in government by the people. In the large view, we have reached a higher degree of comfort and security than ever existed before in the history of the world. Through liberation from widespread poverty we have reached a higher degree of individual freedom than ever before. The devotion to and concern for our institutions are deep and sincere. We are steadily building a new race—a new civilization great in its own attainments. The influence and high purposes of our Nation are respected among the peoples of the world. We aspire to distinction in the world, but to a distinction based

赫伯特·胡佛
Herbert Hoover

胡佛总统就职演说

1929年3月4日

同胞们：

　　此刻我所宣读的，不仅仅是作为一个美国公民承担行政重任的最神圣的誓言，它也是在上帝的旨意下，最高政府机构立志服务于民的一种表示。我以我有限的知识确信，唯有借助于上帝的指引，我才有可能去履行这一日益繁重的任务。

　　秉承历史传统，我必须就当前的一些重要问题，表达我简单、扼要的看法。

我们的进步

　　如果我们探讨国内外的局势，我们会发现有许多情况令人欣慰，也有许多情况令人关切。战后蓬勃有力的复兴，使得我们从第一次世界大战后的损失中摆脱出来。这种力量也使我们对整个世界的复兴和进步做出了贡献。美国的所作所为给予了其他国家和人民以希望和勇气。总的看来，我们现在生活的舒适度和安全度是世界史上前所未有的。从普遍的贫困中解脱出来后，我们得到了空前的个人自由。基于对我们的制度深切而真诚的关注，我们正在逐渐形成一个拥有伟大文化成就的新民族。我国的影响力和崇高的目标获得了全世界许多民族的敬佩。我们渴望获得荣誉，但这一荣誉必须建立在维护我们正义信念的基础之上。在国家复兴的伟大时期，国家深切感谢卡尔文·柯立芝总统的英明领导。

upon confidence in our sense of justice as well as our accomplishments within our own borders and in our own lives. For wise guidance in this great period of recovery the Nation is deeply indebted to Calvin Coolidge.

But all this majestic advance should not obscure the constant dangers from which self-government must be safeguarded. The strong man must at all times be alert to the attack of insidious disease.

The Failure of Our System of Criminal Justice

The most malign of all these dangers today is disregard and disobedience of law. Crime is increasing. Confidence in rigid and speedy justice is decreasing. I am not prepared to believe that this indicates any decay in the moral fiber of the American people. I am not prepared to believe that it indicates an impotence of the Federal Government to enforce its laws.

It is only in part due to the additional burdens imposed upon our judicial system by the eighteenth amendment. The problem is much wider than that. Many influences had increasingly complicated and weakened our law enforcement organization long before the adoption of the eighteenth amendment.

To reestablish the vigor and effectiveness of law enforcement we must critically consider the entire Federal machinery of justice, the redistribution of its functions, the simplification of its procedure, the provision of additional special tribunals, the better selection of juries, and the more effective organization of our agencies of investigation and prosecution that justice may be sure and that it may be swift. While the authority of the Federal Government extends to but part of our vast system of national, State, and local justice, yet the standards which the Federal Government establishes have the most profound influence upon the whole structure.

We are fortunate in the ability and integrity of our Federal judges and attorneys. But the system which these officers are called upon to administer is in many respects ill adapted to present-day conditions. Its intricate and involved rules of procedure have become the refuge of both big and little criminals. There is a belief abroad that by invoking technicalities, subterfuge,

赫伯特·胡佛
Herbert Hoover

然而，我们却不可忽视自治政府时时潜伏的危机。一个坚强的人必须对潜伏的疾病的攻击时时有所警惕。

刑法制度的失败

对法律的轻视和不服从，是当前所有危险中最有害的危险。犯罪的逐渐增加，人们对于严格和迅速的执法的信心正逐渐降低。我不认为这种现象显示了美国人民道德素质的衰退，我更不认为这种现象显示了联邦政府执法律的无能。

部分原因是第十八条宪法修正案增加了我们司法系统的负担。[1]问题还远不止于如此，早在采用第十八条宪法修正案以前，许多影响的存在已经使得执法机关的工作变得复杂而无力。

要重振执法的效力和影响力，我们必须批判地对联邦司法机构进行全面考虑，重新区分功能，简化工作程序，增加特别法庭的条款，严格选择陪审团，更有效地组织调查和执行机构，这样正义才可能有保障，并得到迅速的伸张。尽管联邦政府的权力，只是与州和地方司法系统一起构成我们这个庞大的国家体制的一部分，但是，它对整个结构却具有深远的影响。

幸运的是，我们的联邦法官和律师是有能力的，也是正直的。然而这种依赖于上述人员的制度，从多方面来看，都有不适应今天的条件的地方。它的错综复杂和对工作程序的纠缠，使其成为大大小小罪犯的避难所。国外有一种流行的看法是：那些有钱人通过技术细节的纠缠，巧立名目的延

[1]联邦宪法第十八条修正案禁止酒类的销售和出口。

and delay, the ends of justice may be thwarted by those who can pay the cost.

Reform, reorganization and strengthening of our whole judicial and enforcement system, both in civil and criminal sides, have been advocated for years by statesmen, judges, and bar associations. First steps toward that end should not longer be delayed. Rigid and expeditious justice is the first safeguard of freedom, the basis of all ordered liberty, the vital force of progress. It must not come to be in our Republic that it can be defeated by the indifference of the citizen, by exploitation of the delays and entanglements of the law, or by combinations of criminals. Justice must not fail because the agencies of enforcement are either delinquent or inefficiently organized. To consider these evils, to find their remedy, is the sorest necessity of our times.

Enforcement of the Eighteenth Amendment

Of the undoubted abuses which have grown up under the eighteenth amendment, part are due to the causes I have just mentioned; but part are due to the failure of some States to accept their share of responsibility for concurrent enforcement and to the failure of many State and local officials to accept the obligation under their oath of office zealously to enforce the laws. With the failures from these many causes has come a dangerous expansion in the criminal elements who have found enlarged opportunities in dealing in illegal liquor.

But a large responsibility rests directly upon our citizens. There would be little traffic in illegal liquor if only criminals patronized it. We must awake to the fact that this patronage from large numbers of law-abiding citizens is supplying the rewards and stimulating crime.

I have been selected by you to execute and enforce the laws of the country. I propose to do so to the extent of my own abilities, but the measure of success that the Government shall attain will depend upon the moral support which you, as citizens, extend. The duty of citizens to support the laws of the land is coequal with the duty of their Government to enforce the laws which exist. No greater national service can be given by men and women of good will—who, I know, are not unmindful of the responsibilities of citizenship—than that they

误推迟，最终使正义失败。

多年来，政治家、法官和律师公会曾竭力提倡改革，重组和加强民法及刑法的司法与执行系统。向那个目标跨出第一步，已不容置缓。严正而迅速地伸张正义，是对自由最重要的保护，也是民主制度的基础和人类进步的主要推动力。在我们的共和国中，决不容许因为公民身份的不同以延误和混淆法律或以共同犯罪使正义受到挫折；决不能由于执行机构的失职和组织的无效，而使司法制度遭受失败。思考这些弊端，找出纠正的办法，是我们这个时代最急迫的需要。

第十八条宪法修正案的执行

毫无疑问，由于上述原因，第十八条宪法修正案正在被滥用，这部分是由于有些州不能全力负起执行的责任，有些地方官员也不能尽职尽责地执行法律。所有这一些，都使得罪犯获得了更多的机会去从事不法贩酒勾当。

然而，大量的责任要直接由我们的公民来承担。如果仅仅是罪犯之间的庇护，酒类的非法交易将是微不足道的；相当多的守法公民为其提供的庇护，才鼓励和刺激了犯罪。

本人被你们推选出来执行和加强我们国家的法律，我将尽其所能来做到这一点。但是，政府的成功需依赖公民们道义上的支持。公民对法律的支持和政府对现存法律的执行同等重要。那些知晓公民责任的善良男女们应通过自己的表率帮助铲除犯罪，拒绝参与和谴责非法贩运酒类活动，这是对国家的最大报效。如果执法人员只是有选择性地执行法律，如果公民只是有选择性地支持法律，那么，我们自治政府的整个体制必将崩溃。对某些法律的忽视所造成的最大危害，就是破坏了对所有法律的尊重。如果

should, by their example, assist in stamping out crime and outlawry by refusing participation in and condemning all transactions with illegal liquor. Our whole system of self-government will crumble either if officials elect what laws they will enforce or citizens elect what laws they will support. The worst evil of disregard for some law is that it destroys respect for all law. For our citizens to patronize the violation of a particular law on the ground that they are opposed to it is destructive of the very basis of all that protection of life, of homes and property which they rightly claim under other laws. If citizens do not like a law, their duty as honest men and women is to discourage its violation; their right is openly to work for its repeal.

To those of criminal mind there can be no appeal but vigorous enforcement of the law. Fortunately they are but a small percentage of our people. Their activities must be stopped.

A National Investigation

I propose to appoint a national commission for a searching investigation of the whole structure of our Federal system of jurisprudence, to include the method of enforcement of the eighteenth amendment and the causes of abuse under it. Its purpose will be to make such recommendations for reorganization of the administration of Federal laws and court procedure as may be found desirable. In the meantime it is essential that a large part of the enforcement activities be transferred from the Treasury Department to the Department of Justice as a beginning of more effective organization.

The Relation of Government to Business

The election has again confirmed the determination of the American people that regulation of private enterprise and not Government ownership or operation is the course rightly to be pursued in our relation to business. In recent years we have established a differentiation in the whole method of business regulation between the industries which produce and distribute

公民基于他们的好恶而放纵违反某些法律的行为,那么,他们就破坏了对其生命保障的所有其他法律。公民们若不喜欢某一项法律,作为一个正直的人,也尽可能不要去违背它,但同时有权公正地努力去废止它。

对于那些有犯罪动机的人,应该不是求助于而是强有力地实施法律。幸好这种人为数不多,他们的行为必须受到制止。

全国性的调查

我建议国家委员会调查我们联邦法律体系的整个结构,包括第十八条宪法修正案的执行方法和滥用的原因。其目的在于重新组织对联邦法律和法庭程序的管理,使之更符合需要。同时,应将大部分执行活动从财政部转移到司法部,以作为有效组织的开端。

政府和商业界的关系

这次选举再次证明了美国人民的决心,即将私人企业正规化,但不是将私人企业国有化。这是在我们与商业界的关系中寻求的正确的方针。近年来,在整个商业管理方式中,我们已经在工业企业中确立了一种区别,生产和分配商品的产业为一类,公用事业为另一类。对前者,我们的法律要坚持有效的竞争;对后者,我们以限制竞争的方式充分地给予垄断权,所

commodities on the one hand and public utilities on the other. In the former, our laws insist upon effective competition; in the latter, because we substantially confer a monopoly by limiting competition, we must regulate their services and rates. The rigid enforcement of the laws applicable to both groups is the very base of equal opportunity and freedom from domination for all our people, and it is just as essential for the stability and prosperity of business itself as for the protection of the public at large. Such regulation should be extended by the Federal Government within the limitations of the Constitution and only when the individual States are without power to protect their citizens through their own authority. On the other hand, we should be fearless when the authority rests only in the Federal Government.

Cooperation by the Government

The larger purpose of our economic thought should be to establish more firmly stability and security of business and employment and thereby remove poverty still further from our borders. Our people have in recent years developed a new-found capacity for cooperation among themselves to effect high purposes in public welfare. It is an advance toward the highest conception of self-government. Self-government does not and should not imply the use of political agencies alone. Progress is born of cooperation in the community—not from governmental restraints. The Government should assist and encourage these movements of collective self-help by itself cooperating with them. Business has by cooperation made great progress in the advancement of service, in stability, in regularity of employment and in the correction of its own abuses. Such progress, however, can continue only so long as business manifests its respect for law.

There is an equally important field of cooperation by the Federal Government with the multitude of agencies, State, municipal and private, in the systematic development of those processes which directly affect public health, recreation, education, and the home. We have need further to perfect the means by which Government can be adapted to human service.

以必须管理其服务和收费。唯有严格地执行适用于两种不同企业的法律,才能使全体人民有同等的机会和支配的自由。这将使一般大众受到保护,也使商业界本身能够稳定而繁荣。这些规则必须在不超出宪法的范围内,由联邦政府加以扩展,而这种扩展,只有在各州没有保护其公民的权力后才能得以实现。从另一方面说,只要权威在联邦政府手里,我们就不要害怕。

政府方面的合作

我们经济思想的一个大目标,是使劳资关系更牢固地建立在稳定性和安全性的基础上,使贫困在我们的国土上彻底消失。近年来,我们的人民发现,彼此的协助有助于提高公共福利,这正是迈向自治政府这个最高远设想的一大步。自治政府不是也不应该只是政治机构而已。进步来自社会的合作,而不是来自政府的限制。政府应该合作和鼓励这种集团与集团之间的互助。商业界的合作在提高服务、稳定市场、就业正常化和纠正自身弊病方面取得了巨大的进展。然而,这种进展只有和法律结合起来才可能持续下去。

联邦政府与众多的机构之间,与州政府、市政府和私人之间,也存在着这种重要的合作关系,这些合作关系的系统发展,对于公共健康、娱乐、教育和家庭,都有直接的影响。我们必须进一步使政府的作为与人类的需求相互配合。

Education

Although education is primarily a responsibility of the States and local communities, and rightly so, yet the Nation as a whole is vitally concerned in its development everywhere to the highest standards and to complete universality. Self-government can succeed only through an instructed electorate. Our objective is not simply to overcome illiteracy. The Nation has marched far beyond that. The more complex the problems of the Nation become, the greater is the need for more and more advanced instruction. Moreover, as our numbers increase and as our life expands with science and invention, we must discover more and more leaders for every walk of life. We can not hope to succeed in directing this increasingly complex civilization unless we can draw all the talent of leadership from the whole people. One civilization after another has been wrecked upon the attempt to secure sufficient leadership from a single group or class. If we would prevent the growth of class distinctions and would constantly refresh our leadership with the ideals of our people, we must draw constantly from the general mass. The full opportunity for every boy and girl to rise through the selective processes of education can alone secure to us this leadership.

Public Health

In public health the discoveries of science have opened a new era. Many sections of our country and many groups of our citizens suffer from diseases the eradication of which is mere matters of administration and moderate expenditure. Public health service should be as fully organized and as universally incorporated into our governmental system as is public education. The returns are a thousand fold in economic benefits, and infinitely more in reduction of suffering and promotion of human happiness.

赫伯特·胡佛
Herbert Hoover

教育

　　教育基本上是州政府和当地社会的责任，这当然是正确的，然而，国家作为一个整体，应更多关注教育在各地的发展，以最终实现完全普及并达到高的标准。自治政府之所以能成功，全赖于有教养的选民。我们的目标并不仅仅是消灭文盲，我们的国家早已达到了这一目标。在国家发展中的各种问题愈是复杂，我们所需的教育就愈多。更重要的是，我们的人口和生活水平随着科技发明在增加和发展，我们必须发掘出愈来愈多的不同行业的精英人物。除非我们能从全体人民中吸收所有的精英人物，否则我们没有希望指引这日渐复杂的文明走向光明。正是因为企图从某单一的群体或阶层中获得足够的领导精英，一个又一个文明社会受到破坏。如果我们要阻止阶级差别的扩大，并不断用优秀民众更新领导阶层，我们必须不断地从普通群众中吸收优秀分子。让每个男女都有通过教育的各种选择过程而得到提升的充分机会，这是我们获得领导人才的唯一保证。

公共卫生

　　科学的发展，使得公共卫生进入了一个新的时代。国内有许多地区和人民团体备受病痛的折磨，而疾病知识的教育，仅仅通过行政管理和不大的开支就可做到。公共卫生服务应该充分地组织起来，并像公共教育那样，与政府体制广泛地结合起来。就经济效益来说，我们所得到的回报是上千倍的，无数苦难的消减和人类幸福的增进更不可计数。

World Peace

The United States fully accepts the profound truth that our own progress, prosperity, and peace are interlocked with the progress, prosperity, and peace of all humanity. The whole world is at peace. The dangers to a continuation of this peace to-day are largely the fear and suspicion which still haunt the world. No suspicion or fear can be rightly directed toward our country.

Those who have a true understanding of America know that we have no desire for territorial expansion, for economic or other domination of other peoples. Such purposes are repugnant to our ideals of human freedom. Our form of government is ill adapted to the responsibilities which inevitably follow permanent limitation of the independence of other peoples. Superficial observers seem to find no destiny for our abounding increase in population, in wealth and power except that of imperialism. They fail to see that the American people are engrossed in the building for themselves of a new economic system, a new social system, a new political system all of which are characterized by aspirations of freedom of opportunity and thereby are the negation of imperialism. They fail to realize that because of our abounding prosperity our youth are pressing more and more into our institutions of learning; that our people are seeking a larger vision through art, literature, science, and travel; that they are moving toward stronger moral and spiritual life—that from these things our sympathies are broadening beyond the bounds of our Nation and race toward their true expression in a real brotherhood of man. They fail to see that the idealism of America will lead it to no narrow or selfish channel, but inspire it to do its full share as a nation toward the advancement of civilization. It will do that not by mere declaration but by taking a practical part in supporting all useful international undertakings. We not only desire peace with the world, but to see peace maintained throughout the world. We wish to advance the reign of justice and reason toward the extinction of force.

The recent treaty for the renunciation of war as an instrument of national policy sets an advanced standard in our conception of the relations of nations. Its acceptance should pave the way to greater limitation of armament, the

赫伯特·胡佛
Herbert Hoover

世界和平

美国完全接受这一深刻的真理：我们的进步、繁荣与和平，同全人类的进步、繁荣与和平是不可分割的。整个世界目前是和平的。今天，对于这持续的和平构成威胁的，是仍然不断出现的巨大恐惧和猜疑。当然，没有什么恐惧和猜疑能直接地影响到我国。

对美国有真正了解的人会知道，我们并不希望扩大版图，在经济及其他方面奴役别国人民。那种做法与我们追求人类自由的精神相矛盾。我们的政府形式不适合一直承担限制其他国家民族独立的责任。浅薄的观察家认为，对于我们不断增长的人口、财富和力量来说，除了走帝国主义之路，别无选择。他们忽视了美国人民热衷于自己建立一个新的经济制度、一个新的社会制度、一个新的政治制度这一事实。而这些都是向往自由的理想，与帝国主义是背道而驰的。他们不了解，我们的富足使得我们的年轻人更专注于在我们各学校中的学习；我们的人民正通过艺术、文学、科技和旅行，寻找更宽阔的视野，从而享有更好的精神生活。这种富足，也使我们的同情心远远超出了国家和民族的界限而扩大到全人类。他们看不到美国的理想主义不会引导这一国家走上狭隘、自私的道路，反而会激励她完全投入到文明的进步之中。我们不仅仅是喊口号而已，而是实际地参与、支持所有有益的国际事业。我们不但企求世界和平，更希望这持续的和平能遍及全世界。我们盼望正义和理性的统治，进而消灭武力。

最近一项反对战争的条约[1]，在国与国之间关系方面建立了一种更高

[1]指1928年8月15日由多国共同签订的《凯洛格—布赖恩公约》。该公约明确宣布战争属非法行为，一切国际纠纷必须付诸仲裁。

offer of which we sincerely extend to the world. But its full realization also implies a greater and greater perfection in the instrumentalities for pacific settlement of controversies between nations. In the creation and use of these instrumentalities we should support every sound method of conciliation, arbitration, and judicial settlement. American statesmen were among the first to propose and they have constantly urged upon the world, the establishment of a tribunal for the settlement of controversies of a justifiable character. The Permanent Court of International Justice in its major purpose is thus peculiarly identified with American ideals and with American statesmanship. No more potent instrumentality for this purpose has ever been conceived and no other is practicable of establishment. The reservations placed upon our adherence should not be misinterpreted. The United States seeks by these reservations no special privilege or advantage but only to clarify our relation to advisory opinions and other matters which are subsidiary to the major purpose of the court. The way should, and I believe will, be found by which we may take our proper place in a movement so fundamental to the progress of peace.

Our people have determined that we should make no political engagements such as membership in the League of Nations, which may commit us in advance as a nation to become involved in the settlements of controversies between other countries. They adhere to the belief that the independence of America from such obligations increases its ability and availability for service in all fields of human progress.

I have lately returned from a journey among our sister Republics of the Western Hemisphere. I have received unbounded hospitality and courtesy as their expression of friendliness to our country. We are held by particular bonds of sympathy and common interest with them. They are each of them building a racial character and a culture which is an impressive contribution to human progress. We wish only for the maintenance of their independence, the growth of their stability, and their prosperity. While we have had wars in the Western Hemisphere, yet on the whole the record is in encouraging contrast with that of other parts of the world. Fortunately the New World is largely free from the inheritances of fear and distrust which have so troubled the Old

赫伯特·胡佛
Herbert Hoover

的准则。这项准则的建立，使得更进一步限制军备成为可能。对于这项成就，我们将真诚地扩展至全世界。然而，要充分实现这一点，也意味着应具有越来越完善的和平解决国与国之间争端的手段。为了创造和使用这些手段，我们应当支持每一项合理的方式，包括调停、仲裁和司法解决。美国的政治家率先提出并一直倡导建立具有司法特征的解决争端的法庭。因此，国际司法常设法庭的主要目标，与美国的理想和美国的政治家的风格是特别一致的。为了实现这些目标，再也想不出比这更有效的手段以及更可行的组织机构了。我们关于保留权的信念也不应被曲解，美国寻求这些保留权，不是为了特别的优惠和利益，而仅仅是要阐明我们与那些建设性意见和那些次要事务的关系。我相信，对促进和平有重要意义的方式一定能找到，而我国将在这一运动中起到自己应有的作用。

我们的人民已决定，我国不再像作为国际联盟成员那样，参与政治联盟，那样会使我们作为一个国家卷入到其他国家的争端中去。他们深信，美国从这些义务中解脱出来，能增强其本身参与人类各方面进步的能力。

最近，我刚从西半球各兄弟共和国访问回国。在那里，我受到了热情的招待和礼遇，这是它们对我国友善的表示。对它们的同情和与它们有共同的兴趣，成为约束我们的特殊契约。它们中的每个国家，都正在建立一种对人类进步有显著贡献的种族特征和文化。我们期望它们能继续独立，发展它们的稳定和繁荣。那时我们西半球的作战记录，与世界其他地区相比，大体上说来是令人振奋的。幸而，新世界的大部分已从如此动乱的旧世界所遗留下的恐惧和猜疑中解脱出来了。我们应当保持这种状况。

World. We should keep it so.

It is impossible, my countrymen, to speak of peace without profound emotion. In thousands of homes in America, in millions of homes around the world, there are vacant chairs. It would be a shameful confession of our unworthiness if it should develop that we have abandoned the hope for which all these men died. Surely civilization is old enough; surely mankind is mature enough so that we ought in our own lifetime to find a way to permanent peace. Abroad, to west and east, are nations whose sons mingled their blood with the blood of our sons on the battlefields. Most of these nations have contributed to our race, to our culture, our knowledge, and our progress. From one of them we derive our very language and from many of them much of the genius of our institutions. Their desire for peace is as deep and sincere as our own.

Peace can be contributed to by respect for our ability in defense. Peace can be promoted by the limitation of arms and by the creation of the instrumentalities for peaceful settlement of controversies. But it will become a reality only through self-restraint and active effort in friendliness and helpfulness. I covet for this administration a record of having further contributed to advance the cause of peace.

Party Responsibilities

In our form of democracy the expression of the popular will can be effected only through the instrumentality of political parties. We maintain party government not to promote intolerant partisanship but because opportunity must be given for expression of the popular will, and organization provided for the execution of its mandates and for accountability of government to the people. It follows that the government both in the executive and the legislative branches must carry out in good faith the platforms upon which the party was entrusted with power. But the government is that of the whole people; the party is the instrument through which policies are determined and men chosen to bring them into being. The animosities of elections should have no place in our Government, for government must concern itself alone with the common weal.

赫伯特·胡佛
Herbert Hoover

同胞们，在没有深厚的感情基础上谈论和平是不现实的。在美国成千上万个家庭当中，在世界百万个家庭当中，都有战争牺牲者。假如我们放弃那些很多人为之献身的希望，我们将耻辱地承认我们一钱不值。当然，文明的确是够古老的，人类也的确是够成熟的，正因为如此，我们应在我们的一生中，找到永葆和平的道路。不论东方还是西方，它们的儿子的鲜血在战场上都混合在一起，大部分国家对我们的种族、我们的文化、我们的知识和我们的进步都有所贡献。我们从它们之中形成了完整的语言，而我们制度的精神也取自于它们中的许多国家。它们对和平的期望和我们一样深切、真诚。

唯有重视自己的防御能力才可能对和平做出贡献，限制军备和创造和平解决争端的各种途径，也能促进和平。但是，只有经过自我的约束和积极促进友好与互助，才能使这一切成为现实。我盼望这一届政府能留下进一步对和平事业有所贡献的记录。

政党的职责

我们表达民意的民主形式，只有经过各政党这一媒介才能实现。我国政府维护政党政治并不是提倡狭隘的党派性，而是使得大众的意愿有机会表达。政治组织提供了民意委托的方式和对人民负责的管理机构。接下来，政府的行政与立法部门必须忠实地贯彻政党依此而被委以权力的施政纲领。政府代表人民，政党则是政策决定和选择官员以实施那些政策的工具。各种对选举的敌意在我们的政府中是没有立足之地的，因为政府必须与公共的幸福相一致。

Special Session of the Congress

Action upon some of the proposals upon which the Republican Party was returned to power, particularly further agricultural relief and limited changes in the tariff, cannot in justice to our farmers, our labor, and our manufacturers be postponed. I shall therefore request a special session of Congress for the consideration of these two questions. I shall deal with each of them upon the assembly of the Congress.

Other Mandates from the Election

It appears to me that the more important further mandates from the recent election were the maintenance of the integrity of the Constitution; the vigorous enforcement of the laws; the continuance of economy in public expenditure; the continued regulation of business to prevent domination in the community; the denial of ownership or operation of business by the Government in competition with its citizens; the avoidance of policies which would involve us in the controversies of foreign nations; the more effective reorganization of the departments of the Federal Government; the expansion of public works; and the promotion of welfare activities affecting education and the home.

These were the more tangible determinations of the election, but beyond them was the confidence and belief of the people that we would not neglect the support of the embedded ideals and aspirations of America. These ideals and aspirations are the touchstones upon which the day-to-day administration and legislative acts of government must be tested. More than this, the Government must, so far as lies within its proper powers, give leadership to the realization of these ideals and to the fruition of these aspirations. No one can adequately reduce these things of the spirit to phrases or to a catalogue of definitions. We do know what the attainments of these ideals should be: The preservation of self-government and its full foundations in local government; the perfection of justice whether in economic or in social fields; the maintenance of ordered liberty; the denial of domination by any group or class; the building up and preservation of

赫伯特·胡佛
Herbert Hoover

国会的特别会议

有关共和党取得权力后所应采取行动的建议，特别是进一步的农业救济和有限的关税变动问题，为了对我们的农民、工人和制造商们公正起见，不能再拖延了。因此，我将要求召开一次国会的特别会议来考虑这两个问题。我个人将在国会会议上分别阐述这些问题。

其他的选举委托

在我看来，来自最近选举的最重要的委托是：维护宪法的完整；强有力地执行法律；在公共支出方面继续节俭；否定政府在商业的所有权和经营权，从而与公民竞争；避免那些将使我们陷入外国争议中的各项政策；更有效地重新组织联邦政府的各部门；扩大公共工程；促进影响教育和家庭的福利活动。

以上所述是选举中较明确的决定。然而，更重要的是人民对我们的信任。相信我们不会忽视对深埋心中的美国的理想和抱负的支持，这些理想和抱负是检验政府日常行政和立法活动的试金石。更重要的是，政府在其适当的权限范围内，也必须对这些理想和抱负的实现给予领导。没有人能够将这些事物的精神实质，加以简短的归纳和明确的分类。但我们的确知道如何将这些理想实现：维持自治政府和它在地方政府中完备的基础；完善在经济和社会各方面的正义；保持有秩序的自由；否认任何团体或阶级的支配地位；机会均等的建立和维护；鼓励创造与个性；公共事务中的绝对公正；按适合程度选择官员担任公职；引导经济走向繁荣，进一步减少贫困；舆论的自由；对教育及知识进步的支持；培育宗教精神并容忍所有的信仰；巩固家庭；促进和平。这些抱负的实现是没有捷径的。我们的人民是进取的，然而这种进取的决心必须建立在经验的基础之上，纠正错误

equality of opportunity; the stimulation of initiative and individuality; absolute integrity in public affairs; the choice of officials for fitness to office; the direction of economic progress toward prosperity for the further lessening of poverty; the freedom of public opinion; the sustaining of education and of the advancement of knowledge; the growth of religious spirit and the tolerance of all faiths; the strengthening of the home; the advancement of peace. There is no short road to the realization of these aspirations. Ours is a progressive people, but with a determination that progress must be based upon the foundation of experience. Ill-considered remedies for our faults bring only penalties after them. But if we hold the faith of the men in our mighty past that created these ideals, we shall leave them heightened and strengthened for our children.

Conclusion

This is not the time and place for extended discussion. The questions before our country are problems of progress to higher standards; they are not the problems of degeneration. They demand thought and they serve to quicken the conscience and enlist our sense of responsibility for their settlement. And that responsibility rests upon you, my countrymen, as much as upon those of us who have been selected for office.

Ours is a land rich in resources; stimulating in its glorious beauty; filled with millions of happy homes; blessed with comfort and opportunity. In no nation are the institutions of progress more advanced. In no nation are the fruits of accomplishment more secure. In no nation is the government more worthy of respect. No country is more loved by its people. I have an abiding faith in their capacity, integrity and high purpose. I have no fears for the future of our country. It is bright with hope.

In the presence of my countrymen, mindful of the solemnity of this occasion, knowing what the task means and the responsibility which it involves, I beg your tolerance, your aid, and your cooperation. I ask the help of Almighty God in this service to my country to which you have called me.

的那些考虑不周的方案,只会后患无穷。如果我们忠实于伟大的先辈们所创立的那些理想,那么,当我们再将其传给子孙时,这些理想应该已经得到了提高和巩固。

结论

此时此地不是进一步讨论的时候和场合。我们国家所面临的问题是向更高水平迈进的问题,而不是衰退的问题。这些问题的解决,需要思考也需要我们良心和责任感的支持。同胞们,这就是你们的责任,同样这也是我们这些被选出来担当公职人员的责任。

我们的国家有丰富的资源,有令人振奋的光荣传统,有数以万计的快乐的家庭,也具有舒适的环境和竞争的机会。没有哪个国家的体制比我们的更进步,没有哪个国家取得的成果比我们的更可靠,没有哪个国家的政府比我们的更值得尊重,也没有哪个国家比我们的国家更受人民的爱戴。我坚信我国人民的能力、正直和高尚,我对我们国家的未来没有任何担忧,它充满着希望和光明。

在我的同胞面前,在这种庄严的时刻,我意识到这项任务的意义和责任,我恳求各位的容忍、帮助与合作。我祈求上帝的恩赐,使我能完成你们托付于我的这一任务。

富兰克林·罗斯福
Franklin Roosevelt

富兰克林·罗斯福（Franklin Roosevelt）

生平简介>>

富兰克林·罗斯福是美国第三十二任总统。他于1882年1月30日出生在纽约，哈佛大学毕业，并获得律师资格。1921年8月，他在一次游泳后，患了小儿麻痹症，从此双腿永远残废。1928年，他当选为纽约州州长。

1932年11月，他作为民主党的总统候选人，以"给美国人民带来新政"的许诺，击败了胡佛当选为总统。1936年11月他再次当选。1940年11月，他打破传统第三次当选。1944年11月，他又赢得了第四次大选。

罗斯福是在美国民族丧失信心的时刻，在经济大萧条时期担任总统的，他首先致力于恢复美国人民的自信心，他在第一次当选后的就职演说中最著名的一句话是："我们唯一所恐惧的就是恐惧本身。"在他的领导下，美国度过了历史上最严重的国内危机，并重新获得了自信和力量。

罗斯福于1945年4月12日死于脑出血。按照宪法第二十条修正案规定的总统宣誓就职的新日期，他是最后一个于3月4日和第一个于1月20日宣誓就职的美国总统。他是唯一一位连任四届的总统，也是唯一的残疾人总统。

Franklin Roosevelt
First Inaugural Address

March 4, 1933

I am certain that my fellow Americans expect that on my induction into the Presidency I will address them with a candor and a decision which the present situation of our Nation impels. This is preeminently the time to speak the truth, the whole truth, frankly and boldly. Nor need we shrink from honestly facing conditions in our country today. This great Nation will endure as it has endured, will revive and will prosper. So, first of all, let me assert my firm belief that the only thing we have to fear is fear itself—nameless, unreasoning, unjustified terror which paralyzes needed efforts to convert retreat into advance. In every dark hour of our national life a leadership of frankness and vigor has met with that understanding and support of the people themselves which is essential to victory. I am convinced that you will again give that support to leadership in these critical days.

In such a spirit on my part and on yours we face our common difficulties. They concern, thank God, only material things. Values have shrunken to fantastic levels; taxes have risen; our ability to pay has fallen; government of all kinds is faced by serious curtailment of income; the means of exchange are frozen in the currents of trade; the withered leaves of industrial enterprise lie on every side; farmers find no markets for their produce; the savings of many years in thousands of families are gone.

More important, a host of unemployed citizens face the grim problem of existence and an equally great number toil with little return. Only a foolish optimist can deny the dark realities of the moment.

Yet our distress comes from no failure of substance. We are stricken by no plague of locusts. Compared with the perils which our forefathers conquered because they believed and were not afraid, we have still much to be thankful

富兰克林·罗斯福
Franklin Roosevelt

罗斯福总统首次就职演说

1933年3月4日

我确信,全国同胞们正期待着我在就任总统之时,能坦诚而果断地向他们说明我们民族在目前处境下的前进方向。此刻最宜说的是真话,完全坦白而大胆的真话。我们无须退却,而要诚实地面对我们国家今天所遇到的形势。这个伟大的国家将坚持下去,并将获得新生和繁荣。因此,首先请允许我表明自己坚定的信念,即我们唯一所恐惧的就是恐惧本身——一种无名的、缺乏理性的、没有根据的恐惧,它会把由退却转变为前进所需要的种种努力毁掉。在我们民族生命的每一黑暗的时刻,每个坦诚而富有活力的领导人都得到人民的理解和支持,这是胜利的必要条件。我相信,在这危急的日子里,你们将再次给予领导者以这样的支持。

我和你们都以这样的一种精神,来面对我们共同的困难。感谢上帝,这些困难只涉及物质层面。价值已跌落到难以想象的程度;税收提高了;我们的支付能力降低了;各级政府面临着严重的收入削减;在贸易交往中,交换的手段也被冻结了;工业企业枯萎的落叶随处可见;农民找不到他们的产品市场,成千上万的家庭多年的积蓄用光了。

更为严重的是,一大批失业的人们正面临着严酷的生存问题,同样多的人们则以艰辛的劳动换来少得可怜的报酬。只有愚蠢的乐观主义者才会否认当前这些黑暗的事实。

然而,我们的痛苦不是来自物资的匮乏。我们所遭受的也不是蝗虫的灾害。同我们祖先曾以信念和大无畏精神所克服的各种灾祸相比,我们仍有许多值得庆幸之处。大自然仍在施与它的恩赐,而且人们的努力已使之倍增。

for. Nature still offers her bounty and human efforts have multiplied it. Plenty is at our doorstep, but a generous use of it languishes in the very sight of the supply. Primarily this is because the rulers of the exchange of mankind's goods have failed, through their own stubbornness and their own incompetence, have admitted their failure, and abdicated. Practices of the unscrupulous money changers stand indicted in the court of public opinion, rejected by the hearts and minds of men.

True they have tried, but their efforts have been cast in the pattern of an outworn tradition. Faced by failure of credit they have proposed only the lending of more money. Stripped of the lure of profit by which to induce our people to follow their false leadership, they have resorted to exhortations, pleading tearfully for restored confidence. They know only the rules of a generation of self-seekers. They have no vision, and when there is no vision the people perish.

The money changers have fled from their high seats in the temple of our civilization. We may now restore that temple to the ancient truths. The measure of the restoration lies in the extent to which we apply social values more noble than mere monetary profit.

Happiness lies not in the mere possession of money; it lies in the joy of achievement, in the thrill of creative effort. The joy and moral stimulation of work no longer must be forgotten in the mad chase of evanescent profits. These dark days will be worth all they cost us if they teach us that our true destiny is not to be ministered unto but to minister to ourselves and to our fellow men.

Recognition of the falsity of material wealth as the standard of success goes hand in hand with the abandonment of the false belief that public office and high political position are to be valued only by the standards of pride of place and personal profit; and there must be an end to a conduct in banking and in business which too often has given to a sacred trust the likeness of callous and selfish wrongdoing. Small wonder that confidence languishes, for it thrives only on honesty, on honor, on the sacredness of obligations, on faithful protection, on unselfish performance; without them it cannot live.

Restoration calls, however, not for changes in ethics alone. This Nation

富兰克林·罗斯福
Franklin Roosevelt

丰富的物质财富就在我们门前,只是由于对它的大量耗用而使其供给不足了。这主要是由于人类货物交换的支配者因其顽固和无能所造成的失败,他们已承认了自己的失败,并且退了下来。无耻的金钱交易者的行径在公众舆论的法庭上受到了指控,并将受到人们心灵和理智的唾弃。

的确,他们已经尝试过,但他们的各种努力总是囿于一种陈腐的传统模式中。面对着信贷破产,他们只是一味地借贷更多的金钱。一旦用来诱使人们追逐私利的诱惑失效后,他们又来求助于劝导,含泪求大家恢复信心。他们只懂得利己主义的那一代人的准则,他们缺乏洞察力,而在没有这种洞察力之时,这个民族也就被毁掉了。

金钱的交易者们已从我们文明殿堂的宝座上逃之夭夭了。我们现在可以恢复这一殿堂以古时的原貌,至于恢复的程度要取决于我们使用比纯粹金钱利润更昂贵得多的社会价值的程度。

幸福并不在于只拥有金钱,而在于取得成就的快乐,在于创造性努力的激动之中。工作的快乐和道德感并不一定就会淹没于对过眼云烟的利润的疯狂追逐中。如果这种黑暗的岁月让我们了解到,我们真正的命运不是要别人来侍奉,而是为自己和同胞们服务,那么黑暗让我们付出的所有代价都是值得的。

我们认识到了物质财富不是成功的标准,与之相适应,也必须放弃这样的信念——仅以地位的荣耀以及个人获利的标准来评价公职和政治地位的价值;在银行和企业中也必然会制止一种行为,即过于经常地把神圣的信任混同于冷漠而又自私的不道德行为。少数一些人奇怪,信心为何失落了?因为它只有靠诚实、荣誉、神圣的责任和忠诚的守护以及无私的行为才能得以存在,没有了它,信心就不能产生。

然而,重建所需要的不仅仅是道德上的变革,这个民族需要的是行动,

asks for action, and action now.

Our greatest primary task is to put people to work. This is no unsolvable problem if we face it wisely and courageously. It can be accomplished in part by direct recruiting by the Government itself, treating the task as we would treat the emergency of a war, but at the same time, through this employment, accomplishing greatly needed projects to stimulate and reorganize the use of our natural resources.

Hand in hand with this we must frankly recognize the overbalance of population in our industrial centers and, by engaging on a national scale in redistribution, endeavor to provide a better use of the land for those best fitted for the land. The task can be helped by definite efforts to raise the values of agricultural products and with this the power to purchase the output of our cities. It can be helped by preventing realistically the tragedy of the growing loss through foreclosure of our small homes and our farms. It can be helped by insistence that the Federal, State, and local governments act forthwith on the demand that their cost be drastically reduced. It can be helped by the unifying of relief activities which today are often scattered, uneconomical, and unequal. It can be helped by national planning for and supervision of all forms of transportation and of communications and other utilities which have a definitely public character. There are many ways in which it can be helped, but it can never be helped merely by talking about it. We must act and act quickly.

Finally, in our progress toward a resumption of work we require two safeguards against a return of the evils of the old order; there must be a strict supervision of all banking and credits and investments; there must be an end to speculation with other people's money, and there must be provision for an adequate but sound currency.

There are the lines of attack. I shall presently urge upon a new Congress in special session detailed measures for their fulfillment, and I shall seek the immediate assistance of the several States.

Through this program of action we address ourselves to putting our own national house in order and making income balance outgo. Our international trade relations, though vastly important, are in point of time and necessity

富兰克林·罗斯福
Franklin Roosevelt

而且是即刻的行动。

我们最重要的任务是让人们去工作。如果我们明智而勇敢地面对它的话,这并不是一个无法解决的问题。通过政府直接雇工可部分地做到,对待这项工作就像对待战争的紧急状态一样来处理,同时通过这种就业,圆满地完成一些必需的工程项目,它们将刺激和重组我们对自然资源的使用。

在着手进行这项工作的同时,我们必须坦率地承认,我们工业中心的人口是不平衡的,要在全国范围内重新分配劳力,力图使那些最能善用土地的人们更好地利用土地。这个任务能够借助努力提高各种农产品的价格,并且用这种力量来购买我们城市的产品来完成。它也可以通过避免小家庭和农场无法偿还贷款的悲剧所造成的进一步的损失来完成。它也能借助于联邦、州和各地政府立即行动起来,大幅度地削减费用来完成。它也能借助于把今天经常是分散的、不经济的和不平等的救济活动结合起来来完成。它也能借助于全国性的规划和监督各种形式的交通运输,以及其他具有明确公共性质的事业来完成。完成这一任务,有许多可以借助的方法,但它绝不能借助空话。我们必须行动,必须迅速地行动。

最后,在我们恢复工作的过程中,我们需要有两种保证,以免旧秩序的邪恶卷土重来;必须对所有的银行、信用和投资进行严格的监督;必须禁止用他人的金钱从事投机行为,以及必须提供充足而健全的货币。

着手行动有各条路线。我将在不久召开的特别会议上向新国会力陈实现它们的各种具体措施,而且我要寻求有关各州的立即支援。

通过这个行动纲领,我们要把国家内部治理得井然有序,使收支达到平衡。我们的国际贸易关系,尽管非常重要,但就时间和需要而言,要服从于建立健全的国民经济。作为一个实践方针,我喜欢把最应当先做的事

secondary to the establishment of a sound national economy. I favor as a practical policy the putting of first things first. I shall spare no effort to restore world trade by international economic readjustment, but the emergency at home cannot wait on that accomplishment.

The basic thought that guides these specific means of national recovery is not narrowly nationalistic. It is the insistence, as a first consideration, upon the interdependence of the various elements in all parts of the United States—a recognition of the old and permanently important manifestation of the American spirit of the pioneer. It is the way to recovery. It is the immediate way. It is the strongest assurance that the recovery will endure.

In the field of world policy I would dedicate this Nation to the policy of the good neighbor—the neighbor who resolutely respects himself and, because he does so, respects the rights of others—the neighbor who respects his obligations and respects the sanctity of his agreements in and with a world of neighbors.

If I read the temper of our people correctly, we now realize as we have never realized before our interdependence on each other; that we can not merely take but we must give as well; that if we are to go forward, we must move as a trained and loyal army willing to sacrifice for the good of a common discipline, because without such discipline no progress is made, no leadership becomes effective. We are, I know, ready and willing to submit our lives and property to such discipline, because it makes possible a leadership which aims at a larger good. This I propose to offer, pledging that the larger purposes will bind upon us all as a sacred obligation with a unity of duty hitherto evoked only in time of armed strife.

With this pledge taken, I assume unhesitatingly the leadership of this great army of our people dedicated to a disciplined attack upon our common problems.

Action in this image and to this end is feasible under the form of government which we have inherited from our ancestors. Our Constitution is so simple and practical that it is possible always to meet extraordinary needs by changes in emphasis and arrangement without loss of essential form. That is why our constitutional system has proved itself the most superbly enduring political

富兰克林·罗斯福
Franklin Roosevelt

情最先做。我将不遗余力地调整国际经济来恢复世界贸易，但是国内的紧急状况不能一直等着这项行动纲领的完成。

指导国内复兴的这些特别手段的基本思想并不是狭隘的民族主义。因为它首先要考虑的是坚持美国各地的每个人之间的相互依赖——这是对于先驱者们古老又重要的美国精神的一种认可。它是通向复兴的道路。它是直接的道路，也是这一复兴继续下去的最有力的保证。

在外交政策领域里，我将致力于这个国家的睦邻政策——做一个坚决自尊的邻国，正由于它的自尊，也会尊重其他国家的权利——一个尊重自己所承担义务的邻国，也会维护它与邻国所签订的条约的尊严。

如果我对自己人民的品性认识正确的话，那么我们现在就认识了我们彼此间的相互依赖，这是我们从前从未认识到的；我们不能只是索取，我们必须也要付出；如果我们要前进的话，我们必须像一支训练有素和忠心耿耿的军队那样愿为共同纪律而牺牲，因为没有这种纪律，我们就不能取得进步，领导也无法有效发挥作用。我知道，我们准备好并且愿意使自己的生命和财产顺从这样的纪律，因为它使得一个以更远大利益为目标的领导方针成为可能。这就是我要提供的领导。我发誓，作为一种神圣的职责，这将把我们大家团结在一起，像迄今为止只有在战争时代才唤起的那种共同职责那样。

在做出了这个保证之后，我会毫不犹豫地担负起领导我们这支伟大的人民之军的责任，致力于向我们的共同问题发动一次有序的进攻。

在我们祖先遗留下来的政体下，以这种观念采取行动和达到这一目的是完全可行的。我们的宪法是如此简单而实用，以至于通过调整政策重点和安排计划，而不损害宪法的基本形式就能满足各种特殊需要。这就是为什么我们的宪政制度已被证明是近代世界产生的最经得起考验的政治机制的原因。它已历经了各种紧急状态，如大面积地扩张领土、各地对外战争、

mechanism the modern world has produced. It has met every stress of vast expansion of territory, of foreign wars, of bitter internal strife, of world relations.

It is to be hoped that the normal balance of executive and legislative authority may be wholly adequate to meet the unprecedented task before us. But it may be that an unprecedented demand and need for undelayed action may call for temporary departure from that normal balance of public procedure.

I am prepared under my constitutional duty to recommend the measures that a stricken nation in the midst of a stricken world may require. These measures, or such other measures as the Congress may build out of its experience and wisdom, I shall seek, within my constitutional authority, to bring to speedy adoption.

But in the event that the Congress shall fail to take one of these two courses, and in the event that the national emergency is still critical, I shall not evade the clear course of duty that will then confront me. I shall ask the Congress for the one remaining instrument to meet the crisis—broad Executive power to wage a war against the emergency, as great as the power that would be given to me if we were in fact invaded by a foreign foe.

For the trust reposed in me I will return the courage and the devotion that befit the time. I can do no less.

We face the arduous days that lie before us in the warm courage of the national unity; with the clear consciousness of seeking old and precious moral values; with the clean satisfaction that comes from the stern performance of duty by old and young alike. We aim at the assurance of a rounded and permanent national life.

We do not distrust the future of essential democracy. The people of the United States have not failed. In their need they have registered a mandate that they want direct, vigorous action. They have asked for discipline and direction under leadership. They have made me the present instrument of their wishes. In the spirit of the gift I take it.

In this dedication of a Nation we humbly ask the blessing of God. May He protect each and every one of us. May He guide me in the days to come.

富兰克林·罗斯福
Franklin Roosevelt

剧烈的内乱以及各种世界关系的紧急状态。

人们希望行政权与立法权的平衡能足以完成我们所面临的史无前例的任务。但是一种史无前例和刻不容缓的行动可能会要求暂时背离那种公共程序的正常平衡。

我准备在宪法所赋予我的职责范围内，提出在一个危难的世界中，一个危难的民族所需要采取的各种措施。这些措施，或者像国会出于它的经验和智慧可能制定的其他措施一样，是我在宪法权限之内力求迅速实施的。

但是，在国会不采取这两条路线中的任何一条的情况下，我将不逃避届时摆在我面前的明确的责任。我将向国会要求应付紧急状况的最后一种措施——与这种紧急状况作战的广泛的行政权力，就像如果我们真正遭到一个外敌的侵略时，所赋予我的权力一样大。

对于大家寄予我的厚望，我将以时代所需的勇气和忠诚予以回报。我是这样说的，我也会这样做。
在举国团结的热烈气氛之下，我们面对着眼前的艰难岁月，本着纯真的良心去寻找悠久而珍贵的道德价值，从全体人民坚决履行职责中获得一种完全的满足。我们的目标是保证一种圆满而永久的国民生活。

我们对于真正民主的未来并未失去信心。美国人民并未失败。在他们需要之时，他们已经表达出自己的委托，他们要立即有力地行动起来。他们要求有明确的纪律和方向。他们正在把我当作实现自己各种愿望的现实工具。在这种精神的感召下，我愿做这种工具。

在为这个国家献身之时，我们谦恭地祈求上帝的祝福。希望他保佑我们当中的每一个人，希望他在未来的岁月里指引我。

Franklin Roosevelt
Second Inaugural Address

January 20, 1937

When four years ago we met to inaugurate a President, the Republic, single-minded in anxiety, stood in spirit here. We dedicated ourselves to the fulfillment of a vision—to speed the time when there would be for all the people that security and peace essential to the pursuit of happiness. We of the Republic pledged ourselves to drive from the temple of our ancient faith those who had profaned it; to end by action, tireless and unafraid, the stagnation and despair of that day. We did those first things first.

Our covenant with ourselves did not stop there. Instinctively we recognized a deeper needs—the need to find through government the instrument of our united purpose to solve for the individual the ever-rising problems of a complex civilization. Repeated attempts at their solution without the aid of government had left us baffled and bewildered. For, without that aid, we had been unable to create those moral controls over the services of science which are necessary to make science a useful servant instead of a ruthless master of mankind. To do this we knew that we must find practical controls over blind economic forces and blindly selfish men.

We of the Republic sensed the truth that democratic government has innate capacity to protect its people against disasters once considered inevitable, to solve problems once considered unsolvable. We would not admit that we could not find a way to master economic epidemics just as, after centuries of fatalistic suffering, we had found a way to master epidemics of disease. We refused to leave the problems of our common welfare to be solved by the winds of chance and the hurricanes of disaster.

In this we Americans were discovering no wholly new truth; we were writing

富兰克林·罗斯福

Franklin Roosevelt

罗斯福总统第二次就职演说

1937年1月20日

四年前,当我们举行总统就职典礼时,共和国正以满心的焦虑在等待着。我们致力于一个梦想的实现——让全体人民为追求幸福所必不可少的安全与和平环境早日到来。我们共和国的人民发誓,要从我们古老信念的殿堂中驱赶出那些已亵渎了它的人们;要以坚忍和无畏的行动来结束那个时代的停滞和绝望。我们首先做了这些最先要做的事情。

我们与自己所订的契约并未终止于此。我们本能地认识到一种更深切的需要——通过政府找到实现共同目标的手段,为每个人去解决复杂文明社会所日益产生的各种问题。在没有政府帮助的情况下,努力试图解决这些问题给我们带来了挫折和困惑。因为没有政府的帮助,我们就无法从道德上控制科学,这对使科学成为一个有益的仆人而不是统治人类的残酷主宰是必需的。我们知道,要做到这一点,就要有各种现实的约束,以其约束各种盲目的经济力量以及利令智昏的人。

身在共和国中的我们意识到了一个真理:民主政府生来便具有能力去保护它的人民免遭一度被认为是不可避免的各种灾难,并能够解决曾被认为是无法解决的各种问题。我们不承认自己找不到一条应付经济恐慌的对策,正像经过了几个世纪所谓命中注定的苦难之后,我们已经找到了一条控制流行病的对策一样。我们拒绝把关系到自己共同福祉的问题留给机遇或灾难的狂飙来解决。

在这方面,我们美国人一直没有找到一个全新的真理,我们正在书写

a new chapter in our book of self-government.

This year marks the one hundred and fiftieth anniversary of the Constitutional Convention which made us a nation. At that Convention our forefathers found the way out of the chaos which followed the Revolutionary War; they created a strong government with powers of united action sufficient then and now to solve problems utterly beyond individual or local solution. A century and a half ago they established the Federal Government in order to promote the general welfare and secure the blessings of liberty to the American people.

Today we invoke those same powers of government to achieve the same objectives.

Four years of new experience have not belied our historic instinct. They hold out the clear hope that government within communities, government within the separate States, and government of the United States can do the things the times require, without yielding its democracy. Our tasks in the last four years did not force democracy to take a holiday.

Nearly all of us recognize that as intricacies of human relationships increase, so power to govern them also must increase—power to stop evil; power to do well. The essential democracy of our Nation and the safety of our people depend not upon the absence of power, but upon lodging it with those whom the people can change or continue at stated intervals through an honest and free system of elections. The Constitution of 1787 did not make our democracy impotent.

In fact, in these last four years, we have made the exercise of all power more democratic; for we have begun to bring private autocratic powers into their proper subordination to the public's government. The legend that they were invincible—above and beyond the processes of a democracy—has been shattered. They have been challenged and beaten.

Our progress out of the depression is obvious. But that is not all that you and I mean by the new order of things. Our pledge was not merely to do a patchwork job with secondhand materials. By using the new materials of social justice we have undertaken to erect on the old foundations a more enduring structure for the better use of future generations.

富兰克林·罗斯福
Franklin Roosevelt

自治政府历史的新篇章。

今年，是使我们成为一个独立国家的宪法会议[1]召开150周年。在那个会议上，我们的前人找到了一条摆脱由革命战争所带来的混乱的途径；他们建立了一个强有力的政府，拥有各种团结一致的力量，无论在当时还是现在，都足以解决个人和地方所完全不能解决的问题。一个半世纪以前，他们建立了联邦政府，以此来增进美国人民的普遍福利并确保人民自由幸福。

今天，我们要同样运用政府的力量来达到同样的目的。

四年的新经验符合我们的历史本性。它们表达了一个明确的希望，即各市政府、各州的政府以及联邦政府能够各尽其职地完成历史的使命，而不会放弃民主。在过去的四年里，我们的任务就是极力使民主发扬光大。

几乎我们中的所有人都知道，随着人际关系的日趋复杂，管理它们的力量也必须增强——这也是扬善抑恶的力量。我们国家的真正民主和我们人民的安全并不取决于权力的削减，而取决于它落在哪些人手里——通过诚实而自由的选举制度，每隔一定的时间人们就能够更换或者继续支持他们的代表，1787年的宪法并未使我们的民主软弱无力。

事实上，在过去的四年里，我们使权力的运用更加民主。因为我们已经开始把个人专制的权力恰当地服从于公共的政府。它们是不可战胜的，凌驾和超出各种民主程序的那种神话已经被粉碎了。它们已经遭受到挑战并被击败。

显然，我们的进步已摆脱了萧条。但这完全不是你们和我所指的事物的新秩序。我们的誓言不只是用二等的材料去做修补工作，而是使用社会公正的新材料，从原有的基础上建立一个更持久的结构，让后代们能更好地利用它。

[1]指1787年召开的费城制宪会议。

In that purpose we have been helped by achievements of mind and spirit. Old truths have been relearned; untruths have been unlearned. We have always known that heedless self-interest was bad morals; we know now that it is bad economics. Out of the collapse of a prosperity whose builders boasted their practicality has come the conviction that in the long run economic morality pays. We are beginning to wipe out the line that divides the practical from the ideal; and in so doing we are fashioning an instrument of unimagined power for the establishment of a morally better world.

This new understanding undermines the old admiration of worldly success as such. We are beginning to abandon our tolerance of the abuse of power by those who betray for profit the elementary decencies of life.

In this process evil things formerly accepted will not be so easily condoned. Hard-headedness will not so easily excuse hardheartedness. We are moving toward an era of good feeling. But we realize that there can be no era of good feeling save among men of good will.

For these reasons I am justified in believing that the greatest change we have witnessed has been the change in the moral climate of America.

Among men of good will, science and democracy together offer an ever-richer life and ever-larger satisfaction to the individual. With this change in our moral climate and our rediscovered ability to improve our economic order, we have set our feet upon the road of enduring progress.

Shall we pause now and turn our back upon the road that lies ahead? Shall we call this the promised land? Or, shall we continue on our way? For "each age is a dream that is dying, or one that is coming to birth."

Many voices are heard as we face a great decision. Comfort says, "Tarry a while." Opportunism says, "This is a good spot." Timidity asks, "How difficult is the road ahead?"

True, we have come far from the days of stagnation and despair. Vitality has been preserved. Courage and confidence have been restored. Mental and moral horizons have been extended.

But our present gains were won under the pressure of more than ordinary circumstances. Advance became imperative under the goad of fear and suffering.

富兰克林·罗斯福
Franklin Roosevelt

对于这个目的,我们得益于思想和精神的各种成就的帮助。古老的真理被重温,谬误已被抛弃。我们一直懂得无动于衷的自私是不道德的。我们现在也知道,它是糟糕的经济学。由于繁荣的崩溃,那些自称为切合实际的建设者们已经有了一个信念,即长远看来,坚持经济道德并不吃亏。我们正在开始消除划分现实与理想的界限,并在这个过程中,为建立一个道德更高尚的世界,制作一件力大无比的工具。

这种新的认识摧毁了以追名逐利的成功为荣耀的传统观念。我们开始不再容忍权力被那些为了利益而不顾基本生活礼仪的人所滥用的现象。

在这个过程中,从前认为是邪恶的事情将不会如此轻易地被宽恕。冷静的人们将不会轻易饶恕无情的人。我们正朝着具有美好情感的时代迈进。但是,我们也认识到,如果人们不怀有善良的意愿的话,这一美好情感的时代就不能如愿以偿。

由于这些理由,我相信,我们目睹的最大变化就是美国道德风尚的变化。

在具有善良愿望的人们中间,科学与民主的结合为个人提供了更丰富的生活和更大的满足。随着我们道德风尚的这种变化以及我们重新发现了改进经济秩序的能力,我们已踏上了永久进步之路。

我们将在目前的道路上止步不前或向后转吗?我们能把它称之为大有希望的土地吗?或者,我们将继续走我们的道路吗?因为"每一个时代都是一个正在消逝的梦,抑或是一个即将诞生的梦"[1]。

当我们面临一个伟大的抉择时,我们会听到许多声音。安于现状者说:"歇一会儿吧。"机会主义者说:"这是一个好机会。"懦弱者则问道:"前面的路有多大困难?"

的确,我们已远离了停滞的绝望的岁月,维持了活力,我们已恢复了勇气和信心,开阔了各种思想和道德境界。

但是,我们目前的收获是在超常环境的压力下赢取的。在恐惧与苦难

---

[1]引自亚瑟·奥肖尼西的作品《歌咏之人》。

The times were on the side of progress.

To hold to progress today, however, is more difficult. Dulled conscience, irresponsibility, and ruthless self-interest already reappear. Such symptoms of prosperity may become portents of disaster! Prosperity already tests the persistence of our progressive purpose.

Let us ask again: Have we reached the goal of our vision of that fourth day of March 1933? Have we found our happy valley?

I see a great nation, upon a great continent, blessed with a great wealth of natural resources. Its hundred and thirty million people are at peace among themselves; they are making their country a good neighbor among the nations. I see a United States which can demonstrate that, under democratic methods of government, national wealth can be translated into a spreading volume of human comforts hitherto unknown, and the lowest standard of living can be raised far above the level of mere subsistence.

But here is the challenge to our democracy: In this nation I see tens of millions of its citizens—a substantial part of its whole population—who at this very moment are denied the greater part of what the very lowest standards of today call the necessities of life.

I see millions of families trying to live on incomes so meager that the pall of family disaster hangs over them day by day.

I see millions whose daily lives in city and on farm continue under conditions labeled indecent by a so-called polite society half a century ago.

I see millions denied education, recreation, and the opportunity to better their lot and the lot of their children.

I see millions lacking the means to buy the products of farm and factory and by their poverty denying work and productiveness to many other millions.

I see one-third of a nation ill-housed, ill-clad, ill-nourished.

It is not in despair that I paint you that picture. I paint it for you in hope—because the Nation, seeing and understanding the injustice in it, proposes to paint it out. We are determined to make every American citizen the subject of his country's interest and concern; and we will never regard any faithful law-abiding group within our borders as superfluous. The test of our

富兰克林·罗斯福
Franklin Roosevelt

的驱使下,进步成了必走之路,这个时代有利于进步。

然而,今天要坚持进步就更困难了。麻木不仁、不负责任以及无情的自私已再度出现。这种繁荣的象征有可能变成灾难的预兆!繁荣已在考验我们进步的目标能否持久。

让我们再一次发问:我们已经达到了1933年3月4日那天所梦想的目标了吗?我们已寻找到快乐之谷了吗?

我看到一个处在偌大陆地上的拥有富饶的天然资源的伟大国家。它的一亿三千万人口和平相处,他们正在使自己的国家成为其他民族的好邻居。我看到一个美国,它能够采用民主的管理办法,用国家的财富能够带来迄今为止人所未知的日益广泛的安乐,把最低的生活水准提高到远远超出基本物质需要的程度。

但是,我们的民主也正在受到挑战:在这个国家中,我看到数千万人民——占总人口的很大比例——的大部分此时此刻仍处于今天所称的生活之必需的最起码的标准之下。

我看到数百万家庭依赖低微的收入生存,以至于家庭灾难的阴影日复一日地笼罩着他们。

我看到数百万人们,他们在城市和农村的日常生活仍处在半个世纪前一个所谓的体面社会认为不体面的环境之中。

我看到成百万人得不到教育、娱乐以及改善他们及其子女命运的机会。

我看到数百万人无力购买农产品和工业产品,又因他们的穷困潦倒而无力工作,不能为其他数百万人生产。

我看到全国有三分之一的人口房屋破损,衣衫褴褛,营养不良。

我为你们描绘这个图景时,并没有绝望,我要为你们绘出一幅希望之图——这是因为这个民族已经看到了这是不公正的现象,而准备把它涂掉。我们决心使每一个美国公民成为他的国家施益和关心的臣民,而且我们决不把我们国土之内的任何忠诚守法的群体视为多余。对我们进步的检验不在于我们是否为那些已经拥有了许多东西的人锦上添花,而在于我们

progress is not whether we add more to the abundance of those who have much; it is whether we provide enough for those who have too little.

If I know aught of the spirit and purpose of our Nation, we will not listen to Comfort, Opportunism, and Timidity. We will carry on.

Overwhelmingly, we of the Republic are men and women of good will; men and women who have more than warm hearts of dedication; men and women who have cool heads and willing hands of practical purpose as well. They will insist that every agency of popular government use effective instruments to carry out their will.

Government is competent when all who compose it work as trustees for the whole people. It can make constant progress when it keeps abreast of all the facts. It can obtain justified support and legitimate criticism when the people receive true information of all that government does.

If I know aught of the will of our people, they will demand that these conditions of effective government shall be created and maintained. They will demand a nation uncorrupted by cancers of injustice and, therefore, strong among the nations in its example of the will to peace.

Today we reconsecrate our country to long-cherished ideals in a suddenly changed civilization. In every land there are always at work forces that drive men apart and forces that draw men together. In our personal ambitions we are individualists. But in our seeking for economic and political progress as a nation, we all go up, or else we all go down, as one people.

To maintain a democracy of effort requires a vast amount of patience in dealing with differing methods, a vast amount of humility. But out of the confusion of many voices rises an understanding of dominant public need. Then political leadership can voice common ideals, and aid in their realization.

In taking again the oath of office as President of the United States, I assume the solemn obligation of leading the American people forward along the road over which they have chosen to advance.

While this duty rests upon me I shall do my utmost to speak their purpose and to do their will, seeking Divine guidance to help us each and every one to give light to them that sit in darkness and to guide our feet into the way of peace.

富兰克林·罗斯福
Franklin Roosevelt

是否为那些拥有甚少的人提供富足。

如果我对我们民族的精神和目标还算了解的话,我们将不接受安于现状者、机会主义者以及懦夫们的观点。我们将奋斗下去。

我们共和国绝大多数都是善良的人。他们不仅有非常热情的奉献之心,而且他们还有冷静的头脑和愿为实现目标而工作的双手。他们要求政府机构应能卓有成效地去实现他们的意愿。

当组成政府的所有成员都为了不辜负全民的信任而工作时,政府就是称职的。当它随时了解所有情况时,就能不断取得进步。当人们接受了政府对所做之事的真实报告时,政府才能得到正义的支持和合理的批评。

如果我对我国人民的意愿还算了解的话,他们将要求这些使政府富有成效所必需的条件应建立起来和维持下去。他们将要求一个国家不会由于不公正的弊端而招致破坏,从而,在决心实现和平方面成为各国的楷模。

今天,在突然变化的文明世界中,我们把长久繁荣的理想奉献给我们的祖国。在每一块土地上,总是运转着把人们分离的力量和把人们凝聚的力量。从我们个人的抱负来看,我们是个人主义者。但是,在我们寻求作为一个民族的经济和政治进步时,作为一个整体,要么共同进步腾飞,要么全体倒退沉沦。

坚持民主的力量,需要以极大的耐心去对待方法上的分歧,也需要无比的谦恭。它是从许多声音的混杂中产生的一种对人民大众之需求的理解。由此,政治领导人才能提出共同的理想,并有助于它们的实现。

身为美国总统,我再次发誓,领导美国人民迈向他们已选择的前进道路是我神圣的职责。

当这个职责落在我身上时,我将尽最大努力按照人民的意愿说话,并实现他们的意愿。祈求上帝指引帮助我们之中的每一个人,把光明带给尚在黑暗中的人们,指引我们走上和平之路。

Franklin Roosevelt
Third Inaugural Address

January 20, 1941

On each national day of inauguration since 1789, the people have renewed their sense of dedication to the United States.

In Washington's day the task of the people was to create and weld together a nation.

In Lincoln's day the task of the people was to preserve that Nation from disruption from within.

In this day the task of the people is to save that Nation and its institutions from disruption from without.

To us there has come a time, in the midst of swift happenings, to pause for a moment and take stock—to recall what our place in history has been, and to rediscover what we are and what we may be. If we do not, we risk the real peril of inaction.

Lives of nations are determined not by the count of years, but by the lifetime of the human spirit. The life of a man is three-score years and ten: a little more, a little less. The life of a nation is the fullness of the measure of its will to live.

There are men who doubt this. There are men who believe that democracy, as a form of Government and a frame of life, is limited or measured by a kind of mystical and artificial fate that, for some unexplained reason, tyranny and slavery have become the surging wave of the future — and that freedom is an ebbing tide.

But we Americans know that this is not true.

Eight years ago, when the life of this Republic seemed frozen by a fatalistic terror, we proved that this is not true. We were in the midst of shock—but we acted. We acted quickly, boldly, decisively.

These later years have been living years—fruitful years for the people of this

富兰克林·罗斯福

Franklin Roosevelt

罗斯福总统第三次就职演说

1941年1月20日

　　自1789年以来，每当一任总统就职时，人们都恢复起他们为美国致力奉献的生气。

　　在华盛顿时代，人们的任务是创立、熔铸结合成一个国家。

　　在林肯时代，人们的任务是保护这个国家免其由内部瓦解。

　　在今天，我们的任务是拯救这个国家和它的各种制度，以免受到外部摧毁。

　　在这个瞬息万变的时代，对我们来说，需要有时间稍停片刻，做一番估量——重新回忆一下在历史上我们所处的地位，并且重新发现我们正在扮演的角色以及可能扮演的角色。如果我们不这样做，我们就会因无动于衷而冒真正的危险。

　　国家的寿命并不取决于年代的久远，而是取决于人们的精神的生命力。人的生命是70年，或者多些，或者少些。而一个国家的生命是由它的生存意志程度来决定的。

　　有些人怀疑这一点。有些人相信，民主作为一种政府形式和生活制度，是由一种神秘的和人为的命运来限制和制约的——由于某种无法解释的原因，暴政和奴役已经成为未来汹涌的浪潮——而自由却正在退潮。

　　但我们美国人知道，这是不正确的。

　　八年前，当这个共和国的生命似乎被一种宿命论的恐怖封冻时，我们证明了这不是正确的，我们身处打击之中——但是我们行动起来了。我们迅速地、大胆地、果断地行动起来了。

　　近些年来国家一直生机勃勃，这是处于民主之下的人民的丰收年代。

democracy. For they have brought to us greater security and, I hope, a better understanding that life's ideals are to be measured in other than material things.

Most vital to our present and our future is this experience of a democracy which successfully survived crisis at home; put away many evil things; built new structures on enduring lines; and, through it all, maintained the fact of its democracy.

For action has been taken within the three-way framework of the Constitution of the United States. The coordinate branches of the Government continue freely to function. The Bill of Rights remains inviolate. The freedom of elections is wholly maintained. Prophets of the downfall of American democracy have seen their dire predictions come to naught.

Democracy is not dying.

We know it because we have seen it revive—and grow.

We know it cannot die—because it is built on the unhampered initiative of individual men and women joined together in a common enterprise—an enterprise undertaken and carried through by the free expression of a free majority.

We know it because democracy alone, of all forms of government, enlists the full force of men's enlightened will.

We know it because democracy alone has constructed an unlimited civilization capable of infinite progress in the improvement of human life.

We know it because, if we look below the surface, we sense it still spreading on every continent—for it is the most humane, the most advanced, and in the end the most unconquerable of all forms of human society.

A nation, like a person, has a body—a body that must be fed and clothed and housed, invigorated and rested, in a manner that measures up to the objectives of our time.

A nation, like a person, has a mind—a mind that must be kept informed and alert, that must know itself that understands the hopes and the needs of its neighbors—all the other nations that live within the narrowing circle of the world.

And a nation, like a person, has something deeper, something more

富兰克林·罗斯福
Franklin Roosevelt

丰收的成果已给我们带来了更大的安全,然而我也希望,我们能更充分理解到,生命的理想是由物质之外的事物来衡量的。

对于我们的现在和未来,最为重要的是能成功地经受国内危机的民主尝试,摒除许多邪恶之物;根据持久的路线建立起新的结构,并通过它来坚持民主。

美国宪政的三个组成部分仍在正常运行。政府的各个协调部门仍在自由地继续行使职能。人权法案依旧不容侵犯。选举自由得到了完整的维护。那些预言美国民主制度将崩溃的预言家们,已经看到了自己的可怕预言化成了泡影。

民主并没有死亡。

我们知道这一点,是因为我们已经看到了它的复苏——并且在生长。

我们知道它不能死亡,因为它是建立在一个由共同的事业——一个由自由的大多数通过自由的表达来进行和坚持到底的事业——熔铸在一起的各个男女不屈不挠创造的基础之上。

我们之所以知道这一点,是因为在所有的政体中,只有民主才能谋求到人们开明意志的全力支持。

我们之所以知道这一点,是因为只有民主才会建立起一种无拘无束的文明,它能够在改善人类生活中取得无限的进步。

我们之所以知道这一点,是因为如果我们透过表面看去,我们可以察觉出它正在每块大陆上蔓延,因为它是最人道的、最进步的,并且最终会在人类社会的所有形式中成为最不可征服的。

一个国家如同一个人一样有一个身体,一个必须满足衣食住行得到休养生息的身体,以便在某种程度上,达到我们时代的各种目标。

一个国家如同一个人一样有一个头脑,一个必须保持灵通和警觉的头脑;一个必须了解自我、理解它的邻邦以及生存在这狭小世界范围之内的所有其他民族的希望和要求的头脑。

一个民族如同一个人一样,拥有某种比它各部分的总和更深、更久和

permanent, something larger than the sum of all its parts. It is that something which matters most to its future—which calls forth the most sacred guarding of its present.

It is a thing for which we find it difficult—even impossible—to hit upon a single, simple word.

And yet we all understand what it is—the spirit—the faith of America. It is the product of centuries. It was born in the multitudes of those who came from many lands—some of high degree, but mostly plain people, who sought here, early and late, to find freedom more freely.

The democratic aspiration is no mere recent phase in human history. It is human history. It permeated the ancient life of early peoples. It blazed anew in the middle ages. It was written in Magna Charta.

In the Americas its impact has been irresistible. America has been the New World in all tongues, to all peoples, not because this continent was a new-found land, but because all those who came here believed they could create upon this continent a new life—a life that should be new in freedom.

Its vitality was written into our own Mayflower Compact, into the Declaration of Independence, into the Constitution of the United States, into the Gettysburg Address.

Those who first came here to carry out the longings of their spirit, and the millions who followed, and the stock that sprang from them—all have moved forward constantly and consistently toward an ideal which in itself has gained stature and clarity with each generation.

The hopes of the Republic cannot forever tolerate either undeserved poverty or self-serving wealth.

We know that we still have far to go; that we must more greatly build the security and the opportunity and the knowledge of every citizen, in the measure justified by the resources and the capacity of the land.

But it is not enough to achieve these purposes alone. It is not enough to clothe and feed the body of this Nation, and instruct and inform its mind. For there is also the spirit. And of the three, the greatest is the spirit.

富兰克林·罗斯福
Franklin Roosevelt

更大的东西。它就是某种与未来生死攸关的东西，某种能引发人们保护它神圣存在的东西。

它是一个我们难以寻找，甚至不可能用一个单一简洁的字眼所描述的。

然而我们都理解它是什么——它是精神——是美国人的信念。它是世纪绵延的产物。它是在来自许多土地上的人们的凝聚中产生的，有些人层次高些，但大多数是平民百姓，他们在这里自由地追求，并迟早会得到更多的自由。

对于民主的热望，并不只是人类历史上新近出现的。它本身就是人类的历史。它渗入了早期人类的古老生活，并在中世纪重新燃起火焰。它被载入了英国的大宪章。

在美洲，它的冲击是无法抵挡的。在所有使用不同语言的人们之中，美国已是人们心中的新的世界，这并不是因为这块大陆是一块新发现的土地，而是因为所有来到这里的人们都相信他们能在这块大陆上创造出新的生活——一种自由的新生活。

民主的生命力载入我们的《五月花号公约》[1]中，载入独立宣言中，载入美国的宪法中，载入葛底斯堡的演说中。

那些最先到达这里实现他们精神之热望的人们，连同数百万的跟随者，以及他们的子孙后代，全都不断地、坚定不移地奔向一个理想，每一代人都使之增长和明确起来。

共和国的希望是，永不能允许不应有的贫穷以及自私自利的财富。

我们知道自己还相去甚远，我们必须在自然资源和土地条件允许的情况下，努力为每个公民提供安全、机会和知识。

但是，仅仅实现这些目的是不够的。使这个国家人民有衣穿，有饭吃，并教诲和充实他们的头脑也是不够的。因为还有精神，在这三件东西中，

---

[1]它是1620年"五月花号"船抵达科德角港口时，船上清教徒移民为建立普利茅斯殖民地而订立的自治公约。

Without the body and the mind, as all men know, the Nation could not live.

But if the spirit of America were killed, even though the Nation's body and mind, constricted in an alien world, lived on, the America we know would have perished.

That spirit—that faith—speaks to us in our daily lives in ways often unnoticed, because they seem so obvious. It speaks to us here in the Capital of the Nation. It speaks to us through the processes of governing in the sovereignties of 48 States. It speaks to us in our counties, in our cities, in our towns, and in our villages. It speaks to us from the other nations of the hemisphere, and from those across the seas—the enslaved, as well as the free. Sometimes we fail to hear or heed these voices of freedom because to us the privilege of our freedom is such an old, old story.

The destiny of America was proclaimed in words of prophecy spoken by our first President in his first inaugural in 1789—words almost directed, it would seem, to this year of 1941: "The preservation of the sacred fire of liberty and the destiny of the republican model of government are justly considered ... deeply,... finally, staked on the experiment entrusted to the hands of the American people."

If we lose that sacred fire—if we let it be smothered with doubt and fear—then we shall reject the destiny which Washington strove so valiantly and so triumphantly to establish. The preservation of the spirit and faith of the Nation does, and will, furnish the highest justification for every sacrifice that we may make in the cause of national defense.

In the face of great perils never before encountered, our strong purpose is to protect and to perpetuate the integrity of democracy.

For this we muster the spirit of America, and the faith of America.

We do not retreat. We are not content to stand still. As Americans, we go forward, in the service of our country, by the will of God.

富兰克林·罗斯福
Franklin Roosevelt

它才是最重要的。

没有身体和头脑，所有的人都知道，这个国家是不能生存的。

但是假如美国的精神毁灭了，尽管这个国家的身心在外在世界的压抑下生存着，我们所知道的美国也仍会灭亡。

那种精神——那种信念，在我们的日常生活中，经常以不被注意的方式对我们说话，尽管它们是如此的显而易见。它在国家首都对我们说话，它通过48个州[1]自治管理的程度对我们说话。它在我们的国家、我们的城市、我们的乡镇、我们的村庄对我们说话。它通过这个半球的其他国家，以及横跨大海的那些人——被奴役的，连同自由的人们对我们说话。有时我们没有听到或留意这些自由之声，因为对我们来说，我们的自由特权是一个如此古老的故事。

美国的命运已由我们的首任总统在1789年的就职典礼上，以富有预见性的语言宣告出来，这些话似乎是直接针对1941年所讲的："维护自由的圣火与维护共和政府的命运这两件事，全由美国人民的尝试能否成功而定。"

如果我们失去了那神圣之火，如果我们让它因怀疑和恐惧而熄灭，那么，我们就将抛弃华盛顿曾经用英勇和努力成功建立起来的命运。维护这个国家的精神和信念将对于我们为保卫民族做出的每一个牺牲提供最有力的印证。

面临着前所未有的严峻形势，我们坚持的目的是保护和保持完整的民主。

为此，我们应振作起美国的精神和美国的信念。

我们不能退却，我们不能满足于现状。作为美国人，我们遵从上帝的意志，在为我们国家效力的事业中奋勇向前。

---

[1]夏威夷和阿拉斯加两州当时尚未加入联邦。

哈里·杜鲁门
Harry Truman

哈里·杜鲁门 （Harry Truman）

生平简介 >>

哈里·杜鲁门是美国第三十三任总统。他于1884年5月8日出生在密苏里州。第一次世界大战期间，他自愿从军并当了野战炮兵部队的上尉。1934年被选为密苏里州的参议员。在第二次世界大战期间，他因担任参议院"调查国防计划特别委员会"主席而闻名，这个委员会的工作，使纳税人在战争年代节约了150亿美元的开支。

1944年，他作为罗斯福总统的竞选伙伴而当选为副总统。1945年4月12日，由于罗斯福总统的突然病逝，他成为美国总统。1948年11月，他再次当选为总统。在任期间，他下令向日本投掷原子弹，加速了日本的投降；批准实施了著名的"马歇尔计划"；组建了北大西洋公约组织；命令美国部队参与了朝鲜战争。

退休后，他出版了三卷回忆录，并创建了杜鲁门图书馆。1972年12月26日病逝，终年88岁。

Harry Truman
Inaugural Address

January 20, 1949

Mr. Vice President, Mr. Chief Justice, and fellow citizens, I accept with humility the honor which the American people have conferred upon me. I accept it with a deep resolve to do all that I can for the welfare of this Nation and for the peace of the world.

In performing the duties of my office, I need the help and prayers of every one of you. I ask for your encouragement and your support. The tasks we face are difficult, and we can accomplish them only if we work together.

Each period of our national history has had its special challenges. Those that confront us now are as momentous as any in the past. Today marks the beginning not only of a new administration, but of a period that will be eventful, perhaps decisive, for us and for the world.

It may be our lot to experience, and in large measure to bring about, a major turning point in the long history of the human race. The first half of this century has been marked by unprecedented and brutal attacks on the rights of man, and by the two most frightful wars in history. The supreme need of our time is for men to learn to live together in peace and harmony.

The peoples of the earth face the future with grave uncertainty, composed almost equally of great hopes and great fears. In this time of doubt, they look to the United States as never before for good will, strength, and wise leadership.

It is fitting, therefore, that we take this occasion to proclaim to the world the essential principles of the faith by which we live, and to declare our aims to all peoples.

The American people stand firm in the faith which has inspired this Nation from the beginning. We believe that all men have a right to equal justice under law and equal opportunity to share in the common good. We believe that all

哈里·杜鲁门
Harry Truman

杜鲁门总统就职演说*

1949年1月20日

　　副总统先生、最高法院院长先生及同胞们，我谨以谦卑的心情来接受美国人民赋予我的这一荣誉。我将以竭尽全力为这个国家的利益以及世界和平效力的坚定决心来接受它。

　　在我履行我的职责的过程中，我需要诸位的协助和祈祷。我请求你们给我以鼓励和支持。我们所面临的任务是艰巨的，只有我们携手并肩，才能把它们完成。

　　我们国家历史上的每一阶段都有其特殊的挑战，但今天我们所面临的考验则与以往任何时候比都不逊色。今天不仅标志着一个新时期的开始，而且对于我们和世界来说，将是一个多事之秋，或许也是一个决定性的时候。

　　我们也许注定要经历并在很大程度上促成人类漫长历史上的一个重要转折点。本世纪第一个50年的突出特点是，人权遭到前所未有的野蛮攻击，发生了历史上最令人惊骇的两次世界大战。我们时代至高无上的需要是人们要学会和睦相处。

　　世界各国人民几乎是以一种同时夹杂着热望和恐怖的不定的情绪来迎接未来的。在这迷惘的时刻，他们比以往任何时候更期待美国的善意、力量以及明智的领导。

　　因此，我们最宜在这一时刻向世界宣告我们的生活信念的基本原则，宣告我们全体人民的奋斗目标。

　　美国人民坚定地怀有一种信念，它自开国以来就一直激励着这个民族。我们相信，所有人在法律之下都有权享有公平的待遇，并有同等的机会分享

---

* 本篇有删节。

men have the right to freedom of thought and expression. We believe that all men are created equal because they are created in the image of God.

From this faith we will not be moved.

The American people desire, and are determined to work for, a world in which all nations and all peoples are free to govern themselves as they see fit, and to achieve a decent and satisfying life. Above all else, our people desire, and are determined to work for, peace on earth—a just and lasting peace—based on genuine agreement freely arrived at by equals.

Since the end of hostilities, the United States has invested its substance and its energy in a great constructive effort to restore peace, stability, and freedom to the world.

We have sought no territory and we have imposed our will on none. We have asked for no privileges we would not extend to others.

We have constantly and vigorously supported the United Nations and related agencies as a means of applying democratic principles to international relations. We have consistently advocated and relied upon peaceful settlement of disputes among nations.

We have made every effort to secure agreement on effective international control of our most powerful weapon, and we have worked steadily for the limitation and control of all armaments.

We have encouraged, by precept and example, the expansion of world trade on a sound and fair basis.

Almost a year ago, in company with 16 free nations of Europe, we launched the greatest cooperative economic program in history. The purpose of that unprecedented effort is to invigorate and strengthen democracy in Europe, so that the free people of that continent can resume their rightful place in the forefront of civilization and can contribute once more to the security and welfare of the world.

Our efforts have brought new hope to all mankind. We have beaten back despair and defeatism. We have saved a number of countries from losing their liberty. Hundreds of millions of people all over the world now agree with us, that we need not have war—that we can have peace.

哈里·杜鲁门
Harry Truman

共同的利益。我们相信，所有人都拥有自由思考以及自由言论的权利。我们相信，人类生而平等，乃是因为人是上帝依据自己的形象创造的。

由于这种信念，我们将坚定不移。

美国人民渴望自由，并且决心为一个世界而奋斗，在这一世界里，所有的国家以及所有的人都随心所欲地管理自己，实现一种体面而又心满意足的生活。总之，我们的人民渴望并且决心为地球上的和平——一种建立在以平等所取得的真正自愿的基础之上的——公正而持久的和平而努力。

自从战争结束之后，美国就把它的物资及能量投入到更大的建设性努力中去，用以恢复世界的和平、安定和自由。

我们无意侵略别国领土，我们也没有把我们的意志强加给任何人。我们不要求特权，我们也无意侵犯他人。

我们一贯有力支持联合国以及附属机构，它是把民主原则应用到国际关系中的一个手段。对于各国之间的纠纷，我们一直主张并支持以和平的方式来解决。

我们尽了各种努力去获得对最强大武器进行有效控制的国际协定，我们一直在不断地努力限制和控制各种军备。

经验和教训激励我们在健全而公正的基础上扩大世界贸易。

大约一年前，我们与欧洲16个自由国家合作，我们达成了历史上最伟大的经济合作计划[1]。这一史无前例的努力的目的是激活和加强欧洲的民主，使这块大陆上的自由的人民恢复他们在文明前沿的应有地位，以及能再一次地为世界的福祉与和平做出贡献。

我们的努力已为全人类带来新的希望。我们已经击败了绝望情绪和失败主义。我们已经拯救了许多正在失去自由的国家。全世界千百万人现在都赞成我们，我们不需要战争，我们能够实现和平。

---

[1]指1948年4月通过的援外法案，或称"马歇尔计划"。

The initiative is ours.

We are moving on with other nations to build an even stronger structure of international order and justice. We shall have as our partner's countries which, no longer solely concerned with the problem of national survival, are now working to improve the standards of living of all their people. We are ready to undertake new projects to strengthen the free world.

In the coming years, our program for peace and freedom will emphasize four major courses of action.

First, we will continue to give unfaltering support to the United Nations and related agencies, and we will continue to search for ways to strengthen their authority and increase their effectiveness.

Second, we will continue our programs for world economic recovery.

This means, first of all, that we must keep our full weight behind the European recovery program. We are confident of the success of this major venture in world recovery. We believe that our partners in this effort will achieve the status of self-supporting nations once again.

In addition, we must carry out our plans for reducing the barriers to world trade and increasing its volume. Economic recovery and peace itself depend on increased world trade.

Third, we will strengthen freedom-loving nations against the dangers of aggression.

We are now working out with a number of countries a joint agreement designed to strengthen the security of the North Atlantic area. Such an agreement would take the form of a collective defense arrangement within the terms of the United Nations Charter.

We have already established such a defense pact for the Western Hemisphere by the treaty of Rio de Janeiro.

The primary purpose of these agreements is to provide unmistakable proof of the joint determination of the free countries to resist armed attack from any quarter. Each country participating in these arrangements must contribute all it can to the common defense.

If we can make it sufficiently clear, in advance, that any armed attack

哈里·杜鲁门
Harry Truman

主动权掌握在我们手里。

我们正在与其他国家共建维护国际秩序和公正的一个更强有力的结构。那些不再仅仅关切国家的生存问题、目前正致力于改善全体人民的生活水平的国家,将成为我们的伙伴。我们正打算从事设计新的加强自由世界的计划。

在未来的岁月中,我们的和平与自由的方针将是强调四项重要行动的方针。

第一,我们将继续全力支持联合国及其附属机构,并且继续寻找各种途径来加强它们的权威,增大它们的效力。

第二,我们将继续执行我们恢复世界经济的各项计划。

这就意味着,首先我们必须致力于欧洲复兴的计划。我们自信这一世界复兴的重大事业能够成功。我们相信,我们的友邦在这种努力之中将重获自立的国家地位。

除此之外,我们必须实现自己为了减少世界贸易障碍以及增加世界贸易额的计划。经济复兴与和平本身取决于世界贸易的增长。

第三,我们将加强爱好自由的国家抵抗侵略危险的力量。

我们现在正联合一些国家订立公约,旨在加强北大西洋地区的安全。这样的一个公约将采取符合联合国宪章条款的共同防御协定的形式。

我们已经有了像《里约热内卢条约》那样的西半球的防御条约。

这些协定的主要宗旨是明确地表示,自由的各国团结一致,决心去抵抗任何地区的武力攻击。参与这些协定的每个国家都必须为共同的防御尽一切努力。

如果我们事先能够足以明确,任何影响我国安全的武装侵略都将遭到

affecting our national security would be met with overwhelming force, the armed attack might never occur.

I hope soon to send to the Senate a treaty respecting the North Atlantic security plan.

In addition, we will provide military advice and equipment to free nations which will cooperate with us in the maintenance of peace and security.

Fourth, we must embark on a bold new program for making the benefits of our scientific advances and industrial progress available for the improvement and growth of underdeveloped areas.

More than half the people of the world are living in conditions approaching misery. Their food is inadequate. They are victims of disease. Their economic life is primitive and stagnant. Their poverty is a handicap and a threat both to them and to more prosperous areas.

For the first time in history, humanity possesses the knowledge and the skill to relieve the suffering of these people.

The United States is pre-eminent among nations in the development of industrial and scientific techniques. The material resources which we can afford to use for the assistance of other peoples are limited. But our imponderable resources in technical knowledge are constantly growing and are inexhaustible.

I believe that we should make available to peace-loving peoples the benefits of our store of technical knowledge in order to help them realize their aspirations for a better life. And, in cooperation with other nations, we should foster capital investment in areas needing development.

Our aim should be to help the free peoples of the world, through their own efforts, to produce more food, more clothing, more materials for housing, and more mechanical power to lighten their burdens.

We invite other countries to pool their technological resources in this undertaking. Their contributions will be warmly welcomed. This should be a cooperative enterprise in which all nations work together through the United Nations and its specialized agencies wherever practicable. It must be a worldwide effort for the achievement of peace, plenty, and freedom.

With the cooperation of business, private capital, agriculture, and labor in

哈里·杜鲁门
Harry Truman

毁灭性的反击的话,那么武装侵略就绝不会发生。

我希望不久送交参议院一份有关北大西洋安全计划的条约。

除此之外,我们将为与我们合作的维护和平与安全的各个自由国家提供军事指导和装备。

第四,为了以我们先进的科学和进步的工业帮助改善和发展那些尚未发展起来的地区,我们必须着手一项大胆的新计划。

在这个世界,有半数以上的人们正生活在近乎悲惨的境地之中。他们食物匮乏,饱受疾病的折磨。他们的经济生活既原始又迟缓不振。他们的贫困无论是对他们自己,还是对更繁荣的地区,都构成一种阻碍和威胁。

人类已经掌握了把这些人从苦难中解救出来的知识和技能,这在历史上还是第一次。

在工业和科技发展上,美国在各国中是最卓越的。我们能够提供的用来帮助其他国家人民的物质财富虽然有限,但我们在技术知识方面无法估计的资源则是不断增长的,是取之不尽、用之不竭的。

我相信,我们应该提供我们所有的技术和知识给那些爱好和平的人们,以帮助他们实现追求美好生活的期望,并且在与其他国家的合作中,我们应当促进对需要发展的地区的资本投入。

我们的目的是帮助世界上的自由民族,通过它们自己的努力,去生产更多的食物、更多的衣物、更多的建房材料,以及更多的减轻他们的重负的机械。

我们呼吁其他各国将它们的技术资源投入这一事业,它们的贡献将受到热烈欢迎。这将是一个合作的事业,在这一事业中,所有的国家通过联合国以及它的各个可行的专门机构来共同奋斗。它应当是一项实现和平、富足和自由的世界性努力。

通过我国的商业、私人资本、农业以及劳动力的合作,这个计划能够极

this country, this program can greatly increase the industrial activity in other nations and can raise substantially their standards of living.

Such new economic developments must be devised and controlled to benefit the peoples of the areas in which they are established. Guarantees to the investor must be balanced by guarantees in the interest of the people whose resources and whose labor go into these developments.

The old imperialism—exploitation for foreign profit—has no place in our plans. What we envisage is a program of development based on the concepts of democratic fair-dealing.

All countries, including our own, will greatly benefit from a constructive program for the better use of the world's human and natural resources. Experience shows that our commerce with other countries expands as they progress industrially and economically.

Greater production is the key to prosperity and peace. And the key to greater production is a wider and more vigorous application of modern scientific and technical knowledge.

Only by helping the least fortunate of its members to help themselves can the human family achieve the decent, satisfying life that is the right of all people.

Democracy alone can supply the vitalizing force to stir the peoples of the world into triumphant action, not only against their human oppressors, but also against their ancient enemies—hunger, misery, and despair.

On the basis of these four major courses of action we hope to help create the conditions that will lead eventually to personal freedom and happiness for all mankind.

If we are to be successful in carrying out these policies, it is clear that we must have continued prosperity in this country and we must keep ourselves strong.

Slowly but surely we are weaving a world fabric of international security and growing prosperity.

We are aided by all who wish to live in freedom from fear—even by those who live today in fear under their own governments.

We are aided by all who want relief from the lies of propaganda—who desire truth and sincerity.

大地增强其他国家的工业生产,而且能够充分地提高其人民的生活水平。

这样的新的经济发展必须加以计划和控制,以便给当地的人民带来利益。对投资者的保证必须由对那些人利益的保证来平衡,那些人就是对这种发展提供了资源和劳动力的人们。

老牌的帝国主义——剥夺外国的利益——并没有包括在我们的计划之内。我们所拟订的是一项建立在民主的公平交易观念基础之上的发展计划。

所有的国家,包括我们自己在内,将从更有效地利用世界人力以及自然资源的建设性计划中极大地获益。经验证明,我们与其他国家之间的贸易扩展了,其原因在于它们的工业和经济的进步。

提高生产是带来繁荣与和平的关键,而提高生产的关键是对现代科技知识更广泛、更富有活力的应用。

只有通过帮助那些最不幸的人实现自助,人类大家庭中的所有人才都能享有体面和富足的生活。这是各国人民的权利。

仅凭民主就能提供生机勃勃的力量,激励世界人民走向胜利,不仅仅是反抗他们的人类压迫者,而且反抗他们的古老敌人——饥饿、不幸和绝望。

在四个主要行动方针的基础之上,我们希望帮助建立各种条件,真正引导人们实现个人的自由和全人类的幸福。

如果我们要成功地执行这些政策,我们就必须继续繁荣下去,我们也必须保持自身的强大。

我们正在缓慢而扎实地构造国际安全和日益繁荣的世界性框架。

我们从所有希望摆脱恐惧的人们那里得到帮助,甚至从至今还在他们自己政府统治之下、生活在恐惧之中的人们那里得到帮助。

我们从所有想由宣传的谎言中解脱出来、渴望真理和诚实的人们那里得到帮助。

We are aided by all who desire self-government and a voice in deciding their own affairs.

We are aided by all who long for economic security—for the security and abundance that men in free societies can enjoy.

We are aided by all who desire freedom of speech, freedom of religion, and freedom to live their own lives for useful ends.

Our allies are the millions who hunger and thirst after righteousness.

In due time, as our stability becomes manifest, as more and more nations come to know the benefits of democracy and to participate in growing abundance, I believe that those countries which now oppose us will abandon their delusions and join with the free nations of the world in a just settlement of international differences.

Events have brought our American democracy to new influence and new responsibilities. They will test our courage, our devotion to duty, and our concept of liberty.

But I say to all men, what we have achieved in liberty, we will surpass in greater liberty.

Steadfast in our faith in the Almighty, we will advance toward a world where man's freedom is secure.

To that end we will devote our strength, our resources, and our firmness of resolve. With God's help, the future of mankind will be assured in a world of justice, harmony, and peace.

哈里·杜鲁门
Harry Truman

　　我们从所有渴望自治政府以及拥有决定自己事务的发言权的人们那里得到帮助。

　　我们从所有渴望经济安全，渴求在一个自由的社会中能够享受安全和富足的人们那里得到帮助。

　　我们从所有渴望言论自由、宗教自由以及渴望能为达到有益目标而自由选择生活方式的人们那里得到帮助。

　　我们的联盟者是千千万万如饥似渴地追求正义的人们。

　　在适当的时候，当我们的稳定已得到证明的时候，当愈来愈多的国家了解到民主的益处，以及参加到逐渐富裕起来的行列中的时候，我相信，现在与我们对立的那些国家将放弃它们的幻想，同自由国家一道公正地解决国际分歧。

　　许多事情的发生已给我们的美国民主带来新的影响和新的责任。它们将考验我们的勇气，我们对责任的奉献以及我们的自由信念。

　　但是我要告诉所有人，我们已达到某种程度的自由，我们将会拥有更大的自由。

　　坚定我们对上帝的信念，我们将向一个世界迈进，在这个世界里的人的自由是受到保障的。

　　为了这个目的，我们将奉献我们的力量、我们的资源以及我们坚定的决心。凭借上帝的帮助，人类未来必将生活在一个公正、和谐与和平的世界。

德怀特·艾森豪威尔
Dwight Eisenhower

德怀特·艾森豪威尔（Dwight Eisenhower）

生平简介>>

德怀特·艾森豪威尔是美国第三十四任总统。他于1890年10月14日出生在得克萨斯州。1915年毕业于西点军校，后一直在军队中任职，1941年晋升为准将。1942年6月，他被任命为欧洲战区的司令官，到1944年，他已作为盟军最高司令统率着300万军队。他本人也在这一年成为五星上将，这一军衔由国会在1946年定为永久性的军衔。他在1945年领导盟军最终战胜德国。回国后，他先后任哥伦比亚大学校长和北大西洋公约组织部队的最高司令。

1952年他接受共和党的提名，并以"我喜欢艾克"这一口号，击败了民主党总统候选人、伊利诺伊州州长史蒂文森而当选为总统。1956年，他再次击败史蒂文森连任总统。在他任职期间美国加快了大规模的公路建设计划的实施，修建了41000英里长的州际新公路；扩大和加强了社会安全保障和失业保险事业；把阿拉斯加和夏威夷列为美国的州；建造了圣劳伦斯深水航道；成立了空军学院。

1969年3月28日，他因心脏病发作死于华盛顿的一家陆军医院中。

Dwight Eisenhower
First Inaugural Address

January 20, 1953

My friends, before I begin the expression of those thoughts that I deem appropriate to this moment, would you permit me the privilege of uttering a little private prayer of my own. And I ask that you bow your heads:

Almighty God, as we stand here at this moment my future associates in the executive branch of government join me in beseeching that Thou will make full and complete our dedication to the service of the people in this throng, and their fellow citizens everywhere.

Give us, we pray, the power to discern clearly right from wrong, and allow all our words and actions to be governed thereby, and by the laws of this land. Especially we pray that our concern shall be for all the people regardless of station, race, or calling.

May cooperation be permitted and be the mutual aim of those who, under the concepts of our Constitution, hold to differing political faiths; so that all may work for the good of our beloved country and Thy glory. Amen.

My fellow citizens:

The world and we have passed the midway point of a century of continuing challenge. We sense with all our faculties that forces of good and evil are massed and armed and opposed as rarely before in history.

This fact defines the meaning of this day. We are summoned by this honored and historic ceremony to witness more than the act of one citizen swearing his oath of service, in the presence of God. We are called as a people to give testimony in the sight of the world to our faith that the future shall belong to the free.

Since this century's beginning, a time of tempest has seemed to come upon the continents of the earth. Masses of Asia have awakened to strike off

德怀特·艾森豪威尔
Dwight Eisenhower

艾森豪威尔总统首次就职演说

1953年1月20日

朋友们，在我开始表达我认为最适于此刻的想法之前，请允许我念一小段我个人的祷文。现在就请各位垂首：

全能的主啊，此时此刻，我同将与我在政府行政部门共事的同伴们向您祈求，但愿您保佑我们全心全意为人民以及各地同胞们服务。

我们祈求您赐予我们以明辨是非的能力，允许我们的言行由此来支配，并且受到这块土地上的各种法律的支配。我们还特别祈求，我们的关切将给予所有的人，没有地位的高低以及种族和职业的区分。

在我们的宪法之下，希望持不同政治信仰的人们能够紧密合作，团结一致，为我们所热爱的国家的繁荣以及上帝的荣耀而奋斗。阿门。

同胞们：

世界和我们都已度过了不断遭受挑战的半个世纪。我们大家都深深地感觉到，这种善恶力量大规模地聚集起来、武装起来并互相对峙的情形在历史上也是罕见的。

这一事实表明了今天的意义。在此光荣和历史性的仪式上，我们都被召来为一项比一位公民在上帝面前宣誓就职更有意义的事件做见证。我们都以一个民族的身份被召集起来，并在全世界面前证明我们的信念——相信未来将会属于自由的人们。

本世纪开始以来，动乱似乎就不断地蔓延到世界各地。亚洲的大多数人民已经觉醒，去打碎过去的枷锁。欧洲各大国进行了最血腥的战争，专

shackles of the past. Great nations of Europe have fought their bloodiest wars. Thrones have toppled and their vast empires have disappeared. New nations have been born.

For our own country, it has been a time of recurring trial. We have grown in power and in responsibility. We have passed through the anxieties of depression and of war to a summit unmatched in man's history. Seeking to secure peace in the world, we have had to fight through the forests of the Argonne, to the shores of Iwo Jima, and to the cold mountains of Korea.

In the swift rush of great events, we find ourselves groping to know the full sense and meaning of these times in which we live. In our quest of understanding, we beseech God's guidance. We summon all our knowledge of the past and we scan all signs of the future. We bring all our wit and all our will to meet the question:

How far have we come in man's long pilgrimage from darkness toward light? Are we nearing the light—a day of freedom and of peace for all mankind? Or are the shadows of another night closing in upon us?

Great as are the preoccupations absorbing us at home, concerned as we are with matters that deeply affect our livelihood today and our vision of the future, each of these domestic problems is dwarfed by, and often even created by, this question that involves all humankind.

This trial comes at a moment when man's power to achieve good or to inflict evil surpasses the brightest hopes and the sharpest fears of all ages. We can turn rivers in their courses, level mountains to the plains. Oceans and land and sky are avenues for our colossal commerce. Disease diminishes and life lengthens.

Yet the promise of this life is imperiled by the very genius that has made it possible. Nations amass wealth. Labor sweats to create—and turns out devices to level not only mountains but also cities. Science seems ready to confer upon us, as its final gift, the power to erase human life from this planet.

At such a time in history, we who are free must proclaim anew our faith. This faith is the abiding creed of our fathers. It is our faith in the deathless dignity of man, governed by eternal moral and natural laws.

This faith defines our full view of life. It establishes, beyond debate, those

德怀特·艾森豪威尔
Dwight Eisenhower

制君主被倾覆，他们的帝国也宣告结束，新的国家已经诞生。

就我们自己的国家来说，经历了一段被反复考验的时期。我们的力量和责任都增强了。我们已经度过了极度的经济萧条和战争的恐慌，这在人类历史上是从未有过的。为确保世界和平，我们不得不在阿尔贡的森林里、硫黄岛的海滩上，以及在朝鲜寒冷的山峰上战斗。

在各项重大事件的冲击中，我们发现我们正在逐渐充分地了解和认识我们所处的时代之意义。在寻求了解中，我们祈求上帝的指引。我们运用过去所学的一切知识，也详细地审视了未来的一切迹象，我们将运用一切智慧和所有意志来应付下列问题：

在人类从黑暗走向光明的历程中，我们已经走了多远？我们是否正在接近光明，接近所有人类都应享有的自由和平的一天？还是另一个黑夜的暗幕正在向我们逼近？

在国内，我们正关注于尚待解决的重大问题，也关心那些深深影响我们今后生活和未来理想的因素，国内的每一个问题，与上面那个关系到全人类的问题相比都略逊一筹，甚至通常就是由它而引起的。

当人类创造幸福和驱逐邪恶的能力使我们能看到一切时代中最光明的希望，克服最可怕的恐惧时，这个时候就是我们面临考验的时刻。我们能改变河道，把山川夷为平地，海洋、陆地和天空都是我们的通商大道。疾病减少了，寿命延长了。

然而，就是这种改进人类生活的愿望，使人类的生活陷于危险境地。各国在聚集财富。工人们在流汗中制造出来的工具，不仅可以削平高山，也能夷平城市；科学似乎在准备赐给我们一个最后的礼物——从这个星球上消灭全人类的力量。

在这样一个历史时刻，我们自由的人们必须重申自己的信念。这一信念是我们祖先奉行的信念，是我们对于人性永恒的尊严的信念，这种人性尊严是受着永恒的道德律和自然律支配的。

这个信念说明了我们对生活的整体看法。它无疑确立了造物主所给予

gifts of the Creator that are man's inalienable rights, and that make all men equal in His sight.

In the light of this equality, we know that the virtues most cherished by free people—love of truth, pride of work, devotion to country—all are treasures equally precious in the lives of the most humble and of the most exalted. The men who mine coal and fire furnaces and balance ledgers and turn lathes and pick cotton and heal the sick and plant corn—all serve as proudly, and as profitably, for America as the statesmen who draft treaties and the legislators who enact laws.

This faith rules our whole way of life. It decrees that we, the people, elect leaders not to rule but to serve. It asserts that we have the right to choice of our own work and to the reward of our own toil. It inspires the initiative that makes our productivity the wonder of the world. And it warns that any man who seeks to deny equality among all his brothers betrays the spirit of the free and invites the mockery of the tyrant.

It is because we, all of us, hold to these principles that the political changes accomplished this day do not imply turbulence, upheaval or disorder. Rather this change expresses a purpose of strengthening our dedication and devotion to the precepts of our founding documents, a conscious renewal of faith in our country and in the watchfulness of a Divine Providence.

The enemies of this faith know no god but force, no devotion but its use. They tutor men in treason. They feed upon the hunger of others. Whatever defies them, they torture, especially the truth.

Here, then, is joined no argument between slightly differing philosophies. This conflict strikes directly at the faith of our fathers and the lives of our sons. No principle or treasure that we hold, from the spiritual knowledge of our free schools and churches to the creative magic of free labor and capital, nothing lies safely beyond the reach of this struggle.

Freedom is pitted against slavery; lightness against the dark.

The faith we hold belongs not to us alone but to the free of all the world. This common bond binds the grower of rice in Burma and the planter of wheat in Iowa, the shepherd in southern Italy and the mountaineer in the Andes. It

德怀特·艾森豪威尔
Dwight Eisenhower

人类的那些礼物,即人类各种不能予以剥夺的权利,它使得所有人在上帝面前一律平等。

在这平等的原则中,我们知道,最为自由人所珍爱的是那些美德——爱好真理、以工作为荣、献身国家。这些美德不论是在最卑微的人还是在最高尚的人的生活中,都同样是珍贵的品质。矿工、锅炉工、石匠、车工、棉农、医生和病人以及农民,这些人都和草拟条约的政治家或制定法律的议员一样,同样骄傲地尽心地为美国服务。

这个信念支配着我们整个生活方式。据此信念,人民选举领袖不是为了让他们来统治,而是让他们来服务。它确定我们有选择工作的权利和享受自己劳动所得的权利。它激励着我们的进取精神,使我们的生产力成为世界的奇迹。它也警告我们,企图否定同胞间的平等权利的任何人,都违背了自由的精神,并被人嘲讽为暴君。

因为我们大家都坚守这些原则,今天所完成的政治变革才不至于造成混乱和忧患。相反,这种政治变革的目的是加强我们的奉献以及对所建立的奉献精神的忠诚,并且有意识地重新恢复对国家的信心以及对于上帝监护的信念。

这种信念的敌人是,只知道力量,却忽视上帝的存在,而且吝于奉献,只知使用武力。他们教唆人们叛国,他们垂饵诱惑,对于任何妨碍他们的事物,特别是真理,必定要予以抹杀。

观念上的巨大差异是会引起争论的。这种冲突会直接损伤我们先辈的信念,而且会威胁我们子孙后代的生活。我们所持有的任何原则和财富,从我们在自由的学校和教堂中所领受的精神和知识,到自由劳动和自由资本创造的魔力,无一能安全地逃脱这种争斗。

自由与奴隶制是对立的,光明与黑暗是对立的。

我们所坚持的信念不只属于我们自己,也属于世界上所有的自由人民。这一共同的纽带联结了缅甸的种稻人和爱荷华州的种麦人,南意大利的牧羊人和安第斯山脉的山地人。它把普通人的尊严赐给了那些战死在印度支那

confers a common dignity upon the French soldier who dies in Indo-China, the British soldier killed in Malaya, the American life given in Korea.

We know, beyond this, that we are linked to all free peoples not merely by a noble idea but by a simple need. No free people can for long cling to any privilege or enjoy any safety in economic solitude. For all our own material might, even we need markets in the world for the surpluses of our farms and our factories. Equally, we need for these same farms and factories vital materials and products of distant lands. This basic law of interdependence, so manifest in the commerce of peace, applies with thousand-fold intensity in the event of war.

So we are persuaded by necessity and by belief that the strength of all free peoples lies in unity; their danger, in discord.

To produce this unity, to meet the challenge of our time, destiny has laid upon our country the responsibility of the free world's leadership.

So it is proper that we assure our friends once again that, in the discharge of this responsibility, we Americans know and we observe the difference between world leadership and imperialism; between firmness and truculence; between a thoughtfully calculated goal and spasmodic reaction to the stimulus of emergencies.

We wish our friends the world over to know this above all: we face the threat—not with dread and confusion—but with confidence and conviction.

We feel this moral strength because we know that we are not helpless prisoners of history. We are free men. We shall remain free, never to be proven guilty of the one capital offense against freedom, a lack of stanch faith.

In pleading our just cause before the bar of history and in pressing our labor for world peace, we shall be guided by certain fixed principles.

These principles are:

(1) Abhorring war as a chosen way to balk the purposes of those who threaten us, we hold it to be the first task of statesmanship to develop the strength that will deter the forces of aggression and promote the conditions of peace. For, as it must be the supreme purpose of all free men, so it must be the dedication of their leaders, to save humanity from preying upon itself.

In the light of this principle, we stand ready to engage with any and all others

德怀特·艾森豪威尔

的法国士兵、战死在马来亚的英国士兵以及在朝鲜被夺去生命的美国人。

此外我们也知道,我们与所有自由人民的联系并不只依赖于一个高尚的理想,且依赖于简单的需要。在经济孤立的情况下,没有一个自由民族能够永远拥有特权并获得安全,即使以我们现有的物质力量,我们仍需要在世界市场上销售剩余的农工产品,同样,我们也需要来自远方的重要的农工材料及产品。这种相互依赖的基本法则,在和平时代的贸易中就显出了意义,在战时更具有了千百倍的重要性。

因此,我们已被需要和信念所劝服,以至所有自由世界的力量都要团结一致,我们之所以遭受到危险是由于内部的不和。

为了团结一致和应付时代的挑战,命运已把领导自由世界的责任赋予了我国。

因此,我们再次向我们的朋友保证,在履行这个职责时,我们美国人知道而且也看到世界之领导地位和帝国主义之间的不同、强硬与好战之间的不同、筹划周到的目标与对紧急情况刺激而产生的冲动性反应之间的不同。

我们希望全世界的朋友都能知道这一点:当我们面对威胁时,我们不应恐惧和慌乱,而应满怀信心。

我们之所以会意识到这种道德力量,是因为我们自己并不是无助的历史囚犯,而是自由人。我们将永远维护自由,我们也将永不去犯那种违反自由、丧失信念的重大错误。

在我们面对历史的法庭,为我们的正义事业辩护,并致力于世界和平的时候,我们应当遵循一些既定的原则。

这些原则是:

(一)由于对战争的厌恶,我们将选择一种方式来阻止那些威胁我们的人。我们认为,政治家的首要任务是发展实力,以便阻挡侵略者的力量,创造促进和平的各种条件。因为既然它必定是所有自由人的至高无上的目的,他们的领导者也必须竭尽全力地把人类从无谓的牺牲中解救出来。

基于这个原则,我们准备同所有其他人共同努力,以消除国与国之间的

in joint effort to remove the causes of mutual fear and distrust among nations, so as to make possible drastic reduction of armaments. The sole requisites for undertaking such effort are that—in their purpose—they be aimed logically and honestly toward secure peace for all; and that—in their result—they provide methods by which every participating nation will prove good faith in carrying out its pledge.

(2) Realizing that common sense and common decency alike dictate the futility of appeasement, we shall never try to placate an aggressor by the false and wicked bargain of trading honor for security. Americans, indeed all free men, remember that in the final choice a soldier's pack is not so heavy a burden as a prisoner's chains.

(3) Knowing that only a United States that is strong and immensely productive can help defend freedom in our world, we view our Nation's strength and security as a trust upon which rests the hope of free men everywhere. It is the firm duty of each of our free citizens and of every free citizen everywhere to place the cause of his country before the comfort, the convenience of himself.

(4) Honoring the identity and the special heritage of each nation in the world, we shall never use our strength to try to impress upon another people our own cherished political and economic institutions.

(5) Assessing realistically the needs and capacities of proven friends of freedom, we shall strive to help them to achieve their own security and well-being. Likewise, we shall count upon them to assume, within the limits of their resources, their full and just burdens in the common defense of freedom.

(6) Recognizing economic health as an indispensable basis of military strength and the free world's peace, we shall strive to foster everywhere, and to practice ourselves, policies that encourage productivity and profitable trade. For the impoverishment of any single people in the world means danger to the well-being of all other peoples.

(7) Appreciating that economic need, military security and political wisdom combine to suggest regional groupings of free peoples, we hope, within the framework of the United Nations, to help strengthen such special bonds the world over. The nature of these ties must vary with the different problems of

相互恐惧和猜疑，使大规模的裁减军备成为可能。然而，完成这项任务的唯一先决条件是，在目标方面，他们必须合理而且真诚地为人类谋求和平；在结果方面，他们需提供方法，使每一参加国都有足够的信心履行诺言。

（二）不论从常识还是从常理来看，我们都要认清姑息是毫无用处的，我们不应为了安抚侵略者就以错误和邪恶地出卖荣誉来换取安全。美国人，实际上也是所有自由的人都要记住，在最后的选择中，一个士兵的背包并不像一个囚犯的锁链那样沉重。

（三）我们必须知道，只有一个强大且物产丰富的美国，才能够协助维护世界的自由。因此，我们认为我国的力量与安全，乃是世界各地自由人们真诚的希望寄托。美国的每一位自由公民以及世界上每一位自由公民不可推卸的义务，就是以他们国家的事业为重，然后再求个人的舒适。

（四）我们要尊重世界上每一个国家的认同精神以及特有的传统，且永远不会以我们的力量试图把我们所珍视的政治和经济制度强加于其他民族身上。

（五）在确切地评价那些已经证明是自由之友的国家的需要和能力的基础上，我们将努力帮助它们得到安全和福祉。同样，我们也期待着它们能在现有的资源下，充分而且适当地担负起共同保卫自由的任务。

（六）在认识到经济健全乃是发展军事力量以及促进自由世界和平的重要基础之后，我们将努力帮助各地促进并实施那些能够鼓励生产和有利于贸易的政策。因为世界上任何民族的贫穷都会构成对其他民族幸福的威胁。

（七）我们懂得经济需要、军事安全以及政治哲学等因素会显示出自由国家的多种区域组合，但我们希望在联合国框架内帮助加强全世界各地的这种特殊的结合。然而，这种结合的性质，必须因不同区域的不同问题而有所不同。

different areas.

In the Western Hemisphere, we enthusiastically join with all our neighbors in the work of perfecting a community of fraternal trust and common purpose.

In Europe, we ask that enlightened and inspired leaders of the Western nations strive with renewed vigor to make the unity of their peoples a reality. Only as free Europe unitedly marshals its strength can it effectively safeguard, even with our help, its spiritual and cultural heritage.

(8) Conceiving the defense of freedom, like freedom itself, to be one and indivisible, we hold all continents and peoples in equal regard and honor. We reject any insinuation that one race or another, one people or another, is in any sense inferior or expendable.

(9) Respecting the United Nations as the living sign of all people's hope for peace, we shall strive to make it not merely an eloquent symbol but an effective force. And in our quest for an honorable peace, we shall neither compromise, nor tire, nor ever cease.

By these rules of conduct, we hope to be known to all peoples.

By their observance, an earth of peace may become not a vision but a fact.

This hope—this supreme aspiration—must rule the way we live.

We must be ready to dare all for our country. For history does not long entrust the care of freedom to the weak or the timid. We must acquire proficiency in defense and display stamina in purpose.

We must be willing, individually and as a Nation, to accept whatever sacrifices may be required of us. A people that values its privileges above its principles soon loses both.

These basic precepts are not lofty abstractions, far removed from matters of daily living. They are laws of spiritual strength that generate and define our material strength. Patriotism means equipped forces and a prepared citizenry. Moral stamina means more energy and more productivity, on the farm and in the factory. Love of liberty means the guarding of every resource that makes freedom possible—from the sanctity of our families and the wealth of our soil to the genius of our scientists.

And so each citizen plays an indispensable role. The productivity of our

德怀特·艾森豪威尔
Dwight Eisenhower

在西半球,我们将积极联合所有邻国共同建立一个兄弟般相互信任以及拥有共同目标的社会。

在欧洲,我们请求西欧各国那些开明并具有感召力的领袖们,重新努力使其国民团结一致。只有当自由欧洲团结一致发挥力量时,它才能安全,并在我们的援助下,保卫自己的精神与文化遗产。

(八)鉴于维护自由与自由本身是那样不可分割的整体,我们对各大洲及各民族予以同等的重视和尊敬。我们拒绝任何有关一个种族或另一种族、一国人民或另一国人民在任何意义上是较为低劣的或可作为牺牲品的观点。

(九)尊重联合国,把它看成是所有人民谋求和平的希望之标志,我们将使它不仅仅成为雄辩的象征,而且要使它成为具有实质性的力量,我们在寻求光荣的和平中,既不妥协,也不气馁,更不会止步不前。

我们希望所有民族都能知道这些行为准则。
遵循这些准则,一个和平世界便不会只是理想而是事实。
这种希望,这种至高无上的志向,必定会支配我们的生活道路。
我们必须为我们的国家担当一种风险,因为历史不会把长期捍卫自由的重任交托给弱者和懦夫,我们必须在防务上精益求精,在意志上保持活力。

无论就个人还是就国家而言,我们都必须情愿做出需要我们做出的牺牲,一个把本身的利益看得超过原则的民族,很快就会两者皆失。

这些基本原则并不是与日常事务脱节的抽象概念,它们是精神力量的法则,这些精神力量产生并规定了我们的物质力量。爱国心意味着配备齐全的部队和具有充分准备的人民;道德的持久力意味着在农场和工厂里有更多的能力和更大的生产力;爱好自由意味着保护每一种能使自由成为可能的来源——从家庭的神圣义务、土地的丰富资源到天才的科学家。

因此,每一个公民都扮演着一个不可缺少的角色,我们的头脑、双手,

heads, our hands, and our hearts is the source of all the strength we can command, for both the enrichment of our lives and the winning of the peace.

No person, no home, no community can be beyond the reach of this call. We are summoned to act in wisdom and in conscience, to work with industry, to teach with persuasion, to preach with conviction, to weigh our every deed with care and with compassion. For this truth must be clear before us: whatever America hopes to bring to pass in the world must first come to pass in the heart of America.

The peace we seek, then, is nothing less than the practice and fulfillment of our whole faith among ourselves and in our dealings with others. This signifies more than the stilling of guns, easing the sorrow of war. More than escape from death, it is a way of life. More than a haven for the weary, it is a hope for the brave.

This is the hope that beckons us onward in this century of trial. This is the work that awaits us all, to be done with bravery, with charity, and with prayer to Almighty God.

Dwight Eisenhower
Second Inaugural Address

January 21, 1957

THE PRICE OF PEACE

Mr. Chairman, Mr. Vice President, Mr. Chief Justice, Mr. Speaker, members of my family and friends, my countrymen, and the friends of my country, wherever they may be, we meet again, as upon a like moment four years ago, and again you have witnessed my solemn oath of service to you.

德怀特·艾森豪威尔
Dwight Eisenhower

以及我们的精神生产力,不论是为了使我们的生活富裕,还是为了赢得和平,都是我们所能支配的一切力量的来源。

没有一个人,没有一个家庭,没有一个社会不是在这个责任范围之内为我们所召唤。我们一定要凭借着良知和智慧行事,勤奋地工作,谆谆地善诱他人,以正确的观点来传道,谨慎地并带有情感地衡量我们的每一行动,因为这一真理必须很明确地为大家所了解:凡是美国希望在世界上能够实现的事情,必须首先在美国人的心目中实现。

我们所追求的和平,不过是我们以及与我们有关的其他人之间的整个信念的实现。其意义不仅仅是止住炮声,安抚由战争带来的悲痛,不仅仅是避免死亡,它也是一种生活方式,不仅仅是疲惫者的安息所,它也是勇敢者的希望。

正是这个希望在向我们招手,呼唤着我们在这个忧患重重的世纪里继续向前迈进。这是一个有待于我们大家本着果敢、宽容及对全能的上帝的祈祷来共同完成的事业。

艾森豪威尔总统第二次就职演说*

1957年1月21日

和平的代价

主席先生、副总统先生、首席大法官先生、议长先生、诸位亲友、同胞们、各地的朋友们,我们又见面了,就像四年前的此刻一样,你们再度目睹了本人庄严地宣誓为大家服务的典礼。

---

* 本篇有删节。

I, too, am a witness, today testifying in your name to the principles and purposes to which we, as a people, are pledged.

Before all else, we seek, upon our common labor as a nation, the blessings of Almighty God. And the hopes in our hearts fashion the deepest prayers of our whole people.

May we pursue the right—without self-righteousness.

May we know unity—without conformity.

May we grow in strength—without pride in self.

May we, in our dealings with all peoples of the earth, ever speak truth and serve justice.

And so shall America—in the sight of all men of good will—prove true to the honorable purposes that bind and rule us as a people in all this time of trial through which we pass.

We live in a land of plenty, but rarely has this earth known such peril as today.

In our nation work and wealth abound. Our population grows. Commerce crowds our rivers and rails, our skies, harbors, and highways. Our soil is fertile, our agriculture productive. The air rings with the song of our industry—rolling mills and blast furnaces, dynamos, dams, and assembly lines—the chorus of America the bountiful.

This is our home—yet this is not the whole of our world. For our world is where our full destiny lies—with men, of all people, and all nations, who are or would be free. And for them—and so for us—this is no time of ease or of rest.

In too much of the earth there is want, discord, danger. New forces and new nations stir and strive across the earth, with power to bring, by their fate, great good or great evil to the free world's future. From the deserts of North Africa to the islands of the South Pacific one third of all mankind has entered upon an historic struggle for a new freedom; freedom from grinding poverty. Across all continents, nearly a billion people seek, sometimes almost in desperation, for the skills and knowledge and assistance by which they may satisfy from their own resources, the material wants common to all mankind.

No nation, however old or great, escapes this tempest of change and turmoil.

德怀特·艾森豪威尔
Dwight Eisenhower

今天，我本人也是一位见证人，以你们的名义证明我们作为一个民族，对原则以及目标所做的承诺。

首先，我们依靠全民族的共同努力，寻求全能上帝的祝福。我们内心的这些希望凝结着我们全体人民的最深切的祈祷。

愿我们追求正义而不自以为是。
愿我们懂得在求同存异的基础上保持团结。
愿我们强大而不自傲。
愿我们在与世界各民族交往时，永远说真话，永远主持正义。

这样美国将在所有善意的人的面前证明，它对各项光荣的目标是忠诚的。在我们所经历的充满考验的整个时代里，我们作为一个民族受到这些目标的约束和支配。

我们生活在富饶的土地上，但这儿的人很少经历今天这样的危险。[1]

我们的国家有充分的人力和物质财富，我们的人口日渐增多。商业活动充塞了我们的河流、铁路、天空、港口和公路。我们的土地肥沃，我们的农产品丰盛。天空中鸣奏着我们的工业凯歌，轧钢机、鼓风炉、发电机、水坝以及装备线的声响组合成美国富强之邦的大合唱。

这就是我们的家园，然而这并不是我们的全部世界。因为我们的世界是我们整个命运依托的地方，也是所有自由和即将获得自由的人们与民族的命运依托。为了他们，同样也为了我们，现在还不是安逸和休闲的时候。

世界上还有很多的地方存在着贫困、不和谐和危险。新势力和新国家正遍布于和奋斗在整个地球。它们利用自己的力量，凭借机遇，给自由世界的未来带来更大的利益或更大的灾祸。从北非的沙漠到南太平洋的岛屿，有三分之一的人类开始为摆脱贫困、争取新的自由而进行历史性的努力。遍及大陆的近十亿人正在寻求技术、知识和援助，为此有时甚至不顾一切，以便能够运用自己的资源来满足所有人类的共同需要。

任何国家，不论是古老的还是强大的，都无法逃避这一场动乱的风暴。

---

[1]指与苏联的对抗。

Some, impoverished by the recent World War, seek to restore their means of livelihood. In the heart of Europe, Germany still stands tragically divided. So is the whole continent divided. And so, too, is all the world.

We look upon this shaken earth, and we declare our firm and fixed purpose—the building of a peace with justice in a world where moral law prevails.

The building of such a peace is a bold and solemn purpose. To proclaim it is easy. To serve it will be hard. And to attain it, we must be aware of its full meaning—and ready to pay its full price.

We know clearly what we seek, and why.

We seek peace, knowing that peace is the climate of freedom. And now, as in no other age, we seek it because we have been warned, by the power of modern weapons, that peace may be the only climate possible for human life itself.

Yet this peace we seek cannot be born of fear alone: it must be rooted in the lives of nations. There must be justice, sensed and shared by all peoples, for, without justice the world can know only a tense and unstable truce. There must be law, steadily invoked and respected by all nations, for without law, the world promises only such meager justice as the pity of the strong upon the weak. But the law of which we speak, comprehending the values of freedom, affirms the equality of all nations, great and small.

Splendid as can be the blessings of such a peace, high will be its cost: in toil patiently sustained, in help honorably given, in sacrifice calmly borne.

We are called to meet the price of this peace.

To counter the threat of those who seek to rule by force, we must pay the costs of our own needed military strength, and help to build the security of others.

We must use our skills and knowledge and, at times, our substance, to help others rise from misery, however far the scene of suffering may be from our shores. For wherever in the world a people knows desperate want, there must appear at least the spark of hope, the hope of progress—or there will surely rise at last the flames of conflict.

We recognize and accept our own deep involvement in the destiny of men

德怀特·艾森豪威尔
Dwight Eisenhower

有些被新近的世界大战摧残为贫困的国家，正在设法恢复其生存手段。在欧洲的心脏地带，德国仍处在悲剧性的分裂状态，整个欧洲大陆也同样如此，甚至整个世界也是如此。

我们注视着这一受到震撼的世界，并且宣告我们坚定不移的目标：在这个实行道德和法律的世界中以公正来建立和平。

建立这样一种和平，是一个无畏而严肃的目标。爱好和平说来容易而做来难，而且要达到这个目标，我们必须完全理解它的含义，并且准备为之付出全部代价。

我们十分明白我们所追求的是什么，以及为什么要追求。

我们寻求和平，是因为我们知道和平是自由的基础。而且在现代，与其他时代不同，我们寻求和平是因为我们已被现代武器的威力所警告，和平可能是人类生活本身唯一的可依赖的环境。

然而，我们寻求的这种和平，不能只是因恐惧而产生，它必须深植于各国人民的心目中。必须有一种为所有的世人所感受和分享的正义。因为，没有正义，这个世界只能处于一种紧张而不稳定的暂时休战状态。必须有一种法律并能被所有国家坚决保护和尊重，因为没有这样一种法律，这个世界就只会有那种强者怜悯弱者的无力的正义。而我们所说的具有自由的全部价值的法律，就是要确保所有大小国家一律平等。

这样一种和平能够产生辉煌壮丽的幸福，但它的代价也必定是相当高的，要坚韧地忍受辛劳，正直地给予协助，安然地做出牺牲。

我们被召唤来偿付这种和平的代价。

为对付那些试图用武力统治人们的威胁，我们必须不惜代价建立自己必要的军事力量，并协助其他国家建立安全体系。

不论痛苦发生在世界的哪个地方，我们必须运用我们的技术和知识，有时是物资，来协助其他国家在痛苦和贫困中站起来。因为在世界上的任何地方，一个民族只要知道什么是自己热切需要的，就会满怀希望，一种进步的希望，最终就必定会燃起抗争的烈焰。

我们承认并且接受，各地人的命运与我们息息相关。所以，我们保证尊

everywhere. We are accordingly pledged to honor, and to strive to fortify, the authority of the United Nations. For in that body rests the best hope of our age for the assertion of that law by which all nations may live in dignity.

And, beyond this general resolve, we are called to act a responsible role in the world's great concerns or conflicts—whether they touch upon the affairs of a vast region, the fate of an island in the Pacific, or the use of a canal in the Middle East. Only in respecting the hopes and cultures of others will we practice the equality of all nations. Only as we show willingness and wisdom in giving counsel—in receiving counsel—and in sharing burdens, will we wisely perform the work of peace.

For one truth must rule all we think and all we do. No people can live to itself alone. The unity of all who dwell in freedom is their only sure defense. The economic need of all nations—in mutual dependence—makes isolation an impossibility; not even America's prosperity could long survive if other nations did not also prosper. No nation can longer be a fortress, lone and strong and safe. And any people, seeking such shelter for themselves, can now build only their own prison.

Our pledge to these principles is constant, because we believe in their rightness.

We do not fear this world of change. America is no stranger to much of its spirit. Everywhere we see the seeds of the same growth that America itself has known. The American experiment has, for generations, fired the passion and the courage of millions elsewhere seeking freedom, equality, and opportunity. And the American story of material progress has helped excite the longing of all needy peoples for some satisfaction of their human wants. These hopes that we have helped to inspire, we can help to fulfill.

In this confidence, we speak plainly to all peoples.

We cherish our friendship with all nations that are or would be free. We respect, no less, their independence. And when, in time of want or peril, they ask our help, they may honorably receive it; for we no more seek to buy their sovereignty than we would sell our own. Sovereignty is never bartered among

德怀特·艾森豪威尔
Dwight Eisenhower

重并且努力去加强联合国的权威。因为在这个机构中，有着我们这一代人最美好的希望，它所制定的章程使所有国家都生存在尊严之中。

除了这种总体的决心之外，我们被召唤着在世界重大事件或者冲突中扮演一个负责任的角色，不论是涉及大地区的事务、太平洋岛屿的命运，还是中东一条运河[1]的使用，只有尊重别国的愿望和文化，我们才能实践国与国之间的平等原则。只有在提出忠告、接受建议以及分担责任时，显示出我们的自觉和智慧，我们才能明智地履行和平的任务。

有一条真理规范着我们所想的一切以及我们所做的一切。没有一个民族能够单独存在，团结所有依赖自由的人民，才是唯一可靠的防卫。各国经济需求上的相互依赖使孤立成为不可能。如果别的国家不繁荣，那么恐迫连美国的繁荣也无法长久持续下去。单独一个国家已不再可能成为一座孤独、强大、安全的堡垒。甚至为自己寻求建立这种堡垒的任何民族，到头来也只能为自己建立牢笼。

我们奉行这些原则的誓言是永恒不变的，因为我们相信这些原则的正确性。

我们不怕这个世界有所变化，美国对其精神大多并不陌生。我们到处可见曾使美国本身成长的同样的种子。几代人以来，美国的经验已为各地追求自由、平等和机会的数百万人点燃了热情和勇气的火焰。而且美国物质发展的事迹，已有助于激起所有贫穷者的欲望，以力图稍微满足他们作为人的各种需求。我们既然已经帮助他们激起这些希望，我们也能协助他们实现这些希望。

我们怀着这种信心，坦诚地向所有民族宣布：

我们珍惜同所有自由国家或即将获得自由的国家的友谊，我们同样尊重它们的独立。在它们因贫困和面临危险向我们求援时，它们将不失尊严地得到援助。就如同我们不出卖我们自己的主权一样，我们也决不收买它们的主权。主权绝不会成为自由人之间的交易。

---

[1]指苏伊士运河。1956年埃及将其收归国有。

freemen.

We honor the aspirations of those nations which, now captive, long for freedom. We seek neither their military alliance nor any artificial imitation of our society. And they can know the warmth of the welcome that awaits them when, as must be, they join again the ranks of freedom.

We honor, no less in this divided world than in a less tormented time, the people of Russia. We do not dread, rather do we welcome, their progress in education and industry. We wish them success in their demands for more intellectual freedom, greater security before their own laws, fuller enjoyment of the rewards of their own toil. For as such things come to pass, the more certain will be the coming of that day when our peoples may freely meet in friendship.

So we voice our hope and our belief that we can help to heal this divided world. Thus may the nations cease to live in trembling before the menace of force. Thus may the weight of fear and the weight of arms be taken from the burdened shoulders of mankind.

This, nothing less, is the labor to which we are called and our strength dedicated.

And so the prayer of our people carries far beyond our own frontiers, to the wide world of our duty and our destiny.

May the light of freedom, coming to all darkened lands, flame brightly—until at last the darkness is no more.

May the turbulence of our age yield to a true time of peace, when men and nations shall share a life that honors the dignity of each, the brotherhood of all.

德怀特·艾森豪威尔
Dwight Eisenhower

我们尊重那些现在正被奴役但企盼自由的民族的愿望。我们既不与它们结成军事同盟，也不要求它们对我们的社会进行人为的模仿，而且在它们再度加入自由的行列中来时，它们就能够知道等待着它们的是热忱的欢迎。

在这个分崩离析的世界里，我们仍会像在较为安定的时代那样尊敬俄罗斯人民。我们并不畏惧而是欢迎他们在教育和工业上的进步。我们希望他们有更多的知识自由，在法律面前有更多的安全感，对自己辛勤劳作的报酬有更充分的享受。因为只要这样，我们两国在友谊中自由交往的日子就为期不远了。

我们表达了我们的希望和信念，我们能够弥合这一分裂的世界，唯有如此，各国人民才能不再胆战心惊地生活在武力的威胁之中，由此才能把恐惧和武力的重负从全人类肩上卸下来。

这就是我们被呼唤运用我们的力量完成的一项不折不扣的艰辛工作。

因此，愿我们人民的祈祷，能跨越我们的疆界，传到我们的职责和命运所维系的广阔世界。

愿自由之光，普照一切黑暗的角落，燃起明亮的火焰，直到最终黑暗消失为止。

愿我们动乱的时代为一个真正和平的时代所取代，那时人类和所有国家都享有一种彼此尊重、亲如兄弟的生活。

约翰·肯尼迪
John Kennedy

约翰·肯尼迪（John Kennedy）

生平简介 >>

约翰·肯尼迪是美国第三十五任总统。他于1917年5月29日出生在马萨诸塞州，是第一位出生于20世纪的总统。他毕业于哈佛大学。在第二次世界大战中，他参加了海军，成为一名上尉军官。1947年进入国会众议院，1952年成为参议院议员。

1960年他作为民主党的总统候选人，以"新边疆"的口号参加竞选，并击败共和党候选人尼克松，成为美国有史以来第一位信奉天主教的总统。他的就职演说被认为是美国历史上最精彩的总统就职演说之一，其中有一句最著名的话是："不要问你的国家愿为你做些什么，而要问你愿为你的国家做些什么。"他在最后一刻把讲话稿中的"愿"字改为"能"字。

肯尼迪在任期间，美国在空间领域取得了较大的进展。在外交方面，他成功地处理了1962年的古巴导弹危机，并与苏联达成一项禁止在大气层、空间和水下进行核试验的协议，这是自冷战开始以来缔结的第一个武器控制的条约。

1963年11月22日，当他和夫人乘车经过得克萨斯州的达拉斯市区时，遭到枪击身亡，年仅46岁。

美国历届总统就职演说
THE INAUGURAL ADDRESSES OF THE U.S. PRESIDENTS

John Kennedy
Inaugural Address

January 20, 1961

Vice President Johnson, Mr. Speaker, Mr. Chief Justice, President Eisenhower, Vice President Nixon, President Truman, reverend clergy, fellow citizens, we observe today not a victory of party, but a celebration of freedom—symbolizing an end, as well as a beginning—signifying renewal, as well as change. For I have sworn before you and Almighty God the same solemn oath our forebears prescribed nearly a century and three quarters ago.

The world is very different now. For man holds in his mortal hands the power to abolish all forms of human poverty and all forms of human life. And yet the same revolutionary beliefs for which our forebears fought are still at issue around the globe—the belief that the rights of man come not from the generosity of the state, but from the hand of God.

We dare not forget today that we are the heirs of that first revolution. Let the word go forth from this time and place, to friend and foe alike, that the torch has been passed to a new generation of Americans—born in this century, tempered by war, disciplined by a hard and bitter peace, proud of our ancient heritage—and unwilling to witness or permit the slow undoing of those human rights to which this Nation has always been committed, and to which we are committed today at home and around the world.

Let every nation know, whether it wishes us well or ill, that we shall pay any price, bear any burden, meet any hardship, support any friend, oppose any foe, in order to assure the survival and the success of liberty.

This much we pledge—and more.

To those old allies whose cultural and spiritual origins we share, we pledge the loyalty of faithful friends. United, there is little we cannot do in a host of

约翰·肯尼迪
John Kennedy

肯尼迪总统就职演说

1961年1月20日

首席大法官先生、艾森豪威尔总统、尼克松副总统、杜鲁门总统、牧师和各位公民们，我们没有把今天视为政党的胜利，而把它看成是自由的庆典。它象征着一个结束，也象征着一个开端。它表示更新，也表示变革。因为在诸位以及上帝面前，我宣读了我们的先辈在近175年前拟定的庄严誓言。

如今的世界已大不相同了，人类的巨手掌握着既能消灭人间的各种贫困，又能毁灭人间各种生活的力量。但是革命的信念与我们祖先为之奋斗的信念，即人的权利，不是来自国家的慷慨，而是来自上帝恩赐的信念，仍处在全球性的争辩之中。

今天，我们不敢忘记自己是第一次革命的后代。从此时此地开始，让我们的敌人和朋友听着，火炬已传给新一代的美国人，他们出生于本世纪，经过战火的考验，为艰难困苦与和平所锤炼，更以我们古老的传统而自豪，他们不愿目睹或听任我国一直维护的，而且今天仍在国内外维护的人权被逐渐地剥夺。

让每一个国家都知道，不管它希望我们繁荣还是衰败，我们将不惜任何代价，不惜承担任何责任，不惜应付一切困难，支持所有的朋友，反对任何的敌人，以确保自由的存在和成功。

这是我们所保证的，而且不止于此。

对那些在文化和精神方面跟我们同出一源的老盟友，我们保证给予忠实的朋友的忠诚。团结，将使我们在许多合作事业中无所不能。分裂，我

cooperative ventures. Divided, there is little we can do—for we dare not meet a powerful challenge at odds and split asunder.

To those new States whom we welcome to the ranks of the free, we pledge our word that one form of colonial control shall not have passed away merely to be replaced by a far more iron tyranny. We shall not always expect to find them supporting our view. But we shall always hope to find them strongly supporting their own freedom—and to remember that, in the past, those who foolishly sought power by riding the back of the tiger ended up inside.

To those peoples in the huts and villages across the globe struggling to break the bonds of mass misery, we pledge our best efforts to help them help themselves, for whatever period is required—not because the Communists may be doing it, not because we seek their votes, but because it is right. If a free society cannot help the many who are poor, it cannot save the few who are rich.

To our sister republics south of our border, we offer a special pledge—to convert our good words into good deeds—in a new alliance for progress—to assist free men and free governments in casting off the chains of poverty. But this peaceful revolution of hope cannot become the prey of hostile powers. Let all our neighbors know that we shall join with them to oppose aggression or subversion anywhere in the Americas. And let every other power know that this Hemisphere intends to remain the master of its own house.

To that world assembly of sovereign states, the United Nations, our last best hope in an age where the instruments of war have far outpaced the instruments of peace, we renew our pledge of support—to prevent it from becoming merely a forum for invective—to strengthen its shield of the new and the weak—and to enlarge the area in which its writ may run.

Finally, to those nations who would make themselves our adversary, we offer not a pledge but a request: that both sides begin anew the quest for peace, before the dark powers of destruction unleashed by science engulf all humanity in planned or accidental self-destruction.

We dare not tempt them with weakness. For only when our arms are sufficient beyond doubt can we be certain beyond doubt that they will never be employed.

约翰·肯尼迪
John Kennedy

们将毫无作为，因为我们在争执和四分五裂的状态下，是不敢面对强有力的挑战的。

我们欢迎加入自由行列的新国家，对于它们，我们保证决不允许行将消逝的殖民地统治为一种更强的专制政权所取代。我们并不指望总是看到它们强有力地支持我们的观点，但是我们将永远希望它们强有力地维护自己的自由，并切记，在历史上，凡是愚蠢地骑在虎背上谋求权力的人，最终将被老虎吃掉。

对于地球上那些居住在茅舍和山谷中、正竭力挣脱悲惨处境的民族，我们保证尽最大的努力助其自救，不管这需要的时间有多长——之所以这样做，并不是因为共产主义者可能这样做，不是因为我们想谋求他们的支持，而是因为这是正确的。如果一个自由的社会不能帮助众多穷人的话，它也就无法保全少数富人。

对位于我们南面的姐妹共和国，我们也做出一项特别的保证：把我们的良言化作善行，在争取进步的新联盟中帮助自由的人们以及自由的政府摆脱贫困的枷锁。但是，这种充满希望的和平革命决不可以成为敌对国家的牺牲品。我们要让所有的邻国都知道，我们将与它们团结起来，以反对对美洲的任何地区进行的侵略和颠覆活动，并且也要让其他国家都知道，这个半球的人想永远做自己的主人。

联合国是主权国家的世界性议事场所，是我们在这个战争手段远胜于和平手段的年代里最后的寄托。因此，我们要重申我们对联合国的支持——防止它变成仅供谩骂的场所，加强它对新兴国家和弱国的保护，以及扩大它可以行使权力的领域。

最后，对那些与我们为敌的国家，我们并不提供保证，而是要提出要求：在科学释放出了可怕的破坏力量，把全人类卷入有预谋或意外的自我毁灭的深渊之前，让我们双方都重新开始对和平的探求。

我们不敢以示弱去诱惑他们。因为只有在我们的武力足够强大时，我们才能真正有把握地确信永不使用武力。

But neither can two great and powerful groups of nations take comfort from our present course—both sides overburdened by the cost of modern weapons, both rightly alarmed by the steady spread of the deadly atom, yet both racing to alter that uncertain balance of terror that stays the hand of mankind's final war.

So let us begin anew—remembering on both sides that civility is not a sign of weakness, and sincerity is always subject to proof. Let us never negotiate out of fear. But let us never fear to negotiate.

Let both sides explore what problems unite us instead of belaboring those problems which divide us.

Let both sides, for the first time, formulate serious and precise proposals for the inspection and control of arms—and bring the absolute power to destroy other nations under the absolute control of all nations.

Let both sides seek to invoke the wonders of science instead of its terrors. Together let us explore the stars, conquer the deserts, eradicate disease, tap the ocean depths, and encourage the arts and commerce.

Let both sides unite to heed in all corners of the earth the command of Isaiah—to "undo the heavy burdens ... and to let the oppressed go free."

And if a beachhead of cooperation may push back the jungle of suspicion, let both sides join in creating a new endeavor, not a new balance of power, but a new world of law, where the strong are just and the weak secure and the peace preserved.

All this will not be finished in the first 100 days. Nor will it be finished in the first 1,000 days, nor in the life of this Administration, nor even perhaps in our lifetime on this planet. But let us begin.

In your hands, my fellow citizens, more than in mine, will rest the final success or failure of our course. Since this country was founded, each generation of Americans has been summoned to give testimony to its national loyalty. The graves of young Americans who answered the call to service surround the globe.

Now the trumpet summons us again—not as a call to bear arms, though arms we need; not as a call to battle, though embattled we are—but a call to bear the burden of a long twilight struggle, year in and year out, "rejoicing in hope, patient in tribulation"—a struggle against the common enemies of man:

约翰·肯尼迪
John Kennedy

但是，两个强大的国家集团都不能对当前趋势放心，双方都被现代武器的开支压得透不过气来，双方都惊恐于致命的原子弹不断扩散，然而双方却仍然竞相打破阻止人类最后战争之不确定的恐怖的平衡。

因此，让我们双方重新开始。双方都要记住，谦恭并不是软弱，诚意总是要得到证明。"我们决不因为害怕而谈判，我们也决不害怕谈判。"

让双方都来探讨把我们团结在一起，而不是致力于分裂的东西是什么。

让双方首先提出严格而确定的提案，以监督和控制军备，使摧毁他国的绝对力量置于所有国家的绝对控制之下。

让双方都试图探寻科学的奥秘，而不是科学的恐怖。让我们共同探究星球，治理沙漠，消灭疾病，开发海底资源，鼓励艺术和商业发展。

让双方联合一致，在世界的每一角落都奉行以赛亚的训诫——"解下轭上的索，使被欺压的得自由"[1]。

如果在一个合作的滩头能够逐退猜疑的浪潮，那么就让双方共同做一次新的尝试，不是建立新的力量平衡，而是建立一个新的法治世界。在这里，强者是公正的，弱者是安全的，和平能够得到维持。

所有这些都不可能在第一个百日内完成，也不可能在第一个千日内完成，或者在本届政府任期内完成，甚至不可能在我们有生之年完成这项计划。但是让我们从现在开始。

同胞们，我们事业的最后成功或者失败是掌握在你们手里，而不是在我的手里。自从建国以来，每一代美国人都被召唤去表明对他的国家的忠诚。那些响应召唤而献身的年轻的美国人的坟墓遍布全球。

现在号角又吹响了，它不是在召唤我们拿起武器，尽管我们需要武器；不是召唤我们去作战，尽管我们已准备应战。它召唤我们肩负起持久和胜负未分的斗争，年复一年，"在希望中欢欣，在苦难中经受考验"，这是

[1]引自《圣经·旧约》以赛亚书第五十八章第六节。

tyranny, poverty, disease, and war itself.

Can we forge against these enemies a grand and global alliance, North and South, East and West, that can assure a more fruitful life for all mankind? Will you join in that historic effort?

In the long history of the world, only a few generations have been granted the role of defending freedom in its hour of maximum danger. I do not shrink from this responsibility—I welcome it. I do not believe that any of us would exchange places with any other people or any other generation. The energy, the faith, the devotion which we bring to this endeavor will light our country and all who serve it—and the glow from that fire can truly light the world.

And so, my fellow Americans: ask not what your country can do for you—ask what you can do for your country.

My fellow citizens of the world: ask not what America will do for you, but what together we can do for the freedom of man.

Finally, whether you are citizens of America or citizens of the world, ask of us the same high standards of strength and sacrifice which we ask of you. With a good conscience our only sure reward, with history the final judge of our deeds, let us go forth to lead the land we love, asking His blessing and His help, but knowing that here on earth God's work must truly be our own.

约翰·肯尼迪
John Kennedy

一场反对人类共同的敌人——专制、贫困、疾病和战争本身——的斗争。

为了对抗这些敌人,我们能够组成一个包括东南西北各方的全球性大联盟,以保证全人类享有更丰裕的生活吗?你们愿意加入这一历史性的努力中吗?

在悠久的世界历史中,只有少数几代人有机会在自由蒙受最大危险时,承担起保卫自由的任务。我不会因责任的重大而退却,我欢迎它。我不相信我们中的任何人愿意与其他人或任何其他时代的人交换位置。我们在这场努力中所付出的精力、信心以及贡献,将照亮我们的国家以及所有服务于它的人,而且由此火焰所发出的光焰必能照亮这个世界。

因此,我的美国同胞们,不要问你的国家能为你做些什么,而要问你能为你的国家做些什么。

全世界的公民们,不要问美国将为你们做些什么,而要问我们共同能为人类的自由做些什么。

最后,不论你是美国公民,还是其他国家的公民,请督促我们必定要达到我们向你们要求的崇高的力量和牺牲精神的标准。我们唯一的报酬是问心无愧,我们行为的最后裁判者是历史。我们虽要祈求上帝的祝福和协助,但也要知道,在这个世界里,上帝的工作实际上就是我们自己的工作。让我们奋勇向前,去领导我们所热爱的祖国。

林登·约翰逊
Lyndon Johnson

林登·约翰逊（Lyndon Johnson）

生平简介 >>

林登·约翰逊是美国第三十六任总统。他于1908年8月27日出生在得克萨斯州。1930年毕业于得克萨斯州西南师范学院。1937年，当选为国会众议员。1948年，当选为国会参议员。在参议院工作仅3年，这位年轻的参议员就成为民主党领袖。

1960年，当约翰逊未能获得民主党总统候选人的提名时，他便接受了肯尼迪提名他为副总统的建议。1963年11月22日，肯尼迪遇刺身亡，他身为副总统旋即在达拉斯机场的"空军一号"总统专机的机舱里，宣誓就职。1964年又正式当选为总统。

在内政上，约翰逊总统提出了"伟大社会"的施政纲领。他在位期间，不遗余力地推行各项福利法案、民权法案、消灭贫穷法案和减税法。他著名的"向贫困开战"的口号，引导全国在生活富裕时考虑到饥饿和匮乏的棘手问题。但在外交上，他奉行前任总统所制定的政策，使越战不断升级，这一政策遭到国内外普遍反对。1968年，他宣布不再参与竞选。

1973年1月22日，他在得克萨斯州自己的牧场溘然长逝，享年64岁。

Lyndon Johnson
Inaugural Address

January 20, 1965

My fellow countrymen, on this occasion, the oath I have taken before you and before God is not mine alone, but ours together. We are one nation and one people. Our fate as a nation and our future as a people rest not upon one citizen, but upon all citizens.

This is the majesty and the meaning of this moment.

For every generation, there is a destiny. For some, history decides. For this generation, the choice must be our own.

Even now, a rocket moves toward Mars. It reminds us that the world will not be the same for our children, or even for ourselves in a short span of years. The next man to stand here will look out on a scene different from our own, because ours is a time of change—rapid and fantastic change bearing the secrets of nature, multiplying the nations, placing in uncertain hands new weapons for mastery and destruction, shaking old values, and uprooting old ways.

Our destiny in the midst of change will rest on the unchanged character of our people, and on their faith.

The American Covenant

They came here—the exile and the stranger, brave but frightened—to find a place where a man could be his own man. They made a covenant with this land. Conceived in justice, written in liberty, bound in union, it was meant one day to inspire the hopes of all mankind; and it binds us still. If we keep its terms, we shall flourish.

林登·约翰逊
Lyndon Johnson

约翰逊总统就职演说

1965年1月20日

同胞们,在这个重要时刻,我在上帝和你们面前所宣读的誓言并非我个人的,而是我们大家的。我们同住在一个国家,同属一个民族,国家的命运和民族的前途不能只靠一个公民的努力,而必须靠全体公民的共同努力。

这正是此时此刻的庄严及其意义之所在。

每一代人各有其命运,有些靠历史决定命运,至于我们这一代,命运必须由我们自己来选择。

此时此刻,一枚火箭正向火星飞去。[1]这个事情提醒我们,对我们的子孙以及我们本身而言,这个世界将在短短几年内发生巨大的变化。下一任总统站在这里时,他将看到与我们现在迥然不同的景象。因为我们正处在快速惊人的变革时期,自然的奥秘被揭示,国家的数目成倍增多,许多能征服、毁灭人类的新式武器掌握在不可靠的人手上,许多旧的价值观念在动摇、旧的生活方式在改变。

在这场变革中,我们的命运只有仰赖全国人民始终如一的性格和信念。

美国人的公约

我们的祖先——那些背井离乡的异乡人,勇敢但也受过惊吓的异乡人,来此寻求一块个人可以自主、自由生活的地方。他们和这块土地订下公约,公约的立意是公正,用自由书写,受团结的约束,它注定被用来激发全人类的希望。而且,它现在仍然约束着我们,只要我们遵照其条款,我们就

---

[1]1964年11月28日"水手四号"太空船发射升空,进行火星表面近距离的探测。

Justice and Change

First, justice was the promise that all who made the journey would share in the fruits of the land.

In a land of great wealth, families must not live in hopeless poverty. In a land rich in harvest, children just must not go hungry. In a land of healing miracles, neighbors must not suffer and die unattended. In a great land of learning and scholars, young people must be taught to read and write.

For the more than 30 years that I have served this Nation, I have believed that this injustice to our people, this waste of our resources, was our real enemy. For 30 years or more, with the resources I have had, I have vigilantly fought against it. I have learned, and I know, that it will not surrender easily.

But change has given us new weapons. Before this generation of Americans is finished, this enemy will not only retreat—it will be conquered.

Justice requires us to remember that when any citizen denies his fellow, saying, "His color is not mine," or "His beliefs are strange and different," in that moment he betrays America, though his forebears created this Nation.

Liberty and Change

Liberty was the second article of our covenant. It was self-government. It was our Bill of Rights. But it was more. America would be a place where each man could be proud to be himself: stretching his talents, rejoicing in his work, important in the life of his neighbors and his nation.

This has become more difficult in a world where change and growth seem to tower beyond the control and even the judgment of men. We must work to provide the knowledge and the surroundings which can enlarge the possibilities of every citizen.

一定能繁荣起来。[1]

公正与变革

公正是公约的首项，公正就是承认让所有迁徙到这里的人共享这块土地上的成果。

在这片富饶的土地上，绝不允许任何一个家庭生活于无望的贫困之中。在这片收获丰盛的土地上，绝不允许儿童挨冻受饿。在这片拥有神奇治愈力的土地上，绝不允许邻人痛苦、死亡而无人问津。在这片知识昌明、学者云集的伟大土地上，年轻人必须接受教育，能读会写。

为国家工作三十多年来，我一直认为不公正地待人和浪费资源是我们真正的敌人。三十多年来，我竭尽所能为消灭这些真正的敌人而奋斗，而且我知道也体会到，它们是不会被轻易消除的。

然而，社会的变化却给了我们新的武器。在这一代美国人的有生之年，这些敌人不但会退却，而且最终一定会被征服。

公正就是要我们牢记着：当任何一位公民拒绝承认他的同胞，宣称"他的肤色和我的不同"或是"他的信仰奇特怪异"，他说这种话的时候，他也就背叛了美国，即使他的祖先是这个国家的创建者。

自由与变革

自由是公约的第二项。它是自治。它是我们的权利法案。但并不止于此。美国是人人都会为自己的存在感到自豪的地方，在这里每个人都能施展自己的才能、愉快地工作、在国家和世人的生活中发挥重要的作用。

但是，在一个变化和发展已不是我们所能控制，同时甚至也超出人们的预料的世界里，前面所提到的事项已变得更为困难。所以，我们必须努力提供那种能增加每个公民成功机会的知识和环境。

---

[1] 概指某些南方政治领袖，如阿拉巴马州州长华莱士等，依旧不愿使黑人享有充分的平等自由。

The American covenant called on us to help show the way for the liberation of man. And that is today our goal. Thus, if as a nation there is much outside our control, as a people no stranger is outside our hope.

Change has brought new meaning to that old mission. We can never again stand aside, prideful in isolation. Terrific dangers and troubles that we once called "foreign" now constantly live among us. If American lives must end, and American treasure be spilled, in countries we barely know, that is the price that change has demanded of conviction and of our enduring covenant.

Think of our world as it looks from the rocket that is heading toward Mars. It is like a child's globe, hanging in space, the continents stuck to its side like colored maps. We are all fellow passengers on a dot of earth. And each of us, in the span of time, has really only a moment among our companions.

How incredible it is that in this fragile existence, we should hate and destroy one another. There are possibilities enough for all who will abandon mastery over others to pursue mastery over nature. There is world enough for all to seek their happiness in their own way.

Our Nation's course is abundantly clear. We aspire to nothing that belongs to others. We seek no dominion over our fellow man, but man's dominion over tyranny and misery.

But more is required. Men want to be a part of a common enterprise—a cause greater than themselves. Each of us must find a way to advance the purpose of the Nation, thus finding new purpose for ourselves. Without this, we shall become a nation of strangers.

Union and Change

The third article was union. To those who were small and few against the wilderness, the success of liberty demanded the strength of union. Two centuries of change have made this true again.

No longer need capitalist and worker, farmer and clerk, city and countryside, struggle to divide our bounty. By working shoulder to shoulder, together we can increase the bounty of all. We have discovered that every child who learns,

林登·约翰逊
Lyndon Johnson

美国公约要求我们帮助指出人类解放的途径，这也正是我们今天努力的目标。因此，作为一个国家，世界上我们无法控制的事情太多了；而作为一个民族，我们不会让任何人置身于我们的希望之外。

变革给过去的使命增添了新的意义。我们再也不能冷漠旁观，孤立自傲了。一度我们认为与自己"毫不相干"的危险与麻烦，现在却时时存在于我们中间。如果美国人必须在那些我们知之甚少的国度献出生命、倾注金钱，那便是变革所索取的代价，即我们的信念和我们不朽的公约所需付出的代价。

想想我们是从那艘正驶向火星的火箭上看我们居住的世界，它就好比儿童的地球仪，悬在太空中，依附在上面的许多陆地有如上了颜色的地图。我们都是这小小一块土地上的过客，在飞逝的时光中，我们每个人只是与各自的旅伴一起度过短暂的瞬间。

在这样脆弱的存在中，我们竟彼此仇恨、毁灭，这是多么不可思议？所有愿意放弃主宰他人的人，都有足够的机会来实现对自然的主宰。我坚信，海阔天空，人们总能以自己的方式找到幸福和快乐。

我们所要走的路非常明确，我们不奢求得到别人的东西，我们不企图去统辖我们的同胞，而是要让人类控制住暴政和苦难。

但是这样仍嫌不够。人们想要成为共同事业——比其本身更伟大的目标——的一分子，每个人就必须想方设法为实现国家的目标而奋斗，并为我们自己寻找一个新的目标。若不这样做，我们就会虽然同居一国而形同路人。

团结与变革

公约的第三项是团结。对那些在荒野中奋斗抵抗的弱小的人们而言，要成功地获得自由就需要团结的力量。两个世纪来的变革再度证明团结是正确的。

资本家和工人、农场主和农民、城市和乡村等再也不必为分配利益争斗。只要并肩协力工作，我们就能增进共同的利益。我们已经看到：每个受教育的儿童、每个工作的人，以及每个康复的病人，都像是添加在圣坛

every man who finds work, every sick body that is made whole—like a candle added to an altar—brightens the hope of all the faithful.

So let us reject any among us who seek to reopen old wounds and to rekindle old hatreds. They stand in the way of a seeking nation.

Let us now join reason to faith and action to experience, to transform our unity of interest into a unity of purpose. For the hour and the day and the time are here to achieve progress without strife, to achieve change without hatred—not without difference of opinion, but without the deep and abiding divisions which scar the union for generations.

The American Belief

Under this covenant of justice, liberty, and union we have become a nation—prosperous, great, and mighty. And we have kept our freedom. But we have no promise from God that our greatness will endure. We have been allowed by Him to seek greatness with the sweat of our hands and the strength of our spirit.

I do not believe that the Great Society is the ordered, changeless, and sterile battalion of the ants. It is the excitement of becoming—always becoming, trying, probing, falling, resting, and trying again—but always trying and always gaining.

In each generation, with toil and tears, we have had to earn our heritage again.

If we fail now, we shall have forgotten in abundance what we learned in hardship: that democracy rests on faith, that freedom asks more than it gives, and that the judgment of God is harshest on those who are most favored.

If we succeed, it will not be because of what we have, but it will be because of what we are; not because of what we own, but, rather because of what we believe.

For we are a nation of believers. Underneath the clamor of building and the rush of our day's pursuits, we are believers in justice and liberty and union, and in our own Union. We believe that every man must someday be free. And

上的蜡烛一样,照亮了所有忠诚于公约的人的希望。

所以,我们应该鄙弃我们中间任何企图使旧的创伤复发、旧恨重燃的人,因为他们会阻碍一个正在探索中前进的国家。

现在,让我们把理智和信仰结合起来,把行动和经验结合起来,使我们从利益一致转变到目标一致。在未来的时间里,我们要在没有冲突的情况下取得进步,在没有仇恨的情况下实现变革。当然,这并不是说不允许不同意见存在,而是应该消除在好几代人中都存在的伤害团结的那些根深蒂固的隔阂。

美国人的信仰

在以公正、自由、团结为宗旨的公约指导之下,我们的国家变得繁荣、伟大和强盛,而且我们还保持着自由。但是,我们并未从上帝那里获得保证——我们的伟大会经久不衰。然而上帝曾经容许我们用自己的双手和汗水,用精神上的力量去获得这种伟大。

我并不认为"伟大社会"应像蚁群那样安排有序、一成不变、了无生气。这是一种由"生成"带来的振奋——不停地变革、尝试、探索、失败、休整、再尝试,只要一直在尝试,总会有收获。

我们每一代都必须用我们的辛劳和汗水将我们的传统保持下去。

如果我们现在失败了,是因为我们在富裕中忘却了我们在困苦中学到的东西:民主建立在信仰之上,自由所要求的比它所给予的还多,上帝对那些最受恩泽的人所做的评判也最苛刻。

如果我们成功了,并不是因为我们已经具有了什么,而是因为我们是什么;不是因为我们拥有什么,而是因为我们信仰什么。

因为我们是一个有信仰的国家。在吵闹和日常事务的忙碌下,我们是公正、自由、团结及联邦的信徒。我们相信总有一天每个人都会获得自由,而且我们相信我们能够做到。

we believe in ourselves.

Our enemies have always made the same mistake. In my lifetime—in depression and in war—they have awaited our defeat. Each time, from the secret places of the American heart, came forth the faith they could not see or that they could not even imagine. It brought us victory. And it will again.

For this is what America is all about. It is the uncrossed desert and the unclimbed ridge. It is the star that is not reached and the harvest sleeping in the unplowed ground. Is our world gone? We say "Farewell." Is a new world coming? We welcome it—and we will bend it to the hopes of man.

To these trusted public servants and to my family and those close friends of mine who have followed me down a long, winding road, and to all the people of this Union and the world, I will repeat today what I said on that sorrowful day in November 1963: "I will lead and I will do the best I can."

But you must look within your own hearts to the old promises and to the old dream. They will lead you best of all.

For myself, I ask only, in the words of an ancient leader: "Give me now wisdom and knowledge, that I may go out and come in before this people: for who can judge this thy people, that is so great?"

林登·约翰逊
Lyndon Johnson

我们的敌人每次总是犯着相同的错误,在我的整个一生中——萧条时期和战争时期,他们一直都在等待着我们的失败,但每一回总会从美国人民内心深处涌出他们无法看到或难以想象的信仰。这种信仰带给了我们胜利,这种信仰将会再度带给我们胜利。

因为这就是美国。它是未经跨越的沙漠、未经攀登的峭壁。它是尚未企及的星辰,是沉睡在尚未耕耘的土地上的果实。我们的世界已经逝去了吗?我们对它道声"再见"。新的世界到来了吗?我们欢迎它,并将使它符合人类的希望。

对着这些受重托的公仆,对我的家人,对那些跟随我走过漫长崎岖道路的朋友们,对联邦全体人民和全世界人民,我今天将重复我在1963年11月的那个悲伤的日子[1]所说的话:"我将领导大家并全力以赴。"

但是,你们必须从心底铭记旧日的承诺和旧日的梦想。它是你们最好的向导。

至于我自己,借用古代一位圣贤的话,我只"求你赐我智慧和知识,使我可以领导这人民,不然,谁能治理这么大一个民族呢?"[2]

---

[1]指肯尼迪遇刺身亡后约翰逊紧急接任总统那天。
[2]引自《圣经·旧约》历代志下第一章第十节。

理查德·尼克松
Richard Nixon

理查德·尼克松（Richard Nixon）

生平简介 >>

理查德·尼克松是美国第三十七任总统。他于1913年出生在加利福尼亚州。1940年他与中学教员帕特·瑞安结婚，育有两个女儿。

1946年和1948年他曾两度被选为国会众议员，在此期间，他作为"众议院非美活动调查委员会"的成员而名声大振。1950年当选为参议院议员。

1952年和1956年，他两度被选为艾森豪威尔总统的副总统。1960年，他获共和党总统提名，但被民主党的肯尼迪击败。1962年，他竞选加利福尼亚州州长时，再次失败。之后，他搬到纽约市，加入了一家律师事务所。

1968年，尼克松再度竞选总统，结果击败了民主党人汉弗莱，荣登总统宝座。1972年又获选连任。

在首任期间，尼克松在内政外交方面都取得了巨大成功。在国内，改革选举团、征兵制度、邮政制度、税务制度，并制止了通货膨胀。在国际上，实现了从越南撤军，同中国建立友好关系，并同苏联领导人举行了最高级首脑会议，缓和了世界的紧张局势。1973年，在他连任不久，即卷入了"水门事件"，尼克松在面临弹劾的情况下于1974年8月9日辞职。

尼克松是第一位谋求同中华人民共和国交往的总统，也是第一位任期未满而被迫辞职的总统。

Richard Nixon
First Inaugural Address

January 20, 1969

Senator Dirksen, Mr. Chief Justice, Mr. Vice President, President Johnson, Vice President Humphrey, my fellow Americans—and my fellow citizens of the world community:

I ask you to share with me today the majesty of this moment. In the orderly transfer of power, we celebrate the unity that keeps us free.

Each moment in history is a fleeting time, precious and unique. But some stand out as moments of beginning, in which courses are set that shape decades or centuries.

This can be such a moment.

Forces now are converging that make possible, for the first time, the hope that many of man's deepest aspirations can at last be realized. The spiraling pace of change allows us to contemplate, within our own lifetime, advances that once would have taken centuries.

In throwing wide the horizons of space, we have discovered new horizons on earth.

For the first time, because the people of the world want peace, and the leaders of the world are afraid of war, the times are on the side of peace.

Eight years from now America will celebrate its 200th anniversary as a nation. Within the lifetime of most people now living, mankind will celebrate that great New Year which comes only once in a thousand years—the beginning of the third millennium.

理查德·尼克松
Richard Nixon

尼克松总统首次就职演说

1969年1月20日

德克森参议员、首席大法官先生、副总统先生、约翰逊总统、汉弗莱副总统、同胞们以及世界的公民们：

今天，我请各位和我一起来共度这个庄严的时刻，在这个有秩序的权力移交之际，让我们为保护我们自由的团结而庆祝。

在飞逝的时光中，历史的每一个时刻都是珍贵且独特的，但某些时刻，如在每一个时代的开始，总是特别突出。因为当时所制定的各种方针和政策，将要决定数十年甚至数百年的社会进程。

目前，很可能就是这样的一个时刻。

人类有史以来第一次正在汇集一切力量，使人类许多夙愿最终能够实现成为可能。日新月异的快速变化，使我们在有生之年可以看到在过去可能要用好几个世纪才能出现的进步。

在广泛的太空探测中，我们也发现了地球的新领域。

第一次，由于全世界人民要求和平，世界各国领袖害怕战争的发生，这是一个趋向于和平的时代。[1]

八年以后，美国要庆祝建国200周年，在我们大多数人的有生之年，人类将庆祝极其难逢的千禧年——第三个千年盛世的开始。

---

[1]尼克松执政时，美国在全球的霸权地位已严重衰落，国际形势发生了巨大的变化。尼克松政府决定从越南撤军，并提出了与西欧、苏联发展关系的三点原则，即"伙伴关系""实力地位""谈判时代"，两年后，又提出世界"五极"（美国、西欧、苏联、中国、日本）的概念。

What kind of nation we will be, what kind of world we will live in, whether we shape the future in the image of our hopes, is ours to determine by our actions and our choices.

The greatest honor history can bestow is the title of peacemaker. This honor now beckons America—the chance to help lead the world at last out of the valley of turmoil, and onto that high ground of peace that man has dreamed of since the dawn of civilization.

If we succeed, generations to come will say of us now living that we mastered our moment, that we helped make the world safe for mankind.

This is our summons to greatness.

I believe the American people are ready to answer this call.

The second third of this century has been a time of proud achievement. We have made enormous strides in science and industry and agriculture. We have shared our wealth more broadly than ever. We have learned at last to manage a modern economy to assure its continued growth.

We have given freedom new reach, and we have begun to make its promise real for black as well as for white.

We see the hope of tomorrow in the youth of today. I know America's youth. I believe in them. We can be proud that they are better educated, more committed, more passionately driven by conscience than any generation in our history.

No people has ever been so close to the achievement of a just and abundant society, or so possessed of the will to achieve it. Because our strengths are so great, we can afford to appraise our weaknesses with candor and to approach them with hope.

Standing in this same place a third of a century ago, Franklin Delano Roosevelt addressed a Nation ravaged by depression and gripped in fear. He could say in surveying the Nation's troubles: "They concern, thank God, only material things."

Our crisis today is the reverse.

We have found ourselves rich in goods, but ragged in spirit; reaching with magnificent precision for the moon, but falling into raucous discord on

理查德·尼克松
Richard Nixon

我们的国家将成为怎样的一个国家？我们的世界将成为怎样的一个世界？是否依照我们的希望来塑造未来？这些都依赖于我们的行动和选择来决定。

历史所能赐予我们的最大荣誉，就是和平的缔造者这一桂冠。现在这份殊荣正向美国招手，因为它领导世界走出动乱的幽谷，进入自有文明以来梦寐以求的人类和平的高原的机会已经到来。

如果我们成功了，后代将会说我们这一代把握住了时机，正是我们协力相助使这个世界成为人类的安居之地。

这就是对我们的伟大的呼唤。

我相信，美国人民已准备响应这一呼唤。

本世纪的第二个30年，是一个我们为所达到的成就而感到骄傲的时代，无论在科学、工业还是农业方面我们都有长足的进步。我们比以往任何时候都更广泛地分享着我们的共同财富。我们终于知道如何来管理现代经济，并确保其持续增长。

我们已扩大了自由的领域。不论白人还是黑人，我们已逐步开始实现对他们的自由所做的承诺。

我们从今天的年轻人身上看到了明天的希望，我了解美国的年轻人，我相信他们。他们比过去任何一代所受的教育都多，因此负有更大的责任，也更强烈地接受良心的支配，这些都是我们引以为豪的。

从来没有一个民族如此之接近地达到一个公正且富裕的社会，也从来没有一个民族有如此之坚定的意志要建造这样一个社会。由于我们的力量是如此之大，我们能坦白地检讨自身的缺点，更能怀着希望去改正这些缺点。

30多年前，富兰克林·罗斯福站在这里宣布美国正因经济萧条而陷入恐慌之中，在全面地审视了国家的困难后，他说："感谢上帝，这些困难只是物质方面的。"

今天我们的危机正好相反。

我们的物资充裕，但精神上却感到贫乏；我们能极其准确地登上月球，但地球上却仍是一片紊乱和冲突。

earth.

We are caught in war, wanting peace. We are torn by division, wanting unity. We see around us empty lives, wanting fulfillment. We see tasks that need doing, waiting for hands to do them.

To a crisis of the spirit, we need an answer of the spirit.

To find that answer, we need only look within ourselves.

When we listen to "the better angels of our nature," we find that they celebrate the simple things, the basic things—such as goodness, decency, love, kindness.

Greatness comes in simple trappings.

The simple things are the ones most needed today if we are to surmount what divides us, and cement what unites us.

To lower our voices would be a simple thing.

In these difficult years, America has suffered from a fever of words; from inflated rhetoric that promises more than it can deliver; from angry rhetoric that fans discontents into hatreds; from bombastic rhetoric that postures instead of persuading.

We cannot learn from one another until we stop shouting at one another—until we speak quietly enough so that our words can be heard as well as our voices.

For its part, government will listen. We will strive to listen in new ways—to the voices of quiet anguish, the voices that speak without words, the voices of the heart—to the injured voices, the anxious voices, the voices that have despaired of being heard.

Those who have been left out, we will try to bring in.

Those left behind, we will help to catch up.

For all of our people, we will set as our goal the decent order that makes progress possible and our lives secure.

As we reach toward our hopes, our task is to build on what has gone before—not turning away from the old, but turning toward the new.

In this past third of a century, government has passed more laws, spent more money, initiated more programs, than in all our previous history.

理查德·尼克松
Richard Nixon

我们陷入战争之中,因此希望和平;我们四分五裂,因此需要团结;我们看见周围到处都是空虚的人们,因此需要充实其灵魂;我们看见有很多任务需要完成,正等着人们去行动。

对于精神的危机,我们需要精神的解决方法。

要寻找到答案,我们唯一的办法就是从我们自身上寻找。

当我们聆听"我们天性中的善良天使"时,我们发现她们只赞颂一些简单、基本的习性,诸如善良、宽厚、博爱、仁慈等。

伟大孕育于质朴无华。

如果我们要克服那些使我们分裂的因素,并加强我们的团结,这些简单的事情正是我们目前最需要做的。

压低嗓门就是一件简单的事情。

在那些艰难的岁月里,美国热衷于辞令,轻易地许下诺言,往往却因力不从心而食言;出言激昂,结果却将不满煽动成了仇恨;夸大其词,装腔作势,而没有劝服人的诚意;等等,结果使我们吃尽苦头。

除非我们停止互相叫嚷,除非我们能心平气和地交谈,使对方不仅听清我们的声音,而且理解我们的言辞,否则我们就无法相互学习。

但政府将竭力倾听一切声音——正在默默受苦的声音、无言的倾诉、发自内心的声音、备受伤害者的声音、焦虑者的声音、绝望的声音。

那些被遗弃的人,我们要设法将他们引进我们的队伍中来。

那些落后了的人,我们要帮助他们迎头赶上。

对于全体人民,我们的目标在于建立公平的秩序,以推动社会进步,保障人民安居乐业。

当我们朝着希望迈进时,我们的工作是在过去的基础上继续建设,我们不是抛弃旧的,而是奔向新的目标。

在过去30多年中,政府通过的法律、花费的金钱、启动的计划,超过了我国过去历史的总和。

In pursuing our goals of full employment, better housing, excellence in education; in rebuilding our cities and improving our rural areas; in protecting our environment and enhancing the quality of life—in all these and more, we will and must press urgently forward.

We shall plan now for the day when our wealth can be transferred from the destruction of war abroad to the urgent needs of our people at home.

The American dream does not come to those who fall asleep.

But we are approaching the limits of what government alone can do.

Our greatest need now is to reach beyond government, and to enlist the legions of the concerned and the committed.

What has to be done, has to be done by government and people together or it will not be done at all. The lesson of past agony is that without the people we can do nothing; with the people we can do everything.

To match the magnitude of our tasks, we need the energies of our people—enlisted not only in grand enterprises, but more importantly in those small, splendid efforts that make headlines in the neighborhood newspaper instead of the national journal.

With these, we can build a great cathedral of the spirit—each of us raising it one stone at a time, as he reaches out to his neighbor, helping, caring, doing.

I do not offer a life of uninspiring ease. I do not call for a life of grim sacrifice. I ask you to join in a high adventure—one as rich as humanity itself, and as exciting as the times we live in.

The essence of freedom is that each of us shares in the shaping of his own destiny.

Until he has been part of a cause larger than himself, no man is truly whole.

The way to fulfillment is in the use of our talents; we achieve nobility in the spirit that inspires that use.

As we measure what can be done, we shall promise only what we know we

理查德·尼克松
Richard Nixon

在实现充分就业、改善居住条件、实行优良教育、重建城市和改良农业地区条件等目标上，在保护环境和提高生活水平方面，在所有这些以及其他方面，我们都将加速进行。

我们现在必须做出计划，使得那些用在国外进行毁灭性战争的物力和财力[1]转用于满足国内人民的需要。

美国梦不会降临到那些沉睡不醒的人们中间。

但是我们已经到了政府力所能及的极限。

目前，我们最需要的，就是突破政府的局限，使所有关心者及乐于献身者都来参加这项工作。

那些必须完成的事，应由政府和人民一起来完成，否则就无法实现。过去可悲的教训告诉我们：没有人民的帮助，我们将一事无成；有了人民的帮助，我们就能达到一切目标。

为了完成我们的宏伟大业，我们需要人民贡献自己的力量——不仅要做轰轰烈烈的大事，更重要的是进行那些具体而出色的工作，它们是地区报纸上而不是全国报刊上的头条新闻。

有了这些以后，我们就能筑起一个伟大的精神圣殿——当我们每个人把手伸给邻居，去帮助他，照料他，为他做事时，就如同为我们的精神圣殿添砖加瓦一样。

我并不是在鼓励一种毫无刺激的安逸的生活，我也不要求你们过一种只有无谓的牺牲的生活。我请求各位参与一项崇高的冒险事业——这种事业的内容和人类自身一样丰富多彩，也和我们所处的时代一样激动人心。

自由的本质，是每一个人都为决定自己的命运而努力。

一个人只有使自己成为超越自我的事业的一部分时，才能算是个真正完整无缺的人。

成就感的获得在于运用自己的才能。我们本着一种可以鼓舞我们运用才能解决问题的精神，就能获得巨大的成就。

当我们估量自己能完成什么的时候，我们只就自己知道能做到的事情许

---

[1]越南战争中，美国先后投入兵力250万人，死伤35万人，军费开支浩大，财政赤字增加，黄金储备下降，通货膨胀严重。

can produce, but as we chart our goals we shall be lifted by our dreams.

No man can be fully free while his neighbor is not. To go forward at all is to go forward together.

This means black and white together, as one nation, not two. The laws have caught up with our conscience. What remains is to give life to what is in the law: to ensure at last that as all are born equal in dignity before God, all are born equal in dignity before man.

As we learn to go forward together at home, let us also seek to go forward together with all mankind.

Let us take as our goal: where peace is unknown, make it welcome; where peace is fragile, make it strong; where peace is temporary, make it permanent.

After a period of confrontation, we are entering an era of negotiation.

Let all nations know that during this administration our lines of communication will be open.

We seek an open world—open to ideas, open to the exchange of goods and people—a world in which no people, great or small, will live in angry isolation.

We cannot expect to make everyone our friend, but we can try to make no one our enemy.

Those who would be our adversaries, we invite to a peaceful competition—not in conquering territory or extending dominion, but in enriching the life of man.

As we explore the reaches of space, let us go to the new worlds together—not as new worlds to be conquered, but as a new adventure to be shared.

With those who are willing to join, let us cooperate to reduce the burden of arms, to strengthen the structure of peace, to lift up the poor and the hungry.

But to all those who would be tempted by weakness, let us leave no doubt that we will be as strong as we need to be for as long as we need to be.

Over the past twenty years, since I first came to this Capital as a freshman Congressman, I have visited most of the nations of the world.

I have come to know the leaders of the world, and the great forces, the hatreds, the fears that divide the world.

理查德·尼克松
Richard Nixon

下诺言；但是当我们策划未来时，我们将依自己的理想而定出更高的目标。

当一个人的邻居不能享有自由时，他就不能算是真正享有自由。要前进，就要大家一起前进。

这就是说黑人和白人要共同前进，应团结为一个民族，而不是分裂成两个民族。目前的法律已与我们的良知相符，所差的仅是实践那些法律条款，并确保所有人在他人面前有天生平等的尊严，就像每个人在上帝面前一律平等一样。

当我们懂得在国内携手共进时，让我们也谋求和整个人类共同努力前进。

让我们将下述当作我们的目标：在不知有和平的地方，让那里的人们都能欢迎和平；在和平脆弱的地方，要巩固和平；在和平还短暂易逝的地方，使其持久永存。

经过一段对抗时期以后，我们正进入一个谈判的时代。

让所有的国家都知道，在本届政府执政期间，我们将打开沟通的大门。

我们寻求一个开放的世界——对各种思想开放，对货物交易和人才交流开放。在这个世界中，任何一个民族，无论其大小，都不会生活在怏怏不乐的孤立之中。

我们不奢望每一个人都成为我们的朋友，但我们尽量努力不使任何人成为我们的敌人。

对那些可能与我们为敌的人，我们请他们来进行一次和平竞赛——不是征服地域或扩张霸权，而是使人类的生活富裕起来。

在我们探测宇宙空间的时候，让我们共同进入一个新的世界——不是走向即将被征服的新世界，而是共同进行一次新的探险。

让我们和那些自愿参加者合作，以减少军事负担，加固和平的大厦，使贫穷和饥饿的人脱离困境。

但是，对所有那些见软就欺的人来说，让我们明确表明，我们需要多强大就会多强大，需要强大多久就会强大多久。

自我第一次以国会的新议员的身份进入国会的20多年来，我曾访问过世界上大多数的国家。

我结识了世界各国的领导人，了解到使世界分裂的强大力量，以及各种强烈的仇恨和恐惧。

I know that peace does not come through wishing for it—that there is no substitute for days and even years of patient and prolonged diplomacy.

I also know the people of the world.

I have seen the hunger of a homeless child, the pain of a man wounded in battle, the grief of a mother who has lost her son. I know these have no ideology, no race.

I know America. I know the heart of America is good.

I speak from my own heart, and the heart of my country, the deep concern we have for those who suffer, and those who sorrow.

I have taken an oath today in the presence of God and my countrymen to uphold and defend the Constitution of the United States. To that oath I now add this sacred commitment: I shall consecrate my office, my energies, and all the wisdom I can summon, to the cause of peace among nations.

Let this message be heard by strong and weak alike:

The peace we seek to win is not victory over any other people, but the peace that comes "with healing in its wings"; with compassion for those who have suffered; with understanding for those who have opposed us; with the opportunity for all the peoples of this earth to choose their own destiny.

Only a few short weeks ago, we shared the glory of man's first sight of the world as God sees it, as a single sphere reflecting light in the darkness.

As the Apollo astronauts flew over the moon's gray surface on Christmas Eve, they spoke to us of the beauty of earth—and in that voice so clear across the lunar distance, we heard them invoke God's blessing on its goodness.

In that moment, their view from the moon moved poet Archibald MacLeish to write:

"To see the earth as it truly is, small and blue and beautiful in that eternal silence where it floats, is to see ourselves as riders on the earth together, brothers on that bright loveliness in the eternal cold—brothers who know now they are truly brothers."

理查德·尼克松
Richard Nixon

我知道，和平并不是仅凭愿望就会到来的——除了日复一日、甚至年复一年的耐心而持久的外交努力，别无他法。

我也了解世界各国的人民。

我曾看见无家可归的忍饥挨饿的儿童，在战争中痛苦的受伤者和因失去儿子而悲痛欲绝的母亲。这些饥饿、痛苦、悲伤是没有什么意识形态和种族之分的。

我了解美国，了解美国人的心是善良的。

我从心底里，以及美国人民的心底里，对那些受苦和不幸的人们表示我们最深切的关注。

今天，我在上帝和人民面前宣誓，要拥护和保卫美国的宪法。此外，我现在再补充一项神圣的义务：我将把我的职责、精力和我所拥有的智慧，献给各国间的和平事业。

让强国和弱国都听到这个信息：

我们所寻求的和平并不是打败其他民族，这种和平的到来，伴随着对创伤的医治、对受难者的同情和对反动者的理解，并赋予世界上所有民族决定自己命运的机会。

就在几个星期以前，我们首次分享到了只有上帝才见得到的荣耀——一个在黑暗中辉映光芒的球体。[1]

当"阿波罗号"太空船上的宇航员于圣诞之夜飞临月球灰色的表面时，他们告诉我们地球是多么美丽。在从月球传来的清晰声音中，我们还听到他们祈求上帝赐福于人类。

就在那一刻，他们从月球上看到的景象促使诗人阿克比博·麦克来希写出了下面的诗句：

"茫茫太空，千年沉寂，唯有蔚蓝色的地球，以它那美丽的光环，给宇宙带来了生机。我们共居一乐园，同饮一样的水，我们要真诚相爱，同舟共济，亲如兄弟姐妹。"[2]

---

[1]1968年12月21日，"太阳神八号"进入太空，并绕月球飞行。这批宇宙航行员是进入地球轨道以外遥远太空的第一批人类。宇航船于26日返回地球。

[2]刊于1968年12月25日《纽约时报》头版。

In that moment of surpassing technological triumph, men turned their thoughts toward home and humanity—seeing in that far perspective that man's destiny on earth is not divisible; telling us that however far we reach into the cosmos, our destiny lies not in the stars but on Earth itself, in our own hands, in our own hearts.

We have endured a long night of the American spirit. But as our eyes catch the dimness of the first rays of dawn, let us not curse the remaining dark. Let us gather the light.

Our destiny offers, not the cup of despair, but the chalice of opportunity. So let us seize it, not in fear, but in gladness—and, "riders on the earth together," let us go forward, firm in our faith, steadfast in our purpose, cautious of the dangers; but sustained by our confidence in the will of God and the promise of man.

Richard Nixon

Second Inaugural Address

January 20, 1973

Mr. Vice President, Mr. Speaker, Mr. Chief Justice, Senator Cook, Mrs. Eisenhower, and my fellow citizens of this great and good country we share together:

When we met here four years ago, America was bleak in spirit, depressed by the prospect of seemingly endless war abroad and of destructive conflict at home.

As we meet here today, we stand on the threshold of a new era of peace in the world.

The central question before us is: How shall we use that peace? Let us resolve that this era we are about to enter will not be what other postwar periods have so often been: a time of retreat and isolation that leads to stagnation at home

理查德·尼克松
Richard Nixon

在那科技凌驾一切的胜利时刻，人们想到自己的家园和人类；在那未来的视角之中，看到地球上人类的命运是不可分开的。这告诉我们，不论我们人类在宇宙中走得多远，我们的命运并不能系于星际之间，而只能系于地球本身、我们的手中和心里。

我们已度过了美国精神晦暗不明的漫漫长夜，但是，当我们看到黎明的曙光时，切莫诅咒残留的黑暗，而要积极地将所有的光明集合在一起。

命运所提供给我们的，不是失望，而是机会。因此，让我们毫无畏惧、充满欢愉地抓住机遇吧。"地球的乘客们"，让我们以坚定的信念，朝着既定的目标，谨慎地前进吧！支持我们的是上帝的旨意和人类充满信心的希望。

尼克松总统第二次就职演说

1973年1月20日

副总统先生、众议院议长、首席大法官、库克参议员、艾森豪威尔夫人，以及我的伟大善良的美国同胞们：

四年前我们曾聚集在这里，当时，美国在精神上显得很颓丧，纵观整个世界，国外存在着永无止境的战争，国内则沉浸在破坏性的冲突之中，其情景着实使人感到焦虑。

今天，我们又聚集在这里，我们正站在世界的一个新和平时代的门槛上。

我们目前面临的中心问题是：我们将如何利用这种和平？在这个我们即将进入的时代，让我们下决心避免像过去战后曾经有过的那种情况再次发生，即一个退却与孤立的时代，它导致国内的萧条，在国外诱发新的危险。

and invites new danger abroad.

Let us resolve that this will be what it can become: a time of great responsibilities greatly borne, in which we renew the spirit and the promise of America as we enter our third century as a nation.

This past year saw far-reaching results from our new policies for peace. By continuing to revitalize our traditional friendships, and by our missions to Peking and to Moscow, we were able to establish the base for a new and more durable pattern of relationships among the nations of the world. Because of America's bold initiatives, 1972 will be long remembered as the year of the greatest progress since the end of World War II toward a lasting peace in the world.

The peace we seek in the world is not the flimsy peace which is merely an interlude between wars, but a peace which can endure for generations to come.

It is important that we understand both the necessity and the limitations of America's role in maintaining that peace.

Unless we in America work to preserve the peace, there will be no peace.

Unless we in America work to preserve freedom, there will be no freedom.

But let us clearly understand the new nature of America's role, as a result of the new policies we have adopted over these past four years.

We shall respect our treaty commitments.

We shall support vigorously the principle that no country has the right to impose its will or rule on another by force.

We shall continue, in this era of negotiation, to work for the limitation of nuclear arms, and to reduce the danger of confrontation between the great powers.

We shall do our share in defending peace and freedom in the world. But we shall expect others to do their share.

理查德·尼克松
Richard Nixon

让我们下决心，使这个时代变成肩负历史重任的时代。当美国进入立国的第三个世纪时，则必须重建美国的精神与希望。

我们为寻求和平所采取的新政策，在过去一年中已看出一些影响深远的效果。通过不断地加强和各国的传统友谊，以及政府代表团去北京与莫斯科之行[1]，我们已重建了一种新的和更持久的国际关系的新格局。由于美国的大胆行动，1972年将作为第二次世界大战结束以来，人类在走向世界永久和平道路上最有进展的一年而载入史册。

我们在世界上所谋求的并不是短暂的、昙花一现的和平，而是一个世世代代都能享有的永久的和平。

在维持这种和平中，了解美国所扮演的角色的必要性及其限度是很重要的。

除非我们在美国为维护和平而努力，否则根本不会有和平。

除非我们在美国为维护自由而努力，否则根本不会有自由。

但是，通过我们在过去四年里采取的新的政策所获得的结果，我们必须清楚地了解美国所扮演的角色的新的性质。

我们将尊重我们的条约义务。

我们将全力支持一个原则，这就是没有一个国家有权将其意志或统治强加于另一个国家。

在这个谈判的时代，我们将继续为限制核武器而努力，并减少强国间互相对抗的危险。[2]

我们将奉献自己的一份力量，来保卫世界和平与自由，同时，也期望其他国家贡献它们的力量。

---

[1]尼克松分别于1972年2月及5月赴北京和莫斯科访问。在中国访问期间，与中国政府发表了《上海联合公报》；在苏联访问期间，尼克松与勃列日涅夫在卫生、环境保护、太空和科技合作等方面签订了一些协议。

[2]这之后不久，尼克松与勃列日涅夫举行了华盛顿会谈，于6月18—25日签订了一份保证书，内容是力争在1974年结束核军备竞赛，并避免在国际上发生冲突。

The time has passed when America will make every other nation's conflict our own, or make every other nation's future our responsibility, or presume to tell the people of other nations how to manage their own affairs.

Just as we respect the right of each nation to determine its own future, we also recognize the responsibility of each nation to secure its own future.

Just as America's role is indispensable in preserving the world's peace, so is each nation's role indispensable in preserving its own peace.

Together with the rest of the world, let us resolve to move forward from the beginnings we have made. Let us continue to bring down the walls of hostility which have divided the world for too long, and to build in their place bridges of understanding—so that despite profound differences between systems of government, the people of the world can be friends.

Let us build a structure of peace in the world in which the weak are as safe as the strong—in which each respects the right of the other to live by a different system—in which those who would influence others will do so by the strength of their ideas, and not by the force of their arms.

Let us accept that high responsibility not as a burden, but gladly—gladly because the chance to build such a peace is the noblest endeavor in which a nation can engage; gladly, also, because only if we act greatly in meeting our responsibilities abroad will we remain a great Nation, and only if we remain a great Nation will we act greatly in meeting our challenges at home.

We have the chance today to do more than ever before in our history to make life better in America—to ensure better education, better health, better housing, better transportation, a cleaner environment—to restore respect for law, to make our communities more livable—and to insure the God-given right of every American to full and equal opportunity.

Because the range of our needs is so great—because the reach of our opportunities is so great—let us be bold in our determination to meet those needs in new ways.

Just as building a structure of peace abroad has required turning away from old policies that failed, so building a new era of progress at home requires turning away from old policies that have failed.

理查德·尼克松
Richard Nixon

美国将其他国家内的冲突都视为自己的事情,将其他国家的未来前途视为美国的责任,以及试图告诉其他国家的人民如何管理自己的事务,这样的时代已经过去了。

就像我们尊重每个国家都有决定自己未来前途的权力一样,我们也认为每个国家都有确保自己未来前途的责任。

就像在维护世界和平方面,美国扮演着不可或缺的角色一样,每个国家对于维持本身的和平也同样要担当起重要的责任。

让我们下定决心,与世界其他国家一道,把我们已经开创的事业向前推进。让我们继续不断地努力,拆除那堵把世界长期分裂开来的敌意之墙,代之以相互理解的桥梁——即使各国政治制度间有很大的差别,世界各国人民仍然能成为朋友。

让我们在世界上建立一幢和平大厦,在这幢大厦中,弱国和强国享有一样的安全;每个国家都尊重与自己制度不同的国家的权利,一国不是以武力而是以思想来影响他国。

让我们接受这一崇高的责任,不是将其视为负担,而是欣然地接受,因为建立这种和平大厦是一个国家所能从事的最高尚的努力;也只有勇于承担我们在海外的责任,我们才能继续保持一个大国的地位;而只有继续保持一个大国的地位,我们才能勇于迎接国内的各种挑战。

今天,在改善生活方面,我们有可能做出比以往都多的事情,保证人们享有更好的教育、良好的医疗、舒适的住宅、便利的交通、清洁的环境,恢复对法律的尊重,使我们的社区更生气勃发,保证每一个美国人都享有完全与平等的机会的天赋权利。

由于我们需要的范围是如此广泛,我们的机会所及的范围如此宽广,因此,让我们勇敢地下定决心,以新的方式来满足这些需求。

正如在国外建立一幢和平大厦需要抛弃业已失败的旧政策一样,在国内建设一个进步的新时代也同样需要抛弃已经失败的旧政策。

Abroad, the shift from old policies to new has not been a retreat from our responsibilities, but a better way to peace.

And at home, the shift from old policies to new will not be a retreat from our responsibilities, but a better way to progress.

Abroad and at home, the key to those new responsibilities lies in the placing and the division of responsibility. We have lived too long with the consequences of attempting to gather all power and responsibility in Washington.

Abroad and at home, the time has come to turn away from the condescending policies of paternalism—of "Washington knows best."

A person can be expected to act responsibly only if he has responsibility. This is human nature. So let us encourage individuals at home and nations abroad to do more for themselves, to decide more for themselves. Let us locate responsibility in more places. Let us measure what we will do for others by what they will do for themselves.

That is why today I offer no promise of a purely governmental solution for every problem. We have lived too long with that false promise. In trusting too much in government, we have asked of it more than it can deliver. This leads only to inflated expectations, to reduced individual effort, and to a disappointment and frustration that erode confidence both in what government can do and in what people can do.

Government must learn to take less from people so that people can do more for themselves.

Let us remember that America was built not by government, but by people—not by welfare, but by work—not by shirking responsibility, but by seeking responsibility.

In our own lives, let each of us ask—not just what will government do for me, but what can I do for myself?

In the challenges we face together, let each of us ask—not just how can government help, but how can I help?

Your National Government has a great and vital role to play. And I pledge to you that where this Government should act, we will act boldly and we will lead boldly. But just as important is the role that each and every one of us must

理查德·尼克松
Richard Nixon

在国外，抛弃旧政策改用新政策并不意味着推卸我们肩负的责任，而是开辟通往和平的更佳途径。

在国内，抛弃旧政策而采取新政策也不是推卸我们肩负的责任，而是开辟取得进步的更佳途径。

不论在国外还是在国内，承担这些新的责任的关键在于如何安排和分摊责任。长期以来，我们已经承受了企图将所有权力和责任集中于华盛顿所造成的后果。

不论是在国外还是在国内，如今已到了抛弃那种家长式政治——"华盛顿了解得最清楚"的政策的时候了。

只有在人有了责任以后，才能期望他有负责的行为，这是人的本性。因此，让我们鼓励国内的个人和海外的国家，更多地自立，更多地自决。让我们将责任分摊到更适当的地方，并根据他们为自己所做的事来衡量决定我们要为别人做的事。

这就是为什么今天我不提出所有问题都由美国政府来解决的原因。我们忍受这种错误许诺已经太久了。由于我们过分地信赖政府，我们对政府的要求超过了它的能力所及。这样，只会导致过分的期望以及个人努力的减少，从而造成失望与悲观，这就会侵蚀人们对政府和人民两者的能力所抱的信任。

政府必须尽量减少取之于人民的东西，使他们能为自己多做一些事。

让我们切记美国并不是由政府而是由人民建立起来的；不是由福利，而是由劳动而建立起来的；不是由逃避责任，而是由寻求责任而建立起来的。

在我们自己的生活中，不能只问政府能为我们做什么，而是要问我能为我自己做些什么。

在我们共同面对挑战时，不能只是问政府能提供什么帮助，而是要问我能提供怎样的帮助。

你们的政府扮演着极其重要的角色。我向各位保证，在任何需要政府发挥作用的地方，我们都将大胆地采取行动，勇敢地承担起领导的责任。然而，我们每一个人，无论他是扮演着个人还是社会中一分子的角色，也

play, as an individual and as a member of his own community.

From this day forward, let each of us make a solemn commitment in his own heart: to bear his responsibility, to do his part, to live his ideals—so that together, we can see the dawn of a new age of progress for America, and together, as we celebrate our 200th anniversary as a nation, we can do so proud in the fulfillment of our promise to ourselves and to the world.

As America's longest and most difficult war comes to an end, let us again learn to debate our differences with civility and decency. And let each of us reach out for that one precious quality government cannot provide—a new level of respect for the rights and feelings of one another, a new level of respect for the individual human dignity which is the cherished birthright of every American.

Above all else, the time has come for us to renew our faith in ourselves and in America.

In recent years, that faith has been challenged.

Our children have been taught to be ashamed of their country, ashamed of their parents, ashamed of America's record at home and of its role in the world.

At every turn, we have been beset by those who find everything wrong with America and little that is right. But I am confident that this will not be the judgment of history on these remarkable times in which we are privileged to live.

America's record in this century has been unparalleled in the world's history for its responsibility, for its generosity, for its creativity and for its progress.

Let us be proud that our system has produced and provided more freedom and more abundance, more widely shared, than any other system in the history of the world.

Let us be proud that in each of the four wars in which we have been engaged in this century, including the one we are now bringing to an end, we have fought not for our selfish advantage, but to help others resist aggression.

Let us be proud that by our bold, new initiatives, and by our steadfastness for peace with honor, we have made a break-through toward creating in the world what the world has not known before—a structure of peace that can

理查德·尼克松
Richard Nixon

都是同等重要的。

从今天开始,让我们每一个人都在心里宣誓:负起自己的责任,尽其所能,实践自己的理想。这样,我们就能一起看到美国的一个进步的新时代的来临。我们将以履行对自己及全世界的诺言为荣的心情,来庆祝建国200周年。

在美国最长久最艰难的战争趋于结束之际[1],让我们重新学会就我们之间的分歧以谦恭有礼的态度来辩论。让每一个人都来追求那种政府所无法提供的珍贵的品质,即把尊重彼此之间的权利及感情,对每一个美国人与生俱来的人的尊严的尊重提高到一种新的水平。

更重要的是,现在是恢复我们对自己、对美国的信心的时候了。

近年来,这种信念一直受到挑战。
我们的孩子们一直接受着那种为他们的国家而羞愧,为他们的父母而羞愧,为美国的历史及其在世界上所担当的角色而羞愧的教育。
在每一转折关头,我们都被那些认为美国一无是处的人们所困扰。但我深信,这绝不是历史对我们有幸躬逢其盛的非凡时代所做的评价。

在本世纪,无论就其责任、宽大的风范、创造力还是进步来说,美国在世界历史上都是无与伦比的。
我们骄傲的是,我们的政治制度与世界历史上任何其他制度相比,都为人民提供了更多的自由,而且使国家更富裕,使人们更广泛地分享着劳动的成果。
我们骄傲的是,本世纪我们参与的四次战争[2],包括目前我们正设法结束的这场战争在内,都不是为了自私的利益,而是为了帮助别国抵抗侵略。
我们骄傲的是,由于我们的勇敢创新及执着地追求光荣的和平,因而在创建世界和平大厦方面取得突破性进展;这一和平大厦在世界上前所未

---

[1] 1973年1月27日,《关于在越南结束战争、恢复和平的协定》正式签订。至此,长达12年之久的越南战争结束。
[2] 指"一战"、"二战"、朝鲜战争和越南战争。

last, not merely for our time, but for generations to come.

We are embarking here today on an era that presents challenges great as those any nation, or any generation, has ever faced.

We shall answer to God, to history, and to our conscience for the way in which we use these years.

As I stand in this place, so hallowed by history, I think of others who have stood here before me. I think of the dreams they had for America, and I think of how each recognized that he needed help far beyond himself in order to make those dreams come true.

Today, I ask your prayers that in the years ahead I may have God's help in making decisions that are right for America, and I pray for your help so that together we may be worthy of our challenge.

Let us pledge together to make these next four years the best four years in America's history, so that on its 200th birthday America will be as young and as vital as when it began, and as bright a beacon of hope for all the world.

Let us go forward from here confident in hope, strong in our faith in one another, sustained by our faith in God who created us, and striving always to serve His purpose.

理查德·尼克松
Richard Nixon

有，它将超越我们的时代，一直延续无数代。

今天，我们在这里迈入一个新的时代，它所提出的挑战，是任何一个国家或任何一个时代都未曾面临过的巨大的挑战。

这些年来，我们的所作所为，都对得起上帝、历史及我们的良知。

当我站在这个因历史而神圣的地方，不由得想起在我之前曾站在这里的各位前任，想起他们对美国所抱的各种理想，也想起他们是如何意识到，他们需要远远超出他们自身之外的帮助以实现这些理想。

今天，我请求各位为我祈祷，使我在未来的几年里能得到上帝的帮助，以便所做的决定都是有益于美国的。同时我也祈求各位的帮助，让我们同心协力，接受并战胜挑战。

让我们一起保证，使未来的四年成为美国历史上最繁荣的四年。这样，在美国建国200周年的时候，美国仍像开国时一样年轻、生机勃勃，一样是世界上的一座明亮的希望的灯塔。

让我们满怀希望，彼此信赖，凭借对创造了人类的上帝的信仰，永远奉行上帝的旨意，由此迈步前进吧。

吉米·卡特
Jimmy Carter

吉米·卡特（Jimmy Carter）

生平简介 >>

吉米·卡特是美国第三十九任总统。他于1924年10月1日出生在佐治亚州。他曾就读于佐治亚工技学院和安纳波里斯海军学校，在海军中曾服役7年。1953年，他的父亲去世，他回乡继承了父亲的企业。此后，他成为民政和宗教事业的一位领导人，并以他的影响反对种族隔离。

1962年，他赢得了佐治亚州参议员席位。1970年，他当选为州长。1976年，他被民主党提名为总统候选人，击败共和党人福特，荣登总统宝座。

卡特使美国在1979年1月1日与我国建立正式外交关系，揭开了中美关系的新篇章。

美国历届总统就职演说
THE INAUGURAL ADDRESSES OF THE U.S. PRESIDENTS

Jimmy Carter
Inaugural Address

January 20, 1977

For myself and for our Nation, I want to thank my predecessor for all he has done to heal our land.

In this outward and physical ceremony we attest once again to the inner and spiritual strength of our Nation. As my high school teacher, Miss Julia Coleman, used to say: "We must adjust to changing times and still hold to unchanging principles."

Here before me is the Bible used in the inauguration of our first President, in 1789, and I have just taken the oath of office on the Bible my mother gave me a few years ago, opened to a timeless admonition from the ancient prophet Micah:

"He hath showed thee, O man, what is good; and what doth the Lord require of thee, but to do justly, and to love mercy, and to walk humbly with thy God." (Micah 6:8)

This inauguration ceremony marks a new beginning, a new dedication within our Government, and a new spirit among us all. A President may sense and proclaim that new spirit, but only a people can provide it.

Two centuries ago our Nation's birth was a milestone in the long quest for freedom, but the bold and brilliant dream which excited the founders of this Nation still awaits its consummation. I have no new dream to set forth today, but rather urge a fresh faith in the old dream.

Ours was the first society openly to define itself in terms of both spirituality and of human liberty. It is that unique self-definition which has given us an exceptional appeal, but it also imposes on us a special obligation, to take on those moral duties which, when assumed, seem invariably to be in our own best interests.

吉米·卡特
Jimmy Carter

卡特总统就职演说

1977年1月20日

我谨代表我个人和我们的国家，向前任总统为医治我们国家所做的一切努力致谢。

此刻这一外在的和有形的庆典，再一次验证了我们国家内在的和精神的力量。诚如我的高中老师科尔曼女士所常说的："我们必须适应变化的时代，但仍保持恒定不变的原则。"

现在放在我面前的是1789年我们第一任总统就职时所使用的《圣经》。我刚才宣誓用的是我母亲于几年前送给我的《圣经》，这本《圣经》打开的地方载有古代先知弥迦所留下的一则永恒的训诫：

"世人哪，耶和华已指示你何为善，他向你所要的是什么呢？只要你行公义，好怜悯，存谦卑的心，与你的神同行。"[1]

这个就职典礼标志着一个新的开端，表明我们政府内的人准备进行新的奉献，也意味着我们大家所有人的一种新的精神。一位总统可以了解并宣扬这一新的精神，但这种新精神唯有全体人民才能证明。

两个世纪前，我们国家的诞生，乃是人类在长期寻求自由的过程中的一个里程碑。但是，开国元勋们所追求的勇敢而光辉的理想仍有待完成。今天我不提出新的理想，只是在原有的理想中注入一种新的信念。

我们的社会是有史以来第一个公开以精神价值和人类自由来阐明自己的社会。正是这种独特的自我定义给了我们一种特殊的吸引力，但也同时赋予了我们一种特殊的义务，即承担那些其实对我们非常有利的道德责任。

---

[1] 引自《圣经·旧约》弥迦书第六章第八节。

You have given me a great responsibility—to stay close to you, to be worthy of you, and to exemplify what you are. Let us create together a new national spirit of unity and trust. Your strength can compensate for my weakness, and your wisdom can help to minimize my mistakes.

Let us learn together and laugh together and work together and pray together, confident that in the end we will triumph together in the right.

The American dream endures. We must once again have full faith in our country—and in one another. I believe America can be better. We can be even stronger than before.

Let our recent mistakes bring a resurgent commitment to the basic principles of our Nation, for we know that if we despise our own government we have no future. We recall in special times when we have stood briefly, but magnificently, united. In those times no prize was beyond our grasp.

But we cannot dwell upon remembered glory. We cannot afford to drift. We reject the prospect of failure or mediocrity or an inferior quality of life for any person. Our Government must at the same time be both competent and compassionate.

We have already found a high degree of personal liberty, and we are now struggling to enhance equality of opportunity. Our commitment to human rights must be absolute, our laws fair, our natural beauty preserved; the powerful must not persecute the weak, and human dignity must be enhanced.

We have learned that "more" is not necessarily "better," that even our great Nation has its recognized limits, and that we can neither answer all questions nor solve all problems. We cannot afford to do everything, nor can we afford to lack boldness as we meet the future. So, together, in a spirit of individual sacrifice for the common good, we must simply do our best.

Our Nation can be strong abroad only if it is strong at home. And we know that the best way to enhance freedom in other lands is to demonstrate here that our democratic system is worthy of emulation.

To be true to ourselves, we must be true to others. We will not behave in foreign places so as to violate our rules and standards here at home, for we know that the trust which our Nation earns is essential to our strength.

吉米·卡特
Jimmy Carter

你们赋予我一项重大的责任,这就是要和各位肩并肩地站在一起,不辜负你们的信任,作为展示你们的风貌的代表。让我们共同创造出一种团结与信任的国家精神,你们的力量能够弥补我的弱点,你们的智慧也能帮助我减少错误。

让我们一起学习,一起欢乐,一起工作,一起祷告,并相信站在正义一方的我们终将取得巨大胜利。

"美国梦"历久不衰,我们必须再次对我们的国家及彼此充满信心。我相信美国能够变得更美好,我们能比过去任何时候都更强大。

让我们检讨最近所犯的错误,以便能重拾我国信奉的各项基本原则。因为我们都知道,如果我们蔑视自己的政府,就毫无前途可言。回首往事,在过去一些特殊的时期里,我们曾庄严地团结在一起,虽为时短暂,但意义深远。在那个时候,没有什么是我们不能做到的。

但是,我们不能老是沉湎于过去的功绩中,也不能随波逐流。我们拒绝接受失败的、平庸的或使任何人都过着贫穷生活的远景。我们的政府必须既称职,又富有同情心。

我们已达到了高度的个人自由,目前我们正在尽力实现机会的均等。我们对维护人权的承诺必须是绝对的,我们的法律必须是公平的,而我们原有的美德也必须保持;强者绝不可以欺凌弱者,人性的尊严必须予以加强。

我们已经知道"更多"并不一定就是"更好"。即使我们的国家再伟大,它的能力也有限度。我们既不能回答全部的问题,也无法解决全部的问题。我们虽不能样样事都做,但我们也不能缺乏勇气去应付未来的局面。因此,我们必须怀着一种舍己为大家的精神,尽自己最大的努力做好自己的工作。

我们的国家只有自身强大才能在国外称强。我们知道,促进其他国家自由的最好方法,就是在本国证明我们的民主制度是值得仿效的榜样。

若要忠诚于自己,我们也必须对别人真诚。我们不能在国外违反国内所实施的规范与准则,因为我们知道赢得他国的信任,对加强美国的力量是非常重要的。

The world itself is now dominated by a new spirit. Peoples more numerous and more politically aware are craving and now demanding their place in the sun—not just for the benefit of their own physical condition, but for basic human rights.

The passion for freedom is on the rise. Tapping this new spirit, there can be no nobler nor more ambitious task for America to undertake on this day of a new beginning than to help shape a just and peaceful world that is truly humane.

We are a strong nation, and we will maintain strength so sufficient that it need not be proven in combat—a quiet strength based not merely on the size of an arsenal, but on the nobility of ideas.

We will be ever vigilant and never vulnerable, and we will fight our wars against poverty, ignorance, and injustice—for those are the enemies against which our forces can be honorably marshaled.

We are a purely idealistic Nation, but let no one confuse our idealism with weakness.

Because we are free we can never be indifferent to the fate of freedom elsewhere. Our moral sense dictates a clearcut preference for these societies which share with us an abiding respect for individual human rights. We do not seek to intimidate, but it is clear that a world which others can dominate with impunity would be inhospitable to decency and a threat to the well-being of all people.

The world is still engaged in a massive armaments race designed to ensure continuing equivalent strength among potential adversaries. We pledge perseverance and wisdom in our efforts to limit the world's armaments to those necessary for each nation's own domestic safety. And we will move this year a step toward ultimate goal—the elimination of all nuclear weapons from this Earth. We urge all other people to join us, for success can mean life instead of death.

Within us, the people of the United States, there is evident a serious and purposeful rekindling of confidence. And I join in the hope that when my time as your President has ended, people might say this about our Nation:

—that we had remembered the words of Micah and renewed our search

现在,世界本身正由一种新的精神所支配,那些人数较多、在政治上已经日益觉醒的民族,正在渴望并要求他们在世界上的地位,不仅是为了改善自身的物质条件,而且也是为了获得基本的人权。

对自由热爱的情绪正在高涨。为了发扬这种新精神,在这个新开始的日子,美国当前最高尚最雄心勃勃的工作,莫过于帮助建立一个公正、和平而又真正合乎人性的世界。

我们是一个强大的国家,我们必须保持充足的力量,它不需要经过战争考验的证明,这种从容自如的力量不仅是基于军火库的规模,也是基于思想的高尚。

我们将永远保持警惕,毫不松懈,我们将努力与贫穷、无知和不公正做斗争,因为这些要应付的敌人能将我们光荣地团结起来。

我们是一个以理想主义为荣的国家,但不要让人把我们的理想主义误认为是软弱。

因为我们是自由的,我们绝不能对自由在其他地方的命运漠不关心。我们的道德意识使我们明显地偏爱那些和我们一样对个人人权永远加以尊重的社会。我们并不恫吓别人,但是一个有人可以肆无忌惮作威作福的世界显然是不当的,而且也是对所有人类幸福的一种威胁。

这个世界仍在从事大规模的军备竞赛,以确保能在潜在的对手之间继续维持相等的力量。我们保证要以毅力和智慧努力使世界的军备只限于各国维持自身安全所需的范围。今年我们将开始向着我们的最终目标迈进,即从地球上消灭一切核武器。我们希望其他国家的人民加入我们的行动,因为它的成功即意味着人类生存而不是死亡。

在我们之中,显然有人正在认真而有意识地恢复信心,我也怀着这样一个希望,即在我任期届满时,人们会这样评论我们的国家:

我们记得弥迦的话,重新寻求谦卑、怜悯与公正。

for humility, mercy, and justice;

—that we had torn down the barriers that separated those of different race and region and religion, and where there had been mistrust, built unity, with a respect for diversity;

—that we had found productive work for those able to perform it;

—that we had strengthened the American family, which is the basis of our society;

—that we had ensured respect for the law, and equal treatment under the law, for the weak and the powerful, for the rich and the poor;

—and that we had enabled our people to be proud of their own Government once again.

I would hope that the nations of the world might say that we had built a lasting peace, built not on weapons of war but on international policies which reflect our own most precious values.

These are not just my goals, and they will not be my accomplishments, but the affirmation of our Nation's continuing moral strength and our belief in an undiminished, ever-expanding American dream.

我们已拆除了不同种族、不同地区与不同宗教人们之间的障碍,并在互不信任的地方,以尊重差异来建立团结。

我们已为那些能够胜任的人找到了合适的工作。

我们已巩固了美国的家庭,这是我们的社会基础。

我们已确保法律的尊严,在法律面前不论强弱贫富,一律平等。

我们已使我们的人民重新对自己的政府感到自豪。

我希望那时世界各国都说:我们已建立起一种持久的和平,不是基于战争的武器,而是基于足以反映我们自己最珍贵的价值观念的国际政策。

这些不仅仅是我的目标,也是我们共同的希望。它们将不是我个人的成就,而是我国持续不衰的道德力量以及我们那从未减弱反而日益扩大的"美国梦"的明证。

罗纳德·里根
Ronald Reagan

罗纳德·里根（Ronald Reagan）

生平简介 >>

罗纳德·里根是美国第四十任总统。他于1911年1月6日出生在伊利诺伊州。童年时他过着贫寒的生活。1932年，里根毕业于埃瑞加学院，此后有5年的时间都从事体育节目的播音员工作。1937年，里根改行当电影演员，拍了不少电影。"二战"时他服役于空军。

他曾经是民主党的自由派党员，1962年以后又转变成共和党的一员，并于1966年当选为加利福尼亚州州长。1970年再度获选连任。州长任期届满后，里根成为共和党保守派的发言人，而且差一点赢得1976年共和党总统候选人提名。1980年，他终于获得了总统候选人提名并当选。1984年又获选连任。

20世纪80年代，被作为"里根时代"而铭刻在人们的记忆中。执政的8年间，他恢复了公众对总统职权的信任，并使美国取得了战后历史上最长时期的经济发展。但他在位时的财政预算赤字规模也创造了历史新纪录。

里根的成就还为他的副手布什入主白宫铺平了道路。

里根是第一位遇刺未亡的总统，1981年3月遇刺，经抢救脱险。

Ronald Reagan
First Inaugural Address

January 20, 1981

Senator Hatfield, Mr. Chief Justice, Mr. President, Vice President Bush, Vice President Mondale, Senator Baker, Speaker O'Neill, Reverend Moomaw, and my fellow citizens:

To a few of us here today, this is a solemn and most momentous occasion; and yet, in the history of our Nation, it is a commonplace occurrence. The orderly transfer of authority as called for in the Constitution routinely takes place as it has for almost two centuries and few of us stop to think how unique we really are. In the eyes of many in the world, this every-4-year ceremony we accept as normal is nothing less than a miracle.

Mr. President, I want our fellow citizens to know how much you did to carry on this tradition. By your gracious cooperation in the transition process, you have shown a watching world that we are a united people pledged to maintaining a political system which guarantees individual liberty to a greater degree than any other, and I thank you and your people for all your help in maintaining the continuity which is the bulwark of our Republic.

The business of our nation goes forward. These United States are confronted with an economic affliction of great proportions. We suffer from the longest and one of the worst sustained inflations in our national history. It distorts our economic decisions, penalizes thrift, and crushes the struggling young and the fixed-income elderly alike. It threatens to shatter the lives of millions of our people.

罗纳德·里根
Ronald Reagan

里根总统首次就职演说

1981年1月20日

海特菲尔德议员、首席大法官先生、总统先生、副总统布什先生、副总统蒙代尔先生、贝克议员、议长奥尼尔先生、尊敬的摩麦先生，以及广大支持我的美国同胞们：

对我们今天在场的一些人来说，这是一个庄严和极其重要的时刻。但是，在我国的历史上，这只是一件普通的事情。宪法中所规定的有秩序的权力移交已进行了将近两个世纪，我们当中很少有人会想到这有什么独特之处，但在世界上许多人的眼中，我们视为平常的四年一度的典礼，简直是一个奇迹。

总统先生[1]，我要让同胞们了解，阁下在发扬这一传统中所做的贡献。阁下在移交过程中的密切合作，已向正在注视着我们的世界表明：我们是一个团结的民族，正致力于维持一种比任何其他制度更能确保个人自由的政治制度。感谢阁下及阁下的同僚在维持我们国家支柱的连续性方面所进行的一切努力。[2]

我们国家的事业正继续向前推进，合众国正面临着巨大的经济困难，我们遇到了一次我国历史上最长、最严重的通货膨胀。[3]它破坏了我们的经济政策，导致挥霍浪费，使那些挣扎着谋生的青年人和拿固定工资的中年人受到打击，它威胁着要摧毁千百万人民的生活。

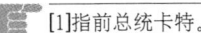

[1]指前总统卡特。
[2]在里根宣誓就职当日，被伊朗扣押的52名美国使馆人员获释。这是卡特政府多方努力的成果，也是献给新一届政府的一份厚礼。
[3]1980年，美国物价指数上涨幅度为13.5%。

Idle industries have cast workers into unemployment, causing human misery and personal indignity. Those who do work are denied a fair return for their labor by a tax system which penalizes successful achievement and keeps us from maintaining full productivity.

But great as our tax burden is, it has not kept pace with public spending. For decades, we have piled deficit upon deficit, mortgaging our future and our children's future for the temporary convenience of the present. To continue this long trend is to guarantee tremendous social, cultural, political, and economic upheavals.

You and I, as individuals, can, by borrowing, live beyond our means, but for only a limited period of time. Why, then, should we think that collectively, as a nation, we are not bound by that same limitation?

We must act today in order to preserve tomorrow. And let there be no misunderstanding—we are going to begin to act, beginning today.

The economic ills we suffer have come upon us over several decades. They will not go away in days, weeks, or months, but they will go away. They will go away because we, as Americans, have the capacity now, as we have had in the past, to do whatever needs to be done to preserve this last and greatest bastion of freedom.

In this present crisis, government is not the solution to our problem.

From time to time, we have been tempted to believe that society has become too complex to be managed by self-rule, that government by an elite group is superior to government for, by, and of the people. But if no one among us is capable of governing himself, then who among us has the capacity to govern someone else? All of us together, in and out of government, must bear the burden. The solutions we seek must be equitable, with no one group singled out to pay a higher price.

We hear much of special interest groups. Our concern must be for a special interest group that has been too long neglected. It knows no sectional boundaries or ethnic and racial divisions, and it crosses political party lines. It is made up of men and women who raise our food, patrol our streets, man our

罗纳德·里根
Ronald Reagan

萧条的工业使工人失业、蒙受痛苦并丧失个人尊严。那些仍拥有工作的人也因税收制度得不到公平的报酬。因为这种税收制度损害了我们事业的成功，使我们不能保持充分的生产力。[1]

但是，尽管我们纳税负担沉重，却一直无法跟上公共支出的增长。几十年来，我们的赤字不断增加[2]，结果只为了眼前一时的利益，把我们的前途和我们子孙的前途都给抵押出去了。这种趋势如果长此以往，必将引起社会、文化、政治与经济的巨大动荡。

作为个人，你们和我能够以借债方式过一种超出我们财力的生活，然而仅能维持一个有限的时期，我们又怎能认为一个国家不会受到同样的限制？

为了明天，我们必须今天就采取行动，请不要有任何误解，我们从今天起就要开始行动。

令我们深受其害的经济弊病，是由几十年累积而来的，这些弊病虽不会在几天、几星期或几个月之内消失，但它们终将会消失。它们之所以会最终消失，是因为现在的美国人和过去一样有能力去做一切需要完成的事，以保护这个最后和最伟大的自由堡垒。

在目前的这场危机中，政府的管理并不是解决问题的答案。

我们常常倾向于认为，社会已变得越来越复杂，以至于不能借自治方式来管理，我们还以为一个由精英集团治理的政府比民治、民享和民有的政府更加优越。试问，如果我们之中没有人能够管理自己，那么谁还有能力去管理他人呢？这个担子要由我们全体，包括政府官员和全体人民来承担。我们谋求的解决办法必须是公平的，不会只让某一团体付出较大的代价。

关于特殊利益集团，我们已听到很多谈论，然而现在我们必须关心一个长期被忽视了的利益集团。这个集团并无区域的界线，也超越了种族和政党的界线。它是由生产粮食、街头巡逻、工作在我们的矿场和工厂、教

---

[1]截至里根就职之日，美国的失业人数已达800万人，失业率达7.6%。
[2]1979年会计年度，联邦政府预算赤字达5800亿美元。

mines and our factories, teach our children, keep our homes, and heal us when we are sick—professionals, industrialists, shopkeepers, clerks, cabbies, and truckdrivers. They are, in short, "We the people," this breed called Americans.

Well, this administration's objective will be a healthy, vigorous, growing economy that provides equal opportunity for all Americans, with no barriers born of bigotry or discrimination. Putting America back to work means putting all Americans back to work. Ending inflation means freeing all Americans from the terror of runaway living costs. All must share in the productive work of this "new beginning" and all must share in the bounty of a revived economy. With the idealism and fair play which is the core of our system and our strength, we can have a strong and prosperous America at peace with itself and the world.

So, as we begin, let us take inventory. We are a nation that has a government—not the other way around. And this makes us special among the nations of the Earth. Our Government has no power except that granted it by the people. It is time to check and reverse the growth of government which shows signs of having grown beyond the consent of the governed.

It is my intention to curb the size and influence of the Federal establishment and to demand recognition of the distinction between the powers granted to the Federal Government and those reserved to the States or to the people. All of us need to be reminded that the Federal Government did not create the States; the States created the Federal Government.

Now, so there will be no misunderstanding, it is not my intention to do away with government. It is, rather, to make it work—work with us, not over us; to stand by our side, not ride on our back. Government can and must provide opportunity, not smother it; foster productivity, not stifle it.

If we look to the answer as to why, for so many years, we achieved so much, prospered as no other people on Earth, it was because here, in this land, we unleashed the energy and individual genius of man to a greater extent than has ever been done before. Freedom and the dignity of the individual have been more available and assured here than in any other place on Earth. The price for this freedom at times has been high, but we have never been unwilling to pay that price.

罗纳德·里根
Ronald Reagan

育我们的子女、管理我们的家务以及治疗我们疾病的人们所组成。他们是专业人员、实业家、店主、小职员、出租车和卡车司机,简言之,他们就是"我们的人民",就是美国人。

本届政府的目标就是建立一个健全、充满生机且不断发展的经济体,排除因偏见或歧视而造成的任何障碍,为所有美国人提供平等的机会。让美国重新运转起来,意味着让所有的美国人恢复工作。终止通货膨胀的意义,在于使所有美国人能从生活费用不断高涨的恐惧中解脱出来。大家都须分担这项"重新开始"的建设性工作,大家也都应分享经济复兴的成果。只要坚持构成我们制度核心的理想主义和公正主义,就能建立一个自身稳定而且能与全世界和平共处的强大、繁荣的美国。

在我们开始之时,首先让我们了解我们自身的情况。我们是一个拥有政府的国家,而不是一个拥有国家的政府。这一点使得我们在世界各国具有独特的地位。除非人民授予,我们的政府便毫无权力可言。目前,政府权力的膨胀已日渐显出有逾越被管理者所同意的范围的迹象,现在正是对这种趋势加以制止并扭转的时候。

我打算限制联邦政府的规模与权力,并要求诸位认识到联邦政府的权力与保留给各州和人民的权力之间的区别。大家都必须牢记不是联邦政府创立了各州,而是各州创立了联邦政府。

我希望大家不要误会,我无意废弃政府[1],而是要使其发挥功能,和我们一起合作,而不是凌驾于我们之上;和我们并肩而立,而不是骑在我们的背上。政府能够而且必须提供机会,而不是扼杀机会;它能够而且必须提高生产力,而不是抑制生产力。

如果我们探讨为什么这么多年来与地球上的其他国家相比,我们所取得的成就如此之多,所获得的繁荣如此之大,其原因是在这片土地上,我们使人的智慧和才能发挥到前所未有的程度。在这里,个人所享有的自由与尊严,超过世界上任何其他地方。虽然为这个自由所付出的代价常常很高,但我们从未因此而吝于付出。

---

[1]里根主张在经济上减轻人民的税务负担,实行财政平衡,废除政府的各种限制;在行政上实现"廉价政府"和"小政府",削减政府开支。

It is no coincidence that our present troubles parallel and are proportionate to the intervention and intrusion in our lives that result from unnecessary and excessive growth of government. It is time for us to realize that we are too great a nation to limit ourselves to small dreams. We are not, as some would have us believe, doomed to an inevitable decline. I do not believe in a fate that will fall on us no matter what we do. I do believe in a fate that will fall on us if we do nothing. So, with all the creative energy at our command, let us begin an era of national renewal. Let us renew our determination, our courage, and our strength. And let us renew our faith and our hope.

We have every right to dream heroic dreams. Those who say that we are in a time when there are no heroes just don't know where to look. You can see heroes every day going in and out of factory gates. Others, a handful in number, produce enough food to feed all of us and then the world beyond. You meet heroes across a counter—and they are on both sides of that counter. There are entrepreneurs with faith in themselves and faith in an idea who create new jobs, new wealth and opportunity. They are individuals and families whose taxes support the Government and whose voluntary gifts support church, charity, culture, art, and education. Their patriotism is quiet but deep. Their values sustain our national life.

I have used the words "they" and "their" in speaking of these heroes. I could say "you" and "your" because I am addressing the heroes of whom I speak—you, the citizens of this blessed land. Your dreams, your hopes, your goals are going to be the dreams, the hopes, and the goals of this administration, so help me God.

We shall reflect the compassion that is so much a part of your makeup. How can we love our country and not love our countrymen, and loving them, reach out a hand when they fall, heal them when they are sick, and provide opportunities to make them self-sufficient so they will be equal in fact and not just in theory?

罗纳德·里根
Ronald Reagan

我们当前所面临的困难，与由于政府不必要的过度膨胀所造成的对我们的生活的干预同步增加，这绝非巧合。我们现在必须了解美国乃是一个泱泱大国，因此绝不能自囿于小小的梦想。虽然有些人企图使我们相信，但我们却不认为那种不可避免的衰退现象是命中注定的事，我也不同意那种不论我们如何努力，某种命运都将落在我们身上的说法，但我相信如果我们听天由命的话，这种命运必将落在我们身上。因此，让我们运用我们掌握的一切创造力开始一个国家复兴的时代吧！让我们重新建立起我们的决心、勇气和力量，让我们重新建立起我们的信仰和希望。

我们完全有权利去做英雄式的梦。有些人说我们处在一个没有英雄的时代，他们只是没有找对地方。每天你都可以看到无数的英雄进出各工厂的大门。其他一些英雄，数目虽少，却生产着足够的粮食以供养我们大家和世界上许多地区。你在柜台旁就能遇见英雄，柜台内外的人都是英雄。那些对自己及其理想有信心并创造出许多新工作、新财富、新机会的企业家们是英雄。那些纳税的个人与家庭也是英雄，因为他们所纳的税支持了政府，他们出于自愿的捐款支持了教会、慈善事业、文化、艺术和教育，他们的爱国主义虽然是默默无声，但却影响深远，他们的价值观念维系着我们国家的生命。

到现在为止，我都用"他们"和"他们的"等字眼来形容这些英雄，我也可以用"你们"和"你们的"，因为我正在对那些我前面提过的英雄们发表演说，那些英雄就是你们，这块上帝赐福的土地上的公民。你们的梦想、希望和目标将是本届政府的梦想、希望和目标。[1]愿上帝帮助我。

本届政府将体现出那已成为你们本性一部分的仁爱之心。我们怎能只爱我们的国家而不爱我们的同胞呢？我们当然爱他们！他们跌倒了，我们伸出援助之手；他们生病了，我们帮着治愈；我们也提供机会，使他们能够自立，使他们在理论上和实际上都享有平等。我们有理由不这样做吗？

---

[1]当时的通货膨胀率及失业率上升，许多美国人都感到悲观失望。美国人对民意测验机构说，这是一个幻想破灭的时代。里根就职时，提出"恢复经济和军事实力"与"重振国威"的口号。里根曾说，"我的美好想法之一是通过使其重新相信自己来帮助美国人摆脱悲观失望情绪"，并要使人民相信，"美国是异乎寻常的，是世界的模范"。

美国历届总统就职演说
THE INAUGURAL ADDRESSES OF THE U.S. PRESIDENTS

Can we solve the problems confronting us? Well, the answer is an unequivocal and emphatic "yes." To paraphrase Winston Churchill, I did not take the oath I have just taken with the intention of presiding over the dissolution of the world's strongest economy.

In the days ahead I will propose removing the roadblocks that have slowed our economy and reduced productivity. Steps will be taken aimed at restoring the balance between the various levels of government. Progress may be slow—measured in inches and feet, not miles—but we will progress. It is time to reawaken this industrial giant, to get government back within its means, and to lighten our punitive tax burden. And these will be our first priorities, and on these principles, there will be no compromise.

On the eve of our struggle for independence a man who might have been one of the greatest among the Founding Fathers, Dr. Joseph Warren, President of the Massachusetts Congress, said to his fellow Americans, "Our country is in danger, but not to be despaired of.... On you depend the fortunes of America. You are to decide the important questions upon which rests the happiness and the liberty of millions yet unborn. Act worthy of yourselves."

Well, I believe we, the Americans of today, are ready to act worthy of ourselves, ready to do what must be done to ensure happiness and liberty for ourselves, our children and our children's children.

And as we renew ourselves here in our own land, we will be seen as having greater strength throughout the world. We will again be the exemplar of freedom and a beacon of hope for those who do not now have freedom.

To those neighbors and allies who share our freedom, we will strengthen our historic ties and assure them of our support and firm commitment. We will match loyalty with loyalty. We will strive for mutually beneficial relations. We will not use our friendship to impose on their sovereignty, for our own sovereignty is not for sale.

As for the enemies of freedom, those who are potential adversaries, they will be reminded that peace is the highest aspiration of the American people. We will negotiate for it, sacrifice for it; we will not surrender for it—now or ever.

Our forbearance should never be misunderstood. Our reluctance for conflict

罗纳德·里根
Ronald Reagan

我们有能力解决面对的问题吗？答案是绝对肯定的。用温斯顿·丘吉尔的话说，我刚才所立的誓言，绝不是想使全球最强大的经济体瓦解。

在未来的日子里，我将计划消除导致我们经济不景气以及生产力下降的许多障碍，我也将采取步骤来恢复各级政府间的平衡。进展将可能很缓慢，只能以英寸、英尺来衡量，而不能以英里来计算，但我们一定会取得进步。唤醒我们这个工业巨人，使政府能够重新量入为出，减轻我们惩罚性的赋税负担，这个时刻已经到来。这些都是我们的当务之急，我们将坚守这些原则，决不妥协。

在我们的国家争取独立战争胜利的前夕，那位如果不是因为发生意外而一定会成为开国元勋的马萨诸塞州议会主席约瑟夫·沃伦博士曾告诉他的美国同胞说："我国正处于危急状态，但不要失望……美国的命运全靠你们。我们未来成千上万的尚未出世的子孙的幸福与自由，也得由你们来决定。努力干吧！不要辜负了你们的职责。"

我相信今天的美国人民已经准备好去行动，以保障我们及子孙后代的幸福与自由。

当我们在自己的国土上发奋图强时，我们在世界就会被认为更加有力量。我们将再次成为自由的典范，给那些还没有获得自由的人们带来希望之光。

对于那些和我们一样具有自由理想的邻国及盟邦，我们将加强彼此间传统性的沟通，并向他们保证我们对他们的支持与坚定的承诺。我们将以诚相待。我们将为互惠的关系而努力，我们决不会利用彼此的友谊骗取他国的主权，因为我们本身的主权同样也是不可出卖的。

对于那些自由的敌人及潜在的对手，我们将提醒他们，和平是美国人民的最高愿望和追求，他们将为它而谈判，为它奋斗和牺牲，但我们决不会为它而投降，不管是现在还是将来。

我们的克制任何时候都不能被误解，我们不愿发生冲突也不应被误认

should not be misjudged as a failure of will. When action is required to preserve our national security, we will act. We will maintain sufficient strength to prevail if need be, knowing that if we do so we have the best chance of never having to use that strength.

Above all, we must realize that no arsenal, or no weapon in the arsenals of the world, is so formidable as the will and moral courage of free men and women. It is a weapon our adversaries in today's world do not have. It is a weapon that we as Americans do have. Let that be understood by those who practice terrorism and prey upon their neighbors.

I am told that tens of thousands of prayer meetings are being held on this day, and for that I am deeply grateful. We are a nation under God, and I believe God intended for us to be free. It would be fitting and good, I think, if on each Inauguration Day in future years it should be declared a day of prayer.

This is the first time in history that this ceremony has been held, as you have been told, on this West Front of the Capitol. Standing here, one faces a magnificent vista, opening up on this city's special beauty and history. At the end of this open mall are those shrines to the giants on whose shoulders we stand.

Directly in front of me, the monument to a monumental man: George Washington, Father of our country. A man of humility who came to greatness reluctantly. He led America out of revolutionary victory into infant nationhood. Off to one side, the stately memorial to Thomas Jefferson. The Declaration of Independence flames with his eloquence.

And then beyond the Reflecting Pool the dignified columns of the Lincoln Memorial. Whoever would understand in his heart the meaning of America will find it in the life of Abraham Lincoln.

Beyond those monuments to heroism is the Potomac River, and on the far shore the sloping hills of Arlington National Cemetery with its row on row of simple white markers bearing crosses or Stars of David. They add up to only a tiny fraction of the price that has been paid for our freedom.

Each one of those markers is a monument to the kinds of hero I spoke of earlier. Their lives ended in places called Belleau Wood, The Argonne, Omaha Beach, Salerno and halfway around the world on Guadalcanal, Tarawa, Pork

罗纳德·里根
Ronald Reagan

为是意志不坚。当必须采取行动来保护我们国家的安全时，我们就会采取行动。如果必要的话，我们也将维持足够的力量去争取优势。因为我们知道，只有这样做我们才最有可能永远避免使用那种力量。

更为重要的是，我们必须认识到世界上没有任何一种武器能比得上自由的人的意志、维护道德的勇气，这种武器是目前世界上任何敌人所没有的，唯有我们美国人民拥有这种武器，一切从事恐怖活动并劫掠其邻国的人最好能了解这一点。

当得知今天举行的祷告会成千上万时，我非常感激。我们是一个在上帝保佑下的国家。我相信上帝希望我们永远享有自由。如果每个就职日都是祈祷日，那将是件非常美好的事。

总统就职典礼在国会大厦西侧举行，这在我国历史上还是第一次。站在此地，我们面对着壮丽的景色，华盛顿的美景和历史古迹都能一览无余。在这条开阔大道的尽头，是一些伟人的纪念堂，我们现在正是站在这些伟人的肩膀上。

我的对面是一位伟人——美国国父乔治·华盛顿——的纪念碑。他是一位谦逊、伟大而不居功的人。他领导美国从革命成功步入一个国家的初创时期。另一边是托马斯·杰斐逊的纪念碑，《独立宣言》由于他的文采而生辉。

在"倒映池"后是由大圆柱组成的庄严的林肯纪念堂，凡是了解"美国"真谛的人，都将会在亚伯拉罕·林肯的一生中找到答案。

在英雄纪念碑之后，就是波托马克河，岸边的山坡上则是阿灵顿国家公墓，其上成排列着简单的白色十字架或大卫之星墓碑，这些仅仅是我们为自由所付出的代价的极小的部分。

那里的每一座墓碑，都是对刚才所提到的那些英雄的纪念，他们在贝洛森林、阿尔贡森林、奥马哈海滩、萨勒诺港，以及东半球的瓜达尔卡纳尔岛、塔拉瓦岛、猪排山、长律湖和越南的稻田、丛林中牺牲了生命。

Chop Hill, the Chosin Reservoir, and in a hundred rice paddies and jungles of a place called Vietnam.

Under one such marker lies a young man—Martin Treptow—who left his job in a small town barber shop in 1917 to go to France with the famed Rainbow Division. There, on the western front, he was killed trying to carry a message between battalions under heavy artillery fire.

We are told that on his body was found a diary. On the flyleaf under the heading, "My Pledge," he had written these words: "America must win this war. Therefore, I will work, I will save, I will sacrifice, I will endure, I will fight cheerfully and do my utmost, as if the issue of the whole struggle depended on me alone."

The crisis we are facing today does not require of us the kind of sacrifice that Martin Treptow and so many thousands of others were called upon to make. It does require, however, our best effort, and our willingness to believe in ourselves and to believe in our capacity to perform great deeds; to believe that together, with God's help, we can and will resolve the problems which now confront us.

And, after all, why shouldn't we believe that? We are Americans. God bless you, and thank you.

Ronald Reagan
Second Inaugural Address

January 21, 1985

Senator Mathias, Chief Justice Burger, Vice President Bush, Speaker O'Neill, Senator Dole, Reverend Clergy, members of my family and friends, and my fellow citizens:

This day has been made brighter with the presence here of one who, for a

罗纳德·里根
Ronald Reagan

这些墓碑下埋葬着一位青年——马丁·特雷普托，他在1917年放弃了他的一个小镇理发厅的工作，随着著名的"彩虹师"前往法国。在法国西部前线的猛烈炮火中为大军传递情报时阵亡。

我们获知在他的遗体上发现了一本日记，他在空白页上写着："我的誓言：美国必须打赢这场战争。因此，我会努力、我会拯救、我会牺牲、我会忍耐、我会尽全力英勇奋战，就像整个战争全靠我一个人一样。"

我们今天面临的危机，并不需要像马丁·特雷普托以及成千上万其他人所做的那种牺牲，但这些危机仍需要我们尽最大的努力，以及我们坚信自己有能力去创造丰功伟绩，坚信通过团结合作，再加上上帝的帮助，我们一定能够解决我们所面临的一切问题。

为什么不相信这些呢？要记住，我们都是美国人！愿上帝保佑我们，谢谢大家。

里根总统第二次就职演说

1985年1月21日

马塞厄斯参议员、伯格首席大法官、布什副总统、奥尼尔议长、多尔参议员、尊敬的牧师、我的家人和同胞们：

今天由于一个人的出席，使得典礼光辉夺目，这个人曾暂时离开过我

time, has been absent—Senator John Stennis.

God bless you and welcome back.

There is, however, one who is not with us today: Representative Gillis Long of Louisiana left us last night. I wonder if we could all join in a moment of silent prayer. (Moment of silent prayer.) Amen.

There are no words adequate to express my thanks for the great honor that you have bestowed on me. I will do my utmost to be deserving of your trust.

This is, as Senator Mathias told us, the 50th time that we the people have celebrated this historic occasion. When the first President, George Washington, placed his hand upon the Bible, he stood less than a single day's journey by horseback from raw, untamed wilderness. There were 4 million Americans in a union of 13 States. Today we are 60 times as many in a union of 50 States. We have lighted the world with our inventions, gone to the aid of mankind wherever in the world there was a cry for help, journeyed to the Moon and safely returned. So much has changed. And yet we stand together as we did two centuries ago.

When I took this oath four years ago, I did so in a time of economic stress. Voices were raised saying we had to look to our past for the greatness and glory. But we, the present-day Americans, are not given to looking backward. In this blessed land, there is always a better tomorrow.

Four years ago, I spoke to you of a new beginning and we have accomplished that. But in another sense, our new beginning is a continuation of that beginning created two centuries ago when, for the first time in history, government, the people said, was not our master, it is our servant; its only power that which we the people allow it to have.

That system has never failed us, but, for a time, we failed the system. We asked things of government that government was not equipped to give. We yielded authority to the National Government that properly belonged to States or to local governments or to the people themselves. We allowed taxes and inflation to rob us of our earnings and savings and watched the great industrial machine that had made us the most productive people on Earth slow down and the number of unemployed increase.

罗纳德·里根
Ronald Reagan

们，他就是约翰·斯坦尼斯参议员。

上帝保佑你，欢迎你的归来。

但是，今天也有一个人没有能和我们在一起，他是路易斯安那州的吉利斯·朗议员，他昨天晚上离开了我们，请让我们默默地为他祈祷吧！阿门！

对各位给予我的殊荣，我找不到恰当的语言来表达我的感激之情。我将尽我最大的努力，不负你们对我的重托。

正如马塞厄斯参议员所说，这已是我们的人民第50次庆祝这一历史仪式。当第一位总统乔治·华盛顿把他的手放在这本《圣经》上的时候，我们的地域不大，若骑上一匹马，仅仅一天时间即可穿过原始的、尚未开发的荒野。那时候，13个州的联盟共有400万人。而今，我们已是50个州的联盟，人口是原来的60倍。我们的发明和创造照亮了这个世界，无论来自世界哪个角落的呼救我们都曾给予了他们最大的帮助。我们曾踏上月球，并安全返回。变化如此之大，然而我们一起站在这里，仍像200年前那样。

四年前我宣誓的时候，正值我国经济困难时期。有些人大声疾呼，我们应该回首过去的伟大和光荣。但是，我们今天的美国人不应一味向后看。在这块上帝保佑的土地上，明天总是更美好的。

四年前，我曾对你们说起一个新的开端，现在我们已经实现了。然而，从另一种意义上来讲，这种新的开端不过是两个世纪前创造的开端的继续。那时候，人们在历史上第一次这样宣称，政府不是我们的主人，它是我们的公仆。这是我们人民允许它拥有的唯一的权力。

这种制度从未令我们失望过，而我们却曾一度有负于这个制度。我们要求政府给予我们的东西是它没有能力提供的。我们把原应当属于州政府、地方政府或人民自己的权力交给了联邦政府。我们听任税收和通货膨胀劫取了我们的所得和积蓄。我们看到巨大的工业机构使得地球上最富生产能力的民族衰退下来，失业的人数剧增。

美国历届总统就职演说
THE INAUGURAL ADDRESSES OF THE U.S. PRESIDENTS

By 1980, we knew it was time to renew our faith, to strive with all our strength toward the ultimate in individual freedom consistent with an orderly society.

We believed then and now there are no limits to growth and human progress when men and women are free to follow their dreams.

And we were right to believe that. Tax rates have been reduced, inflation cut dramatically, and more people are employed than ever before in our history.

We are creating a nation once again vibrant, robust, and alive. But there are many mountains yet to climb. We will not rest until every American enjoys the fullness of freedom, dignity, and opportunity as our birthright. It is our birthright as citizens of this great Republic, and we'll meet this challenge.

These will be years when Americans have restored their confidence and tradition of progress; when our values of faith, family, work, and neighborhood were restated for a modern age; when our economy was finally freed from government's grip; when we made sincere efforts at meaningful arms reduction, rebuilding our defenses, our economy, and developing new technologies, and helped preserve peace in a troubled world; when Americans courageously supported the struggle for liberty, self-government, and free enterprise throughout the world, and turned the tide of history away from totalitarian darkness and into the warm sunlight of human freedom.

My fellow citizens, our Nation is poised for greatness. We must do what we know is right and do it with all our might. Let history say of us, "These were golden years—when the American Revolution was reborn, when freedom gained new life, when America reached for her best."

Our two-party system has served us well over the years, but never better than in those times of great challenge when we came together not as Democrats or Republicans, but as Americans united in a common cause.

Two of our Founding Fathers, a Boston lawyer named Adams and a Virginia planter named Jefferson, members of that remarkable group who met in Independence Hall and dared to think they could start the world over again, left us an important lesson. They had become political rivals in the Presidential

罗纳德·里根
Ronald Reagan

直到1980年,我们知道该是我们恢复信心、全力以赴争取与有序社会相一致的个人自由的时候了。

我们总是相信,当人们能自由地追寻他们的理想时,社会的发展和人类的进步就没有极限。

我们的信念是正确的。现在税率已经降低,通货膨胀也大幅下降,就业的人数比我国以往历史上任何时候都多。

我们正在重新创造一个国家,使它无比强大,充满活力。然而,仍有许多高山要攀登,我们将永不停息,努力奋斗,直到所有的美国人都充分享受到自由、尊严和机会这些我们与生俱有的权利。这种权利是伟大的合众国每一位公民都享有的权利。我们将迎接这一挑战。

我们一旦接受这一挑战,就要在数年时间里恢复信心和进步传统;重申信仰、家庭、工作和睦邻的价值;摆脱政府对我们经济的控制;为有意义的裁减军备做出真诚的努力,重建我们的国防,发展我们的经济和新技术,在这纷杂的世界上维护世界和平;勇敢地支持全世界人民争取自由、自治和自由企业制度,并使历史的潮流从极权主义的黑暗中转向人类自由温暖的阳光下。

亲爱的同胞们,我们的国家正蓄势而上,我们必须懂得去做我们认为正确的事情,并且不遗余力。要让历史这样评价我们:在那些金色的岁月里,美国精神得到了振兴,自由获得了新生,美国获得了丰硕的成果。

应当说,在过去的许多年中,我们的两党制为美国带来了巨大的好处,为我们解决了许多问题。但是,我们还有比这种制度更好的东西,当我们面临挑战的时候,我们走到一起,不是作为共和党或民主党,而是作为美国人,为了共同的事业,团结在一起。

我们的两位立国之父,一位是波士顿的律师亚当斯,另一位是弗吉尼亚的种植园主杰斐逊,他们是那个时代的杰出代表。这两位伟人相聚在独立大厅,他们敢于设想自己能开创新的世界。他们给我们留下了重要的训诫。在1800年的总统选举中,他们成为政敌。然而,多年之后,他们退离了工作岗

election of 1800. Then years later, when both were retired, and age had softened their anger, they began to speak to each other again through letters. A bond was reestablished between those two who had helped create this government of ours.

In 1826, the 50th anniversary of the Declaration of Independence, they both died. They died on the same day, within a few hours of each other, and that day was the Fourth of July.

In one of those letters exchanged in the sunset of their lives, Jefferson wrote: "It carries me back to the times when, beset with difficulties and dangers, we were fellow laborers in the same cause, struggling for what is most valuable to man, his right to self-government. Laboring always at the same oar, with some wave ever ahead threatening to overwhelm us, and yet passing harmless ... we rode through the storm with heart and hand."

Well, with heart and hand, let us stand as one today: One people under God determined that our future shall be worthy of our past. As we do, we must not repeat the well-intentioned errors of our past. We must never again abuse the trust of working men and women, by sending their earnings on a futile chase after the spiraling demands of a bloated Federal Establishment. You elected us in 1980 to end this prescription for disaster, and I don't believe you reelected us in 1984 to reverse course.

At the heart of our efforts is one idea vindicated by 25 straight months of economic growth: Freedom and incentives unleash the drive and entrepreneurial genius that are the core of human progress. We have begun to increase the rewards for work, savings, and investment; reduce the increase in the cost and size of government and its interference in people's lives.

We must simplify our tax system, make it more fair, and bring the rates down for all who work and earn. We must think anew and move with a new boldness, so every American who seeks work can find work; so the least among us shall have an equal chance to achieve the greatest things—to be heroes who heal our sick, feed the hungry, protect peace among nations, and leave this world a better place.

The time has come for a new American emancipation—a great national

罗纳德·里根
Ronald Reagan

位,年龄的增长驱散了他们心头的怨恨,他们又开始了通信交谈,帮助建立我们这个政府的两位先生之间又重新建立起新的纽带。

1826年,当纪念《独立宣言》发表50周年时,他们二人去世了。他们逝世在同一天,只相差几个小时。那一天是7月4日。

在他们垂暮之年的通信中,杰斐逊写道:"它把我带回到那个时代,那时,我们面临重要困难和危险。我们是同胞,都在为一个事业,人类最宝贵的东西——自治的权力而奋斗。像同划着一支桨一样,前面总有恶浪企图吞没我们,然而风浪过去之后,我们却毫无伤害……我们的心紧紧连在一起,手挽着手闯过了这些风暴。"

今天,让我们也同样紧密团结在一起,在上帝指引下,使我们的未来无愧于我们的过去。要做到这一点,我们就绝对不能重蹈覆辙。我们不能再次辜负劳动大众,把他们所创造的财富用在满足膨胀的联邦权力机构提出的需求上。1980年你们选举我们以便结束这场灾难。我相信1984年你们再次选举我们不是为了使历史逆转。

连续25个月经济的持续增长证明了一个观点:自由与激励使企业家的能动性和天才得到了发挥,这是人类进步的核心。我们增加了对工作、储蓄和投资的奖励,缩减了政府的规模和开支,减少了政府对人民生活的干预。

我们必须简化我们的税收制度,使之更公平,要减少对所有靠工作挣钱的人的税收。我们必须重新考虑采取更新、更大胆的举动,以便使每一个寻找工作的美国人都能找到工作,并使我们当中的最普通的人也能得到一个平等的机会,去进行他们最伟大的事业,成为治愈疾病的英雄,从事慈善的英雄,维持国际和平的英雄,以使这个世界更美好。

新的美国解放的时刻已经到来——这是一场全国范围的摧毁阻碍经济发

drive to tear down economic barriers and liberate the spirit of enterprise in the most distressed areas of our country. My friends, together we can do this, and do it we must, so help me God.

From new freedom will spring new opportunities for growth, a more productive, fulfilled and united people, and a stronger America—an America that will lead the technological revolution, and also open its mind and heart and soul to the treasures of literature, music, and poetry, and the values of faith, courage, and love.

A dynamic economy, with more citizens working and paying taxes, will be our strongest tool to bring down budget deficits. But an almost unbroken 50 years of deficit spending has finally brought us to a time of reckoning. We have come to a turning point, a moment for hard decisions. I have asked the Cabinet and my staff a question, and now I put the same question to all of you: If not us, who? And if not now, when? It must be done by all of us going forward with a program aimed at reaching a balanced budget. We can then begin reducing the national debt.

I will shortly submit a budget to the Congress aimed at freezing government program spending for the next year. Beyond that, we must take further steps to permanently control Government's power to tax and spend. We must act now to protect future generations from Government's desire to spend its citizens' money and tax them into servitude when the bills come due. Let us make it unconstitutional for the Federal Government to spend more than the Federal Government takes in.

We have already started returning to the people and to State and local governments responsibilities better handled by them. Now, there is a place for the Federal Government in matters of social compassion. But our fundamental goals must be to reduce dependency and upgrade the dignity of those who are infirm or disadvantaged. And here a growing economy and support from family and community offer our best chance for a society where compassion is a way of life, where the old and infirm are cared for, the young and, yes, the unborn protected, and the unfortunate looked after and made self-sufficient.

And there is another area where the Federal Government can play a part.

展障碍,在我国最贫困地区发扬进取精神的运动。朋友们,我们团结一心,我们就可以完成这一事业,我们一定要完成这项事业。愿上帝护佑我们。

新的自由会带来新的发展机会,一个更富有创造性、更勇于实现自己抱负和更团结的美国;新的自由也会使美国更加强大。美国将领导新的技术革命。面对文学、音乐和诗歌的宝库,面对忠诚、勇气和仁爱的价值观,美国人民将敞开他们的胸怀。

有更多公民工作和纳税的充满活力的经济,是我们减少预算赤字的最强大的工具。连续50年的财政赤字,已到了我们对它进行彻底清算的时候了。现在,我们已到了一个转折点,到了做出艰难抉择的关头。我已向内阁和我的助手们提出一个问题,现在我把这个问题摆在你们的面前。如果不是由我们还能由谁来清算?如果不是现在又更待何时?这些事必须由我们全体共同去做,即制订出一个旨在达到预算平衡的计划,然后削减国家债务。

我将尽快向国会提交一份旨在明年冻结政府计划支出的预算报告。除此之外,我们必须采取进一步的措施,以便永远控制政府对税收和支出的权限。现在我们就必须做出反应,保护未来的几代人,使他们免遭政府挥霍公民的钱以及向他们征税的欲望,免遭当他们的账单到期时无钱兑付之苦。联邦政府如果寅吃卯粮便是违法的行为。

我们已开始交回那些人民、州和地方政府能够处理得更好的事务的权力。对联邦政府来说,现在有一项社会关爱工作。但是,对那些年老体弱、无生活能力的人,我们最基本的目标必须是减少他们的依赖性,提高他们的社会尊严。日益增长的经济和来自家庭及社团的支持,为我们提供了一个最好的机会来建立一种社会。在这个社会中,仁爱是一种生活方式;在这个社会中,老弱病残者将得到关心,年幼的和尚未出生的婴儿将受到保护,不幸者将受到照顾并使之自立。

现在,还有另一个领域联邦政府可以发挥其作用。作为一个上了年纪的

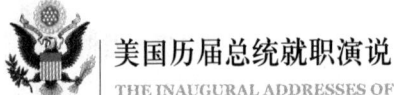

As an older American, I remember a time when people of different race, creed, or ethnic origin in our land found hatred and prejudice installed in social custom and, yes, in law. There is no story more heartening in our history than the progress that we have made toward the "brotherhood of man" that God intended for us. Let us resolve there will be no turning back or hesitation on the road to an America rich in dignity and abundant with opportunity for all our citizens.

Let us resolve that we the people will build an American opportunity society in which all of us—white and black, rich and poor, young and old—will go forward together arm in arm. Again, let us remember that though our heritage is one of blood lines from every corner of the Earth, we are all Americans pledged to carry on this last, best hope of man on Earth.

I have spoken of our domestic goals and the limitations which we should put on our National Government. Now let me turn to a task which is the primary responsibility of National Government—the safety and security of our people.

Today, we utter no prayer more fervently than the ancient prayer for peace on Earth. Yet history has shown that peace will not come, nor will our freedom be preserved, by good will alone. There are those in the world who scorn our vision of human dignity and freedom. One nation, the Soviet Union, has conducted the greatest military buildup in the history of man, building arsenals of awesome offensive weapons.

We have made progress in restoring our defense capability. But much remains to be done. There must be no wavering by us, nor any doubts by others, that America will meet her responsibilities to remain free, secure, and at peace.

There is only one way safely and legitimately to reduce the cost of national security, and that is to reduce the need for it. And this we are trying to do in negotiations with the Soviet Union. We are not just discussing limits on a further increase of nuclear weapons. We seek, instead, to reduce their number. We seek the total elimination one day of nuclear weapons from the face of the Earth.

Now, for decades, we and the Soviets have lived under the threat of mutual assured destruction; if either resorted to the use of nuclear weapons, the other could retaliate and destroy the one who had started it. Is there either logic or

罗纳德·里根
Ronald Reagan

美国人，我曾记得有一个时期，在我们这块土地上出生的不同种族、不同信仰或不同民族的人民发现，我们的社会风俗和法律中存在着偏见和相互间的仇恨。在我们的历史上，没有任何一件事比我们在"人人皆兄弟"这方面取得的进步更振奋人心。这也是上帝对我们的期望。美国要人人有尊严，每一个公民都可以享有充分的机会，在这条道路上，我们决不反悔也决不犹豫。

让我们决心把美国建成一个机会均等的社会，在这里，无论白人还是黑人，无论富人还是穷人，无论年轻人还是老年人，都能携手并肩共同前进。让我们再次记住，尽管我们的祖先来自世界各个角落，拥有不同血统，然而，我们都是美国人，我们立志要实现人类最终也是最美好的希望。

我已谈了国内我们要实现的目标和我们应对联邦政府施加的各种限制。现在让我们转向另一项任务，它也是联邦政府的一个基本任务，即我国人民的安全保障。

今天，我们对任何一件事的祈祷也不像对古老的和平的祈祷那样热诚。然而，历史已经证明和平与我们的自由不会因为良好的愿望而自动到来和持续下去。世界上还有些人嘲笑我们对人类尊严和自由的远见。有一个国家叫苏联，进行着人类的历史上最庞大的军事准备，建立了令人畏惧的攻击性武器库。

在恢复我们的防卫能力方面，我们已取得了进展，但是还有更多的事情要做，我们决不动摇，别人也不应怀疑，美国一定不负使命，保持自由、安定与和平。

削减国防开支的唯一可靠合理的途径，就是削减国防开支的需求。我们在同苏联的谈判中正努力这样做。我们不仅仅讨论对核武器进一步加以限制，而且我们正寻求减少核武器的数量。我们在寻求有一天在地球上最终全面销毁核武器。

几十年来，我们同苏联都生活在一种可能相互毁灭的威胁之下，如果任何一方使用核武器，另一方将实施报复，毁灭首先使用核武器的一方。[1]这

---

[1] 据1985年统计资料显示，在运载工具方面，美国有1966件，苏联有2495件；在弹头数量方面，美国拥有11262枚，苏联有9524枚。

morality in believing that if one side threatens to kill tens of millions of our people, our only recourse is to threaten killing tens of millions of theirs?

I have approved a research program to find, if we can, a security shield that would destroy nuclear missiles before they reach their target. It wouldn't kill people, it would destroy weapons. It wouldn't militarize space, it would help demilitarize the arsenals of Earth. It would render nuclear weapons obsolete. We will meet with the Soviets, hoping that we can agree on a way to rid the world of the threat of nuclear destruction.

We strive for peace and security, heartened by the changes all around us. Since the turn of the century, the number of democracies in the world has grown fourfold. Human freedom is on the march, and nowhere more so than our own hemisphere. Freedom is one of the deepest and noblest aspirations of the human spirit. People, worldwide, hunger for the right of self-determination, for those inalienable rights that make for human dignity and progress.

America must remain freedom's staunchest friend, for freedom is our best ally.

And it is the world's only hope, to conquer poverty and preserve peace. Every blow we inflict against poverty will be a blow against its dark allies of oppression and war. Every victory for human freedom will be a victory for world peace.

So we go forward today, a nation still mighty in its youth and powerful in its purpose. With our alliances strengthened, with our economy leading the world to a new age of economic expansion, we look forward to a world rich in possibilities. And all this because we have worked and acted together, not as members of political parties, but as Americans.

My friends, we live in a world that is lit by lightning. So much is changing and will change, but so much endures, and transcends time.

History is a ribbon, always unfurling; history is a journey. And as we continue our journey, we think of those who traveled before us. We stand together again at the steps of this symbol of our democracy—or we would have been standing at the steps if it hadn't gotten so cold. Now we are standing inside this symbol of our democracy. Now we hear again the echoes of our past: a

罗纳德·里根
Ronald Reagan

样一来，如果对方威胁要毁灭我们成千上万的人，我们唯一的行动便是威胁毁灭他们成千上万的人，这难道符合逻辑或道德吗？

我刚刚批准了一项研究发明安全防卫方法的计划[1]。这就是在导弹未到达目标之前，就将其摧毁。它将不会伤害人民，而只是摧毁武器；它也不会使空间军事化，而是将使地球上各种武器库实现非军事化，使核武器成为废物。我们将会见苏联人并希望达成一项协议，使整个世界摆脱核毁灭的威胁。

世界的巨大变化鼓舞着我们去为和平与安全而奋斗。自本世纪以来，世界上民主国家的数量已增长了四倍。人类争取自由的斗争在我们这一半球上比在任何地方都大踏步地前进；自由是人类精神世界中最深邃、最高尚的追求之一。全世界的人民都渴望享有自决的权利，渴望享有对于人类的尊严和进步的不可剥夺的权利。

美国必须继续成为自由最坚定的朋友，因为自由是我们最好的盟友。

自由是维护和平、消灭饥饿的唯一希望。我们对贫穷的每一次打击都是对压迫和战争这个贫穷的黑色联盟的打击。我们为人类自由而获得的每一次胜利，都将是争取世界和平的胜利。

因此，我们今天仍在向前发展，这个民族仍处在它年轻的强盛时期，并执着、坚定地追求自己的目标。随着我们联盟的加强，我们的经济领导世界走向经济发展的新时代，展望未来，我们充满无限的潜力。这一切之所以成为可能，就是因为我们共同工作共同行动，不是作为政党的一员，而是作为美国人。

朋友们，我们生活在一个电闪雷鸣的世界里。这个世界在发生着巨大的变化，并将继续发生变化，如此多的东西将长存并超越时代。

历史是一条不断展开的缎带，历史也是一次旅程。当我们继续行进的时候，我们一定会想到走在我们前面的人。原本，我们要再次站在象征着我国民主制的国会大厦的台阶上，但由于天气太冷，我们站在国会大厦里

---

[1]指"星球大战"计划。

general falls to his knees in the hard snow of Valley Forge; a lonely President paces the darkened halls, and ponders his struggle to preserve the Union; the men of the Alamo call out encouragement to each other; a settler pushes west and sings a song, and the song echoes out forever and fills the unknowing air.

It is the American sound. It is hopeful, big-hearted, idealistic, daring, decent, and fair. That's our heritage; that is our song. We sing it still. For all our problems, our differences, we are together as of old, as we raise our voices to the God who is the Author of this most tender music. And may He continue to hold us close as we fill the world with our sound—sound in unity, affection, and love—one people under God, dedicated to the dream of freedom that He has placed in the human heart, called upon now to pass that dream on to a waiting and hopeful world.

God bless you and may God bless America.

罗纳德·里根
Ronald Reagan

面。[1]此时我们耳畔回荡着历史的回声,我们仿佛看见:一位将军在福吉谷寒冷的冰雪中跪倒;一位孤独的总统徘徊在黑暗的大厅,考虑着为维护联邦的战斗;美国西南部的人喊叫着互相鼓舞;一位开拓者向西部挺进,他唱着一首歌,这首歌永不消逝,回荡在未知的天空中。

这就是美国之声:它充满了希望,雄心勃勃,潇洒自如,公正无比。这是我们的遗产,这是我们的歌。这首歌我们现在依然在唱。尽管我们还有许多困难,并存在着许多分歧,我们仍像我们的前辈一样团结在一起。这是上帝谱写的曲子,我们高声欢唱这首歌,把它献给上帝。愿上帝保佑我们紧密团结、友爱,一如既往。在上帝的指引下,我们将把一切奉献给上帝赐予人类的自由理想,并努力将它传给充满希望的未来。让这个世界充满我们的声音。愿上帝继续让我们紧密地团结在一起。在上帝指引下的民族,会将一切都奉献给上帝赐予人类心中的自由理想,并号召把这一理想传给正在等待和充满希望的世界。

愿上帝保佑你们,保佑美国。

---

  [1]就职典礼原定在国会大厦西门廊举行,但由于天气太冷,改在国会大厦的圆形大厅举行,故出此语。

乔治·布什
George Bush

乔治·布什（George Bush）

生平简介 >>

乔治·布什是美国第四十一任总统。他于1924年6月12日出生在马萨诸塞州。18岁那年，布什应征入伍参加了海军。退役后，考进耶鲁大学攻读经济学。毕业后，移居"石油之城"得克萨斯州的奥德萨。20世纪50年代末60年代初，布什由于经营石油生意有方，成为"百万富翁"。

1964年，布什成了得克萨斯州共和党主席。1966年当选为联邦众议院议员。1971年任美国驻联合国大使，1973年任共和党全国委员会主席，1974—1975年，被尼克松总统任命为美国驻中国联络办事处主任。1976—1977年被福特总统调任为中央情报局局长。1977年民主党人执政，布什的这一职务被解除，但此举却促使布什走上了竞选1980年总统之路。经过激烈的角逐，里根最终获得了共和党总统候选人的提名，布什居第二，成为副总统候选人。

1988年的总统竞选，布什战胜了强劲的对手民主党人杜卡基斯成为总统。

布什政策的特点为：经济上，不增税，反对保护主义；国防上，花更多的钱增强实力；外交上，对苏采取强硬政策，使北约盟国更多地承担欧洲防务费用，还希望在太平洋创建一个类似北约的联盟以确保安全。

George Bush
Inaugural Address

January 20, 1989

Mr. Chief Justice, Mr. President, Vice President Quayle, Senator Mitchell, Speaker Wright, Senator Dole, Congressman Michel, and fellow citizens, neighbors, and friends:

There is a man here who has earned a lasting place in our hearts and in our history. President Reagan, on behalf of our Nation, I thank you for the wonderful things that you have done for America.

I have just repeated word for word the oath taken by George Washington 200 years ago, and the Bible on which I placed my hand is the Bible on which he placed his. It is right that the memory of Washington be with us today, not only because this is our Bicentennial Inauguration, but because Washington remains the Father of our Country. And he would, I think, be gladdened by this day; for today is the concrete expression of a stunning fact: our continuity these 200 years since our government began.

We meet on democracy's front porch, a good place to talk as neighbors and as friends. For this is a day when our nation is made whole, when our differences, for a moment, are suspended.

And my first act as President is a prayer. I ask you to bow your heads:

Heavenly Father, we bow our heads and thank You for Your love. Accept our thanks for the peace that yields this day and the shared faith that makes its continuance likely. Make us strong to do your work, willing to heed and hear your will, and write on our hearts these words: "Use power to help people." For we are given power not to advance our own purposes, nor to make a great show in the world, nor a name. There is but one just use of power, and it is to serve people. Help us to remember it, Lord. Amen.

乔治·布什
George Bush

布什总统就职演说

1989年1月20日

首席大法官先生、总统先生、奎尔副总统、米切尔参议员、怀特议长、多尔参议员、米歇尔议员，睦邻好友，同胞们：

我们之中有这样一个人，他在我们心中和我们的历史上赢得了永恒的地位，这就是里根总统。我代表我们的国家和民族，向您致谢，因为您为美国做出了出色的贡献。

我刚刚逐字逐句宣读了乔治·华盛顿200年前所做的誓言，也将我的手放在了他的手曾放过的《圣经》上。今天我们在这里怀念他是对的，不仅仅因为今天这次典礼是我国首位总统就职200周年的纪念，还因为华盛顿始终是我们的国父。我想今天他一定会含笑九泉的。一个令人惊奇的事实今天在这里得到了充分体现，那便是开国以来我们已经延续了200年。

我们聚会在民主大厦的前廊，这是大家以邻居和朋友身份交谈的好地方，这一天使我们的"民族"成为一个整体，我们的纷争也暂告停息。

作为总统，我的第一个举动便是祷告——我请求大家垂首：

"伟大的上帝，我们向您致意，感谢您恩赐予我们的爱。我们感谢促成今日盛典的安宁祥和局面，感谢您使我们拥有使这种局面长存的共同信念。请让我们强盛起来去完成您的意愿，听从并跟随您的意志，让我们在心中铭刻下这样的话语：'用权力去帮助人民。'因为给我们权力并不是让我们追求个人正当目的，也不是为了在世上显赫一时，更不是为了追名逐利。使用权力只有一个正当目的，那便是为公众服务。请让我们永远牢记这一点——上帝，阿门。"

I come before you and assume the Presidency at a moment rich with promise. We live in a peaceful, prosperous time, but we can make it better. For a new breeze is blowing, and a world refreshed by freedom seems reborn; for in man's heart, if not in fact, the day of the dictator is over. The totalitarian era is passing, its old ideas blown away like leaves from an ancient, lifeless tree. A new breeze is blowing, and a nation refreshed by freedom stands ready to push on. There is new ground to be broken, and new action to be taken. There are times when the future seems thick as a fog; you sit and wait, hoping the mists will lift and reveal the right path. But this is a time when the future seems a door you can walk right through into a room called tomorrow.

Great nations of the world are moving toward democracy through the door to freedom. Men and women of the world move toward free markets through the door to prosperity. The people of the world agitate for free expression and free thought through the door to the moral and intellectual satisfactions that only liberty allows.

We know what works: Freedom works. We know what's right: Freedom is right. We know how to secure a more just and prosperous life for man on Earth: through free markets, free speech, free elections, and the exercise of free will unhampered by the state.

For the first time in this century, for the first time in perhaps all history, man does not have to invent a system by which to live. We don't have to talk late into the night about which form of government is better. We don't have to wrest justice from the kings. We only have to summon it from within ourselves. We must act on what we know. I take as my guide the hope of a saint: In crucial things, unity; in important things, diversity; in all things, generosity.

America today is a proud, free nation, decent and civil, a place we cannot help but love. We know in our hearts, not loudly and proudly, but as a simple fact, that this country has meaning beyond what we see, and that our strength is a force for good. But have we changed as a nation even in our time? Are we enthralled with material things, less appreciative of the nobility of work and sacrifice?

My friends, we are not the sum of our possessions. They are not the measure

乔治·布什
George Bush

　　我站在你们的面前,承担起总统的重任。此时此刻前景无限。我们生活在一个和平昌盛的时代,然而我们还能使之更加美好。因为一股新风徐徐吹来,自由使得这个世界重新获得了新生。也许事实并非如此,但在人们心中,独裁者的时代已经结束,极权主义者的时代已一去不复返,旧的观念像枯树上的叶子随风飘去。一股新风徐徐吹来,经过自由洗礼的民族随时准备奋勇向前。我们要开垦新的土地,我们要采取新的行动。有的时候前途充满浓重的迷雾,你要静静地等待,期待迷雾消散,显出正确的道路。然而此时此刻未来看起来就像一座大门,你可以径直走进那被称之为明天的房间。

　　世界上伟大的民族正是经过这个自由的通道走向民主,全世界人民也正经过这个繁荣之道走向自由市场,世界人民为了自由地表达和自由地思想而疾呼,他们通过这条路达到理智和道德上的满足,这种满足只有自由可以实现。

　　我们知道什么能发挥作用,自由就能发挥作用;我们懂得什么是正确的,自由就是正确的。我们也知道怎样去为地球上的人类争得更加公正和富足的生活,那便是通过自由市场、自由言论、自由选举和不受国家干涉的自由意志。

　　本世纪第一次——也许是整个历史的第一次,人类不必再去发明创造一种他们赖以生存的制度了。我们不必讨论至深夜,探讨哪种形式的政府更好一些。公正不必从国王那里去争得,只需从我们自身召唤。我们必须按照我们所知的事物去行动。我把一位圣人的话作为我的座右铭:关键的时候要团结一心,重要关头要博采众议,对一切事情要宽宏大量。

　　今天的美国是一个骄傲、自由的礼仪之邦——对待这块土地我们只有奉献我们的爱。我们不必张扬和自负,但我们内心深深懂得这样一个简单的道理:这个国家的意义远远超出我们所能看到的,我们的力量永远为善而用。当下,我们作为一个民族,是否已经变化了?我们是否被物质的力量所迷惑,不再推崇那高尚的工作和牺牲精神了?

　　朋友们,我们并不等于我们财富的总和,它们并不是评价我们生活的尺

of our lives. In our hearts we know what matters. We cannot hope only to leave our children a bigger car, a bigger bank account. We must hope to give them a sense of what it means to be a loyal friend, a loving parent, a citizen who leaves his home, his neighborhood and town better than he found it. What do we want the men and women who work with us to say when we are no longer there? That we were more driven to succeed than anyone around us? Or that we stopped to ask if a sick child had gotten better, and stayed a moment there to trade a word of friendship?

No President, no government, can teach us to remember what is best in what we are. But if the man you have chosen to lead this government can help make a difference; if he can celebrate the quieter, deeper successes that are made not of gold and silk, but of better hearts and finer souls; if he can do these things, then he must.

America is never wholly herself unless she is engaged in high moral principle. We as a people have such a purpose today. It is to make kinder the face of the Nation and gentler the face of the world. My friends, we have work to do. There are the homeless, lost and roaming. There are the children who have nothing, no love, no normalcy. There are those who cannot free themselves of enslavement to whatever addiction—drugs, welfare, the demoralization that rules the slums. There is crime to be conquered, the rough crime of the streets. There are young women to be helped who are about to become mothers of children they can't care for and might not love. They need our care, our guidance, and our education, though we bless them for choosing life.

The old solution, the old way, was to think that public money alone could end these problems. But we have learned that is not so. And in any case, our funds are low. We have a deficit to bring down. We have more will than wallet; but will is what we need. We will make the hard choices, looking at what we have and perhaps allocating it differently, making our decisions based on honest need and prudent safety. And then we will do the wisest thing of all: We will turn to the only resource we have that in times of need always grows—the goodness and the courage of the American people.

I am speaking of a new engagement in the lives of others, a new activism,

乔治·布什
George Bush

度。在我们心中我们懂得什么至关重要。我们不能只想着留给我们的孩子一辆更豪华的轿车,更多的银行存款。我们必须让他们知道如何成为忠诚的朋友、慈爱的父母和一名让社区和家乡变得更好的公民。当我们离开的时候,会让那些同我们一起工作的人说些什么呢?说我们比周围任何人都更致力追求成功?还是说我们会停下来询问那生病的孩子是否有所好转,并说一些温存、关心的话?

没有一位总统,也没有一届政府能告诉我们并让我们记住对于我们来说什么是最好的。但是你们选定的统率这个政府的人,如果他能取得许多不显眼的但意义重大的成就,当然这些成就不只是黄金与丝绸的堆积,而且还包括人们的心灵变得更加美好,灵魂变得更加纯净,如果可以做到这一切,那么,他就应当去做。

美国人民只有具备了高尚的道德情操,美国才会真正完全实现自我。作为一个民族,今天我们应具有这样的目的:使世界的面貌变得更加美好,美国的面貌更加仁慈。朋友们,我们有很多事情要做。世界上还有许多无家可归、迷惘无援、四处流浪的人们。还有那些一无所有的儿童,没有爱,没有正常的生活。有许多人沉沦于吸毒而不能自拔,或沾染上笼罩着贫民窟的堕落习气。大街上猖狂的犯罪必须予以严厉地打击。许多即将成为孩子母亲的未成年妇女需要帮助,她们对那些孩子无力抚养和照顾,或不会加以爱护。她们需要我们的关心,需要我们的指导和教育,我们乞求上帝保佑她们能选择自己的生活。

过去的方式和方法总是让我们认为公共开支就完全可以解决这些问题,但我现在懂得了事实并非如此。无论如何,我们的资金还不很充足,我们有赤字需要削减,我们的愿望总是超过我们钱包的支付能力,而愿望又是我们最为需要的。我们将进行艰难的抉择,看一看我们拥有什么,或许还要做出有区别的分配,使我们的决策建立在真正的需要和谨慎的安全之上,然后,我们便可做出最明智之举。我们将求助于随需求的增长而增长的唯一资源,它便是美国人民的善良和勇气。

我此刻讲的是对于他人生活的一种新参与———一种新的行动主义,亲力

hands-on and involved, that gets the job done. We must bring in the generations, harnessing the unused talent of the elderly and the unfocused energy of the young. For not only leadership is passed from generation to generation, but so is stewardship. And the generation born after the Second World War has come of age.

I have spoken of a thousand points of light, of all the community organizations that are spread like stars throughout the Nation, doing good. We will work hand in hand, encouraging, sometimes leading, sometimes being led, rewarding. We will work on this in the White House, in the Cabinet agencies. I will go to the people and the programs that are the brighter points of light, and I will ask every member of my government to become involved. The old ideas are new again because they are not old, they are timeless: duty, sacrifice, commitment, and a patriotism that finds its expression in taking part and pitching in.

We need a new engagement, too, between the Executive and the Congress. The challenges before us will be thrashed out with the House and the Senate. We must bring the Federal budget into balance. And we must ensure that America stands before the world united, strong, at peace, and fiscally sound. But, of course, things may be difficult. We need compromise; we have had dissension. We need harmony; we have had a chorus of discordant voices.

For Congress, too, has changed in our time. There has grown a certain divisiveness. We have seen the hard looks and heard the statements in which not each other's ideas are challenged, but each other's motives. And our great parties have too often been far apart and untrusting of each other. It has been this way since Vietnam. That war cleaves us still. But, friends, that war began in earnest a quarter of a century ago; and surely the statute of limitations has been reached. This is a fact: The final lesson of Vietnam is that no great nation can long afford to be sundered by a memory. A new breeze is blowing, and the old bipartisanship must be made new again.

To my friends—and yes, I do mean friends—in the loyal opposition—and yes, I mean loyal: I put out my hand. I am putting out my hand to you, Mr. Speaker. I am putting out my hand to you, Mr. Majority Leader. For this is

乔治·布什
George Bush

亲为,把事情做好。我们必须激励几代人,利用老一代未充分使用的智慧,开发尚未集中的年轻一代的活力。因为不仅领导权要一代一代地传下去,对国家事务的管理同样如此。第二次世界大战后出生的一代已成长起来。

我已谈及千万盏明灯的作用,即像星星一样散布在全国各地做好事的社团组织。我们将携手并进、互相鼓舞,有时去领导,有时被领导,不断取得收获。在白宫里,在内阁中,我们将照此工作。我将求助于人民,求助于我们的纲领,这是光明中更加夺目的闪光点。我将请求政府的每一位成员一起参与。旧的观念会再次成为新的观念,因为它们不是旧的,而是永恒的;责任、牺牲、承诺,以及一种爱国主义,这种爱国主义体现在参与和投入中。

在行政部门和国会之间,我们也需要新关系。我们面前的挑战将通过白宫与众议院、参议院商讨解决。我们还必须使得联邦预算保持平衡,必须保证美国在全世界面前是团结、强大、和睦的,并在经济上是无懈可击的,当然事情也许是困难的。我们中间存在着意见分歧,我们需要让步和妥协,我们已有诸多不和谐的因素,我们需要和谐。

国会在我们时代也正在变化,有一些分歧正在继续,我们曾经看到人们怒气满面,听到人们发表各种声明,不是互相质疑各自的观点,而是质疑对方的动机。我们的两党总是相距甚远,彼此之间互不信任。自从越南战争起便一直是这样。那场战争把我们分成了两派。但是,朋友们,那场战争是在25年前真正开始的;当然,诉讼时效已经到了。越战的最后教训就是:一个民族,即使再伟大,也无法长期承受由一件往事造成的分裂。一股新风正徐徐吹来,陈旧的两党关系必须更新。

面对我忠诚的朋友们——是的,我的确用了"忠诚的"和"朋友们"——我向你们伸出了我的手。我把我的手伸给你,议长先生;我把我的手伸给你,多数党领袖先生。事情就是如此,这是握手言和的时代。我

the thing: This is the age of the offered hand. We can't turn back clocks, and I don't want to. But when our fathers were young, Mr. Speaker, our differences ended at the water's edge. And we don't wish to turn back time, but when our mothers were young, Mr. Majority Leader, the Congress and the Executive were capable of working together to produce a budget on which this nation could live. Let us negotiate soon and hard. But in the end, let us produce. The American people await action. They didn't send us here to bicker. They ask us to rise above the merely partisan. "In crucial things, unity"—and this, my friends, is crucial.

To the world, too, we offer new engagement and a renewed vow: We will stay strong to protect the peace. The "offered hand" is a reluctant fist; but once made, strong, and can be used with great effect. There are today Americans who are held against their will in foreign lands, and Americans who are unaccounted for. Assistance can be shown here, and will be long remembered. Good will begets good will. Good faith can be a spiral that endlessly moves on.

Great nations like great men must keep their word. When America says something, America means it, whether a treaty or an agreement or a vow made on marble steps. We will always try to speak clearly, for candor is a compliment, but subtlety, too, is good and has its place. While keeping our alliances and friendships around the world strong, ever strong, we will continue the new closeness with the Soviet Union, consistent both with our security and with progress. One might say that our new relationship in part reflects the triumph of hope and strength over experience. But hope is good, and so are strength and vigilance.

Here today are tens of thousands of our citizens who feel the understandable satisfaction of those who have taken part in democracy and seen their hopes fulfilled. But my thoughts have been turning the past few days to those who

乔治·布什
George Bush

们不能让时间倒转,我也不想这样做。然而,当我们的父亲年轻的时候,议长先生,我们的分歧在国内就结束了。我们不期望时间倒转,但是当我们的母亲年轻的时候,多数党领袖先生,国会和行政当局能够携手工作,共同制定对国家有利的预算。让我们尽快地进行认真的会谈,并结出果实。美国人民等待着行动,他们让我们到这里来并不是为了争吵不休,他们要求我们摆脱党派之争。关键时刻要团结一心,朋友们,现在便是关键的时候了。

  我们也向全世界奉献我们新的承诺和誓言。我们将保持强大,以便保卫和平。我们"伸出去的手"是一个不太情愿的拳头。然而一旦握手言和,那将是十分有力的,足以产生巨大的影响和威力。今天有一些美国人被强制扣留在国外[1],也有一些美国人下落不明。援助体现在这里,并将永远被记住。好意总会得到好报;忠诚会像螺旋式的上升,永无止境。

  伟大的民族就像伟人一样永不食言。无论是一个条约、一个协议,还是在这大理石石阶上做出的诺言。美国人民言必信,行必果。我们将力求直来直去,因为坦率就是美德,但是巧妙也同样有它的地位。在整个世界范围内,除了巩固我们与同盟国之间的友谊外,我们也要同苏联继续保持密切的关系,这与我们的安全和进步的需要相一致。[2]有人也许会说,我们这种新型的关系在一定程度上反映了希望和力量战胜了经验,然而希望总是好的,力量和警惕也是好的。

  今天在场的公民成千上万,他们都感到,那些已加入民主行列并看到自己的希望得以实现的人们所抱有的喜悦心情,是可以理解的。但是我的

---

[1]指被扣押在黎巴嫩的人质。由于美国及西方国家在中东长期以来采取偏袒以色列的政策,因此,这些国家在中东的人员成为绑架者打击的主要目标。1984年3月,在贝鲁特发生的第一起绑架事件就是美国驻黎巴嫩使馆一等秘书、美中央情报局黎巴嫩站站长巴克利被绑架。后来在黎巴嫩被扣的20多名人质中,有9名是美国人。

[2]当时,美、苏关系取得了长足的进展。1985年至1988年,美、苏最高首脑连续四次会晤,并签订了《苏联和美国消除两国中程和中短程导弹条约》以消除中远程核武器。1988年12月7日,戈尔巴乔夫在联大宣布苏联单方面裁军50万。

would be watching at home, to an older fellow who will throw a salute by himself when the flag goes by, and the women who will tell her sons the words of the battle hymns. I don't mean this to be sentimental. I mean that on days like this, we remember that we are all part of a continuum, inescapably connected by the ties that bind.

Our children are watching in schools throughout our great land. And to them I say, thank you for watching democracy's big day. For democracy belongs to us all, and freedom is like a beautiful kite that can go higher and higher with the breeze. And to all I say: No matter what your circumstances or where you are, you are part of this day, you are part of the life of our great nation.

A President is neither prince nor pope, and I don't seek a window on men's souls. In fact, I yearn for a greater tolerance, an easy-goingness about each other's attitudes and way of life.

There are few clear areas in which we as a society must rise up united and express our intolerance. The most obvious now is drugs. And when that first cocaine was smuggled in on a ship, it may as well have been a deadly bacteria, so much has it hurt the body, the soul of our country. And there is much to be done and to be said, but take my word for it: This scourge will stop.

And so, there is much to do; and tomorrow the work begins. I do not mistrust the future; I do not fear what is ahead. For our problems are large, but our heart is larger. Our challenges are great, but our will is greater. And if our flaws are endless, God's love is truly boundless.

Some see leadership as high drama, and the sound of trumpets calling, and sometimes it is that. But I see history as a book with many pages, and each day we fill a page with acts of hopefulness and meaning. The new breeze blows, a page turns, the story unfolds. And so today a chapter begins, a small and stately story of unity, diversity, and generosity—shared, and written, together.

Thank you. God bless you and God bless the United States of America.

乔治·布什
George Bush

思绪已在过去的几天中转移到了那些可能在家中关注我们的人们。当我们的旗帜飘过的时候,一位老者肯定会自觉地向它致敬;一位妇女也会将战歌的词句教给她的儿子。我并不认为这是感情用事。我的意思是,在今天这样的日子,我们是一个有机的整体,我们被一条纽带连在一起,任何人都不可能例外。

在祖国的大地上,我们的孩子们在学校注视着我们,我向他们致以深切的谢意,感谢他们关注着民主的盛大节日。因为民主属于我们每一个人,而自由像一只风筝乘风而上。我还要对所有的人这样说:无论你们处境如何,无论你们身在何处,你们都是这个节日的一部分,你们都是我们伟大民族生命的一部分。

一位总统,他既不是君主,也不是教皇。当然我也并不奢望看透"人类的心灵之窗",事实上,对于人与人之间的态度和他们的生活方式,我倒希望更加随和,更加宽容。

而对于某些问题,作为整个社会的一员,我们必须团结起来,以示毫不容忍。目前最明显的便是毒品。[1]当第一批可卡因用船走私进来时,就像一批死亡的病菌,伤害着我们国家的肌体和灵魂。对此,我们要说的和要做的事情太多太多,但请记住我的话:这种灾难即将终止。

如此众多的事情、工作从明天就要着手进行。对于未来,我充满希望。无论前面是什么,我都无所畏惧。因为尽管我们面前的问题如此巨大,但我们的决心更大;无论我们面前的挑战多么严峻,我们的意志却更为坚强;即使我们有无数的缺点,但上帝的恩爱定会无穷无尽。

有人以为领导是极富戏剧性的,长号声声亮。有些时候的确是这样。然而我把历史看作一部巨著,每天我们都用希望和富有意义的行动书写一页。一股新风徐徐吹来,吹开了新的一页,故事又展开了——今天就开始了新的一章;我们将共同书写和分享这个团结一心、博采众议、宽容大量的庄严的小故事。

谢谢各位。上帝保佑你们。上帝保佑美利坚合众国!

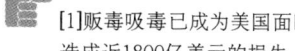

[1]贩毒吸毒已成为美国面临的危机。1989年国会的一份调查估计,吸毒和酗酒每年给国家造成近1800亿美元的损失。据对全美1000家最大的私人企业进行的调查,每年有520亿美元的产值因吸毒而损失。

比尔·克林顿
Bill Clinton

比尔·克林顿（Bill Clinton）

生平简介 >>

比尔·克林顿是美国第四十二任总统，1946年8月19日出生于美国南部的阿肯色州。1963年夏，他在"中学模拟政府"的竞选中被选为"参议员"，获得去华盛顿旅行的奖励。在华盛顿，他受到约翰·肯尼迪总统的接见，并合影留念。华盛顿之行，使克林顿立下了攀登美国权力顶峰的宏愿。

1976年，他当选为阿肯色州政府司法部长，两年后，在他32岁时，他首次参加州长竞选，结果角逐成功，成为美国当时最年轻的州长，被誉为民主党的"童星"。1980年，他竞选连任未成。在经过两年"卧薪尝胆"后，终于再次夺得州长职务。此后，他又连任四届州长，这在美国历史上也是没有先例的。任职期间，他使阿肯色州的经济增长达29%，就业率和收入增长率也高于全国平均数。1991年6月克林顿被《新闻周刊》评为全美处理政务效率最高的州长之一。

1991年10月，克林顿正式宣布参加1992年的总统竞选，以绝对多数票击败共和党在任总统布什和无党派总统候选人佩罗。

比尔·克林顿是美国20世纪以来第一位"二战"后出生的总统。克林顿是美国历史上第五任左撇子总统，在他之前的四位左撇子总统，除布什外，还有詹姆斯·加菲尔德、哈里·杜鲁门和杰拉尔德·福特。

美国历届总统就职演说

Bill Clinton
First Inaugural Address

January 20, 1993

My fellow citizens:

Today we celebrate the mystery of American renewal.

This ceremony is held in the depth of winter. But, by the words we speak and the faces we show the world, we force the spring. A spring reborn in the world's oldest democracy, that brings forth the vision and courage to reinvent America.

When our founders boldly declared America's independence to the world and our purposes to the Almighty, they knew that America, to endure, would have to change. Not change for change's sake, but change to preserve America's ideals—life, liberty, the pursuit of happiness. Though we march to the music of our time, our mission is timeless. Each generation of Americans must define what it means to be an American.

On behalf of our nation, I salute my predecessor, President Bush, for his half-century of service to America. And I thank the millions of men and women whose steadfastness and sacrifice triumphed over Depression, fascism and Communism.

Today, a generation raised in the shadows of the Cold War assumes new responsibilities in a world warmed by the sunshine of freedom but threatened still by ancient hatreds and new plagues.

Raised in unrivaled prosperity, we inherit an economy that is still the world's strongest, but is weakened by business failures, stagnant wages, increasing inequality, and deep divisions among our people.

When George Washington first took the oath I have just sworn to uphold, news traveled slowly across the land by horseback and across the ocean by boat.

比尔·克林顿
Bill Clinton

克林顿总统首次就职演说

1993年1月20日

同胞们：

今天，我们庆祝美国复兴的奇迹。

这个仪式是在隆冬举行的，但是，我们通过自己的言语和向世界展示的面貌，促使春天的到来。春天又降临到世界上这个最古老的民主国家，它带来了重塑美国的远见和勇气。

当我国的缔造者大胆地向世界宣布美国独立并向上帝表明我们的目的时，他们知道，美国要世世代代存在下去，就必须变革。不是为变革而变革，而是为了保持美国的理想——为了生命、自由和对幸福的追求而变革。虽然我们是踏着时代的旋律前进的，但是我们的使命是永恒的。每一代美国人都必须明确作为一个美国人意味着什么。

我代表我们国家，向我的前任布什总统致敬，他为美国服务了半个世纪；我也感谢千百万男女同胞，是他们以其坚定和牺牲战胜了大萧条、法西斯和共产主义。

今天，在冷战阴影下成长的一代人，在一个虽然刚从自由的阳光中得到温暖却仍受到旧仇新祸威胁的世界中承担着新的责任。

我们在无与伦比的繁荣中成长，继承了仍然是全世界最强大的经济，但是企业的倒闭、工资增长的停滞[1]、不平等程度的加深以及我们人民之间的急剧分化，使经济受到了削弱。

当乔治·华盛顿第一次宣读我刚才发出的誓言时，那个消息在陆地上

---

[1] 1988年，典型的美国家庭收入为37579美元，1992年为35939美元，四年下降了4%。

Now, the sights and sounds of this ceremony are broadcast instantaneously to billions around the world.

Communications and commerce are global; investment is mobile; technology is almost magical; and ambition for a better life is now universal. We earn our livelihood in peaceful competition with people all across the earth.

Profound and powerful forces are shaking and remaking our world, and the urgent question of our time is whether we can make change our friend and not our enemy.

This new world has already enriched the lives of millions of Americans who are able to compete and win in it. But when most people are working harder for less; when others cannot work at all; when the cost of health care devastates families and threatens to bankrupt many of our enterprises, great and small; when fear of crime robs law-abiding citizens of their freedom; and when millions of poor children cannot even imagine the lives we are calling them to lead—we have not made change our friend.

We know we have to face hard truths and take strong steps. But we have not done so. Instead, we have drifted, and that drifting has eroded our resources, fractured our economy, and shaken our confidence.

Though our challenges are fearsome, so are our strengths. And Americans have ever been a restless, questing, hopeful people. We must bring to our task today the vision and will of those who came before us.

From our revolution, the Civil War, to the Great Depression to the civil rights movement, our people have always mustered the determination to construct from these crises the pillars of our history.

Thomas Jefferson believed that to preserve the very foundations of our nation, we would need dramatic change from time to time. Well, my fellow citizens, this is our time. Let us embrace it.

Our democracy must be not only the envy of the world but the engine of our own renewal. There is nothing wrong with America that cannot be cured by what is right with America.

And so today, we pledge an end to the era of deadlock and drift—a new season of American renewal has begun. To renew America, we must be bold.

比尔·克林顿
Bill Clinton

是靠驿站、在海洋是靠木船缓慢传递的。而现在这个仪式的情景和声音正通过广播电视即刻向全世界几十亿人播放。

通信和商务具有全球性;投资具有流动性;技术近乎具有魔力;改善生活的愿望现在遍及全球。今天美国人通过与世界各地人民和平竞争来谋求生存。

各种深刻而强大的力量正在动摇和重新塑造我们的世界,我们时代的紧迫问题是,我们是否能使变革成为我们的朋友,而不是敌人。

这个新世界已经使几百万能够竞争并在竞争中取胜的美国人的生活富裕起来。但是,当多数人工作增加而收入减少的时候;当一些人根本无法工作的时候;当医疗开支给家庭造成沉重负担并给大大小小的企业带来破产威胁的时候;当遵纪守法的公民因为惧怕犯罪活动而失去行动自由的时候;当数百万贫困的儿童甚至无法想象我们呼吁他们去过的那种生活的时候,我们并没有使变革成为自己的朋友。

我们知道我们不得不正视艰难的现实和采取有力的措施。但我们并没有这样做,而是放任自流。这种做法已经侵蚀了我们的资源,破坏了我们的经济,动摇了我们的信心。

虽然我们面临的挑战是令人生畏的,但是我们的力量也同样不可小觑。美国人始终是永不满足、勇于追求和大有希望的人民。我们必须以我们前人的远见和意志来完成我们今天的任务。

从独立战争到南北战争,从大萧条到民权运动,我们的人民始终蕴聚决心,从历次危机中构筑我国历史的支柱。

托马斯·杰斐逊认为,为维护我国的根基,我们需要时常进行激动人心的变革。那么,我的同胞们,我们的时代就是变革的时代。让我们拥抱这个时代吧。

我们的民主制度必须不仅是世界的典范,而且还应是我们自己振兴的动力。美国没有任何错误的东西不能被正确的东西所纠正。

所以,今天,我们立下誓言,要结束这个僵持停顿和放任自流的时代,开启美国振兴的新时期。要振兴美国,我们必须无所畏惧。我们必须做前

We must do what no generation has had to do before. We must invest more in our own people, in their jobs, in their future, and at the same time cut our massive debt. And we must do so in a world in which we must compete for every opportunity. It will not be easy; it will require sacrifice. But it can be done, and done fairly, not choosing sacrifice for its own sake, but for our own sake. We must provide for our nation the way a family provides for its children.

Our Founders saw themselves in the light of posterity. We can do no less. Anyone who has ever watched a child's eyes wander into sleep knows what posterity is. Posterity is the world to come—the world for whom we hold our ideals, from which we have borrowed our planet, and to whom we bear sacred responsibility. We must do what America does best: offer more opportunity to all and demand responsibility from all.

It is time to break the bad habit of expecting something for nothing, from our government or from each other. Let us all take more responsibility, not only for ourselves and our families but for our communities and our country. To renew America, we must revitalize our democracy.

This beautiful capital, like every capital since the dawn of civilization, is often a place of intrigue and calculation. Powerful people maneuver for position and worry endlessly about who is in and who is out, who is up and who is down, forgetting those people whose toil and sweat sends us here and pays our way.

Americans deserve better, and in this city today, there are people who want to do better. And so I say to all of us here, let us resolve to reform our politics, so that power and privilege no longer shout down the voice of the people. Let us put aside personal advantage so that we can feel the pain and see the promise of America. Let us resolve to make our government a place for what Franklin Roosevelt called "bold, persistent experimentation," a government for our tomorrows, not our yesterdays. Let us give this capital back to the people to whom it belongs.

To renew America, we must meet challenges abroad as well at home. There is no longer division between what is foreign and what is domestic—the world economy, the world environment, the world AIDS crisis, the world arms race—they affect us all.

比尔·克林顿
Bill Clinton

人没有做过的事情。我们必须对我们的人民,以及他们的工作和他们的未来给予更多的投入,同时减少我们的巨额债务。而且,我们必须在一个每个机会都要竞争的世界中去做这些事。这不会是轻而易举的,它要求做出牺牲。但这是可以做到并且可以做得公平合理的,不是为牺牲而牺牲,而是为我们自己而牺牲。我们必须要像家庭供养孩子那样供养我们的国家。

我们的开国元勋是以未来的眼光来看待他们自己的。我们也能够这样做。曾见过孩子眼睛蒙眬进入梦乡的人知道后世是什么。后世是行将到来的世界——我们对它寄托我们的理想,向它借用了这块地球,我们对它负有神圣的责任。我们必须充分发挥美国的最大优势:向所有人提供更多的机会,要求所有人承担其责任。

现在已经到了破除那种只求向政府或者别人免费索取的恶习的时候了。让我们大家都担负起更大的责任,不仅为了我们自己和我们的家庭,也为我们的社会和我们的国家。为了振兴美国,我们必须恢复我们民主制度的活力。

这个美丽的首都,同文明之初以来的每一个首都一样,常常是一个勾心斗角、尔虞我诈的地方。掌权者们为争名夺利和宦海沉浮而无休止地争斗,却忘了那些用辛勤和汗水把我们送到这里并养活了我们的人们。

美国人理应生活得更好。在今天的这个城市里,这里的人们就想把事情办得更好。所以,我要向这里的各位说,让我们决心进行政治改革,以便使权力和特权不再盖过人民的声音。让我们撇开个人利益,这样我们才能觉察美国的病痛,看到它的前途。让我们决心使我们的政府成为一个富兰克林·罗斯福所称的"大胆持久的试验"的场所,也就是一个为我们的未来服务的政府,而不是一个留恋过去的政府。让我们把这个首都还给它所属的人。

为振兴美国,我们必须应付国内外的种种挑战。现在内政与外交之间已不再有明确的界限——世界经济、世界环境、世界艾滋病危机、世界军备竞赛,这一切都影响着我们。

Today, as an old order passes, the new world is freer but less stable. Communism's collapse has called forth old animosities and new dangers. Clearly America must continue to lead the world we did so much to make.

While America rebuilds at home, we will not shrink from the challenges, nor fail to seize the opportunities, of this new world. Together with our friends and allies, we will work to shape change, lest it engulf us.

When our vital interests are challenged, or the will and conscience of the international community is defied, we will act—with peaceful diplomacy when ever possible, with force when necessary. The brave Americans serving our nation today in the Persian Gulf, in Somalia, and wherever else they stand are testament to our resolve.

But our greatest strength is the power of our ideas, which are still new in many lands. Across the world, we see them embraced—and we rejoice. Our hopes, our hearts, our hands, are with those on every continent who are building democracy and freedom. Their cause is America's cause.

The American people have summoned the change we celebrate today. You have raised your voices in an unmistakable chorus. You have cast your votes in historic numbers. And you have changed the face of Congress, the presidency and the political process itself. Yes, you, my fellow Americans have forced the spring. Now, we must do the work the season demands.

To that work I now turn, with all the authority of my office. I ask the Congress to join with me. But no president, no Congress, no government, can undertake this mission alone. My fellow Americans, you, too, must play your part in our renewal. I challenge a new generation of young Americans to a season of service—to act on your idealism by helping troubled children, keeping company with those in need, reconnecting our torn communities. There is so much to be done — enough indeed for millions of others who are still young in spirit to give of them in service, too.

In serving, we recognize a simple but powerful truth—we need each other. And we must care for one another. Today, we do more than celebrate America;

比尔·克林顿
Bill Clinton

今天,随着旧秩序的消失,新世界更加自由,但更不稳固。共产主义的瓦解唤醒了旧的仇恨,带来了新的危险[1]。显然,美国必须继续领导这个我们过去为之付出许多的世界。

在美国国内进行重建的同时,我们不会面对这个新世界的挑战退缩不前,也不会错失这个新世界所带来的机会。我们将同我们的朋友和盟国一起努力塑造变革,以防我们被变革吞没。

当我们至关重要的利益受到挑战的时候,或者当国际社会的意志和良知遭到蔑视的时候,我们将采取行动——只要有可能,就进行和平外交活动,如果有必要,就使用武力。今天在波斯湾、索马里以及任何其他地方为我们国家效力的美国勇士们,就是我们决心的明证。

但是,我们最强有力的是我们思想的威力,它在许多地方仍然是新鲜的。我们为看到这些思想在世界各地被接受而欢欣鼓舞。我们的希望、我们的心、我们的手同那些在各大洲创建民主和自由的人们连在一起。他们的事业就是美国的事业。

美国人民唤来了我们今天庆祝的变革。你们毫不含糊地齐声疾呼。你们以前所未有的人数参加投票。你们改变了国会、总统职务和政治进程本身的面貌。是的,美国同胞们,你们使春天提前来临。现在,我们必须去做这个季节需要做的工作。

从现在起,我将运用总统职务所赋予我的全部权力来致力于这项工作。我请求国会同我一道做这项工作。任何总统、任何国会、任何政府都不可能单独完成这一使命。同胞们,你们也一样,必须在我们的复兴事业中负起你们的责任。我要求新一代的美国年轻人做出贡献,按照你们的理想主义行动起来,帮助那些陷入困境的孩子们,使贫困的人们得到关怀,使我们四分五裂的社会重新融为一体。有如此多的事情有待完成——对于那些在精神上仍然年轻的几百万人来说,也可以为此去贡献自己的力量。

在做出贡献的时候,我们认识到一个简单而又重要的真理:我们相互需要,我们也必须相互关心。今天,我们不仅是在赞颂美国,我们再一次

[1]指苏东剧变。

we rededicate ourselves to the very idea of America.

An idea born in revolution and renewed through two centuries of challenge. An idea tempered by the knowledge that, but for fate, we—the fortunate and the unfortunate—might have been each other. An idea ennobled by the faith that our nation can summon from its myriad diversity the deepest measure of unity. An idea infused with the conviction that America's long heroic journey must go forever upward.

And so, my fellow Americans, at the edge of the 21st century, let us begin with energy and hope, with faith and discipline, and let us work until our work is done. The scripture says, "And let us not be weary in well-doing, for in due season, we shall reap, if we faint not."

From this joyful mountaintop of celebration, we hear a call to service in the valley. We have heard the trumpets. We have changed the guard. And now, each in our way, and with God's help, we must answer the call.

Thank you and God bless you all.

Bill Clinton
Second Inaugural Address

January 20, 1997

My fellow citizens:

At this last presidential inauguration of the 20th century, let us lift our eyes toward the challenges that await us in the next century. It is our great good fortune that time and chance have put us not only at the edge of a new century, in a new millennium, but on the edge of a bright new prospect in human affairs—a moment that will define our course, and our character, for decades to come. We must keep our old democracy forever young. Guided by the ancient vision of a promised land, let us set our sights upon a land of new promise.

把自己奉献给美国的理想：

这个理想在革命中诞生，在两个世纪的挑战中更新；这个理想经受了认识的考验，大家认识到，若不是命运的安排，幸运者或不幸者有可能互换位置；这个理想由于一种信念而变得崇高，即我们国家能够在千变万化的多样性中实现最大程度的统一；这个理想洋溢着一种信念，即美国漫长而英勇的旅程一定能够永远继续。

同胞们，当我们即将跨入21世纪的时候，让我们以活力和希望、信念和纪律为开端。让我们努力奋斗，直到实现目标。正如《圣经》所说："我们应不厌其烦地行善，只要不气馁，到一定时候，当有所得。"

在这个充满欢乐的山巅，我们听到山谷里传来的要我们为国效力的呼唤。我们听到了号声。我们已经换班。现在，我们必须以自己的方式在上帝的帮助下响应这一召唤。

谢谢，上帝将福佑众生。

克林顿总统第二次就职演说

1997年1月20日

同胞们：

在20世纪最后一次总统就职典礼上，让我们放眼下个世纪等待我们的艰巨任务。非常幸运的是，时间和机遇使我们不仅处于新的世纪、新的千年即将到来的时刻，而且处于人世间光明的新前景即将展现的时刻——确定我们今后几十年的道路和特性的时刻。我们必须使我们古老的民主永葆青春。在"应许之地"这一古老憧憬的指引下，让我们放眼于新的希望之地。

美国历届总统就职演说

THE INAUGURAL ADDRESSES OF THE U.S. PRESIDENTS

The promise of America was born in the 18th century out of the bold conviction that we are all created equal. It was extended and preserved in the 19th century, when our nation spread across the continent, saved the union, and abolished the awful scourge of slavery.

Then, in turmoil and triumph, that promise exploded onto the world stage to make this the American Century.

And what a century it has been. America became the world's mightiest industrial power; saved the world from tyranny in two world wars and a long cold war; and time and again, reached out across the globe to millions who, like us, longed for the blessings of liberty.

Along the way, Americans produced a great middle class and security in old age; built unrivaled centers of learning and opened public schools to all; split the atom and explored the heavens; invented the computer and the microchip; and deepened the wellspring of justice by making a revolution in civil rights for African Americans and all minorities, and extending the circle of citizenship, opportunity and dignity to women.

Now, for the third time, a new century is upon us, and another time to choose. We began the 19th century with a choice, to spread our nation from coast to coast. We began the 20th century with a choice, to harness the Industrial Revolution to our values of free enterprise, conservation, and human decency. Those choices made all the difference. At the dawn of the 21st century a free people must now choose to shape the forces of the Information Age and the global society, to unleash the limitless potential of all our people, and, yes, to form a more perfect union.

When last we gathered, our march to this new future seemed less certain than it does today. We vowed then to set a clear course to renew our nation.

In these four years, we have been touched by tragedy, exhilarated by challenge, strengthened by achievement. America stands alone as the world's indispensable nation. Once again, our economy is the strongest on Earth. Once again, we are building stronger families, thriving communities, better educational opportunities, a cleaner environment. Problems that once seemed destined to deepen now bend to our efforts: our streets are safer and record

比尔·克林顿
Bill Clinton

源自所有生命生而平等的勇敢信念，美国的宣言于18世纪诞生。在19世纪，我们国家横跨整个大陆，挽救了联邦，废除了恐怖的奴隶制，这一信念得以流传和扩展。[1]

接着，在动荡与胜利之中，这一信念迅速传遍整个世界，使这个世纪成为美国世纪。

这是怎样的一个世纪啊！美国成为世界上最强大的工业国，从两次世界大战和漫长的冷战的暴虐中拯救了世界，一次次向全球数百万渴望自由的人伸出援助之手。

在此过程中，美国造就了人数众多的中产阶级，并使老年人有所保障；建立了无可比拟的学习中心，并对所有人开放公立学校；使原子发生裂变，并对太空进行探索；发明了计算机和微芯片；通过发起一场非裔美国人和所有少数民族的民权革命，以及扩大妇女的公民权、就业机会和尊严，而深掘了公正之泉。

现在，我们第三次面临一个新世纪，再次需要做出抉择。在19世纪之初，我们决定把我国从东海岸扩展到西海岸。在20世纪之初，我们决定利用工业革命加强主张自由经营、保护资源和维护人类尊严的价值观。这些抉择带来了巨大变化。在21世纪即将来临的时候，自由的人民必须做出抉择，去打造信息时代和全球一体化的力量，发挥全体人民无穷的潜力，建设一个更加完美的联邦。

上次我们聚集在这里时，对走向这个新的未来没有今天这样自信。当时我们发誓要确定明确的路线，振兴国家。

在这四年中，悲惨事件牵动了我们的心，挑战使我们兴奋，成就给我们增添了力量。美国作为世界上不可缺少的国家巍然挺立。我们的经济实力再次成为全世界最强大的。再一次，我们建立起更加牢固的家庭和欣欣向荣的社区，创造了更好的教育机会和更加清洁的环境。一度似乎肯定要恶化的问题现在屈服于我们的努力之下：我们的街道比过去安全了，从领

---

[1]指19世纪美国向西部的扩张，南北战争以及1862年林肯签署的《解放黑奴宣言》。

numbers of our fellow citizens have moved from welfare to work.

And once again, we have resolved for our time a great debate over the role of government. Today we can declare: Government is not the problem, and government is not the solution. We—the American people—we are the solution. Our founders understood that well and gave us a democracy strong enough to endure for centuries, flexible enough to face our common challenges and advance our common dreams in each new day.

As times change, so government must change. We need a new government for a new century—humble enough not to try to solve all our problems for us, but strong enough to give us the tools to solve our problems for ourselves; a government that is smaller, lives within its means, and does more with less. Yet where it can stand up for our values and interests in the world, and where it can give Americans the power to make a real difference in their everyday lives, government should do more, not less. The preeminent mission of our new government is to give all Americans an opportunity—not a guarantee, but a real opportunity—to build better lives.

Beyond that, my fellow citizens, the future is up to us. Our founders taught us that the preservation of our liberty and our union depends upon responsible citizenship. And we need a new sense of responsibility for a new century. There is work to do, work that government alone cannot do: teaching children to read; hiring people off welfare rolls; coming out from behind locked doors and shuttered windows to help reclaim our streets from drugs and gangs and crime; taking time out of our own lives to serve others.

Each and every one of us, in our own way, must assume personal responsibility—not only for ourselves and our families, but for our neighbors and our nation. Our greatest responsibility is to embrace a new spirit of community for a new century. For any one of us to succeed, we must succeed as one America.

The challenge of our past remains the challenge of our future—will we be one nation, one people, with one common destiny, or not? Will we all come together, or come apart?

The divide of race has been America's constant curse. And each new wave

比尔·克林顿
Bill Clinton

取福利救济转而参加工作的公民人数达到创纪录的水平。

我们再次为我们时代有关政府作用的大辩论找到了结论。今天我们可以宣布：政府不是问题的生产者，也不是问题的解决者。我们——美国人民——才是问题的解决者。我们的开国元勋们对这一点很清楚，给我们建立了民主制度，这个制度强大得足以存在几百年，灵活得足以在每天新的情况下面对我们共同的挑战和推进我们共同的理想。

政府必须随时代的变化而变化。我们在新世纪需要一个新政府，一个谦逊得不力图解决所有问题，但强大得足以赋予我们解决问题的工具的政府，一个规模更小、量入而出、少花钱多办事的政府。在能够维护我们的价值观和利益的地方，在能够给美国人力量，使他们的日常生活发生真正变化的地方，政府应该多干，而不是少干。我们新政府的首要任务是给所有美国人一个机会，而不是一个保证，一个建设更加美好生活的真正的机会。

除此以外，同胞们，未来要靠我们去建设。我们的开国元勋们教导我们，要保住我们的自由和团结需要依靠负责任的公民来实现。我们在新世纪需要新的责任感。我们有很多工作要做，而政府不能把这些工作包下来：要教育儿童读书；要给人们提供工作，让他们摆脱福利救济；要走出封闭的家园，帮助人们远离毒品、黑社会和犯罪；要从我们的生活中抽出时间服务于他人。

我们每一个人都必须按照自己的方式承担起个人的责任——不仅是对自己和家庭的责任，而且是对社会和国家的责任。我们最大的责任是要有一种新世纪应有的新的集体精神。为了每一个人的成功，作为整体的美国必须成功。

我们过去遇到的挑战仍将是我们今后面临的挑战——我们是要作为一个国家、一个民族，命运与共，还是相反？我们是要联合在一起，还是要四分五裂？

种族分裂始终是美国的祸根，每一次新的移民潮都使旧的偏见有了新

of immigrants gives new targets to old prejudices. Prejudice and contempt, cloaked in the pretense of religious or political conviction are no different. These forces have nearly destroyed our nation in the past. They plague us still. They fuel the fanaticism of terror. And they torment the lives of millions in fractured nations all around the world.

These obsessions cripple both those who hate and, of course, those who are hated, robbing both of what they might become. We cannot, we will not, succumb to the dark impulses that lurk in the far regions of the soul everywhere. We shall overcome them. And we shall replace them with the generous spirit of a people who feel at home with one another.

Our rich texture of racial, religious and political diversity will be a Godsend in the 21st century. Great rewards will come to those who can live together, learn together, work together, forge new ties that bind together.

As this new era approaches we can already see its broad outlines. Ten years ago, the Internet was the mystical province of physicists; today, it is a commonplace encyclopedia for millions of schoolchildren. Scientists now are decoding the blueprint of human life. Cures for our most feared illnesses seem close at hand.

The world is no longer divided into two hostile camps. Instead, now we are building bonds with nations that once were our adversaries. Growing connections of commerce and culture give us a chance to lift the fortunes and spirits of people the world over. And for the very first time in all of history, more people on this planet live under democracy than dictatorship.

My fellow Americans, as we look back at this remarkable century, we may ask, can we hope not just to follow, but even to surpass the achievements of the 20th century in America and to avoid the awful bloodshed that stained its legacy? To that question, every American here and every American in our land today must answer a resounding "Yes."

This is the heart of our task. With a new vision of government, a new sense of responsibility, a new spirit of community, we will sustain America's journey. The promise we sought in a new land we will find again in a land of new promise.

In this new land, education will be every citizen's most prized possession.

比尔·克林顿
Bill Clinton

的靶子。在宗教和政治信仰掩盖下的偏见和轻蔑是一丘之貉。过去它们差一点毁灭我们,现在它们依然缠绕着我们。它们助长恐怖的狂热,它们折磨着全世界支离破碎的国家数百万人的生命。

这些执迷伤害了被仇恨者,当然也伤害了仇恨者,使他们不能达到他们可能达到的境界。我们不能——也决不会——屈从于藏在灵魂深处无论哪个角落的罪恶的冲动。我们将克服它们,代之以一种能同别人和睦相处的民族宽容精神。

在21世纪,种族、宗教和政治的多样性将成为我们得天独厚的优势。那些能一起生活、一起学习、一起工作和缔造把大家维系在一起的新联系的人将得到丰厚的报偿。

随着这个新时代日益临近,我们已经可以看清它的大致轮廓了。十年之前,互联网一度是物理学家的神秘领域,如今,它已成为数百万学童寻常的百科全书。科学家们现在正在破译人的生命原型的密码。医治人类一些最可怕的疾病的办法看来也已指日可待了。

世界已不再分成两个敌对的阵营。相反,我们现在正在同以前曾是我们的敌人的国家建立联系。商业和文化交往的发展使我们有可能增加全世界的财富,提升全世界人民的精神水平。现在,有史以来第一次,这个星球上生活在民主制度下的人民多于生活在独裁统治下的人民。

我的美国同胞们,当我们回顾这个了不起的世纪之时,我们也许会问:"我们能否不仅是延续、而且超越美国在20世纪取得的成就,避免发生玷污先辈英明的可怕的流血事件?"对于这个问题,在场的每一位美国人以及全国的每一位美国人今天都应当响亮地回答:"能!"

这是我们的核心任务。伴随着政府新的政见、新的责任感、新的团体精神,我们将继续美国之旅。我们在新的土地上寻求的承诺,我们将再次在新的希望之地找到。

在这片新希望之地上,教育将是每个公民最可贵的财富。我们的学校

美国历届总统就职演说
THE INAUGURAL ADDRESSES OF THE U.S. PRESIDENTS

Our schools will have the highest standards in the world, igniting the spark of possibility in the eyes of every girl and every boy. And the doors of higher education will be open to all. The knowledge and power of the Information Age will be within reach not just of the few, but of every classroom, every library, every child. Parents and children will have time not only to work, but to read and play together. And the plans they make at their kitchen table will be those of a better home, a better job, the certain chance to go to college.

Our streets will echo again with the laughter of our children, because no one will try to shoot them or sell them drugs anymore. Everyone who can work, will work, with today's permanent under class part of tomorrow's growing middle class. New miracles of medicine at last will reach not only those who can claim care now, but the children and hardworking families too long denied.

We will stand mighty for peace and freedom, and maintain a strong defense against terror and destruction. Our children will sleep free from the threat of nuclear, chemical or biological weapons. Ports and airports, farms and factories will thrive with trade and innovation and ideas. And the world's greatest democracy will lead a whole world of democracies.

Our land of new promise will be a nation that meets its obligations—a nation that balances its budget, but never loses the balance of its values. A nation where our grandparents have secure retirement and health care, and their grandchildren know we have made the reforms necessary to sustain those benefits for their time. A nation that fortifies the world's most productive economy even as it protects the great natural bounty of our water, air, and majestic land.

And in this land of new promise, we will have reformed our politics so that the voice of the people will always speak louder than the din of narrow interests—regaining the participation and deserving the trust of all Americans.

Fellow citizens, let us build that America, a nation ever moving forward toward realizing the full potential of all its citizens. Prosperity and power—yes, they are important, and we must maintain them. But let us never forget: The greatest progress we have made, and the greatest progress we have yet to make, is in the human heart. In the end, all the world's wealth and a thousand armies

比尔·克林顿
Bill Clinton

将具有世界最高水平,能在每一个少男少女的眼中点燃希望的火花。高等教育的大门将对所有人敞开。信息时代的知识和力量将不只为少数人所独享,而是为每一间教室、每一个图书馆和每一个儿童所共有。家长不仅有时间工作,而且有时间与孩子们一道阅读和玩耍。他们在餐桌上谈论的将是买更好的房子、找更好的职业以及寻求读大学的机会。

我们的街道上将再度回响起孩子们的笑声,因为不会有人再试图朝他们开枪或向他们兜售毒品。每个有能力工作的人都会有工作,今天久处下层社会的人明天将是不断扩大的中产阶级的一员。新研制的药物终将不仅造福于现在能得到医疗照顾的人,而且将造福于长期以来得不到这种照顾的儿童和勤奋工作的家庭。

我们将是维护和平与自由的强大力量,持续有力抵御恐怖与破坏活动。我们的儿童将可以在不受核武器、化学武器或生物武器威胁的环境中安睡。港口和机场、农场和工厂都会随着贸易、创新方法和新思想的增多而繁荣兴旺。这个世界上最伟大的民主国家将引领整个世界的民主政治潮流。

我们的新希望之地将是一个履行自己的义务的国家,是一个既要实现预算平衡又不放弃价值平衡的国家,是一个祖父母享受着退休和医疗保障、孙辈知道我们进行了为使他们到时候也能得到这些福利所需要的改革的国家,是一个在保护大自然慷慨赐予我们的水、空气和壮丽河山的同时发展着这个世界上最有生产力的经济的国家。

而且,在这片新希望之地上,我们将改革我们的政治,使人民的声音永远高过狭隘利益集团的鼓噪,重新实现所有美国人的参政,不辜负所有美国人的信任。

同胞们,让我们建设这样一个美国吧,建设一个永远前进、朝着充分发挥其所有公民的潜能的方向前进的国家吧。繁荣和强大确实重要,我们也必须保持繁荣和强大,但是,让我们不要忘记,我们业已取得的和将要取得的最大成就在于人民内心。归根到底,世界上的一切财富以及万马千军都无法与人类的精神力量与精神文明相匹敌。

are no match for the strength and decency of the human spirit.

Thirty-four years ago, the man whose life we celebrate today spoke to us down there, at the other end of this Mall, in words that moved the conscience of a nation. Like a prophet of old, he told of his dream that one day America would rise up and treat all its citizens as equals before the law and in the heart. Martin Luther King's dream was the American Dream. His quest is our quest: the ceaseless striving to live out our true creed. Our history has been built on such dreams and labors. And by our dreams and labors we will redeem the promise of America in the 21st century.

To that effort I pledge all my strength and every power of my office. I ask the members of Congress here to join in that pledge. The American people returned to office a President of one party and a Congress of another. Surely, they did not do this to advance the politics of petty bickering and extreme partisanship they plainly deplore. No, they call on us instead to be repairers of the breach, and to move on with America's mission.

America demands and deserves big things from us—and nothing big ever came from being small. Let us remember the timeless wisdom of Cardinal Bernardin, when facing the end of his own life. He said: "It is wrong to waste the precious gift of time, on acrimony and division."

Fellow citizens, we must not waste the precious gift of this time. For all of us are on that same journey of our lives, and our journey, too, will come to an end. But the journey of our America must go on.

And so, my fellow Americans, we must be strong, for there is much to dare. The demands of our time are great and they are different. Let us meet them with faith and courage, with patience and a grateful and happy heart. Let us shape the hope of this day into the noblest chapter in our history. Yes, let us build our bridge. A bridge wide enough and strong enough for every American to cross over to a blessed land of new promise.

比尔·克林顿
Bill Clinton

34年前,有一个人,他的一生为我们今天所歌颂,他就在那边,在这个广场的另一端对我们演讲,他的话打动了国家的良知。就像一位古代先知那样,他谈到了他的梦想:有朝一日,美国将站起来,在法律面前和人们心中所有公民都能被平等对待。马丁·路德·金的梦就是美国之梦。他的追求就是我们的追求——为实现我们真正的信仰而永不停息地努力。[1]我们的历史建立在这样的梦想和努力的基础之上。通过我们的梦想和努力,我们一定会重塑21世纪美国的希望。

为了这一努力,我郑重保证,我将付出我的所有力量,运用我的职位赋予我的一切权力。我请求在场的所有国会议员与我一道做此郑重保证。美国人民把总统职位交给了一个党,把国会交给了另一个党。他们这样做肯定不是为了促进他们显然深感厌恶的为小事争吵不休、极端维护党派利益的政治。不是的。相反,他们要求我们所有人弥合裂痕,继续完成美国的使命。[2]

国家要求我们成就大事,我们也理应为它成就大事,而计较小事是绝不能成就大事的。让我们记住贝尔纳丁红衣主教临终时的至理名言。他说:"把宝贵的时间浪费在尖刻与隔阂上是错误的。"

美国同胞们,我们不应当浪费当前宝贵的时间,因为我们大家都处在相同的生命旅途中。我们的生命旅途总有完结之时,但我们的美国之旅却应当继续下去。

因此,我的同胞们,我们必须强大,因为挑战很多。我们这个时代的要求是很高的,也是与以往不同的。让我们带着信念和勇气、带着耐心和感恩快乐的心去迎接这些挑战。让我们把今天的希望变成历史上最辉煌的篇章。是的,让我们架设我们的桥梁——一座又宽广又坚固的桥梁,一座

---

[1]著名黑人民权运动领袖马丁·路德·金,1963年领导25万人向华盛顿进军"大游行",为黑人争取自由平等和就业。马丁·路德·金在华盛顿林肯纪念堂发表了《我有一个梦想》的著名演说。

[2]美国总统选举采用选举人制度。美国宪法第二条第一款规定,"得票最多者,如其所得票数超过全体选举人的半数,即当选为总统。"1996年11月总统大选,克林顿得选举人票379张,远远超出所需半数的270票,以高票当选。共和党候选人多尔获159张,也就是说,有三分之一的选民投票给了共和党。所以,在就职演说中,安抚共和党选民的情绪是必要的。

May those generations whose faces we cannot yet see, whose names we may never know, say of us here that we led our beloved land into a new century with the American Dream alive for all her children; with the American promise of a more perfect union a reality for all her people; with America's bright flame of freedom spreading throughout all the world.

From the height of this place and the summit of this century, let us go forth. May God strengthen our hands for the good work ahead—and always, always bless our America.

足以使每一个美国人走向充满新希望之地的桥梁。

但愿我们现在还看不到他们的面孔、永远不会知道他们的名字的后代在谈到我们这些人的时候能够说，我们是在美国儿女依旧怀着对美国之梦的憧憬、美国许诺的一个更加完美的联邦对于它的全体人民已经变成现实、美国光焰夺目的自由之火正在燃遍全世界的情况下，带领我们可爱的国家进入一个新世纪的。

让我们从这个高台之上，从这个世纪之巅继续前进。愿上帝给我们以力量，使我们做好今后的工作；愿上帝永远永远保佑我们美国。

乔治·沃克·布什
George Walker Bush

乔治·沃克·布什（George Walker Bush）

生平简介 >>

　　乔治·沃克·布什是美国第四十三任总统，1946年7月6日出生于康涅狄格州。1964年就读于耶鲁大学历史系。1968年至1973年在国家空军警卫队服役。1975年获哈佛商学院MBA硕士学位。1988年帮助其父乔治·布什竞选美国总统，出任高级顾问。1994年11月当选为得克萨斯州州长，1998年连任。1999年6月12日，布什正式宣布参加2000年总统选举，2000年8月2日在费城召开的共和党全国代表大会上被提名为总统候选人。2001年1月20日宣誓就任总统，他是继美国第六任总统亚当斯之后第二位踏着父亲的足印入主白宫的总统。他任内发生了"9·11"事件，随后他发动阿富汗战争、伊拉克战争等一系列反恐战争并取得较大成效。2004年11月总统选举中布什再次赢得大选。

美国历届总统就职演说

THE INAUGURAL ADDRESSES OF THE U.S. PRESIDENTS

George Walker Bush
First Inaugural Address

January 20, 2001

  Chief Justice Rehnquist, President Carter, President Bush, President Clinton, distinguished guests and my fellow citizens, the peaceful transfer of authority is rare in history, yet common in our country. With a simple oath, we affirm old traditions and make new beginnings.

  As I begin, I thank President Clinton for his service to our nation.

  And I thank Vice President Gore for a contest conducted with spirit and ended with grace.

  I am honored and humbled to stand here, where so many of America's leaders have come before me, and so many will follow.

  We have a place, all of us, in a long story—a story we continue, but whose end we will not see. It is the story of a new world that became a friend and liberator of the old, a story of a slave-holding society that became a servant of freedom, the story of a power that went into the world to protect but not possess, to defend but not to conquer.

  It is the American story—a story of flawed and fallible people, united across the generations by grand and enduring ideals.

  The grandest of these ideals is an unfolding American promise that everyone belongs, that everyone deserves a chance, that no insignificant person was ever born.

  Americans are called to enact this promise in our lives and in our laws. And though our nation has sometimes halted, and sometimes delayed, we must follow no other course.

  Through much of the last century, America's faith in freedom and democracy was a rock in a raging sea. Now it is a seed upon the wind, taking root in many nations.

乔治·沃克·布什
George Walker Bush

布什总统首次就职演说

2001年1月20日

尊敬的芮恩奎斯特大法官，卡特总统，布什总统，克林顿总统，尊敬的来宾们，我的同胞们：和平的权力移交在历史上较为罕见，但在美国却是一件普遍的事。我们以朴素的誓言肯定了古老的传统，同时也开创了新的起点。

首先，我要感谢克林顿总统对我们国家的贡献。

感谢戈尔副总统在整个竞选过程中所展现出的英勇精神和优雅风度。

我很荣幸站在这里，同时也感到谦卑。许多美国领导人曾经从这里起步，以后也会有很多领导人从这里继续开拓。

我们每个人在美国悠久的历史故事中都有属于自己的位置。我们正在继续抒写这个故事，但却无法看到它的尽头。这是一个有关新世界的故事，一个对旧世界友好和解放的故事，一个由奴隶制社会发展为崇尚自由的社会的故事，一个强国去保护、捍卫世界而不是占有并征服世界的故事。

这就是美国的故事，几代并非十全十美的美国人民在伟大和永恒的理想中团结奋进的故事。

这些理想中最伟大的便是美国对每个人都应有的承诺，每个人都有自身的价值，每个人都有成功的机会，每个人天生都会有所作为。

美国人竭力把在生活和法律中兑现这一承诺视为使命。虽然我们曾在追求实现这个承诺的过程中停滞不前甚至倒退，但我们仍将坚定不移地完成这一使命。

上世纪大部分时候，美国自由民主的信念就像汹涌大海中的岩石，而现在，它更像风中的种子，已在许多国家扎根。

美国历届总统就职演说
THE INAUGURAL ADDRESSES OF THE U.S. PRESIDENTS

Our democratic faith is more than the creed of our country, it is the inborn hope of our humanity, an ideal we carry but do not own, a trust we bear and pass along. And even after nearly 225 years, we have a long way yet to travel.

While many of our citizens prosper, others doubt the promise, even the justice, of our own country. The ambitions of some Americans are limited by failing schools and hidden prejudice and the circumstances of their birth. And sometimes our differences run so deep, it seems we share a continent, but not a country. We do not accept this, and we will not allow it. Our unity, our union, is the serious work of leaders and citizens in every generation. And this is my solemn pledge: I will work to build a single nation of justice and opportunity. I know this is in our reach because we are guided by a power larger than ourselves who creates us equal in His image. And we are confident in principles that unite and lead us onward.

America has never been united by blood or birth or soil. We are bound by ideals that move us beyond our backgrounds, lift us above our interests and teach us what it means to be citizens. Every child must be taught these principles. Every citizen must uphold them. And every immigrant, by embracing these ideals, makes our country more, not less, American.

Today, we affirm a new commitment to live out our nation's promise through civility, courage, compassion and character. America, at its best, matches a commitment to principle with a concern for civility. A civil society demands from each of us good will and respect, fair dealing and forgiveness.

Some seem to believe that our politics can afford to be petty because, in a time of peace, the stakes of our debates appear small. But the stakes for America are never small. If our country does not lead the cause of freedom, it will not be led. If we do not turn the hearts of children toward knowledge and character, we will lose their gifts and undermine their idealism. If we permit our economy to drift and decline, the vulnerable will suffer most.

We must live up to the calling we share. Civility is not a tactic or a sentiment. It is the determined choice of trust over cynicism, of community over chaos. And this commitment, if we keep it, is a way to shared accomplishment.

America, at its best, is also courageous.

乔治·沃克·布什
George Walker Bush

民主的信仰在美国不仅仅是国家层面的信条,更是人类与生俱来的希望。我们承载希望,但不会独占民主。我们会将民主铭记于心并不断传播。225年过去了,我们仍有很长的路要走。

在我们许多公民走向成功的同时,也有人对我们国家所许下的诺言甚至正义表示怀疑,由于失败的教育、潜在的偏见以及出身环境遏制了一些美国人的雄心壮志,有时,我们的分歧是如此之深,似乎我们虽身处同一个大陆,但不属于同一个国家。对此,我们无法接受,也不允许这样。团结和统一是每一代领导人和美国公民的庄严使命。我郑重宣誓:努力构建一个正义与机遇并存的国家。我知道这是我们可以达到的目标,因为上帝按照自己的形象创造了我们,并以其高于一切的力量指引我们向前。我们对这些把我们团结起来并引领我们开拓前进的原则充满信心。

美国从未被血统、出身或者地域联结起来。只有理想使我们心系一处,超越了自己的背景和个人利益,并教诲我们成为一个公民的意义。这些原则应该教给每一个孩子,每一个公民也应该坚持这些原则。每一个移民也会通过拥护这些理想,使我们国家不丧失且更具美国特色。

今天,我们要明确一个新的信念,通过文明、勇气、同理心和品格来履行我们国家的诺言。美国在其鼎盛时期也没忘记遵循谦卑有礼的原则,一个文明的社会需要我们每个人充满善意、尊重他人、公平处事和宽宏大量。

有人认为我们的政治制度很微弱,因为在和平时期,我们所争辩的话题都是无意义的。但是,对于美国而言,所有这些问题的探讨都不是小事。如果我们不来倡导自由,那么自由将不会被倡导。如果我们不引导孩子们热爱知识、发扬品格,那么就会扼杀他们的天赋,难以让其实现理想。如果我们任凭经济衰落,那么弱势群体将会是最大的受害者。

我们应该响应时代的号召。文明有礼不是一种战术策略,也不是感情用事。这是我们在愤恨声中获取信任、在混乱局势中寻求统一的最坚定的选择。如果我们坚定这样的信念,就会实现共同的成就。

美国正处在最好的时候,将勇往直前。

Our national courage has been clear in times of depression and war, when defending common dangers defined our common good. Now we must choose if the example of our fathers and mothers will inspire us or condemn us. We must show courage in a time of blessing by confronting problems instead of passing them on to future generations.

Together, we will reclaim America's schools, before ignorance and apathy claim more young lives.

We will reform Social Security and Medicare, sparing our children from struggles we have the power to prevent. And we will reduce taxes, to recover the momentum of our economy and reward the effort and enterprise of working Americans.

We will build our defenses beyond challenge, lest weakness invite challenge.

We will confront weapons of mass destruction, so that a new century is spared new horrors.

The enemies of liberty and our country should make no mistake: America remains engaged in the world by history and by choice, shaping a balance of power that favors freedom. We will defend our allies and our interests. We will show purpose without arrogance. We will meet aggression and bad faith with resolve and strength. And to all nations, we will speak for the values that gave our nation birth.

America, at its best, is compassionate. In the quiet of American conscience, we know that deep, persistent poverty is unworthy of our nation's promise.

And whatever our views of its cause, we can agree that children at risk are not at fault. Abandonment and abuse are not acts of God, they are failures of love.

And the proliferation of prisons, however necessary, is no substitute for hope and order in our souls.

Where there is suffering, there is duty. Americans in need are not strangers, they are citizens, not problems, but priorities. And all of us are diminished when any are hopeless.

Government has great responsibilities for public safety and public health, for civil rights and common schools. Yet compassion is the work of a nation, not

乔治·沃克·布什
George Walker Bush

美国国民英勇的精神,在经济大萧条和战争时期展现得淋漓尽致,在抵御共同的危险中体现了我们共同的优秀品格。现在,我们要做出选择,选择的正确与否将会决定我们的祖先是勉励还是谴责我们。我们必须在上帝的眷顾中展现我们的勇气,勇于直面问题,而不是把问题留给子孙后代。

我们要携手并进,重振美国的学校教育,不让无知与冷漠毁掉更多年轻的生命。

我们要改革社会保障和医疗制度,尽全力让孩子们免于痛苦挣扎。我们将降低税收,恢复经济发展,奖励努力为事业奋斗的美国人民。

我们要建立抵抗挑战的防御体系,以防弱点再带来挑战。

我们要抵挡大规模毁灭性武器,以便在新世纪摆脱新形式的恐怖威胁。

反对自由和美国的人们应该清楚,美国将继续积极参与国际事务,以求世界力量的均衡,使自由的力量遍及全球。[1]这是历史的选择。我们会捍卫我们的盟国及自身的利益。[2]我们要谦逊地向世界展示我们的目标,也将坚决打击各种侵略和不守信用的行径。我们要向世界传递孕育了我们伟大民族的价值观。

正处于鼎盛时期的美国也不缺乏同理心。当我们静心思考,我们就会明了根深蒂固的贫穷与美国做出的承诺不相符。

不管我们对贫困原因的看法如何,我们都明白处于危险中的儿童没有过错。放弃和虐待他们不是上帝的作为,而是爱的缺失。

监狱数量的增多,无论多么必要,都无法替代我们灵魂中的希望和秩序。

哪里有痛苦,我们的义务就在哪里。对我们来说,需要帮助的美国人不是陌生人,而是我们的公民;不是包袱,而是急需救助的对象。如果有人陷入绝望的话,我们大家都会因此显得渺小。

政府在公共安全、卫生、民权和学校教育方面都负有重大责任。然而,

---

[1]指北约东扩:波兰、匈牙利、捷克于1999年3月正式加入北约。

[2]当时美海外军事基地374个,分布在140多个国家和地区,驻军30万人。

just a government. And some needs and hurts are so deep they will only respond to a mentor's touch or a pastor's prayer. Church and charity, synagogue and mosque lend our communities their humanity, and they will have an honored place in our plans and in our laws.

Many in our country do not know the pain of poverty, but we can listen to those who do. And I can pledge our nation to a goal: When we see that wounded traveler on the road to Jericho, we will not pass to the other side.

America, at its best, is a place where personal responsibility is valued and expected.

Encouraging responsibility is not a search for scapegoats, it is a call to conscience. And though it requires sacrifice, it brings a deeper fulfillment. We find the fullness of life not only in options, but in commitments. And we find that children and community are the commitments that set us free.

Our public interest depends on private character, on civic duty and family bonds and basic fairness, on uncounted, unhonored acts of decency which give direction to our freedom.

Sometimes in life we are called to do great things. But as a saint of our times has said, every day we are called to do small things with great love. The most important tasks of a democracy are done by everyone.

I will live and lead by these principles: to advance my convictions with civility, to pursue the public interest with courage, to speak for greater justice and compassion, to call for responsibility and try to live it as well. In all these ways, I will bring the values of our history to the care of our times.

What you do is as important as anything government does. I ask you to seek a common good beyond your comfort; to defend needed reforms against easy attacks; to serve your nation, beginning with your neighbor. I ask you to be citizens: citizens, not spectators; citizens, not subjects; responsible citizens, building communities of service and a nation of character.

Americans are generous and strong and decent, not because we believe in ourselves, but because we hold beliefs beyond ourselves. When this spirit of citizenship is missing, no government program can replace it. When this spirit

乔治·沃克·布什
George Walker Bush

同理心不仅仅是政府的职责,也是整个国家的义务。有些需求和伤痕是如此的迫切和深刻,只有通过导师的爱抚和牧师的祷告才能有所感触。不论是教堂还是慈善机构、犹太会堂还是清真寺,都使我们的社区更加人性化,因此它们理应在我们的建设规划和法律中受到尊重。

许多人不理解贫穷的痛苦,但我们可以聆听那些颇有感触的人是如何诉说的。我可以保证美国会实现一个目标:当我们看到受伤的旅者倒在通往耶利哥的路上时,我们不会袖手旁观。

处在鼎盛期的美国很看重每个人应担负起的责任。

鼓励人们勇于承担责任不是要寻找替罪羊,而是对人的良知的呼唤。尽管需要牺牲,但它也给人们带来了更深刻的成就感。我们发现生活的充实不仅在于选择,也在于承诺。我们通过对社会和孩子尽责而获得最终的自由。

我们的公共利益取决于每个人的品行,公民义务和家庭纽带以及最基本的公平性,无数默默无闻的体面行为,都为我们的自由指明了方向。

在生活中,我们时常被召唤去做一些伟大的事情。但是,正如我们所处时代的一位圣人所言,每一天我们都被召唤以大爱去做一些小事。民主制度中最重要的任务是由每一个人来完成的。

我将遵循以下原则来指导我的生活,坚定自己的信念但不强加于人,为公众的利益勇往直前,追求正义和同理心,并且勇于承担责任,通过这些方式,把我们的历史价值带入我们的时代。

您所做的一切与政府所做的任何一件事同等重要。我恳请大家可以超越自己的利益而考虑公众的利益,捍卫必要的改革,使其不要轻易受到攻击,从身边小事做起,为国家效力。希望大家成为真正的公民,而不是旁观者,也不是臣民。大家应成为有责任心的公民,共同建设一个互助的社会和有品格的国家。

美国人慷慨、坚强和体面,不是因为我们相信自己,而是因为我们拥有超越自己的信念。当缺少这种公民精神时,任何政府计划都不能取而代之。只要有这种精神,任何错误都无法抗衡它。

is present, no wrong can stand against it.

After the Declaration of Independence was signed, Virginia statesman John Page wrote to Thomas Jefferson: "We know the race is not to the swift nor the battle to the strong. Do you not think an angel rides in the whirlwind and directs this storm?"

Much time has passed since Jefferson arrived for his inauguration. The years and changes accumulate. But the themes of this day he would know: our nation's grand story of courage and its simple dream of dignity.

We are not this story's author, who fills time and eternity with his purpose. Yet his purpose is achieved in our duty, and our duty is fulfilled in service to one another.

Never tiring, never yielding, never finishing, we renew that purpose today, to make our country more just and generous, to affirm the dignity of our lives and every life.

This work continues. This story goes on. And an angel still rides in the whirlwind and directs this storm.

God bless you all, and God bless America.

George Walker Bush
Second Inaugural Address

January 20, 2005

Vice President Cheney, Mr. Chief Justice, President Carter, President Bush, President Clinton, members of the United States Congress, reverend clergy, distinguished guests, fellow citizens:

On this day, prescribed by law and marked by ceremony, we celebrate the durable wisdom of our Constitution, and recall the deep commitments that

乔治·沃克·布什
George Walker Bush

《独立宣言》签署之后,弗吉尼亚州的政治家约翰·佩齐在给托马斯·杰弗逊的信中说:"我们知道,敏锐的身手不一定可以赢得比赛,力量强大也不一定可以在战争中取胜。这不都是冥冥之中上帝的安排吗?"

自从杰斐逊总统就职典礼以来,已经过去了很长时间,美国也发生了翻天覆地的变化,但有一点他可以肯定,我们这个时代的主题仍然是续写我们国家开拓向前的宏伟故事和追求尊严的纯朴梦想。

我们不是这个故事的作者,杰斐逊总统本人的远大目标穿越时空,在我们的职责中得以实现,而我们通过每个人的努力履行着各自的职责。

我们从不劳累、屈服、完竭,今天我们重申这一目标:使我们的国家更加公正和慷慨,确保我们每个人、每个生命的尊严。

这项工作会继续进行下去,这个故事也还在延续。上帝也仍然在驾驭我们的远行。

上帝保佑大家!上帝保佑美国!

布什总统第二次就职演说

2005年1月20日

切尼副总统、首席法官先生、卡特总统、布什总统、克林顿总统、国会议员们、牧师大人、尊敬的来宾、同胞们:

今天,我们依法以这个仪式来庆祝我们宪法持久不衰的智慧,回顾将我们国家团结在一起的坚定信念。我很感激此时此刻获得的荣耀,想到今后我

unite our country. I am grateful for the honor of this hour, mindful of the consequential times in which we live, and determined to fulfill the oath that I have sworn and you have witnessed.

At this second gathering, our duties are defined not by the words I use, but by the history we have seen together. For a half a century, America defended our own freedom by standing watch on distant borders. After the shipwreck of communism came years of relative quiet, years of repose, years of sabbatical—and then there came a day of fire.

We have seen our vulnerability—and we have seen its deepest source. For as long as whole regions of the world simmer in resentment and tyranny—prone to ideologies that feed hatred and excuse murder—violence will gather, and multiply in destructive power, and cross the most defended borders, and raise a mortal threat. There is only one force of history that can break the reign of hatred and resentment, and expose the pretensions of tyrants, and reward the hopes of the decent and tolerant, and that is the force of human freedom.

We are led, by events and common sense, to one conclusion: The survival of liberty in our land increasingly depends on the success of liberty in other lands. The best hope for peace in our world is the expansion of freedom in all the world.

America's vital interests and our deepest beliefs are now one. From the day of our Founding, we have proclaimed that every man and woman on this earth has rights, and dignity, and matchless value, because they bear the image of the Maker of Heaven and earth. Across the generations we have proclaimed the imperative of self-government, because no one is fit to be a master, and no one deserves to be a slave. Advancing these ideals is the mission that created our Nation. It is the honorable achievement of our fathers. Now it is the urgent requirement of our nation's security, and the calling of our time.

So it is the policy of the United States to seek and support the growth of democratic movements and institutions in every nation and culture, with the ultimate goal of ending tyranny in our world.

This is not primarily the task of arms, though we will defend ourselves and our friends by force of arms when necessary. Freedom, by its nature, must

们即将度过的日子,我决心履行自己在你们的见证下宣读的誓言。

在这第二次聚会上,我们的职责不是由我说的话而是由我们共同目睹的历史所决定的。半个世纪以来,美国守护了遥远的边疆,捍卫了我们自己的自由。东欧剧变后,我们度过了相对平静、安宁、悠闲的一段时光。而接下来,一个灾难性的日子降临了。

我们看到了自己的脆弱,也看到了它的深刻根源。只要世界各地还在仇恨和暴政中煎熬,暴力活动就会增加,这些倾向于滋生仇恨并为杀戮寻找借口的意识形态,其破坏力就会成倍加强,并穿越大多数边防线,构成一种致命的威胁。在历史上,只有一种力量能够打破仇恨和怨忿的束缚,撕下暴君的伪装,满足那些宽容大度的正派人士的愿望,那就是人类自由的力量。

我们从一些事件和常识中得出了一个结论:自由能否在我们的国家继续存在下去,越来越多地取决于自由能否在其他国家取得成功。要实现世界和平,最好的途径就是在全世界范围内传播自由。

如今,美国的重要利益和我们的坚定信念是一致的。从我们建国的那一天起,我们就一直宣称,地球上的每个人都拥有权利、尊严和无可比拟的价值,因为他们都是造世主的产物。历代以来,我们一直宣扬自治的必要性,因为没有人有资格成为主人,也没有人应该成为奴隶。追求这些理想的使命促使我们建立了国家。这是我们祖先取得的光辉成就。现在,它是我们的国家安全提出的迫切要求,是我们这个时代的呼唤。

因此,寻求和支持民主运动和民主制度在各个国家和各种文化下的发展成为美国的政策,其最终目标是结束我们这个世界上的暴政。

这项任务并非主要由武装暴力来达成,尽管我们会在必要的时候依靠军队来保护我们自己和我们的朋友。由于自由本身的特点,它必须由公民

be chosen, and defended by citizens, and sustained by the rule of law and the protection of minorities. And when the soul of a nation finally speaks, the institutions that arise may reflect customs and traditions very different from our own. America will not impose our own style of government on the unwilling. Our goal instead is to help others find their own voice, attain their own freedom, and make their own way.

The great objective of ending tyranny is the concentrated work of generations. The difficulty of the task is no excuse for avoiding it. America's influence is not unlimited, but fortunately for the oppressed, America's influence is considerable, and we will use it confidently in freedom's cause.

My most solemn duty is to protect this nation and its people from further attacks and emerging threats. Some have unwisely chosen to test America's resolve, and have found it firm.

We will persistently clarify the choice before every ruler and every nation: The moral choice between oppression, which is always wrong, and freedom, which is eternally right. America will not pretend that jailed dissidents prefer their chains, or that women welcome humiliation and servitude, or that any human being aspires to live at the mercy of bullies.

We will encourage reform in other governments by making clear that success in our relations will require the decent treatment of their own people. America's belief in human dignity will guide our policies, yet rights must be more than the grudging concessions of dictators; they are secured by free dissent and the participation of the governed. In the long run, there is no justice without freedom, and there can be no human rights without human liberty.

Some, I know, have questioned the global appeal of liberty—though this time in history, four decades defined by the swiftest advance of freedom ever seen, is an odd time for doubt. Americans, of all people, should never be surprised by the power of our ideals. Eventually, the call of freedom comes to every mind and every soul. We do not accept the existence of permanent tyranny because we do not accept the possibility of permanent slavery. Liberty will come to those who love it.

Today, America speaks anew to the peoples of the world:

乔治·沃克·布什
George Walker Bush

来选择和捍卫,并依靠法治和保护少数民族的措施来维系。当一个民族最终发出自己的心声时,它所建立的制度可能反映出与我们截然不同的习俗和传统。美国不会把我们自己的执政方式强加在不愿意接受它的国家身上。相反,我们的目标是帮助其他人找到他们自己的心声,获得他们自己的自由,并开创自己的自由之路。

实现结束暴政这一伟大目标需要几代人全力以赴的工作。这项任务的艰巨性不能成为逃避它的借口。美国的影响力并非毫无局限,但幸运的是,对于那些受压迫的人来说,美国的影响力是相当大的,而我们将充满自信地在自由事业中发挥这一影响力。

我最庄重的职责就是努力保护美国及其人民免受新的恐怖袭击和威胁。有些人非常愚蠢地选择试探美国的决心,最终发现美国决心坚定。

我们将坚定地表明摆在每个统治者和每个国家面前的选择,是关乎终究错误的压迫与永远正确的自由之间的道义的选择。美国不会佯称,被关押的异见分子更青睐束缚他们的枷锁,或者妇女喜欢遭受屈辱和奴役,以及有人愿意听人摆布。

我们明确表示,要想同我国建立良好关系,须体面地对待自己的国民,并以此来鼓励其他国家政府进行改革。美国对人类尊严的信念影响着我们的政策,然而,权利不是独裁者做出的勉强让步,而必须要靠自由地发表意见和人民的参与来得到保障。毕竟,没有自由就没有正义,没有人类自由就没有人权。

我知道,有些人对全世界的自由呼声提出了质疑,尽管自由在过去40年中取得了前所未有的飞速进步。美国人民永远不应该为信念所产生的力量感到意外。最终,自由的呼声定能深入人心。我们不允许暴君的长久存在,因为我们不允许出现持久的奴役。只有热爱自由的人才会得到自由。

今天,美国再次对全世界各族人民说:

All who live in tyranny and hopelessness can know: the United States will not ignore your oppression, or excuse your oppressors. When you stand for your liberty, we will stand with you.

Democratic reformers facing repression, prison, or exile can know: America sees you for who you are: the future leaders of your free country.

The rulers of outlaw regimes can know that we still believe as Abraham Lincoln did: "Those who deny freedom to others deserve it not for themselves; and, under the rule of a just God, cannot long retain it."

The leaders of governments with long habits of control need to know: To serve your people you must learn to trust them. Start on this journey of progress and justice, and America will walk at your side.

And all the allies of the United States can know: we honor your friendship, we rely on your counsel, and we depend on your help. Division among free nations is a primary goal of freedom's enemies. The concerted effort of free nations to promote democracy is a prelude to our enemies' defeat.

Today, I also speak anew to my fellow citizens:

From all of you, I have asked patience in the hard task of securing America, which you have granted in good measure. Our country has accepted obligations that are difficult to fulfill, and would be dishonorable to abandon. Yet because we have acted in the great liberating tradition of this nation, tens of millions have achieved their freedom. And as hope kindles hope, millions more will find it. By our efforts, we have lit a fire as well—a fire in the minds of men. It warms those who feel its power, it burns those who fight its progress, and one day this untamed fire of freedom will reach the darkest corners of our world.

A few Americans have accepted the hardest duties in this cause—in the quiet work of intelligence and diplomacy...the idealistic work of helping raise up free governments...the dangerous and necessary work of fighting our enemies. Some have shown their devotion to our country in deaths that honored their whole lives—and we will always honor their names and their sacrifice.

All Americans have witnessed this idealism, and some for the first time. I ask our youngest citizens to believe the evidence of your eyes. You have seen duty and allegiance in the determined faces of our soldiers. You have seen that

所有生活在暴政和绝望下的人都应该知道：美国不会无视你们所受到的压迫，不会饶恕你们的压迫者。当你们支持自由时，美国将与你们站在一起。

面临镇压、囚禁或者流亡的民主改革人士知道：美国了解你们，把你们看成自由国家未来的领袖。

非法政府的统治者知道，我们仍然像亚伯拉罕·林肯总统一样认为："那些不让别人享有自由的人自己不配拥有自由，而且也不会长久地享有自由。"

那些习惯于控制人民的统治者需要知道：要想服务于民就必须学会信任他们。从这一进步与正义之旅开始，美国将伴你左右。

美国的所有盟友都应该知道：我们尊重与你们的友谊，我们依靠你们的忠告，我们依赖于你们的帮助。分裂自由国家的团结是自由之敌的目的。自由国家共同努力推动民主是我们的敌人走向失败的开始。

今天，我再次对我的美国人民说：

在保护美国安全的艰难时刻，我请求你们给予我足够的耐心。我们国家承担了难以完成且不应放弃的责任。正因为我们国家继续着解放被压迫者的传统，使得数亿人获得了自由。正如希望会点燃希望，还会有更多的人获得自由。经过不懈的努力，我们点燃了人们心中希望的火种。它温暖了那些感觉到它力量的人，它为那些奋勇前进的人照亮了方向，有朝一日，它将把自由的火种撒播到世界最黑暗的角落。

一些美国人已经承担起了这一最艰巨的职责：那些情报界和外交界默默无闻的工作，那些被理想主义激励帮助自由政府所做的工作，以及打击敌人这一危险而又必不可少的工作。有些人甚至将自己的生命奉献给了我们的祖国——我们将永远铭记他们的名字以及他们所做出的牺牲。

所有美国人都见证了这种理想主义，有些人是第一次看到。我希望我们的青年相信你们的所见。你们从美军士兵坚毅的表情中看到了责任和忠诚。你们看到生命是脆弱的，邪恶是真实存在的，勇气获得了胜利。加入这项更

life is fragile, and evil is real, and courage triumphs. Make the choice to serve in a cause larger than your wants, larger than yourself—and in your days you will add not just to the wealth of our country, but to its character.

America has need of idealism and courage, because we have essential work at home—the unfinished work of American freedom. In a world moving toward liberty, we are determined to show the meaning and promise of liberty.

In America's ideal of freedom, citizens find the dignity and security of economic independence, instead of laboring on the edge of subsistence. This is the broader definition of liberty that motivated the Homestead Act, the Social Security Act, and the G.I. Bill of Rights. And now we will extend this vision by reforming great institutions to serve the needs of our time. To give every American a stake in the promise and future of our country, we will bring the highest standards to our schools, and build an ownership society. We will widen the ownership of homes and businesses, retirement savings and health insurance—preparing our people for the challenges of life in a free society. By making every citizen an agent of his or her own destiny, we will give our fellow Americans greater freedom from want and fear, and make our society more prosperous and just and equal.

In America's ideal of freedom, the public interest depends on private character—on integrity, and tolerance toward others, and the rule of conscience in our own lives. Self-government relies, in the end, on the governing of the self. That edifice of character is built in families, supported by communities with standards, and sustained in our national life by the truths of Sinai, the Sermon on the Mount, the words of the Koran, and the varied faiths of our people. Americans move forward in every generation by reaffirming all that is good and true that came before—ideals of justice and conduct that are the same yesterday, today, and forever.

In America's ideal of freedom, the exercise of rights is ennobled by service, and mercy, and a heart for the weak. Liberty for all does not mean independence from one another. Our nation relies on men and women who look after a neighbor and surround the lost with love. Americans, at our best, value the life we see in one another, and must always remember that even the unwanted

伟大的事业吧，它比你个人的需要重要得多，比个人伟大得多。有生之年，你不仅为我们的国家增添了财富，你还会帮助它增光添彩。

美国需要理想和勇气，因为我们在国内还有重要的工作，那就是尚未完成的美国自由的未竟之业。在一个走向自由的世界里，我们决心彰显自由的真义和承诺。

在美国自由的理想信念中，公民们享有经济独立带来的尊严和保障，而不是徘徊在生存边缘的辛苦劳作。这是更广义的自由的定义，它推动了《宅地法案》《社会保障法案》和《退伍军人权利法案》的制定。现在，我们通过改革总体制度，满足时代需求，来扩展这一定义。为了使每一个美国人都与我们国家的希望和未来息息相关，我们要以最高标准发展学校教育、建设所有权社会。我们将扩大人们对房屋和企业、退休储蓄和医疗保险的所有权，让我们的人民做好准备，应对自由社会中的生活挑战。通过使每一位公民成为自己命运的主宰者，我们将使美国同胞更加远离贫困和恐惧，使我们的社会更加繁荣、公正、平等。

在美国的自由理念中，公众利益依赖于个人品格，正直、对他人的宽容以及我们自己生活中的道德准则。民主自治最终要依赖对自我的管理。品格的大厦建立在家庭之上，由规范的邻里社区关系来支撑，凭借西奈的真理、登山宝训、《古兰经》上的话语以及各种信仰的支持，树立在我们的国家生活之中。一代又一代美国人通过弘扬过去创造的一切美好正确的东西而前进。这些思想和准则昨天、今天、永远都是如此。

在美国的自由理念中，助人、仁慈和对弱者的同情，使个人的权利变得更加崇高。全面的自由并不意味着人们互不相干。我们国家依赖于那些照顾邻里、关爱失意者的人们。美国人珍视每个人的生活，而且要永远记得，那些所谓的无用之辈也有他们的价值。我们的国家必须抛弃所有种族主义的恶习，因为我们不能在传递自由信息的同时还携带着偏见的包袱。

have worth. And our country must abandon all the habits of racism, because we cannot carry the message of freedom and the baggage of bigotry at the same time.

From the perspective of a single day, including this day of dedication, the issues and questions before our country are many. From the viewpoint of centuries, the questions that come to us are narrowed and few. Did our generation advance the cause of freedom? And did our character bring credit to that cause?

These questions that judge us also unite us, because Americans of every party and background, Americans by choice and by birth, are bound to one another in the cause of freedom. We have known divisions, which must be healed to move forward in great purposes—and I will strive in good faith to heal them. Yet those divisions do not define America. We felt the unity and fellowship of our nation when freedom came under attack, and our response came like a single hand over a single heart. And we can feel that same unity and pride whenever America acts for good, and the victims of disaster are given hope, and the unjust encounter justice, and the captives are set free.

We go forward with complete confidence in the eventual triumph of freedom. Not because history runs on the wheels of inevitability; it is human choices that move events. Not because we consider ourselves a chosen nation; God moves and chooses as He wills. We have confidence because freedom is the permanent hope of mankind, the hunger in dark places, the longing of the soul. When our Founders declared a new order of the ages; when soldiers died in wave upon wave for a union based on liberty; when citizens marched in peaceful outrage under the banner "Freedom Now"—they were acting on an ancient hope that is meant to be fulfilled. History has an ebb and flow of justice, but history also has a visible direction, set by liberty and the Author of Liberty.

When the Declaration of Independence was first read in public and the Liberty Bell was sounded in celebration, a witness said, "It rang as if it meant something." In our time it means something still. America, in this young century, proclaims liberty throughout all the world, and to all the inhabitants thereof. Renewed in our strength—tested, but not weary—we are ready for

乔治·沃克·布什
George Walker Bush

单从一天来看，包括我发表就职演说的今天，摆在我们国家面前的事务和问题繁多。从几个世纪的角度来看，我们遇到的这些问题又算不了什么。我们这一辈人是否推动了自由事业的发展？我们有没有给这项事业增光添彩？

这些对我们做出裁量的问题也把我们团结在一起，因为不同党派和背景的美国人，无论是移民还是本土公民，都在自由事业中凝心聚力。我们意识到了分歧，必须消除它们才能坚定前进，我将矢志不渝地为之奋斗。这些分歧不是美国的特色。当自由遭受侵犯时，我们能感受到我们国家的团结和友情，我们齐心协力。每当美国主持正义、受灾者得到希望、不公正的现象被审判以及囚徒获得自由时，我们便同样能感受到这种团结和自豪。

在前进的道路上，我们坚信自由会取得最终的胜利。这不是历史的必然性所致，而是人民的选择；也不是因为我们把自己看作是受上帝垂爱的国家，而是上帝自己的意志和选择。我们信心十足，因为自由是人类永恒的希望，是黑暗中的明灯，是灵魂的期盼。当我们的立国先贤宣布新时代的准则时，当一批批战士为了自由的联邦而献身时，当人们在"自由"的口号下激愤地进行和平抗议时，他们都在实践着那古老的愿望，这愿望也必将成为现实。正义在历史的长河中也有起伏，但历史有一个明确的方向，那就是由自由和自由之神所确立的方向。

当《独立宣言》首次公布于众时，自由的钟声在庆典上响起，一位与会者说："它的敲响意味深长。"如今，它仍然蕴涵深意。在新的世纪，美国向全世界及所有人宣告自由。我们历经考验，却依然不倦不息，我们将重振雄风，时刻准备迎接人类自由历史上最伟大的成就。

the greatest achievements in the history of freedom.

May God bless you, and may He watch over the United States of America.

愿上帝保佑你们，眷顾美国。

巴拉克·奥巴马
Barack Obama

巴拉克·奥巴马（Barack Obama）

生平简介 >>

巴拉克·奥巴马是美国第四十四任总统，1961年8月4日出生在夏威夷檀香山。奥巴马两岁多时，父母婚姻破裂。6岁时，奥巴马随母亲和继父前往印度尼西亚生活。

1997年，奥巴马进入政坛，当选伊利诺伊州参议员，并连任8年。2000年，他竞选联邦众议员，但没有成功。尽管如此，他已在全国政坛崭露头角，并应邀在2004年民主党全国代表大会上发表主题演讲。同年11月，他在国会选举中当选伊利诺伊州联邦参议员。

2007年2月，奥巴马正式宣布竞选总统。他在竞选中以"变革"为主题，强调结束伊拉克战争、实现能源自给、停止减税政策和普及医疗保险等，并承诺实现党派团结、在国际上重建同盟关系、恢复美国领导地位。

2008年8月27日，奥巴马在民主党全国代表大会上获得总统候选人提名。在11月4日的总统大选中，他成功当选。2012年，获得连任。

美国历届总统就职演说 | THE INAUGURAL ADDRESSES OF THE U.S. PRESIDENTS

Barack Obama
First Inaugural Address

January 20, 2009

My fellow citizens:

I stand here today humbled by the task before us, grateful for the trust you have bestowed, mindful of the sacrifices borne by our ancestors. I thank President Bush for his service to our nation, as well as the generosity and cooperation he has shown throughout this transition.

Forty-four Americans have now taken the presidential oath. The words have been spoken during rising tides of prosperity and the still waters of peace. Yet, every so often the oath is taken amidst gathering clouds and raging storms. At these moments, America has carried on not simply because of the skill or vision of those in high office, but because We the People have remained faithful to the ideals of our forbearers, and true to our founding documents.

So it has been. So it must be with this generation of Americans.

That we are in the midst of crisis is now well understood. Our nation is at war, against a far-reaching network of violence and hatred. Our economy is badly weakened, a consequence of greed and irresponsibility on the part of some, but also our collective failure to make hard choices and prepare the nation for a new age. Homes have been lost; jobs shed; businesses shuttered. Our health care is too costly; our schools fail too many; and each day brings further evidence that the ways we use energy strengthen our adversaries and threaten our planet.

These are the indicators of crisis, subject to data and statistics. Less measurable but no less profound is a sapping of confidence across our land—a nagging fear that America's decline is inevitable, that the next generation must lower its sights.

巴拉克·奥巴马
Barack Obama

奥巴马总统首次就职演说

2009年1月20日

同胞们：

今天我站在这里，深感面前使命的重大，深谢你们赋予的信任，并铭记我们前辈们为了这个国家所做的牺牲。我感谢布什总统对国家的贡献，也感谢他在两届政府过渡阶段给予的慷慨协作。

迄今为止，已经有44名美国人进行过总统宣誓。[1]这些宣誓词曾在蒸蒸日上的繁荣时期和宁静安详的和平年代诵读，但也响彻在阴云密布、风暴降临的时刻。美国能够历经这些时刻而勇往直前，不仅仅是因为领导人的能力和远见，更是因为"我们的人民"始终坚信我们先辈的理想，对我们的建国理念忠贞不渝。

过去如此。我们这一代美国人也要如此。

我们都很清楚，目前我们正处于危机之中。我们的国家正在进行战争，打击分布广泛的暴力和仇恨势力。[2]我们的经济受到严重的削弱，其原因部分归咎于一些人的贪婪和不负责任，同时也因为在做出艰难选择和准备迎接新时代方面，我们的决策出现了集体性失误。如今，有人失去住房，就业减少，商业破产。医疗卫生耗费巨大；学校质量没有保障；而每一天都在不断证明，我们使用能源的方式助长了敌对势力，同时也威胁着我们的星球。

这些是统计数据和指标传达出的危机信号。而更难以衡量但同样意义深远的是美国人自信心的丧失。现在一种认为美国衰落不可避免，我们的下一代必须降低生活预期的言论正在吞噬着人们的自信。

[1]这里所说的44人有误，实为43人。格罗弗·克利夫兰分别当选美国第22任和24任总统。
[2]美国正在进行两场战争，分别是阿富汗战争和伊拉克战争。

Today I say to you that the challenges we face are real. They are serious and they are many. They will not be met easily or in a short span of time. But know this, America—they will be met.

On this day, we gather because we have chosen hope over fear, unity of purpose over conflict and discord.

On this day, we come to proclaim an end to the petty grievances and false promises, the recriminations and worn-out dogmas that for far too long have strangled our politics.

We remain a young nation, but in the words of Scripture, the time has come to set aside childish things. The time has come to reaffirm our enduring spirit; to choose our better history; to carry forward that precious gift, that noble idea, passed on from generation to generation: the God-given promise that all are equal, all are free, and all deserve a chance to pursue their full measure of happiness.

In reaffirming the greatness of our nation, we understand that greatness is never a given. It must be earned. Our journey has never been one of shortcuts or settling for less. It has not been the path for the faint-hearted—for those who prefer leisure over work, or seek only the pleasures of riches and fame. Rather, it has been the risk-takers, the doers, the makers of things—some celebrated but more often men and women obscure in their labor, who have carried us up the long, rugged path towards prosperity and freedom.

For us, they packed up their few worldly possessions and traveled across oceans in search of a new life.

For us, they toiled in sweatshops and settled the West; endured the lash of the whip and plowed the hard earth.

For us, they fought and died, in places like Concord and Gettysburg; Normandy and Khe Sahn.

Time and again these men and women struggled and sacrificed and worked till their hands were raw so that we might live a better life. They saw America as bigger than the sum of our individual ambitions; greater than all the differences of birth or wealth or faction.

巴拉克·奥巴马
Barack Obama

今天，我告诉大家，我们面临的挑战是真实存在的，并且严峻和繁杂。它们不可能轻易地或在短时间内被克服。但是，请记住这句话：它们终将被征服。

今天，我们聚集在这里是因为我们选择希望而不是恐惧，选择齐心协力而不是冲突对立。

今天，我们在这里宣告，让牵制我国政治为时太久的斤斤计较与虚假承诺、相互指责和陈词滥调就此完结。

我们仍是一个年轻的国家，但借用《圣经》的话说，放弃幼稚的时代已经到来了。现在应是我们重树坚韧精神的时候，应是选择创造更佳历史业绩的时候，应是将代代相传的宝贵财富、崇高理想向前发展的时候：上帝赋予所有人平等、所有人自由和所有人充分追求幸福的机会。

在重申我们国家的伟大的同时，我们深知伟大从来不是上天赐予的，伟大需要努力赢得。我们的历程从来不是走捷径或退而求其次的历程。它不是弱者的道路——它不属于好逸恶劳或只图名利享受的人；这条路属于冒险者、实干家、创造者——尽管有些人享有盛名，但更多的人在默默无闻地耕耘劳作，正是这些人带领我们走过了漫长崎岖的征程，带领我们走向富强和自由。

为了我们，他们背起简单的行囊上路，远涉重洋，追求新生活。

为了我们，他们在条件恶劣的工厂劳作，在西部原野拓荒，忍着鞭笞之痛在坚硬的土地上耕耘。

为了我们，他们奔赴疆场，英勇捐躯，长眠于康科德、葛底斯堡、诺曼底和溪山。[1]

为了我们，他们前赴后继，历尽艰辛，全力奉献，不辞劳苦，直至双手结起层层老茧，就是要让我们能够过上更好的生活。在他们眼里，美国的强盛与伟大超越了个人的雄心，也超越了所有种族、贫富和派系的差异。

---

[1]康科德：独立战争中的战场；葛底斯堡：南北战争时的战场；诺曼底：第二次世界大战中的战场；溪山：越战中的战场。

This is the journey we continue today. We remain the most prosperous, powerful nation on Earth. Our workers are no less productive than when this crisis began. Our minds are no less inventive, our goods and services no less needed than they were last week or last month or last year. Our capacity remains undiminished. But our time of standing pat, of protecting narrow interests and putting off unpleasant decisions—that time has surely passed. Starting today, we must pick ourselves up, dust ourselves off, and begin again the work of remaking America.

For everywhere we look, there is work to be done. The state of our economy calls for action, bold and swift, and we will act—not only to create new jobs, but to lay a new foundation for growth. We will build the roads and bridges, the electric grids and digital lines that feed our commerce and bind us together. We will restore science to its rightful place, and wield technology's wonders to raise health care's quality and lower its cost. We will harness the sun and the winds and the soil to fuel our cars and run our factories. And we will transform our schools and colleges and universities to meet the demands of a new age. All this we can do. All this we will do.

Now, there are some who question the scale of our ambitions—who suggest that our system cannot tolerate too many big plans. Their memories are short. For they have forgotten what this country has already done; what free men and women can achieve when imagination is joined to common purpose, and necessity to courage.

What the cynics fail to understand is that the ground has shifted beneath them—that the stale political arguments that have consumed us for so long no longer apply. The question we ask today is not whether our government is too big or too small, but whether it works—whether it helps families find jobs at a decent wage, care they can afford, a retirement that is dignified. Where the answer is yes, we intend to move forward. Where the answer is no, programs will end. And those of us who manage the public's dollars will be held to account—to spend wisely, reform bad habits, and do our business in the light of day—because only then can we restore the vital trust between a people and their government.

巴拉克·奥巴马
Barack Obama

今天，作为后来者，我们踏上了这一未尽的旅程。我们依然是地球上最繁荣、最强大的国家。我们的劳动者的创造力并没有因为眼前的这场危机而减弱。我们的头脑依然富于创造力。我们的产品与服务仍旧像上星期、上个月或去年一样受人欢迎。我们的能力从未衰退。但是，维持现状、着眼小利以及面对艰难决定一再拖延的时代已经过去了。从今天起，我们必须振作起来，扫去阴霾，开启再造美国的事业。

无论我们把目光投向何处，都有工作在等待着我们。经济形势要求我们果敢而迅速地行动，我们将不辱使命，不仅要创造新的就业机会，而且要打下新的增长基础。我们将建造道路和桥梁，架设电网，铺设电子通信网络，不仅是为了促进商业，也是为了把我们紧密相连。我们将恢复尊重科学的传统，利用高新技术的超常潜力提高医疗保健质量并降低成本。我们将利用太阳能、风力和地热为车辆和工厂提供能源。我们将改造我们的中小学和高等院校，以应对新时代的挑战。这一切我们都能做到，这一切我们必将做到。

现在，有人怀疑我们的雄心壮志，他们说我们的体制不能承受太多的宏伟规划。他们太健忘了，因为他们忘记了这个国家已经取得的成就，忘记了一旦共同的目标插上理想的翅膀、现实的要求鼓起勇气的风帆，自由的人民就会爆发出无穷的创造力。

这些怀疑论者没有认识到美国正在发生的改变，那些长期以来空耗我们的精力的陈腐政治观点已经过时。我们今天提出的问题不是我们的政府太大还是太小，而是它是否行之有效，它是否能够帮助人们找到报酬合理的就业机会，是否能够为他们提供费用适度的医疗保健服务，是否能够确保他们在退休后不失尊严。哪个方案能给予肯定的答案，我们就推进哪个方案。哪个方案的答案是否定的，我们就选择终止它。作为公共资金的管理者，我们必须承担责任，明智地使用资金，抛弃坏习惯，在阳光下履行职责，因为只有这样我们才能恢复人民对政府的至关重要的信任。[1]

---

[1] 奥巴马的救市计划为8190亿美元，其中的2750亿美元将用于退税，而用5440亿美元进行投资。据称这个计划要为美国创造300万个以上的就业机会。

Nor is the question before us whether the market is a force for good or ill. Its power to generate wealth and expand freedom is unmatched, but this crisis has reminded us that without a watchful eye, the market can spin out of control—the nation cannot prosper long when it favors only the prosperous. The success of our economy has always depended not just on the size of our Gross Domestic Product, but on the reach of our prosperity; on the ability to extend opportunity to every willing heart—not out of charity, but because it is the surest route to our common good.

As for our common defense, we reject as false the choice between our safety and our ideals. Our Founding Fathers, faced with perils that we can scarcely imagine, drafted a charter to assure the rule of law and the rights of man, a charter expanded by the blood of generations. Those ideals still light the world, and we will not give them up for expedience's sake. And so to all the other peoples and governments who are watching today, from the grandest capitals to the small village where my father was born: know that America is a friend of each nation and every man, woman, and child who seeks a future of peace and dignity, and we are ready to lead once more.

Recall that earlier generations faced down fascism and communism not just with missiles and tanks, but with the sturdy alliances and enduring convictions. They understood that our power alone cannot protect us, nor does it entitle us to do as we please. Instead, they knew that our power grows through its prudent use; our security emanates from the justness of our cause, the force of our example, the tempering qualities of humility and restraint.

We are the keepers of this legacy. Guided by these principles once more, we can meet those new threats that demand even greater effort—even greater cooperation and understanding between nations. We will begin to responsibly leave Iraq to its people, and forge a hard-earned peace in Afghanistan. With old friends and former foes, we will work tirelessly to lessen the nuclear threat, and roll back the specter of a warming planet. We will not apologize for our way of life, nor will we waver in its defense, and for those who seek to advance their aims by inducing terror and slaughtering innocents, we say to you now that our spirit is stronger and cannot be broken; you cannot outlast us, and

巴拉克·奥巴马
Barack Obama

我们面临的问题也并不是市场好坏的问题。市场创造财富、拓展自由的能力无可匹敌，但这场危机提醒我们：没有严格的监督，市场就会失控，如果一个国家仅仅施惠于富裕者，其富裕便不能持久。我们的经济成功从来不是仅仅取决于国内生产总值的规模，还取决于繁荣的普及面，即为每一位愿意致富的人取决于提供机会的能力，我们这样做不是出于慈善，而是因为这才是最可靠的共同富裕之路。

就共同防御而言，我们决不接受安全与理念不可两全的荒谬论点。建国先贤面对我们难以想见的险恶局面，起草了一部保障法治和人权的宪章，一部子孙后代以自己的鲜血使之更加完美的宪章。今天，这些理念仍然照耀着世界，我们不会为一时之利而弃之。因此，对于今天正在观看这一仪式的其他国家的人民和政府——从最繁华的首都到我父亲出生的小村庄——我要对你们说的是：凡追求和平与尊严的国家以及每一位男人、妇女和儿童，美国都是你们的朋友。我们已经做好准备，再一次走在前面担当领导。

回想我们的先辈们，他们在战胜法西斯主义时依靠的不仅仅是导弹和坦克，更是牢固的联盟和不渝的信念。他们懂得单凭武力无法保护我们的安全，也不能让我们随心所欲。相反，他们知道审慎使用实力会使我们更强大；我们的安全源于事业的正义性、典范的感召力，以及谦卑和克制的融合。

我们是这一传统的继承者。我们只要重新以这些原则为指导，就能应对这些需要投入更多努力、更多国与国的合作及理解的崭新挑战。我们将开始以负责任的方式把伊拉克移交给伊拉克人民，并在阿富汗巩固来之不易的和平。[1]我们将与多年的朋友和昔日的对手一道不懈地努力，减轻核威胁，扭转全球变暖的趋势。我们不会在价值观念上退缩，也不会动摇捍卫它的决心，对于那些妄图以煽动恐怖和屠杀无辜的手段达到其目的的人，我们现在就告诉你们，我们的意志更加顽强、坚不可摧；你们无法拖垮我

---

[1]奥巴马在竞选时承诺要在16个月内撤出驻伊美军，与此同时，阿富汗将重新成为美国的反恐中心。

we will defeat you.

For we know that our patchwork heritage is a strength, not a weakness. We are a nation of Christians and Muslims, Jews and Hindus—and non-believers. We are shaped by every language and culture, drawn from every end of this Earth; and because we have tasted the bitter swill of civil war and segregation, and emerged from that dark chapter stronger and more united, we cannot help but believe that the old hatreds shall someday pass; that the lines of tribe shall soon dissolve; that as the world grows smaller, our common humanity shall reveal itself; and that America must play its role in ushering in a new era of peace.

To the Muslim world, we seek a new way forward, based on mutual interest and mutual respect. To those leaders around the globe who seek to sow conflict, or blame their society's ills on the West—know that your people will judge you on what you can build, not what you destroy. To those who cling to power through corruption and deceit and the silencing of dissent, know that you are on the wrong side of history; but that we will extend a hand if you are willing to unclench your fist.

To the people of poor nations, we pledge to work alongside you to make your farms flourish and let clean waters flow; to nourish starved bodies and feed hungry minds. And to those nations like ours that enjoy relative plenty, we say we can no longer afford indifference to the suffering outside our borders; nor can we consume the world's resources without regard to effect. For the world has changed, and we must change with it.

As we consider the road that unfolds before us, we remember with humble gratitude those brave Americans who, at this very hour, patrol far-off deserts and distant mountains. They have something to tell us, just as the fallen heroes who lie in Arlington whisper through the ages. We honor them not only because they are the guardians of our liberty, but because they embody the spirit of service; a willingness to find meaning in something greater than themselves. And yet, at this moment—a moment that will define a generation—it is precisely this spirit that must inhabit us all.

巴拉克·奥巴马
Barack Obama

们,我们必将战胜你们。[1]

因为我们知道,我们由衲而成的传统是一种优势,而不是劣势。我们是一个由基督教徒和穆斯林、犹太教徒和印度教徒以及无宗教信仰者组成的国家。我们受惠于地球上四面八方每一种语言和文化的影响。由于我们饮过南北战争和种族隔离的苦水,走出了那个黑暗时代并变得更加坚强和团结,我们不能不相信昔日的仇恨终有一天会成为过去;种族之间的界线很快会消失;随着世界变得越来越小,人类的共有品性将得到彰显;美国必须为迎来一个和平的新纪元发挥自己的作用。

面对穆斯林世界,我们寻求一条新的前进道路,以共同利益和相互尊重为基础。对于世界上那些妄图制造矛盾、将自己社会的弊端归罪于西方的领导人,我们奉劝你们:你们的人民将以你们的建设成就而不是你们的毁灭能力来评判你们。对于那些依靠腐败、欺骗、压制不同意见等手段固守权势的人,我们提醒你们:你们站在了历史错误的一边;但只要你们放弃压迫,我们仍将伸出友谊之手。

对于贫困国家的人民,我们保证同你们并肩努力,让你们的农田丰收,让清洁的用水取之不竭;使饥饿的身体得以饱食,使饥渴的心灵受到滋润。对于那些像我们一样富饶的国家,我们要说我们再不能对他人的苦难无动于衷,也再不能肆意消耗世界的资源。世界已经改变,我们必须随之改变。

在思索我们面前的道路时,我们怀着崇敬的心情感谢此刻正在偏远的沙漠和山区巡逻的英勇无畏的美国人。他们向我们述说着什么,正如在阿灵顿公墓长眠的阵亡英雄在漫漫岁月中低浅的吟诵。我们崇敬他们,不仅因为他们捍卫着我们的自由,而且因为他们代表着献身精神,体现了超越个人、寻求远大理想的意愿。而在这个时刻,这个具有划时代意义的时刻,我们大家所必须具备的正是这种精神。

---

[1]就在奥巴马就职前不到一个月,以色列与加沙又燃战火。奥巴马上台伊始,便面临中东的动乱局势。奥巴马在就职后的第一个工作日,就给巴民族权力机构主席阿巴斯通电话,承诺努力实现中东地区的"持久和平"。

美国历届总统就职演说
THE INAUGURAL ADDRESSES OF THE U.S. PRESIDENTS

For as much as government can do and must do, it is ultimately the faith and determination of the American people upon which this nation relies. It is the kindness to take in a stranger when the levees break, the selflessness of workers who would rather cut their hours than see a friend lose their job which sees us through our darkest hours. It is the firefighter's courage to storm a stairway filled with smoke, but also a parent's willingness to nurture a child, that finally decides our fate.

Our challenges may be new. The instruments with which we meet them may be new. But those values upon which our success depends—honesty and hard work, courage and fair play, tolerance and curiosity, loyalty and patriotism—these things are old. These things are true. They have been the quiet force of progress throughout our history. What is demanded then is a return to these truths. What is required of us now is a new era of responsibility—a recognition, on the part of every American, that we have duties to ourselves, our nation, and the world, duties that we do not grudgingly accept but rather seize gladly, firm in the knowledge that there is nothing so satisfying to the spirit, so defining of our character, than giving our all to a difficult task.

This is the price and the promise of citizenship.

This is the source of our confidence—the knowledge that God calls on us to shape an uncertain destiny.

This is the meaning of our liberty and our creed—why men and women and children of every race and every faith can join in celebration across this magnificent mall, and why a man whose father less than sixty years ago might not have been served at a local restaurant can now stand before you to take a most sacred oath.

So let us mark this day with remembrance, of who we are and how far we have traveled. In the year of America's birth, in the coldest of months, a small band of patriots huddled by dying campfires on the shores of an icy river. The capital was abandoned. The enemy was advancing. The snow was stained with blood. At a moment when the outcome of our revolution was most in doubt, the father of our nation ordered these words be read to the people:

"Let it be told to the future world ... that in the depth of winter, when

巴拉克·奥巴马
Barack Obama

虽然政府能有许多作为也必须有许多作为,但最终离不开美国人民的信仰和决心,这便是我国的立国之本。正是因为人们在大堤崩裂时接纳陌生人的关爱之情,正是因为工人们宁愿减少自己的工时而不愿看到朋友失去工作的无私精神,才使我们度过了最暗淡的时光。正是因为消防队员们冲进浓烟滚滚的楼道的无畏勇气,也正是因为父母培养孩子的无私之心,最终决定我们的命运。

我们面临的挑战可能前所未闻。我们迎接挑战的方式也可能前所未有。然而,我们赖以成功的价值观——诚实和勤奋、勇气和公平、宽容心和探索精神、忠诚和爱国——从未改变。这些价值观都是千真万确的。这些价值观是我国整个历史过程中一股无声的进步力量。现在需要的便是重归这些真理。我们现在需要做的是开创负责任的新时代——每一个美国人都需要认识到我们对自己、对国家、对全世界都承担着义务。对于这些义务,我们并非勉强接受,而是心甘情愿主动承担,同时坚信我们为艰巨的使命付出一切,没有任何事可以如此满足我们的道义感,也没有任何事能如此体现我们的特性。

这是公民的义务和承诺。
这是我们自信的来源——上帝赐予我们知识,以应对未知的命运。

这就是我们的自由和我们坚守的信念的意义——这就是为什么今天不同种族和不同信仰的男女老少能在这个宏伟的大草坪上欢聚一堂,这就是为什么近六十年前,一位父亲走进当地餐厅甚至无人理睬,而今天他的儿子可以在这里,在你们面前,许下庄严的誓言。

为此,让我们记住这一天,记住我们是什么样的人,记住我们已经走过了多长的路。在美利坚诞生的年月,在那些最寒冷的日子里,为数不多的爱国者聚集在一条冰河的岸边,身旁的篝火即将熄灭。首都已经沦陷,敌人正在逼近,鲜血染红了白雪。在不知道我们的革命何去何从,战局最为艰难的时刻,我们的国父们这样说:

"让我们昭告未来的世界……在这个酷寒的冬季,万物萧疏,只有希

nothing but hope and virtue could survive ... that the city and the country, alarmed at one common danger, came forth to meet ... it."

America! In the face of our common dangers, in this winter of our hardship, let us remember these timeless words. With hope and virtue, let us brave once more the icy currents, and endure what storms may come. Let it be said by our children's children that when we were tested we refused to let this journey end, that we did not turn back nor did we falter; and with eyes fixed on the horizon and God's grace upon us, we carried forth that great gift of freedom and delivered it safely to future generations.

Thank you. God bless you. And God bless the United States of America.

Barack Obama
Second Inaugural Address

January 21, 2013

Vice President Biden, Mr. Chief Justice, Members of the United States Congress, distinguished guests, and fellow citizens:

Each time we gather to inaugurate a president, we bear witness to the enduring strength of our Constitution. We affirm the promise of our democracy. We recall that what binds this nation together is not the colors of our skin or the tenets of our faith or the origins of our names. What makes us exceptional—what makes us American—is our allegiance to an idea, articulated in a declaration made more than two centuries ago:

"We hold these truths to be self-evident, that all men are created equal, that they are endowed by their Creator with certain unalienable rights, that among these are Life, Liberty, and the pursuit of Happiness."

Today we continue a never-ending journey, to bridge the meaning of those words with the realities of our time. For history tells us that while these truths may be self-evident, they have never been self-executing; that while freedom is a gift from God, it must be secured by His people here on Earth. The patriots

望和美德可以长存……这个城市和这个国家,在共同的危机下团结起来,共同面对前方的艰难。"

这就是美国。在我们面临共同危难之际,在我们遇到艰难险阻的深冬,让我们牢记这些永恒的话语。心怀希望和勇气,让我们再一次不惧严寒,勇为中流砥柱,不论什么风暴来袭,我们必将坚不可摧。今后,让我们的后代子孙如此评说:在面临挑战的时候,我们没有屈服,我们没有逃避也没有犹豫;我们在上帝的关爱下眺望远方,发扬自由这个宝贵的传统,将它平稳地传递给未来的世世代代。

谢谢。上帝保佑你们。天佑美国。

奥巴马总统第二次就职演说

2013年1月21日

拜登副总统、首席大法官、国会议员们、尊敬的各位嘉宾、亲爱的公民们:

每一次我们集会庆祝总统就职都是在见证美国宪法的持久力量。我们都是在肯定美国民主的承诺。我们重申,将这个国家紧密联系在一起的不是我们的肤色,也不是我们信仰的教条,更不是我们名字的来源。让我们与众不同,让我们成为美国人的是我们对于一种理念的恪守。200多年前,这一理念在一篇宣言中被清晰阐述:

"我们认为下述真理是不言而喻的,人人生而平等。造物主赋予他们若干不可剥夺的权利,包括生存、自由和追求幸福的权利。"

今天,我们继续着这一未竟的征程,架起这些理念与我们时代现实之间的桥梁。因为历史告诉我们,即便这些真理是不言而喻的,它们也从来不会自动生效。因为虽然自由是上帝赋予的礼物,但仍需要世间的子民去捍卫。1776年,美国的爱国先驱们推翻国王的暴政不是为了实现少数人的

of 1776 did not fight to replace the tyranny of a king with the privileges of a few or the rule of a mob. They gave to us a Republic, a government of, and by, and for the people, entrusting each generation to keep safe our founding creed.

For more than two hundred years, we have.

Through blood drawn by lash and blood drawn by sword, we learned that no union founded on the principles of liberty and equality could survive half-slave and half-free. We made ourselves anew, and vowed to move forward together.

Together, we determined that a modern economy requires railroads and highways to speed travel and commerce; schools and colleges to train our workers.

Together, we discovered that a free market only thrives when there are rules to ensure competition and fair play.

Together, we resolved that a great nation must care for the vulnerable, and protect its people from life's worst hazards and misfortune.

Through it all, we have never relinquished our skepticism of central authority, nor have we succumbed to the fiction that all society's ills can be cured through government alone. Our celebration of initiative and enterprise; our insistence on hard work and personal responsibility, these are constants in our character.

But we have always understood that when times change, so must we; that fidelity to our founding principles requires new responses to new challenges; that preserving our individual freedoms ultimately requires collective action. For the American people can no more meet the demands of today's world by acting alone than American soldiers could have met the forces of fascism or communism with muskets and militias. No single person can train all the math and science teachers we'll need to equip our children for the future, or build the roads and networks and research labs that will bring new jobs and businesses to our shores. Now, more than ever, we must do these things together, as one nation, and one people.

This generation of Americans has been tested by crises that steeled our resolve and proved our resilience. A decade of war is now ending. An economic recovery has begun. America's possibilities are limitless, for we possess all

巴拉克·奥巴马
Barack Obama

特权或建立暴民的统治。先驱们留给我们一个共和国，一个民有、民治、民享的政府。他们委托每一代美国人捍卫我们的建国信条。

在过去的200多年里，我们做到了。

从奴役的血腥枷锁和刀剑的血光厮杀中我们懂得了，建立在自由与平等原则之上的联邦不能永远维持半奴隶和半自由的状态。我们赢得了新生，发誓共同前进。

我们共同决定，现代经济需要铁路与高速公路以加速旅行和商业交流，需要中小学校与大学来培训我们的工人。

我们共同发现，自由市场的繁荣只能建立在保障竞争与公平竞争的原则之上。

我们共同决定，一个伟大的国家必须关照弱势群体，保护其人民不受生命威胁和不幸的侵扰。

一路走来，我们从未放弃对集权的质疑。我们同样不屈服于这一谎言：一切社会弊端都只能靠政府来解决。我们对积极向上与奋发进取的赞扬，我们对努力工作与个人责任的坚持，这些都是美国精神的基本要义。

我们也理解，时代在变化，我们同样需要变革。对建国精神的忠诚，需要我们迎接新的挑战。保护我们的个人自由，最终需要所有人的共同努力。因为美国人不能再独自迎接当今世界的挑战，正如美国士兵们不能再像先辈一样，用步枪和民兵同敌人——法西斯主义与共产主义——作战。一个人无法培训所有的数学与科学老师，我们需要他们为了未来去教育孩子们。一个人无法建设道路、铺设网络、建立实验室来为国内带来新的工作岗位和商业机会。现在，与以往任何时候相比，我们都更需要团结合作，作为一个国家、一个民族团结起来。

这一代美国人经历了危机的考验，经济危机坚定了我们的决心，证明了我们的韧性。长达十年的战争正在结束，经济的复苏已经开始。美国的可能性是无限的，因为我们拥有当今没有边界的世界所需要的所有品质：年轻

the qualities that this world without boundaries demands: youth and drive; diversity and openness; an endless capacity for risk and a gift for reinvention. My fellow Americans, we are made for this moment, and we will seize it — so long as we seize it together.

For we, the people, understand that our country cannot succeed when a shrinking few do very well and a growing many barely make it. We believe that America's prosperity must rest upon the broad shoulders of a rising middle class. We know that America thrives when every person can find independence and pride in their work; when the wages of honest labor liberate families from the brink of hardship. We are true to our creed when a little girl born into the bleakest poverty knows that she has the same chance to succeed as anybody else, because she is an American, she is free, and she is equal, not just in the eyes of God but also in our own.

We understand that outworn programs are inadequate to the needs of our time. We must harness new ideas and technology to remake our government, revamp our tax code, reform our schools, and empower our citizens with the skills they need to work harder, learn more, and reach higher. But while the means will change, our purpose endures: a nation that rewards the effort and determination of every single American. That is what this moment requires. That is what will give real meaning to our creed.

We, the people, still believe that every citizen deserves a basic measure of security and dignity. We must make the hard choices to reduce the cost of health care and the size of our deficit. But we reject the belief that America must choose between caring for the generation that built this country and investing in the generation that will build its future. For we remember the lessons of our past, when twilight years were spent in poverty, and parents of a child with a disability had nowhere to turn. We do not believe that in this country, freedom is reserved for the lucky, or happiness for the few. We recognize that no matter how responsibly we live our lives, any one of us, at any time, may face a job loss, or a sudden illness, or a home swept away in a terrible storm. The commitments we make to each other — through Medicare, and Medicaid, and Social Security — these things do not sap our initiative; they strengthen

巴拉克·奥巴马
Barack Obama

与活力、多样性与开放、无穷的冒险精神以及创造的天赋。我亲爱的同胞们，我们正是为此刻而生，我们更要在此刻团结一致，抓住当下的机会。

因为我们——美国人民——清楚，如果只有不断萎缩的少数群体获得成功，而大多数人不能成功，我们的国家就无法成功。我们相信，美国的繁荣必须建立在不断扩大的中产阶级的宽阔臂膀之上。我们知道，只有当每个人都能在工作中找到自立与自豪时，只有当诚实劳动获得的薪水足够让家庭摆脱困苦时，美国的繁荣才能实现。我们如此才算忠诚于我们的信念：一个出生于最贫穷环境中的小女孩都能知道，她有同其他所有人一样的成功机会，因为她是一个美国人，她是自由的、平等的，不仅在上帝眼中，而且在我们自己的眼中。

我们知道，我们已然陈旧的方案不足以满足时代的需要。我们必须应用新理念和新技术重塑我们的政府，改进我们的税法，改革我们的学校，让我们的公民拥有他们所需要的技能，以便更加努力地工作，学更多的知识，向更高处发展。我们的方法虽然有改变，但目的始终如一：国家对每个美国人的努力和决心给予奖励。这是现在需要的。这将给我们的信条赋予真正的意义。

我们，即美国人民，仍然认为，每个公民都应当获得基本的安全和尊严。我们必须做出艰难抉择，降低医疗费用，缩减赤字规模。但我们拒绝在照顾建设国家的这一代和投资即将建设国家的下一代间做出选择。因为我们记得过去的教训：老年人的夕阳时光在贫困中度过，家有残障儿童的父母无处求助。我们相信，在这个国家，自由不只是那些幸运儿的专属，或者说幸福只属于少数人。我们知道，不管我们怎样负责任地生活，我们任何人在任何时候都可能面临失业、突发疾病或住房被可怕的飓风摧毁的风险。我们通过医疗保险、联邦医疗补助计划、社会保障项目向每个人做出承诺，这些不会让我们的创造力衰竭，而是会让我们更强大。这些不会让我们成为充满不劳而获者的国度，这些让我们敢于承担风险，让国家伟大。

us. They do not make us a nation of takers; they free us to take the risks that make this country great.

We, the people, still believe that our obligations as Americans are not just to ourselves, but to all posterity. We will respond to the threat of climate change, knowing that the failure to do so would betray our children and future generations. Some may still deny the overwhelming judgment of science, but none can avoid the devastating impact of raging fires, and crippling drought, and more powerful storms. The path towards sustainable energy sources will be long and sometimes difficult. But America cannot resist this transition; we must lead it. We cannot cede to other nations the technology that will power new jobs and new industries — we must claim its promise. That is how we will maintain our economic vitality and our national treasure—our forests and waterways; our croplands and snowcapped peaks. That is how we will preserve our planet, commanded to our care by God. That's what will lend meaning to the creed our fathers once declared.

We, the people, still believe that enduring security and lasting peace do not require perpetual war. Our brave men and women in uniform, tempered by the flames of battle, are unmatched in skill and courage. Our citizens, seared by the memory of those we have lost, know too well the price that is paid for liberty. The knowledge of their sacrifice will keep us forever vigilant against those who would do us harm. But we are also heirs to those who won the peace and not just the war, who turned sworn enemies into the surest of friends, and we must carry those lessons into this time as well.

We will defend our people and uphold our values through strength of arms and rule of law. We will show the courage to try and resolve our differences with other nations peacefully—not because we are naive about the dangers we face, but because engagement can more durably lift suspicion and fear. America will remain the anchor of strong alliances in every corner of the globe; and we will renew those institutions that extend our capacity to manage crisis abroad, for no one has a greater stake in a peaceful world than its most powerful nation. We will support democracy from Asia to Africa; from the Americas to the Middle East, because our interests and our conscience compel us to act

巴拉克·奥巴马
Barack Obama

　　我们，即美国人民，仍然相信，我们作为美国人的义务不只是对我们自己而言，还包括对子孙后代。我们将应对气候变化的威胁，认识到不采取措施应对气候变化就是对子孙后代的背叛。一些人可能仍在否定科学界的压倒性判断，但没有人能够避免熊熊火灾、严重旱灾、更强力风暴带来的灾难性打击。通向可持续能源的道路是漫长的，有时是困难的，但美国不能抵制这种趋势，我们必须引领这种趋势。我们不能把制造新就业机会和新行业的技术让给其他国家，我们必须明确这一承诺。这是我们保持经济活力和国家财富——我们的森林和航道，我们的农田与雪峰——的方法。这将是我们保护我们星球的办法，上帝把这个星球托付给了我们。这将给我们的建国之父们曾宣布的信条赋予意义。

　　我们，即美国人民，仍然相信持久的安全与和平，不需要持续的战争。我们勇敢的士兵经受了战火的考验，他们的技能和勇气是无可匹敌的。我们的公民依然铭记着那些阵亡者，非常清楚我们为自由付出的代价，明白他们的牺牲将让我们永远对那些试图伤害我们的势力保持警惕。但我们也是那些赢得和平而不只是战争的人们的后代，他们将仇敌转变成最可靠的朋友，我们也必须把这些经验带到这个时代。

　　我们将通过强大的军力和法治保护我们的人民，捍卫我们的价值观。我们将展现试图和平解决与其他国家分歧的勇气，但这不是因为我们对面临的危险持幼稚的态度，而是因为接触能够更持久地化解疑虑和恐惧。美国将在全球保持强大的联盟，我们将维护这些能扩展我们应对海外危机能力的机制。因为作为世界上最强大的国家，我们在世界和平方面拥有最大的利益。我们将支持从亚洲到非洲、从美洲至中东的民主国家，因为我们的利益和良心驱使我们代表那些想获得自由的人们采取行动。我们必须成为贫困者、病患者、被边缘化人士、异见受害者的希望来源，不仅仅是出于慈善，也是因为这个时代的和平需要不断推进我们共同信念中的原则：

on behalf of those who long for freedom. And we must be a source of hope to the poor, the sick, the marginalized, the victims of prejudice — not out of mere charity, but because peace in our time requires the constant advance of those principles that our common creed describes: tolerance and opportunity; human dignity and justice.

We, the people, declare today that the most evident of truths — that all of us are created equal — is the star that guides us still; just as it guided our forebears through Seneca Falls, and Selma, and Stonewall; just as it guided all those men and women, sung and unsung, who left footprints along this great Mall, to hear a preacher say that we cannot walk alone; to hear a King proclaim that our individual freedom is inextricably bound to the freedom of every soul on Earth.

It is now our generation's task to carry on what those pioneers began. For our journey is not complete until our wives, our mothers, and daughters can earn a living equal to their efforts. Our journey is not complete until our gay brothers and sisters are treated like anyone else under the law — for if we are truly created equal, then surely the love we commit to one another must be equal as well. Our journey is not complete until no citizen is forced to wait for hours to exercise the right to vote. Our journey is not complete until we find a better way to welcome the striving, hopeful immigrants who still see America as a land of opportunity; until bright young students and engineers are enlisted in our workforce rather than expelled from our country. Our journey is not complete until all our children, from the streets of Detroit to the hills of Appalachia to the quiet lanes of Newtown, know that they are cared for, and cherished, and always safe from harm.

That is our generation's task—to make these words, these rights, these values—of Life, and Liberty, and the Pursuit of Happiness—real for every American. Being true to our founding documents does not require us to agree on every contour of life; it does not mean we will all define liberty in exactly the same way, or follow the same precise path to happiness. Progress does not compel us to settle centuries-long debates about the role of government for all time — but it does require us to act in our time.

宽容和机遇，人类尊严与正义。

我们，即美国人民，今天宣布，最不言自明的真理——所有人都是生而平等的——一直是引领我们的恒星。它引领我们的先辈穿越纽约塞尼卡瀑布城(女权抗议事件)、塞尔玛(黑人权力事件)和石墙(同性恋与警察发生的暴力事件)，引领着所有在伟大征程中一路留下足迹的男性和女性，留下姓名和没有留下姓名的人，去聆听一位牧师说，我们不能独自前行，去聆听马丁·路德·金说，我们个人的自由与地球上每个灵魂的自由不可分割。

继续先辈开创的事业是我们这代人的任务。直到我们的妻子、母亲和女儿的待遇能够与她们的努力相称，我们的征途才会结束。直到我们同性恋的兄弟姐妹在法律之下得到与其他人同样的待遇，我们的征途才会结束。因为如果我们真正是生而平等的，那么我们对彼此的爱也应该是平等的。直到没有公民需要等待数个小时去行使投票权，我们的征途才会结束。直到我们找到更好的方法迎接努力、有憧憬的移民，他们依旧视美国为一块充满机会的土地；直到聪颖年轻的学生和工程师为我们所用，而不是被逐出美国，我们的征途才会结束。直到我们所有的儿童，从底特律的街道到阿巴拉契亚的山岭，再到纽敦镇安静的小巷，知道他们被关心和珍视，永远远离伤害，我们的征途才会结束。

那是我们这一代的任务——让生存、自由和追求幸福的言语、权利和价值切实体现在每个美国人的身上。忠实于我们的立国文本不是要将每个人的生活一致化，也并不意味着，我们会以完全一样的方式去定义自由，沿着同样的道路通向幸福。进步不会终止几个世纪以来一直纠结的关于政府角色的争论，但它确实要求我们现在就采取行动。

For now decisions are upon us, and we cannot afford delay. We cannot mistake absolutism for principle, or substitute spectacle for politics, or treat name-calling as reasoned debate. We must act, knowing that our work will be imperfect. We must act, knowing that today's victories will be only partial, and that it will be up to those who stand here in four years, and forty years, and four hundred years hence to advance the timeless spirit once conferred to us in a spare Philadelphia hall.

My fellow Americans, the oath I have sworn before you today, like the one recited by others who serve in this Capitol, was an oath to God and country, not party or faction — and we must faithfully execute that pledge during the duration of our service. But the words I spoke today are not so different from the oath that is taken each time a soldier signs up for duty, or an immigrant realizes her dream. My oath is not so different from the pledge we all make to the flag that waves above and that fills our hearts with pride.

They are the words of citizens, and they represent our greatest hope.

You and I, as citizens, have the power to set this country's course.

You and I, as citizens, have the obligation to shape the debates of our time — not only with the votes we cast, but with the voices we lift in defense of our most ancient values and enduring ideals.

Let each of us now embrace, with solemn duty and awesome joy, what is our lasting birthright. With common effort and common purpose, with passion and dedication, let us answer the call of history, and carry into an uncertain future that precious light of freedom.

Thank you, God Bless you, and may He forever bless these United States of America.

巴拉克·奥巴马
Barack Obama

我们现在就要做出选择,我们不能拖延。我们不能误将绝对主义当作原则,或者以作秀代替政治,或将中伤视作理性的辩论。我们必须行动,要意识到我们的工作并不完美。我们必须行动,要意识到今天的胜利是并不完全的,需要靠未来4年、40年或是400年致力于这项事业的人,去推进当年在费城制宪会议大厅传承给我们的永恒精神。

我的美国同胞,我今天在你们面前宣读的誓词,如同在国会山服务的其他人曾宣读过的誓词一样,是对上帝和国家的誓词,不是对党派或是派别的,我们必须在任期内忠实地履行这些承诺。但我今天宣读的誓词与士兵报名参军或者是移民实现梦想时所宣读的誓词没有多少差别。我的誓词与我们所有的人向我们头顶飘扬的、让我们心怀自豪的国旗所表达的誓言没有多大差别。

这些是公民的心声,代表着我们最伟大的希望。

你们和我,作为公民,都有权力决定这个国家前进的道路。

你们和我,作为公民,都有义务塑造我们时代的辩题,不仅通过我们的选票,而且通过为捍卫悠久的价值观和持久的理想而发出的声音。

现在让我们带着庄严的责任和无比的快乐,拥抱我们永恒的与生俱来的权利。凭借共同的努力和共同的目标,凭借热情与奉献,让我们回应历史的召唤,将珍贵的自由之光带入未知的未来。

感谢你们,上帝保佑你们,愿上帝永远保佑美利坚合众国。

唐纳德·特朗普
Donald Trump

唐纳德·特朗普（Donald Trump）

生平简介>>

唐纳德·特朗普是美国第四十五任总统。他于1946年6月14日出生在纽约市。1964年毕业于纽约军事学校。特朗普曾经是美国最具知名度的房地产商之一，人称"地产之王"。1975年，他以1000万美元的价格买进纽约中央车站附近的破旧旅馆，将其重建后打造成著名的"凯悦酒店"，这成为他房地产事业上的重要里程碑。2015年6月17日，特朗普在纽约市第五大道特朗普大厦宣布参加美国总统竞选。2015年12月7日，特朗普入围美国知名新闻周刊《时代》2015年度人物的候选名单。2016年7月21日，特朗普正式接受美国共和党总统候选人提名。2016年11月9日，当选总统。2017年1月20日中午，特朗普在美国首都华盛顿宣誓就职。

Donald Trump
Inaugural Address

January 20, 2017

Chief Justice Roberts, President Carter, President Clinton, President Bush, President Obama, fellow Americans and people of the world, thank you.

We, the citizens of America, are now joined in a great national effort to rebuild our country and restore its promise for all of our people. Together we will determine the course of America and the world for many, many years to come.

We will face challenges. We will confront hardships. But we will get the job done. Every four years, we gather on these steps to carry out the orderly and peaceful transfer of power.

And we are grateful to President Obama and First Lady Michelle Obama for their gracious aid throughout this transition. They have been magnificent. Thank you.

Today's ceremony, however, has very special meaning. Because today, we are not merely transferring power from one administration to another or from one party to another.

But we are transferring power from Washington D.C. and giving it back to you, the people.

For too long, a small group in our nation's capital has reaped the rewards of government while the people have borne the cost. Washington flourished, but the people did not share in its wealth. Politicians prospered, but the jobs left. And the factories closed.

The establishment protected itself but not the citizens of our country. Their victories have not been your victories. Their triumphs have not been your triumphs. And while they celebrated in our nation's capital, there was little to celebrate for struggling families all across our land. That all changes

唐纳德·特朗普
Donald Trump

特朗普总统就职演说

2017年1月20日

首席大法官罗伯茨先生,卡特总统,克林顿总统,布什总统,奥巴马总统,各位美国同胞,世界人民,感谢你们!

各位美国公民,我们正参与一项伟大的全国性事业:重建我们的国家,重塑对全体人民的承诺。我们将一起决定未来很多年内美国乃至全世界的道路。

我们会遭遇挑战。我们会遇到困难。但是我们能将这项事业完成。每过四年,我们都相聚在这里进行有序和平的权力交接。

我们应该感谢总统奥巴马和第一夫人米歇尔·奥巴马,他们在权力交接中,慷慨地给予我以帮助。他们真的很棒。谢谢你们。

今天的就职典礼有着特殊的意义。因为今天我们不只是将权力由一任总统交接到下一任总统,由一个政党交接给另一政党。

今天我们是将权力由华盛顿交接到了人民的手中,即你们的手中。

长久以来,华盛顿的一小群人攫取了利益果实,代价却要由人民来承受。华盛顿欣欣向荣,人民却没有分享到财富。政客们塞满了腰包,工作机会却越来越少,无数工厂关门。

建制派保护的是他们自己,而不是我们国家的公民。他们的成功不属于你们,他们的胜利也不是你们的胜利。当他们在我们的首都欢呼庆祝时,这片土地上无数在挣扎奋斗的家庭却没有什么可以庆祝的。但这些都会改变,在此地改变,在此时改变。因为你们的时刻来临了,这一刻属于你们。

starting right here and right now. Because this moment is your moment. It belongs to you.

It belongs to everyone gathered here today and everyone watching all across America. This is your day. This is your celebration. And this, the United States of America, is your country.

What truly matters is not which party controls our government but whether our government is controlled by the people. January 20th, 2017 will be remembered as the day the people became the rulers of this nation again.

The forgotten men and women of our country will be forgotten no longer.

Everyone is listening to you now. You came by the tens of millions to become part of a historic movement, the likes of which the world has never seen before.

At the center of this movement is a crucial conviction—that a nation exist to serve its citizens. Americans want great schools for their children, safe neighborhoods for their families and good jobs for themselves.

These are just and reasonable demands of righteous people and a righteous public. But for too many of our citizens, a different reality exist. Mothers and children trapped in poverty in our inner cities, rusted out factories scattered like tombstones across the landscape of our nation, an education system flushed with cash but which leaves our young and beautiful students deprived of all knowledge. And the crime, and the gangs, and the drugs that have stolen too many lives and robbed our country of so much unrealized potential. This American carnage stops right here and stops right now.

We are one nation, and their pain is our pain. Their dreams are our dreams, and their success will be our success. We share one heart, one home and one glorious destiny.

The oath of office I take today is an oath of allegiance to all Americans. For many decades, we've enriched foreign industry at the expense of American industry, subsidized the armies of other countries while allowing for the very sad depletion of our military.

We defended other nation's borders while refusing to defend our own.

And spent trillions and trillions of dollars overseas while America's infrastructure has fallen into disrepair and decay.

唐纳德·特朗普
Donald Trump

  这次胜利属于今天聚集在这里的所有人以及全国正在看这次典礼的所有美国人。这是属于你们的一天。这是你们的庆祝日。我们所在的美利坚合众国，是你们的国家。

  真正重要的并不是政府由哪个党派掌控，而是政府是否由人民做主。2017年1月20日，这一天将会被铭记，美国人重新成为国家的主宰者。

  曾经被忽视的美国人不会继续被忽视。

  现在，所有人都在倾听你们。你们数以千万计地投入到这场历史运动中，这样的事情世界上从来没有过。

  这一就职典礼的核心是一种信念——我们坚信国家是为服务人民而存在的。我们国家想要为孩子们提供优良的学校教育，为家庭提供安全的生活环境，为每个人提供好的就业岗位。

  这些是正直的人民、正直的公众发出的合理诉求，但是很多人面对的现实却与我们的期望不相符。在内城区，母亲和孩子正陷于贫困之中，生锈的工厂像墓碑一样布满我们国家的土地，教育系统资金充裕，我们年轻又俊俏的学生们却没有学到任何知识。犯罪团体和毒品夺走了许多生命，阻碍了我们国家未开发潜力的释放。我们国家中的这些屠杀行为将永久结束在此地、结束在此刻。

  我们同属一个国家，他们的痛苦就是我们的痛苦。他们的梦想也是我们的梦想，他们的成就将是我们的成就。我们万众一心，同住一个家园，将会共享耀眼的成就。

  今天我所做的就职誓言是对所有美国人的效忠。几十年来，我们以美国工业的衰落为代价为别国的工业输送营养，为别国军队施以援助，但对我国军力的耗损视而不见。

  我们曾经致力于保卫其他国家的领地，却忽略了我们自己的领土安全。

  我们曾经将成千上万亿美元投入海外，我们自己的基础设施却年久失修、长年荒废。

We've made other countries rich while the wealth, strength, and confidence of our country has dissipated over the horizon. One by one, the factories shuttered and left our shores with not even a thought about the millions and millions of American workers that were left behind.

The wealth of our middle class has been ripped from their homes and then redistributed all across the world.

But that is the past and now we are looking only to the future.

We assembled here today are issuing a new decree to be heard in every city, in every foreign capital and in every hall of power. From this day forward, a new vision will govern our land. From this day forward, it's going to be only America first—America first.

Every decision on trade, on taxes, on immigration, on foreign affairs will be made to benefit American workers and American families. We must protect our borders from the ravages of other countries making our products, stealing our companies and destroying our jobs.

Protection will lead to great prosperity and strength. I will fight for you with every breath in my body. And I will never, ever let you down.

America will start winning again, winning like never before.

We will bring back our jobs. We will bring back our borders. We will bring back our wealth, and we will bring back our dreams. We will build new roads and highways and bridges and airports and tunnels and railways all across our wonderful nation. We will get our people off of welfare and back to work rebuilding our country with American hands and American labor. We will follow two simple rules—buy American and hire American.

We will seek friendship and goodwill with the nations of the world.

But we do so with the understanding that it is the right of all nations to put their own interests first. We do not seek to impose our way of life on anyone but rather to let it shine as an example. We will shine for everyone to follow.

We will reinforce old alliances and form new ones. And unite the civilized world against radical Islamic terrorism, which we will eradicate completely from the face of the earth.

At the bedrock of our politics will be a total allegiance to the United

唐纳德·特朗普
Donald Trump

我们帮助其他国家走上了富裕之路，我们自己的财富、力量和自信却逐渐消失在地平线上。我们的工厂一个接一个倒闭，而成千上万落在后面的工人被长久忽视。

我们中产阶级的财富被剥削，再被分配给世界其他国家。

但这些都是过去了，我们现在要看向未来。

我们今天聚集于此，是为了颁布新的命令，让它在每个城市、每个国家的首都、每座权力的殿堂回响。从今天开始，我们的国家将拥有新的愿景。从今天开始，只有美国优先——美国优先。

每一个关于贸易、关于税收、关于移民、关于外交的决定，都会为了美国工人和美国家庭的利益而做出。我们要保护我们的国界不受其他国家的破坏，这些国家生产了本属于我们的商品，偷走了本来要投资在我们国土上的公司，毁掉了我们的工作机会。

只有保护，才能有真正的富强。我会拼尽每一口气，为你们奋战到底，而且我永远，永远不会让你们失望。

美国会重新成为胜者，它的胜利将远超昔日的荣光。

我们会拿回属于我们的工作。我们会重新守卫住国界。我们会夺回我们的财富和我们的梦想。在我们辽阔伟大的国土上，我们要建立新的道路、高速公路、桥梁、机场、隧道和铁路，人民不再依靠福利，而是回到工作岗位，依靠美国人的双手，美国人的劳动，重建我们的国家。我们将遵循两条最简单的原则——买美国的商品，雇美国的工人。

我们会同世界其他国家和睦修好。

但是我们这样做是基于以下共识：所有国家都有权以自己的利益为先。我们不寻求将自己的生活方式强加于人，更期望它能自己发光发亮成为榜样。所有愿意效仿我们的人都能感受到这种光亮。

我们会加固与旧盟友的关系，建立新的联盟。文明世界的国家会团结起来，以抵御激进的伊斯兰恐怖主义，我们会把他们从地球表面全部清除。

政治必须以完全拥护我们自己的国家为基础。通过忠诚于我们的国

States of America and through our loyalty to our country, we will rediscover our loyalty to each other. When you open your heart to patriotism, there is no room for prejudice.

The Bible tells us how good and pleasant it is when God's people live together in unity. We must speak our minds openly, debate our disagreement honestly but always pursue solidarity. When America is united, America is totally unstoppable.

There should be no fear. We are protected, and we will always be protected. And most importantly, we will be protected by the great men and women of our military and law enforcement. We will be protected by God.

Finally, we must think big and dream even bigger. In America, we understand that a nation is only living as long as it is striving. We will no longer accept politicians who are all talk and no action, constantly complaining but never doing anything about it.

The time for empty talk is over. Now arrives the hour of action.

Do not allow anyone to tell you that it cannot be done. No challenge can match the heart and fight and spirit of America. We will not fail. Our country will thrive and prosper again. We stand at the birth of a new millennium, ready to unlock the mysteries of space, to free the earth from the miseries of disease and to harness the energies, industries and technologies of tomorrow. A new national pride will stir ourselves, lift our sights and heal our divisions. It's time to remember that old wisdom our soldiers will never forget—that whether we are black or brown or white, we all bleed the same red blood of patriots.

We all enjoyed the same glorious freedoms, and we all salute the same great American flag.

And whether a child is born in the urban sprawl of Detroit or the windswept plains of Nebraska, They look up at the same night sky, they build a heart with the same dreams and they are infused with the breath of life by the same Almighty Creator.

So to all Americans in every city near and far, small and large, from mountain to mountain, from ocean to ocean, hear these words—you will never be ignored again.

家，我们会实现我们彼此之间的忠诚。当你心怀爱国主义，你便不会再心存偏见。

《圣经》告诉我们，当上帝的子民团结一致，那情景将是妙不可言的。我们必须坦率地表达我们的观点，真诚地就不同观点进行辩论，但同时，我们也要追求团结一致。当美国人民团结在一起时，美国会变得势不可当。

我们不需要再心存恐惧。我们会被保护，我们会永远被保护。来自军队和执法部门的这些优秀的男男女女，将会保护我们。更重要的是，上帝会保佑我们。

最后，在美国，我们要敢想，更要敢做梦。我们必须理解，一个国家只有不断进取，才能生存下去。我们不再接纳那些只说不做、只会抱怨而从不试图做出改变的政客。

讲空话的时代已经结束了。现在是行动的时间。

不要听信任何人说你不可能成功。美国人的决心、战斗力和精神可以克服任何挑战。我们不会失败。我们的国家会重新发展和繁荣起来。我们即将迎来新的一个世纪，准备好了破解太空的奥秘，将世界从疾病的痛苦中解脱，驾驭未来的新能源、新产业和新技术。一种新的国家荣誉感在我们心中激荡，提升我们的视野、缝合我们的分裂。现在是时候让美国的"斗士们"再次记起一种古老的智慧——不管我们是黑皮肤、棕色皮肤，还是白皮肤，我们都流着爱国者的红色血液。

我们共同享受自由的光辉，我们共同向伟大的美国国旗致敬。

我们的孩子，不管是出生在底特律城郊，还是内布拉斯加州被风吹拂的平原上，他们仰望的都是同一片夜空，他们的内心都承载着同样的梦想，他们的生命都由同一个万能的主所赋予。

所有的美国人，无论远近，即使远隔千山万水，你们也要记住：你再也不会被忽视。

Your voice, your hopes and your dreams will define our American destiny. Together, And your courage and goodness and love will forever guide us along the way. We will make America strong again. We will make America wealthy again. We will make America proud again. We will make America safe again. And yes, together, thank you. We will make America great again. God bless you. And God bless America. Thank You.

唐纳德·特朗普
Donald Trump

你们的声音,你们的希望和你们的梦想,将定义美国的命运。你们的勇气、善意和爱将永远指引我们的方向。我们会让美国再次强大。我们会让美国再次富有。我们会让美国再次骄傲。我们会让美国再次安全。当然,我们将共同做到这些,谢谢你们,让美国再次强大。上帝保佑你们。上帝保佑美利坚。谢谢!

约瑟夫·拜登
Joseph Biden

约瑟夫·拜登（Joseph Biden）

生平简介>>

约瑟夫·拜登是美国第四十六任总统。他于1942年11月20日出生在宾夕法尼亚州。拜登毕业于雪城大学，当过一段时间律师，1970年进入政界，1972年11月当选联邦参议员并六次连任至2009年。1988年和2007年两度竞选美国总统，均未成功。2008年和2013年两度成为奥巴马的竞选搭档，并于2009—2017年任副总统。2019年4月25日拜登宣布参选美国总统。2021年1月7日当选。2023年4月25日是拜登宣布参加2020年总统选举四周年纪念日，这一日拜登在社交媒体上正式宣布将竞选连任美国总统。

Joseph Biden

Inaugural Address

January 20, 2021

Chief Justice Roberts, Vice President Harris, Speaker Pelosi, Leader Schumer, Leader McConnell, Vice President Pence, my distinguished guests, and my fellow Americans.

This is America's day. This is democracy's day, a day of history and hope of renewal and resolve. Through a crucible for the ages, America has been tested anew and America has risen to the challenge. Today, we celebrate the triumph not of a candidate, but of a cause, the cause of democracy. The people... The will of the people, has been heard and the will of the people has been heeded.

We've learned again that democracy is precious, democracy is fragile and, at this hour my friends, democracy has prevailed. So now on this hallowed ground where just a few days ago violence sought to shake the Capitol's very foundations, we come together as one nation under God, indivisible, to carry out the peaceful transfer of power as we have for more than two centuries.

As we look ahead in our uniquely American way, restless, bold, optimistic, and set our sights on a nation we know we can be and must be, I thank my predecessors of both parties. I thank them from the bottom of my heart. And I know the resilience of our Constitution and the strength, the strength of our nation, as does President Carter, who I spoke with last night who cannot be with us today, but who we salute for his lifetime of service.

I've just taken a sacred oath each of those patriots have taken, the oath first sworn by George Washington. But the American story depends not on any one of us, not on some of us, but on all of us. On we the people who seek a more perfect union. This is a great nation, we are good people. And over the centuries through storm and strife in peace and in war we've come so far. But we still have far to go.

约瑟夫·拜登

Joseph Biden

拜登总统就职演说

2021年1月20日

首席大法官罗伯茨、副总统哈里斯、众议院议长佩洛西、民主党领袖舒默、共和党领袖麦康奈尔、副总统彭斯，尊敬的各位来宾，以及亲爱的美国同胞们。

这是属于美国的日子。这是属于民主的日子。这是历史和希望的日子，复苏和决心的日子。历经多年考验，美国经受了新的考验，美国已奋起迎接挑战。今天，我们庆祝的不是一位候选人的胜利，而是一项事业，一项民主事业的胜利。人民以及人民的意愿得到倾听和关注。

我们再次意识到，民主的可贵和脆弱。朋友们，民主在此刻获胜。朋友们，在这一时刻，民主占了上风。因此，就在这片几天前曾发生暴力、撼动国会大厦根基的神圣土地上，在上帝的指引下，我们作为一个不可分割的国家团结在一起，遵照我们两个多世纪以来的传统，进行权力的和平交接。

当我们以我们独特的美国方式，以悸动、勇敢、乐观展望未来，并将目光投向我们知道我们能够、而且必须成为的国家上时，我感谢两党的前辈们，我要从心底里感谢他们。我知道我们宪法的坚韧和强大，知道我们国家的力量。同样的，我也要感谢卡特前总统，我昨晚曾与他交谈，尽管他今天无法出席，但我们仍要为他的毕生奉献致敬。

我刚刚宣读了每位爱国者都曾宣读过的神圣誓言。这份誓言是由乔治·华盛顿首次宣读的。但美国的故事并不取决于我们中的任何一个人或一些人，而是取决于所有美国人，取决于我们那些追求建立更完美联邦国家的人。这是一个伟大的国家，我们是善良的人民。经过几百年的洗礼，经过风暴与冲突，和平与战争，我们走了这么远。但是我们还有很长的路要走。

美国历届总统就职演说
THE INAUGURAL ADDRESSES OF THE U.S. PRESIDENTS

We'll press forward with speed and urgency for we have much to do in this winter of peril and significant possibility. Much to do, much to heal, much to restore, much to build and much to gain. Few people in our nation's history have been more challenged or found a time more challenging or difficult than the time we're in now. A once in a century virus that silently stalks the country has taken as many lives in one year as in all of World War Two.

Millions of jobs have been lost. Hundreds of thousands of businesses closed. A cry for racial justice, some 400 years in the making, moves us. The dream of justice for all will be deferred no longer. A cry for survival comes from the planet itself, a cry that can't be any more desperate or any more clear. And now, the rise of political extremism, white supremacy, domestic terrorism, that we must confront and we will defeat.

To overcome these challenges, to restore the soul and secure the future of America, requires so much more than words. It requires the most elusive of all things in a democracy: unity. Unity. In another January on New Year's Day in 1863 Abraham Lincoln signed the Emancipation Proclamation. When he put pen to paper the president said, and I quote, "if my name ever goes down in history, it'll be for this act, and my whole soul is in it".

My whole soul is in it today, on this January day. My whole soul is in this. Bringing America together, uniting our people, uniting our nation. And I ask every American to join me in this cause. Uniting to fight the foes we face: anger, resentment and hatred. Extremism, lawlessness, violence, disease, joblessness, and hopelessness.

With unity we can do great things, important things. We can right wrongs, we can put people to work in good jobs, we can teach our children in safe schools. We can overcome the deadly virus, we can rebuild work, we can rebuild the middle class and make work secure, we can secure racial justice and we can make America once again the leading force for good in the world.

I know speaking of unity can sound to some like a foolish fantasy these days. I know the forces that divide us are deep and they are real. But I also know they are not new. Our history has been a constant struggle between the American ideal, that we are all created equal, and the harsh ugly reality that

约瑟夫·拜登
Joseph Biden

我们带着速度和紧迫感前进，因为在这个险境重重的冬天我们有很多要完成的事情和重要的可能性。在我们国家的历史中，很少有先贤遇到过比这更大的挑战，也很少有先贤遇到过像今天这般充满挑战和困难的时代。百年一遇的病毒潜入我们的国家，在一年中夺走的生命比整个"二战"还要多。

数百万人失业，数十万的生意关门。几百年来对种族平等的呼声推动了我们前进。公正的梦想不再推迟。地球本身发出了生存的呐喊，这一声呐喊从未像现在这样迫切和清晰。政治极端主义、白人至上、国内恐怖主义兴起，我们必须与之斗争，并且我们会战胜他们。

解决这些挑战，恢复人们的信念和确保美国的未来，需要的不仅仅是言语。我们需要民主中最难以捉摸的东西，那就是团结。团结。在1863年新年的那天，亚伯拉罕·林肯签署了《解放黑奴宣言》。当他把笔放在纸上的那一刻，林肯总统说道，"如果我的名字能在历史上留下，那必定是因为这一举动。我的整个灵魂都献给此事。"

今天，在一月的这一天，我也将整个灵魂献于此事：把美国团结起来，让人民团结，让国家团结。我呼吁每个美国人都加入这项事业。团结起来对抗我们面临的敌人，对抗愤怒、怨恨和仇恨，以及极端主义、违法、暴力、疾病、失业和绝望。

只有团结起来，我们才能做出伟大的事、做成重要的事。我们可以纠正错误，可以让人们有一份好工作，可以在安全的学校里教我们的孩子，可以战胜致命的病毒，可以恢复我们的工作、重振中产阶级并提供医疗保健用以保护所有人。我们能实现种族公正，让美国再次成为世界积极的领导力量。

我知道，现在谈论团结可能听起来像是愚蠢的幻想。我知道分裂我们的力量很深厚，而且是真实存在的。但我也知道它们并不新鲜。我们的历史是美国理想不断斗争的过程。我们生来平等，种族主义、本土保护主义和恐惧这些丑陋残酷的现实将我们撕裂。这场战斗是长期的，而且胜负难料。

racism, nativism and fear have torn us apart. The battle is perennial and victory is never secure.

Through civil war, the Great Depression, World War, 9/11, through struggle, sacrifice, and setback, our better angels have always prevailed. In each of our moments enough of us have come together to carry all of us forward and we can do that now. History, faith and reason show the way, the way of unity.

We can see each other not as adversaries but as neighbors. We can treat each other with dignity and respect. We can join forces, stop the shouting and lower the temperature. For without unity there is no peace, only bitterness and fury, no progress, only exhausting outrage. No nation, only a state of chaos. This is our historic moment of crisis and challenge. And unity is the path forward. And we must meet this moment as the United States of America.

If we do that, I guarantee we will not fail. We have never, ever, ever, ever failed in America when we've acted together. And so today at this time in this place, let's start afresh, all of us. Let's begin to listen to one another again, hear one another, see one another. Show respect to one another. Politics doesn't have to be a raging fire destroying everything in its path. Every disagreement doesn't have to be a cause for total war and we must reject the culture in which facts themselves are manipulated and even manufactured.

My fellow Americans, we have to be different than this. We have to be better than this and I believe America is so much better than this. Just look around. Here we stand in the shadow of the Capitol dome. As mentioned earlier, completed in the shadow of the Civil War, when the union itself was literally hanging in the balance, we endure, we prevail. Here we stand, looking out on the great Mall, where Dr King spoke of his dream.

Here we stand, where 108 years ago at another inaugural, thousands of protesters tried to block brave women marching for the right to vote. And today we mark the swearing in of the first woman elected to national office, Vice President Kamala Harris. Don't tell me things can change. Here we stand where heroes who gave the last full measure of devotion rest in eternal peace.

And here we stand just days after a riotous mob thought they could use violence to silence the will of the people, to stop the work of our democracy,

约瑟夫·拜登
Joseph Biden

经历了内战、大萧条、世界大战、"9·11"事件,经历了斗争、牺牲和挫折,我们本性中"更善良的天使"一直占上风。在所有的时刻,有足够的我们团结一心向前走,我们现在也能做到。历史、信仰和理性为我们指明道路,那是团结之路。

我们可以把彼此视为邻居,而不是对手。我们给予彼此尊严和尊重。我们可以联合起来,停止喊叫,减少愤怒。没有团结就没有和平,没有团结就只剩苦涩和愤怒,没有进步,只有筋疲力尽的暴行。没有国家,只有混乱的状态。这是我们面临危机和挑战的历史性时刻。团结才是前进的道路。我们必须以美利坚合众国的名义迎接这一时刻。

如果我们能做到,我保证我们不会失败。只要我们团结,美国就永远永远不会失败。今天,此刻此地,让我们所有人重新开始。让我们开始倾听彼此,看见彼此,尊重彼此。政治不一定非得是熊熊大火,摧毁它行进道路上的一切。每一个分歧都不一定是全面战争的原因,我们必须拒绝这种事实本身被操纵甚至被捏造的文化。

我的同胞们,我们需要比当下更多样。我们需要比当下更好。我相信美国一定能更好。看看四周,我们站在国会大厦穹顶的影子下。当时联邦本身岌岌可危。我们坚韧不屈,我们取得胜利。我们站在这里,眺望着马丁·路德·金谈论他的梦想的大广场。

108年前,我们所站之处,在另一场就职演说上,几千名抗议者试图阻止勇敢的女性为获得投票权而游行。而今天,我们为第一位当选为国家级公职的女性,卡玛拉·哈里斯宣誓就职副总统而见证。不要告诉我世事会变。我们所站立的地方,是英雄们奉献出全部、在永恒和平中安息的地方。

也就在我们所站立的地方,几天前,一群暴徒认为他们可以使用暴力压制人民的意愿,阻止我们的民主事业,把我们从这片神圣的土地上赶走。

to drive us from this sacred ground. It did not happen, it will never happen, not today, not tomorrow, not ever. Not ever. To all those who supported our campaign, I'm humbled by the faith you placed in us. To all those who did not support us, let me say this. Hear us out as we move forward. Take a measure of me and my heart.

If you still disagree, so be it. That's democracy. That's America. The right to dissent peacefully within the guardrail of our democracy is perhaps our nation's greatest strength. If you hear me clearly, disagreement must not lead to disunion. And I pledge this to you. I will be a President for all Americans, all Americans. And I promise you I will fight for those who did not support me as for those who did.

Many centuries ago, St Augustine, the saint of my church, wrote that a people was a multitude defined by the common objects of their love, defined by the common objects of their love. What are the common objects we as Americans love, that define us as Americans? I think we know. Opportunity, security, liberty, dignity, respect, honor, and yes, the truth.

Recent weeks and months have taught us a painful lesson. There is truth and there are lies. Lies told for power and for profit. And each of us has a duty and a responsibility as citizens as Americans and especially as leaders. Leaders who are pledged to honor our Constitution to protect our nation, to defend the truth and defeat the lies.

Look, I understand that many of my fellow Americans view the future with fear and trepidation. I understand they worry about their jobs. I understand like their dad they lay in bed at night staring at the ceiling thinking: Can I keep my healthcare? Can I pay my mortgage? Thinking about their families, about what comes next. I promise you, I get it. But the answer's not to turn inward. To retreat into competing factions. Distrusting those who don't look like you, or worship the way you do, who don't get their news from the same source as you do.

We must end this uncivil war that pits red against blue, rural versus urban, conservative versus liberal. We can do this if we open our souls instead of hardening our hearts, if we show a little tolerance and humility, and if we're

约瑟夫·拜登
Joseph Biden

那没有发生,也永远不会发生,今天不会,明天不会,永远不会,永远都不会。对支持我们竞选的人们,我们感激你们对我们的信念。对没有支持我们的人,请关注我们前进的步伐,监督我和我的心。

如果你仍然有异议,那就有异议。这就是民主,这就是美国,拥有和平表达异议的权利。保卫我们的民主也许是我们国家最强大的力量。意见不同不一定要导致分裂。我向你们保证。我将会是所有美国人的总统,所有的美国人。我承诺,我会捍卫支持我和不支持我的人的权利。

许多世纪以前,我的教会的圣徒圣奥古斯丁写道,一个民族是由他们共同热爱的目标所定义的群体。由他们共同的目标来定义。我们美国人所热爱的、能将我们定义为美国人的共同目标是什么?我想我们都知道,那就是机会、安全、自由、尊严、尊重、荣誉,是的,还有真理。

最近几周和几个月,我们学到了惨痛的教训。其中有真相,也有谎言。为了权力和利益而说谎。作为美国公民,尤其是作为领导者,我们每个人都有责任,也有义务。那些承诺遵守宪法的领导者,只为保护我们国家,捍卫真理,击败谎言。

我理解我的许多美国同胞对未来充满恐惧和恐惧。我理解他们担心自己的工作。我理解他们就像他们的父亲一样,会在晚上躺在床上盯着天花板想:我还能继续享受医疗保健吗?我可以支付我的抵押贷款吗?他们考虑着家人,思索着接下来会怎么样。我保证,我理解这种感受。然而答案不在内心煎熬,不是内部斗争,不是不相信与你容貌、信仰或是认知不同的人。

我们必须结束这场两党之间、农村与城市之间、保守派与自由派之间的无礼之战。如果我们敞开灵魂,而不是心如坚石,我们就能够做到。如果我们展现出一点容忍和谦卑,如果我们愿意替对方着想就好了,就像我

willing to stand in the other person's shoes, as my mom would say. Just for a moment, stand in their shoes.

Because here's the thing about life: There's no accounting for what fate will deal you. Some days you need a hand. There are other days when we're called to lend a hand. That's how it has to be, that's what we do for one another. And if we are that way our country will be stronger, more prosperous, more ready for the future. And we can still disagree.

My fellow Americans, in the work ahead of us we're going to need each other. We need all our strength to persevere through this dark winter. We're entering what may be the darkest and deadliest period of the virus. We must set aside politics and finally face this pandemic as one nation, one nation. And I promise this, as the Bible says, Weeping may endure for a night, joy cometh in the morning. We will get through this together. Together.

Look folks, all my colleagues I serve with in the House and the Senate up here, we all understand the world is watching, watching all of us today. So here's my message to those beyond our borders. America has been tested and we've come out stronger for it. We will repair our alliances, and engage with the world once again. Not to meet yesterday's challenges but today's and tomorrow's challenges. And we'll lead not merely by the example of our power but the power of our example.

Fellow Americans, moms, dads, sons, daughters, friends, neighbors and co-workers. We will honor them by becoming the people and the nation we can and should be. So I ask you let's say a silent prayer for those who lost their lives, those left behind and for our country. Amen.

Folks, it's a time of testing. We face an attack on our democracy, and on truth, a raging virus, a stinging inequity, systemic racism, a climate in crisis, America's role in the world. Any one of these would be enough to challenge us in profound ways. But the fact is we face them all at once, presenting this nation with one of the greatest responsibilities we've had. Now we're going to be tested. Are we going to step up?

It's time for boldness for there is so much to do. And this is certain, I promise you. We will be judged, you and I, by how we resolve these cascading crises

约瑟夫·拜登
Joseph Biden

的母亲常说的那样,"站在他们角度想想,哪怕就一瞬间。"

因为人生就是这样。没人算得出命运将会如何待你。在有些日子里你会需要帮助,在另一些日子里,别人需要我们的帮助。就该是这样,这就是我们为彼此做的事情。这样一来,我们的国家会更加强大、更加繁荣、更有准备迎接未来。而且我们仍然可以保留异议。

我的同胞们,前方的事业决定了我们需要彼此。我们需要所有的力量来度过寒冬。我们处在病毒最黑暗和最致命的阶段。我们必须把政治放在一边,以一个国家的姿态面对疫情。我保证,正如《圣经》中所说:一宿虽然有哭泣,早晨便必欢呼。我们将一起度过,携手同行。

看,各位,以及我在众议院和参议院的各位同事们,我们都明白全世界都在看着,看着我们今天在场的所有人。这是我给美国以外的人们传达的信息:美国经受住了考验,我们因此变得更加强大。我们将修复我们的同盟,并再次与世界接触。不只是迎接昨天的挑战,还要迎接今天和明天的挑战。我们将引领世界,不只是因为我们所显示的实力,而是因为我们所树立的榜样。

美国同胞们、母亲们、父亲们、儿子们、女儿们、朋友们、邻居们和同事们,我们将以他们为荣,成为我们能够且应该成为的人民和国家。所以,我请求你们,让我们为那些失去生命的人、那些还在的人和我们的国家默默祈祷。阿门。

各位,这是一个考验的时刻。我们面临着对我们民主和真理的攻击,正在肆虐的疫情、让人痛心的不平等、系统性的种族歧视、气候危机,以及美国在世界上的角色危机。其中任何一个问题都足够让我们面临巨大的挑战。然而我们现在在同时面临着所有这些问题,也赋予我们整个国家举足轻重的责任。如今我们经历着考验。我们能迎难而上吗?

是时候勇敢一点了,因为我们还有很多事需要去做。我向你们保证,这是肯定的。我们如何解决我们这个时代的级联危机,将成为评判我们的标

of our era. We will rise to the occasion. Will we master this rare and difficult hour? Will we meet our obligations and pass along a new and better world to our children? I believe we must and I'm sure you do as well. I believe we will, and when we do, we'll write the next great chapter in the history of the United States of America, the American story.

A story that might sound like a song that means a lot to me, it's called American Anthem. And there's one verse that stands out at least for me and it goes like this: The work and prayers of century have brought us to this day, which shall be our legacy, what will our children say? Let me know in my heart when my days are through, America, America, I gave my best to you.

Let us add our own work and prayers to the unfolding story of our great nation. If we do this, then when our days are through, our children and our children's children will say of us: They gave their best, they did their duty, they healed a broken land.

My fellow Americans I close the day where I began, with a sacred oath. Before God and all of you, I give you my word. I will always level with you. I will defend the Constitution, I'll defend our democracy. I'll defend America and I will give all — all of you — keep everything I do in your service, thinking not of power but of possibilities. Not of personal interest but of public good.

And together we will write an American story of hope, not fear, of unity not division, of light not darkness. A story of decency and dignity, love and healing, greatness and goodness. May this be the story that guides us, the story that inspires us. And the story that tells ages yet to come that we answered the call of history, we met the moment. Democracy and hope, truth and justice, did not die on our watch but thrive.

That America secured liberty at home and stood once again as a beacon to the world. That is what we owe our forbearers, one another, and generations to follow.

So with purpose and resolve, we turn to those tasks of our time. Sustained by faith, driven by conviction and devoted to one another and the country we love with all our hearts. May God bless America and God protect our troops.

Thank you, America.

约瑟夫·拜登
Joseph Biden

准。我们将迎难而上。我们可以掌控这罕见且艰难的时刻吗？我们会履行我们的义务，把一个新的、更美好的世界传给我们的孩子吗？我认为我们必须这样做，并且我肯定你们也这样认为。我相信我们将会做到，并且当我们做到的时候，我们将书写美利坚历史上下一个伟大篇章，美国的故事。

有个叫《美国国歌》的故事对我有重要的意义，这个故事的名字像是一首歌。其中有一段是这样的："百年的劳作和祷告把我带到今日，这是我们的遗产，我们的孩子们会怎么说？当我时日将近，我问心无愧，美国啊美国，我把最好的给了你。"

让我们把努力和祷告带入美国的故事中。如果我们做得到，我们的日子就有盼头，我们的孩子和他们的孩子会这样评价我们："他们竭尽所能，履行了责任，他们治愈了破碎的国家。"

我的同胞们，让我以开场时宣誓的方式结束就职演说。在上帝和人民面前，我宣誓：我将永远与你们一样平等；我将捍卫宪法，捍卫民主，捍卫美国；我会为你们全心付出，你们所有人，让我做的一切是为了服务你们。我所想的不是权力而是可能性，不为个人利益而为公共谋利。

我们将共同书写一个充满希望而非恐惧、充满团结而非分裂、充满光明而非黑暗的美国故事，一个关于正派和尊严、爱和疗愈、伟大和善良的故事。愿这个故事可以指引我们、激励我们，告诉未来的世世代代，我们回应了历史的召唤，我们相遇在此刻。民主和希望，真理和正义，在我们这里没有消亡，而是愈加繁盛。

美国保证了国家的自由，再一次以灯塔的姿态立于全世界。这是我们需要向前辈和后代交代的。

我们带着使命感和决心，面对时代的任务。信仰永存，信念驱使，彼此奉献，全心全意地热爱我们所爱的国家。愿上帝保佑美国，愿上帝保佑我们的军队。

感谢你，美国。